AUGUSTINE: EARLIER WRITINGS

THE LIBRARY OF CHRISTIAN CLASSICS

ICHTHUS EDITION

AUGUSTINE: EARLIER WRITINGS

Selected and translated
with Introductions by

JOHN H. S. BURLEIGH

Philadelphia
THE WESTMINSTER PRESS

Published simultaneously in Great Britain and the United States of America by the S.C.M. Press, Ltd., London, and The Westminster Press, Philadelphia.

First published MCMLIII

Library of Congress Catalog Card No. 53-13043

9 8 7 6 5 4 3 2 1

Printed in the United States of America

GENERAL EDITORS' PREFACE

The Christian Church possesses in its literature an abundant and incomparable treasure. But it is an inheritance that must be reclaimed by each generation. THE LIBRARY OF CHRISTIAN CLASSICS is designed to present in the English language, and in twenty-six volumes of convenient size, a selection of the most indispensable Christian treatises written prior to the end of the sixteenth century.

The practice of giving circulation to writings selected for superior worth or special interest was adopted at the beginning of Christian history. The canonical Scriptures were themselves a selection from a much wider literature. In the Patristic era there began to appear a class of works of compilation (often designed for ready reference in controversy) of the opinions of well-reputed predecessors, and in the Middle Ages many such works were produced. These medieval anthologies actually preserve some noteworthy materials from works otherwise lost.

In modern times, with the increasing inability even of those trained in universities and theological colleges to read Latin and Greek texts with ease and familiarity, the translation of selected portions of earlier Christian literature into modern languages has become more necessary than ever; while the wide range of distinguished books written in vernaculars such as English makes selection there also needful. The efforts that have been made to meet this need are too numerous to be noted here, but none of these collections serves the purpose of the reader who desires a library of representative treatises spanning the Christian centuries as a whole. Most of them embrace only the age of the Church Fathers, and some of them have long been out of print. A fresh translation of a work already translated may shed much new light upon its meaning. This is true even of Bible translations despite the work of many experts through the centuries. In some instances old translations have been adopted in this series, but wherever necessary or desirable, new ones have been made. Notes have been supplied where these were needed to explain the author's meaning. The introductions provided for the several treatises and extracts will, we believe, furnish welcome guidance.

JOHN BAILLIE
JOHN T. MCNEILL
HENRY P. VAN DUSEN

CONTENTS

PREFACE

The editor of a volume entitled *Augustine: Earlier Writings* would seem to be faced with the necessity in the first place of determining his *terminus ad quem*. This is not an altogether simple matter. All the extant writings are subsequent to the decisive event of his life, his conversion in 386, described in Books VII and VIII of the *Confessions*. Now the *Confessions* were written some fourteen years after the event, and many scholars have maintained that they give a highly romanticized version of what actually took place. Relying on works written before 391, and especially on those of the Cassiciacum period, they have asserted, in Alfaric's words, that it was "to Neoplatonism that he was converted, rather than to the Gospel." They have pointed out that abandonment of the world for the life of philosophic contemplation was entirely in the Platonist manner, and that St. Augustine devoted himself, with a group of like-minded friends, not to the study of the Bible or of specifically Christian doctrines, but to the discussion of general philosophic questions, increasingly in the light of the *Enneads* of Plotinus. Of the growing influence of Plotinus upon his thought Alfaric has brought together an impressive mass of detailed evidence. From this point of view his ordination to the presbyterate in 391 marks the end of his early period.

It is true, of course, that there was development in St. Augustine's thought, and that his ordination marks an important stage in it. His call to become a "minister of God's Word and Sacrament" necessitated a closer and more continuous study of Scripture, and with that would come a strengthening of his grasp on Biblical truth, and a profounder acquaintance with Christian doctrine. But that there was anything like an abandonment of philosophy in favour of theology, or any easy substitution of faith in place of reason, is disproved by the manifest continuity of his central ideas before and after 391. The *Cassiciacum Dialogues* must not be taken as reflecting fully his intellectual and spiritual activity during that period. In part they are exercises in philosophical disputation for the training of his two young pupils. But also they give clear indications of devotional exercises and Scripture study going on at that time. He was certainly making a careful study of the Epistles of St. Paul, in which for some time already he had been deeply interested. Due weight must also be given to the passage (*Contra Academ.* III. xix. 43) in which he says: "No one doubts that we are impelled to learn by the twofold forces of authority and reason. I have determined henceforth never to depart from the authority of Christ, for I find none more valid. But as regards that which must be pursued with subtle reasoning, my disposition now is impatiently to long to apprehend the truth not only by faith but also with the understanding; and I am confident that meantime I shall find in the Platonists something that is not incompatible with our [Christian] sacred things." Here his programme is announced. After laying the spectre of academic doubt with the argument, among others, that doubt itself implies a standard of certainty, he is going on to work out a system of Christian philosophy in which the articles of the Christian faith will be interpreted to the understanding with the aid of clues that Platonism will supply. Before 391 this had been achieved. The philosophy then arrived at was, in its main features, to be his for the rest of his life. When he wrote the *Retractations* only minor details were found requiring correction.

In the *Retractations* St. Augustine himself marks the division between his early and his later writings. That work is in two Books, of which the former reviews his writings previous to his elevation to the episcopate in 395/6; and the second begins with a review of his answers to the *Questions* of Simplicianus, written "at the beginning of my episcopate." To this work he frequently refers later as setting forth his final understanding of the Pauline doctrine of grace. Here if anywhere we may choose to fix the point at which the "earlier" gives place to the "later" Augustine, remembering that any such choice is somewhat arbitrary.

Of the numerous works written before 395 naturally a selection had to be made. Some of them are already available in English translations, and weight was given to this consideration. In spite, however, of the fact that the *Soliloquies* have been beautifully translated with Notes and Introduction by Rose Elizabeth Cleveland (Williams and Norgate, London, 1910) its claim to be included here seemed irresistible. Of the *De Libero Arbitrio* there is an American translation, but, as it is not widely accessible, it too is included. On the other hand the absence of a translation determined the inclusion of the *De Natura Boni*, in spite of its date, in preference to the "Reply to the Fundamental Epistle of Manes," which will be found in the Edinburgh translation (T. and T. Clark). It has an interest of its own in the attempt there made to give Scripture proofs for a metaphysic essentially Neoplatonist. Reluctantly it was decided to include none of the anti-Donatist works, partly because the more important ones are later than 395, and are already available in translation, but also because they represent an aspect of St. Augustine's thought and work, important no doubt, but lying somewhat apart from the main stream of his development. The present selection is offered in the hope that it may give an adequate representation of the working out of the system, metaphysical, epistemological, ethical and withal Biblical, which may justly be called "Augustinianism."

To the translation of each work there has been prefixed St. Augustine's own review of it in the *Retractations*, and a brief Introduction; while to facilitate reference, and to indicate the plan of the argument an analysis of each work has been given where it appeared necessary.

JOHN H. S. BURLEIGH.

University of Edinburgh.

The Soliloquies

St. Augustine's Review of the Soliloquies. Retractations I, IV

1. Meantime I wrote two other books on matters touching my earnest quest for truth concerning problems whose solution was my chief desire. They were written as a dialogue between myself and Reason, as if there were two of us present, though actually I was alone. To this work I gave the name *Soliloquies*. It remained unfinished. In the First Book the question was: What kind of man he ought to be who wishes to lay hold on wisdom, which is grasped by the mind and not by bodily sense; and the answer was in a measure made clear. At the end of the book it was concluded as the result of a logical proof that things which truly are, are immortal. In the Second Book there is a long argument about the immortality of the soul, but the subject was not fully dealt with.

2. In these Books there are some things of which I do not approve. I do not approve of what I said in my prayer: "God who willest not that any should know the truth but those that are pure." It could be replied to this that many who are not pure know many true things. It was not defined what was the truth that none but the pure could know, nor indeed what knowing is. And there is the sentence: "God whose kingdom is this whole world which sense knows not." If the relative clause is to be taken as referring to God, some words ought to have been added, for example, "whom the sense of a mortal body knows not." If it was meant that the world was not known by sense, the world must be understood to be the future world in which there will be a new heaven and a new earth. Even so, I should have added the words "of the mortal body." But at that time I was still using the word, "sense," to express what is properly to be called "bodily sense." I need not repeat continually what I have just said, but

it should be remembered wherever that expression occurs in my writings.

3. Where I have said of the Father and the Son that "he who begets and he who is begotten is one," I ought to have said "are one," for the Truth says openly "I and my Father are one." Nor am I satisfied with the statement that when God is known in this life the soul is already happy, except, of course, by hope. Again the statement: "Not by one way only is wisdom approached," does not sound well; as if there were another way besides Christ, who said: I am the Way. This offence to religious ears should have been avoided. Christ is the Way universally, and these are different ways of which we sing in the psalm: "Show me thy ways, O Lord, and teach me thy paths." In the sentence: "These sensible things are to be utterly avoided," care should have been taken to avoid being thought to hold the opinion of the false philosopher Porphyry, who said everything corporeal is to be avoided. Of course, I did not say "all sensible things" but "these sensible things," meaning corruptible things. But it would have been better to have said so. Sensible things which are corruptible will not exist in the new heaven and the new earth of the age to come.

4. Again (in Bk. II, xx, 35) I said that those who are educated in the liberal arts doubtless, in learning them, draw them out from the oblivion which has overwhelmed them, or dig them out, as it were. I do not approve of this. When even untrained persons, suitably questioned, are able to return correct answers about some of the arts, a more credible reason is that they have according to their natural capacity the presence of the light of eternal reason. Hence they catch a glimpse of immutable truth. The reason is not that they once knew it and have forgotten, as Plato and others like him have thought. Against their opinion I have argued in *De Trinitate*, Bk. XII, as far as the subject of that work gave me occasion. The *Soliloquies* begin with the words: *Volventi mihi multa ac varia.*

The Soliloquies

INTRODUCTION

In *De Ordine* (I. iii. 6) St. Augustine tells us of his habit, during the sojourn at Cassiciacum, of lying awake in bed for half the night thinking his own thoughts, undisturbed by the two young pupils for whose education he was responsible, and for whose philosophical awakening the three disputations of that period were in part designed. The *Soliloquies*, we may suppose, represent these private meditations and show us the kind of question that he felt to be most urgent. But they also reveal the manner of man he was in the crucial period between his conversion and his baptism. In this respect they invite comparison with the *Confessions*. No doubt the *Soliloquies* must suffer thereby. The subject, God and the soul, is fundamentally the same, but the treatment is incomparably narrower, being primarily metaphysical rather than biographical. Nevertheless here too his spiritual history has a place; the cultivation of the liberal arts, here regarded more favourably than in the *Confessions*; the reading of the *Hortensius* with the deep impression it made upon him; the influence of Ambrose; his ill-health; his abandonment of the world, riches, fame and wife; the conscientious examination of his moral state, with the claim to have progressed and the admission that temptation was not wholly overcome. There is here no philosophic calm. With all the Neoplatonic colouring, there is a quite un-Plotinian intensity of feeling, the restless heart of the *Confessions* that can find rest only in God. This passionate religious quest really dominates the work in spite of the weary stretches of inconclusive argument, in logical proof of the immortality of the soul, which occupy so much of the Second Book. The whole is conceived in a framework of prayer. If the lengthy opening prayer, made up of phrases gathered from Plotinus and from the Bible, may seem to be overloaded, it must be regarded as his sincere and earnest confession of faith. It is remarkable how little in the *Soliloquies* had to be retracted later. Only one major correction had to be made, viz., the substitution for the Platonic doctrine of reminiscence of the genuinely Augustinian doctrine of Divine Illumination.

ANALYSIS

Book I

i, 1. Introduction.

2–6. Prayer of Invocation.
Enumeration of the attributes, perfections, and gracious acts of God. "I spoke not what I knew, but what I had gathered from many quarters and committed to memory, and in which I have put such faith as I was able."

ii, 7—v, 11. Knowledge of God a Unique form of Knowledge.
(7) I desire to know God and the soul. Nothing else besides. But knowledge of God is unique. (8) It is quite unlike sense-knowledge. Even knowledge of one's best friend is no adequate analogy. (9) Plato and Plotinus may have spoken true things about God without knowing him. (10) Knowledge of mathematical truth is real knowledge, but (12) is also inadequate, for it does not lead to beatitude. "The intelligible beauty of God is superior to the certain truths of mathematics."

vi, 12—viii, 15. Analogy of Sensual and Intelligible Vision.
(12) Common vision requires (*a*) possession of sound eyes, (*b*) the act of directing them towards an object. So, with the vision of God, the mind (*a*) must have sound eyes that can look beyond temporal things. They must be healed by faith, hope and love. (13) (*b*) It must direct its regard to the right object, i.e., it must have right reason, which again demands faith, hope and love. (14) When the vision of God has been attained these three will still be required in this life, but in the life to come faith becomes knowledge, hope becomes possession, only love must remain and increase. (15) As in the sensible world all objects to be seen must be illumined, so also in the intelligible world. As the sun is to the sensible world, so is God to the intelligible world.

ix, 16—xiv, 26. Examination of his Moral State.
(16) He still fears pain, death and loss of friends, but claims

to have made progress in the moral life. (17) Since reading the *Hortensius*, fourteen years before, he has ceased to desire riches. He has recently come to despise fame and marriage. Pleasures of the table do not entice him. (18) Riches, fame, wife, might still be desirable but only as means to the cultivation of wisdom. (19) They are not desired for their own sake and therefore cannot be called cupidities. (20) So with friendships, health, life itself and even immortality. (21) Bodily pain distracts the mind and may be the chief evil, but it can be endured. (22) Why then is wisdom withheld? (23) Long training is necessary, just as eyes must be gradually accustomed to look at the sun. This is the function of the school disciplines. (24) (Next day) "When you achieve the condition of finding no delight at all in earthly things, in that moment you will have wisdom." (25–6) Proof that sensual temptation still has power over him.

xv, 27–30. Epilogue.

(28) Truth is eternal, and (29) must exist in something equally eternal. Whatever truly exists must exist eternally. (30) Augustine will ponder this and pray for power to understand its import.

Book II

i, 1. The Problem stated anew.

Augustine knows that he exists, lives and has intelligence, and that ignorance is misery. He wants to have it proved (*a*) that he will live eternally, and (*b*) that he will know eternally. [(*b*) is not dealt with in the *Soliloquies*, but in its sequel, *De Immortalitate Animae*.]

ii, 2—v, 8. Truth and Falsehood in Sense-knowledge.

(2) Truth is logically indestructible, but (3) the soul perceives reality by means of the senses which are deceptive. Falsehood is that which appears to the percipient other than it truly is. (4) If you allow that falsehood is inevitable and eternal as truth, and that it can only be perceived by a sentient, i.e., living, soul, the soul is proved to be immortal! (5) Without a percipient there can be neither truth nor falsehood, and (7) on these terms there is no escape from solipsism.

vi, 9—x, 18. Truth and Falsehood inevitably intertwined in Sense-knowledge.

(10) The false has some resemblance to the true, exemplified

by a classification of all kinds of resemblance. (13) But the false is also unlike the true. (16) Resemblance may be intended to deceive, but it can also be intended harmlessly to amuse. (17) Painters, sculptors, artists generally, try to produce imitations of the true. (18) Roscius is a real man, but in order to be a true tragedian he must be a false Hecuba, Priam or the like. But we must seek an absolute truth unmixed with falsehood.

xi, 19—xiii, 24. The School Disciplines teach absolute Truth.

(19) The school disciplines are true without admixture of falsehood, because they teach ordered scientific knowledge. Dialectic with its definitions and divisions is the norm, and may be called truth itself. (20) Even literary studies, though they deal with the falsehoods of poetry and fables, deal with them in an objective way, giving ordered knowledge about them. (22) A quality may inhere in a subject as essence or as accident. That which exists inseparably in a subject cannot exist when the subject is destroyed. (23) Soul being essentially life cannot admit of death, though there is the depressing analogy of light which may not admit of darkness, but may be removed to give place to darkness. (24) The school disciplines are truth. They exist in the mind. Therefore the mind is immortal.

xiv, 25–26. Further Difficulties.

(25) The argument is over-subtle. (26) We have no books, and friends who might have helped are absent. Ambrose could have solved the problem but perhaps did not even know there was a problem.

xv, 27—xix, 33. Recapitulation.

(28) Truth is indestructible. (29–30) Truth and falsehood, resemblance and difference. (31) Problem of the void. (32) Matter, form and mathematical figures. (33) Mathematical figures transcend all material things which imitate them but do not fully exemplify them. They are in the mind and they are eternal. Therefore the mind is eternal.

xx, 34 to the end. Epilogue.

(34) Phenomena of memory and forgetfulness. (35) Knowledge may be Reminiscence. At all events it has nothing to do with the senses but belongs to the mind or reason. (36) The problem of the eternal life of the soul has been solved as far as possible. There remains that of its eternal possession of intelligence.

The Soliloquies

THE TEXT

Book I

i, 1. For long I had been turning over in my mind many various thoughts. For many days I had been earnestly seeking to know myself and my chief good and what evil was to be shunned. Suddenly someone spoke to me, whether it was myself or someone else from without or from within I know not. Indeed, to know that is my main endeavour. At any rate someone, let us call him Reason, said to me: Suppose you have discovered some truth. To whom will you entrust it in order that you may proceed to further thoughts? *Augustine.*—To my memory, I suppose. *Reason.*—Can your memory properly preserve all your thoughts. *Augustine.*—That would be difficult, nay impossible. *Reason.*—Then you must write it down. But what do you do when your health will not allow the labour of writing? These thoughts must not be dictated, for they require complete solitude. *A.*—True. I do not know what I am to do, then. *R.*—Pray for health and for aid to attain to what you desire; and write this down that you may become more spirited in your quest. Then briefly summarize your conclusions in a few short theses. Do not look to attract a multitude of readers. This will be sufficient for the few who share your fellowship. *A.*—I shall do as you say.

2. O God, Creator of the universe, give me first that I may pray aright, then that I may conduct myself worthily of being heard by thee, and finally that I may be set free by thee. God, by whom all things come into existence which by themselves would not exist; who permittest not to perish even that which destroys itself; who out of nothing didst create this world which the eyes of all perceive to be most beautiful; who doest no evil so that existence is good because it is thy work; who showest

that evil is nothing to the few who take refuge in the truth; by whom the universe even with its sinister aspects is perfect; by whom there is no absolute disharmony because bad and good together harmonize; whom everything capable of loving loves consciously or unconsciously; in whom are all things yet so that thou art unharmed by the baseness, malice or error of any of thy creatures; who hast willed that none but the pure can know the truth; Father of Truth, of Wisdom, of the True and Perfect Life, of Beatitude, of the Good and Beautiful, of the Intelligible Light, Father of our awakening and of our illumination, of the sign by which we are admonished to return to thee.

3. Thee I invoke, O God, the Truth, in, by and through whom all truths are true; the Wisdom, in, by and through whom all are wise who are wise; the True and Perfect Life, in, by and through whom live all who live truly and perfectly; the Beatitude, in, by and through whom all the blessed are blessed; the Good and the Beautiful, in, by and through whom all good and beautiful things have these qualities; the Intelligible Light, in, by and through whom all intelligible things are illumined; whose kingdom is this whole world unknown to corporeal sense; whose kingdom gives the Law also to these mundane realms; from whom to be turned is to fall; to whom to be turned is to rise; in whom to abide is to stand fast; from whom to depart is to die; to whom to return is to revive; in whom to dwell is to live; whom no man loses unless he be deceived; whom no man seeks unless he has been admonished; whom no man finds unless he has been purified; whom to abandon is to perish; to reach out to whom is to love; to see whom is true possession. I invoke thee, O God, to whom faith calls us, hope lifts us, and charity unites us; by whom we overcome the enemy and are delivered from utter destruction; by whom we are admonished to awake; by whom we distinguish good from evil and shun evil and follow after good; by whom we yield not to adversities; our rightful Lord, whom we rightly serve; by whom we learn that those things are alien which once we thought were ours and that those things are ours which once we thought were alien; by whom we do not cleave to the delights and enticements of wicked men, and are delivered from becoming insignificant through attention to trifles; by whom our better part is not left subject to our lower part; by whom death is swallowed up in victory; who convertest us to thyself; who divestest us of what is not, that thou mayest clothe us with what is; who hearest and defendest us and leadest us into all truth; who speakest to us all

good words and neither makest us nor allowest us to be made foolish; who recallest us to the Way, bringest us to the Door and causest it to be opened to them that knock; who givest us the Bread of Life and causest us to thirst after that water of which having drunk, we thirst no more; who reprovest the world concerning sin, righteousness and judgment; by whom unbelievers do not distress us, and we repudiate the error of those who think that souls have no merit with thee; by whom we serve not the weak and beggarly elements. God, who purgest us and preparest us for divine rewards, come propitiously to my aid.

4. In all that I say come to my aid, thou who art alone God, one substance eternal and true, where there is no strife, no confusion, no transition, no lack, no death, but absolute concord, absolute clearness, constancy, plenitude, life, where nothing is lacking, nothing redundant, and where he who begets and he who is begotten are one. God, whom all serve, and whom every good soul obeys; by whose laws the heavens rotate, the stars hold on their courses, the sun rules the day and the moon the night, and the whole world keeps the mighty constancy of things, so far as sensible matter permits, according to the order and recurrence of times—daily light alternates with darkness; monthly the moon waxes and wanes; yearly there is the succession of spring, summer, autumn, winter; over longer periods there is the perfection of the course of the sun, and in their vast circles the stars return to the place of their rising. God, by whose laws, established for ever, the unstable movement of mutable things is not permitted to be disordered, but is ever reduced to apparent stability by the reins which hold in the revolving ages; by whose laws the soul's will is free, and by unalterable necessity rewards are distributed to the good and punishments to the evil. God, from whom all good things flow down to us, and by whom all evil is warded off from us, above whom is nothing, outside of whom is nothing, without whom is nothing, under whom, in whom and with whom are all things; who hast made man in thine own image and similitude, which every one acknowledges who knows himself. Hear me, my God, my Lord, my King, my Father, my Cause, my Hope, my Riches, my Honour, my Home, my Fatherland, my Health, my Light, my Life. Hear me, hear me, in thine own way known to but few.

5. Now thee only I love; thee only I follow; thee only I seek; thee only am I ready to serve. Because thou alone art justly Lord, I desire to be under thy jurisdiction. Command, I beseech thee, as thou wilt, but heal and open my ears that I may

hear thy voice. Heal and open my eyes that I may see thy beckoning. Drive madness from me that I may recognize thee. Tell me whither I must go that I may behold thee; and I hope to do all that thou dost command. Receive, I pray, thy fugitive, most clement Father and Lord. Already I have been punished enough. Enough have I served thine enemies whom thou hast put under thy feet. Enough have I been the plaything of deceits. Receive me, thy servant, now fleeing from these things, as they formerly received me, a stranger, when I was fleeing from thee. I perceive I must return to thee. Let thy door be opened to me when I knock. Teach me how to come to thee. I have nothing else but the will to come. I know nothing save that transient dying things are to be spurned, certain and eternal things to be sought after. This only I know, O Father, but how to come to thee I know not. Tell me. Show me. Provide for my journey. If those who take refuge in thee find thee by faith, give me faith; if by virtue, give me virtue; if by knowledge, give knowledge. Increase in me faith, hope and charity, O thou admirable and unequalled Goodness.

6. I come to thee, and how to come I ask thee again. For if thou dost leave a man he perishes. But thou dost not, for thou art the highest good which no man hath rightly sought and failed to find. Every man hath rightly sought to whom thou hast given the power to do so. Make me to seek thee, Father. Free me from error. As I seek thee, may nothing else substitute itself for thee. If I desire nothing else but thee, may I at last find thee, Father, I beseech thee. But if there be in me the desire for anything superfluous, do thou thyself cleanse me and make me fit to see thee. Concerning the health of this my mortal body, so long as it is of some use to me, or to those whom I love, I leave it to thee, most kind and wise Father, and I will pray for relief from the scourge wherewith thou dost now chasten me.[1] Only I beseech thy most excellent clemency to convert me wholly to thyself, to allow nothing to gainsay me as I draw near to thee and to bid me while I bear and wear this mortal body to be pure, generous, just and prudent, a perfect lover and receiver of thy Wisdom and worthy to dwell in thy most blessed kingdom. Amen. Amen.

ii, 7. I have made my prayer to God. *Reason.*—What then do you wish to know? *Augustine.*—All that I have mentioned in my prayer. *Reason.*—Briefly summarize it. *Augustine.*—I desire to know God and the soul. *R.*—Nothing more? *A.*—Nothing

1 A reference to his chest trouble.

whatever. *R.*—Begin your quest, then. But first explain what manner of demonstration of God would appear to you satisfying. *A.*—I do not know what kind of demonstration would satisfy me, for I do not think I know anything as I desire to know God. *R.*—What, then, is your difficulty? Don't you think you must first know what is a satisfying knowledge of God, beyond which you will make no further inquiry? *A.*—Certainly; but I do not see how it can be defined. Have I ever had knowledge of anything comparable with God, so that I could say I want to know God as I know that? *R.*—If you do not yet know God how do you know that you know nothing similar to God? *A.*—If I knew anything similar to God I would doubtless love it. But I love nothing but God and the soul, and I know neither. *R.*—Don't you love your friends? *A.*—How could I not love them seeing I love the soul? *R.*—For the same reason do you love fleas and bugs? *A.*—I said I loved the soul, not animals.[1] *R.*—Either your friends are not men or you do not love them. For man is an animal, and you said you did not love animals. *A.*—Indeed they are men and I love them, not because they are animals but because they are men, that is, they have rational souls which I love even in robbers. I can love reason in any man even while I justly hate the man who misuses what I love. I love my friends the more, the better they use their rational souls, or at all events the more they desire to use them well.

iii, 8. *R.*—I agree. But if anyone promised to give you a knowledge of God like the knowledge you have of Alypius, would not you be grateful and say it was enough? *A.*—Indeed I should be grateful, but I should not say it was enough. *R.*—Pray why? *A.*—I do not know God as I know Alypius, but even Alypius I do not know sufficiently well. *R.*—Are you not shameless in wanting to know God better than you know Alypius? *A.*—That does not follow. In comparison with the heavenly bodies nothing is of less account than my dinner. I do not know what I shall have for dinner to-morrow, and yet I do know in what sign of the zodiac the moon will be. There is nothing shameless in that. *R.*—So a sufficient knowledge of God would resemble the knowledge you have of the course of the moon? *A.*—No; because the latter is sense-knowledge. I do not know whether God or some hidden natural cause may suddenly alter the ordinance and course of the moon. Were that to happen all that I had assumed would be false. *R.*—You

1 Anima (soul) is also the life principle of animate beings (animals).

believe that might happen? *A.*—No, I don't. But my question is not about what I believe but about what I know. Possibly we may be rightly said to believe everything we know, but not to know what we only believe. *R.*—In this matter, then, you reject entirely the testimony of the senses. *A.*—Entirely. *R.*—Well now, take your friend Alypius, whom you have just said you do not know sufficiently. Do you wish to know him by sense-knowledge or by intellectual knowledge? *A.*—What I know of him by sense-knowledge—if it can be called knowledge—is insignificant and yet sufficient so far as it goes. But I desire to reach by intellect a knowledge of that part of him, namely, his mind, where he is truly my friend. *R.*—Can he be known otherwise? *A.*—By no means. *R.*—Do you dare to say that your most familiar friend is unknown to you? *A.*—There is no daring about it. I think that law of friendship is most just which lays down that a man shall love his friend as himself, neither less nor more. So, seeing that I do not know myself, how can I be reproached for saying that I do not know him, especially since, I dare say, he does not profess to know himself either. *R.*—If the knowledge you seek is of the kind which is attained by the intellect alone, you had no right, when I said it was shameless of you to seek to know God while professing ignorance of Alypius, to offer the analogy of your dinner and the moon, for these things, as you say, belong to the world of the senses. iv, 9. But no matter. Answer me this: If the statements of Plato and Plotinus concerning God are true, would you be satisfied to know God as they knew him? *A.*—Even if their statements are true, it does not necessarily follow that they knew him. Many speak at great length of things they do not know, just as I said I desire to know all the things I mentioned in my prayer. I could not desire to know what I already knew. How then was I able to speak of these things? I spoke not that which I understood with my mind, but that which I have gathered from many quarters and committed to memory and in which I have put such faith as I was able. To know is quite another matter. *R.*—Tell me this. You know what a line is in geometry. *A.*—Yes, that I clearly know. *R.*—In saying so you are not afraid of the Academics. *A.*—Not at all. They wanted to avoid philosophical error. I am no philosopher, so I am not afraid to profess knowledge of the things I know. But if I reach Wisdom as I desire I shall do as she directs. *R.*—Quite right. But to return to my question. You know what a line is. Do you also know the round object which is called a sphere? *A.*—I do.

R.—Every point on the circumference is equidistant from the centre. *A.*—Exactly. *R.*—Have you gained this knowledge by the senses or by the intellect? *A.*—In this matter I have found the senses to be like a ship. They brought me to my destination, but when I dismissed them and began to think about these things in my mind I was still as one on the high seas and my footsteps long faltered. It seems to me one might more readily sail on dry land than learn geometry by the senses, and yet they seem to be of some use to beginners. *R.*—You do not doubt, then, that whatever you have learned of these things is to be called knowledge? *A.*—The Stoics would not permit me, for they attribute knowledge to none but the Sage. I do not deny that I have such perception of these matters as they concede even to fools. But I have no fear of the Stoics. Certainly I have knowledge of those things about which you asked me. Go on and let me see the purpose of your questioning. *R.*—There is no need for haste. We are at leisure. Just be careful to make no rash concessions. I am trying to give you confidence in matters in which you need fear no fall, and, as if that were a small business, you bid me hasten on. *A.*—May God do as you say. Ask as you see fit, and rebuke me more severely if I become impatient again.

10. *R.*—It is manifest to you, then, that a line cannot by any possibility be divided lengthwise? *A.*—It is. *R.*—But across? *A.*—It is infinitely divisible. *R.*—Similarly it is clear that a sphere cannot have more than one point from which circles may be drawn. *A.*—Quite so. *R.*—Are lines and spheres the same or do they differ? *A.*—Obviously they differ very much. *R.*—If they differ very much, as you say, and yet you know both of them equally, the knowledge remains the same even if its objects differ. *A.*—No one denied that. *R.*—Oh yes, you did a moment ago. When I asked what kind of knowledge of God would satisfy you, you replied that you could not explain it because you had grasped nothing as you desired to know God, that you knew nothing comparable to God. Now does the line resemble the sphere? *A.*—Who would say such a thing? *R.*—My question was not *what* you know but *how* you know. Have you any knowledge that resembles knowledge of God? Your knowledge of the line and the sphere is the same knowledge though its objects differ. Tell me, would you be satisfied to know God as you know the mathematical sphere, that is, to have no more doubt in the one case than in the other?

v, 11. *A.*—You press me hard and almost convince me, but I

dare not say that I wish to know God as I know these things. Not only the things but the knowledge, too, seem to me to be different. First, because the line and the sphere do not differ so much that knowledge of them cannot be contained within the framework of one science. Now no geometer ever professed to teach about God. Secondly, if knowledge of God were the same as knowledge of mathematical figures, I would rejoice as much in the knowledge of them as I expect to rejoice when I come to know God. But in comparison with the latter I despise the former so much that it sometimes seems to me that all these things would perish from my mind if I should come to know him and to see him in the manner in which he can be seen. Even now compared to love of him these things hardly enter my mind. *R.*—Granted that you would rejoice more in the knowledge of God than in the knowledge of these things, the difference would be due to the objects known not to the knowing. No doubt looking at a serene sky gives you much greater pleasure than looking at the earth, yet the seeing would be the same. If you were asked whether you were as certain of your seeing the earth as of your seeing the sky, I believe you would have to reply—unless your eyes were at fault—that you were just as certain, even though you had greater pleasure in the beauty and lustre of the heaven. *A.*—I confess your similitude affects me, and I am induced to assent up to a point. As the sky is superior to the earth in its peculiar beauty, so is the intelligible beauty of God superior to the certain truths of mathematics.

vi, 12. *R.*—You do well to be so affected. For Reason who speaks with you promises to let you see God with your mind as the sun is seen with the eye. The mind has, as it were, eyes of its own, analogous to the soul's senses. The certain truths of the sciences are analogous to the objects which the sun's rays make visible, such as the earth and earthly things. And it is God himself who illumines all. I, Reason, am in minds as the power of looking is in the eyes. Having eyes is not the same thing as looking, and looking is not the same as seeing. The soul therefore needs three things: eyes which it can use aright, looking and seeing. The eye of the mind is healthy when it is pure from every taint of the body, that is, when it is remote and purged from desire of mortal things. And this, faith alone can give in the first place. It is impossible to show God to a mind vitiated and sick. Only the healthy mind can see him. But if the mind does not believe that only thus will it attain vision, it will not seek healing. Even if it believes that this is true, and that only so will it attain the vision, but at the same time despairs of healing, will it not abandon the quest and refuse to obey the precepts of the physician? *A.*—Most assuredly, especially because its disease must have sharp remedies. *R.*—So to faith must be added hope. *A.*—That I believe. *R.*—Suppose it believes all this is true and hopes that healing is possible, but does not love and desire the promised light, and thinks it must meantime be content with its darkness which through habit has become pleasant, will it not, no less, spurn the physician? *A.*—Perfectly true. *R.*—Therefore a third thing is necessary, love. *A.*—There is nothing more necessary. *R.*—Without these three no soul is healed so that it may see, that is, know God.

13. When its eyes are healed, what next? *A.*—It must look. *R.*—Yes. Reason is the power of the soul to look, but it does not follow that every one who looks, sees. Right and perfect looking which leads to vision is called virtue. For virtue is right and perfect reason. But even looking cannot turn eyes already healed to the light unless these three things are present: faith that believes that the object to which our looking ought to be directed can, when seen, make us blessed; hope which is assured that vision will follow right looking; love which longs to see and to enjoy. Then looking is followed by the vision of God, its true end in the sense that there is nothing more to look for. This truly is perfect virtue, reason achieving its end, which is the happy life. This vision is knowledge compounded of the knower and that which is known; just as vision in the ordinary sense is compounded of the sense of sight and the sensible object, of which if either is lacking there is no seeing.

vii, 14. Now let us see whether these three things are still necessary when the soul has attained the vision, that is the knowledge, of God. Why should faith be necessary when vision is already attained? And hope, too, when that which was hoped for is grasped? From love alone nothing can be taken away, but rather much must be added. For when the soul sees that unique and true Beauty it will love it more. Unless it fix its eye upon it with strong love and never leave off looking towards it, it will not be able to abide in that most blessed vision. But while the soul inhabits this mortal body, even if it fully sees, that is, knows, God, the bodily senses perform their proper functions. They may not have power to lead astray, but at least they can make things difficult. Faith may be called that which resists the senses and believes that the world of the mind is better. Again, in this life, though the soul may be blessed by the knowledge of God, nevertheless it has to bear many bodily troubles. It must hope that all these disadvantages will cease after death. In this life hope never departs from the soul. But when after this life the soul gives itself wholly to God, love remains to hold it fast. Faith cannot be said to be, where truth is assailed by no falsehood. Nothing is left to hope for when everything is securely possessed. There are three stages in the soul's progress: healing, looking, seeing. Likewise there are three virtues: faith, hope, love. For healing and looking, faith and hope are always necessary. For seeing, all three are necessary in this life, but in the life to come love only.

viii, 15. Now listen while I teach you something concerning God from the analogy of sensible things, so far as the present time demands. God, of course, belongs to the realm of intelligible things, and so do these mathematical symbols, though there is a great difference. Similarly the earth and light are visible, but the earth cannot be seen unless it is illumined. Anyone who knows the mathematical symbols admits that they are true without the shadow of a doubt. But he must also believe that they cannot be known unless they are illumined by something else corresponding to the sun. About this corporeal sun notice three things. It exists. It shines. It illumines. So in knowing the hidden God you must observe three things. He exists. He is known. He causes other things to be known. I am venturing to teach you how to know God and yourself. But how will you take what I say? as probable or as true? *A.*—As probable assuredly, but I must confess I am aroused to a greater hope. I know that what you have said about the line and the sphere is true, but I would not dare to say of any of your other statements that I know it. *R.*—That is not surprising, for nothing has been expounded hitherto which demands comprehension.

ix, 16. But now let us get on without delay, and let us begin with the first question of all, whether we are healed and sound. *A.*—That we shall discover by investigating your inward state or mine. Do you ask and I shall give my opinions in reply. *R.*—Is there anything you love besides knowledge of yourself and of God? *A.*—I could, of course, reply that in my present mood there is nothing that I love more, but it would be safer to say that I do not know. My experience has been that often, when I supposed that nothing could move me, something has come into my mind which has affected me more than I imagined. It may not have completely drawn me away from my thoughts, but in fact it has interrupted them more than I supposed. It would seem that I can be affected by three things chiefly, fear of losing my friends, fear of pain and fear of death. *R.*—So you love your health, your own life in the body, and to be surrounded by your friends. Otherwise you would not dread the loss of these things. *A.*—I confess that is so. *R.*—So your mind is somewhat disturbed because all your friends are not here with you, and because your health is not very good. That is the point. *A.*—You are right. I cannot deny it. *R.*—If you were suddenly to become sound and well, and to see all your friends around you enjoying peace and cultured leisure, you would be transported with joy. *A.*—Yes, to some extent. And if it all happened suddenly, as you put it, how could I contain myself? How could I be expected to dissimulate transports of joy. *R.*—So up till now you are agitated by the well-known diseases and perturbations of the mind. What impudence for such eyes to wish to see the sun of the intellectual realm! *A.*—You have jumped to conclusions as if I did not feel that I had made any moral progress, that some temptations had lost their power and that some resistance had been offered. Ask about this.

x, 17. *R.*—Don't you see that corporeal eyes even when sound are often smitten by the light of the sun and have to be averted and find refuge in darkness? Why then do you speak of progress, and not only of what you wish to see? Nevertheless let us discuss the progress we think we have made. Do you desire riches? *A.*—No, not for a long time. I am now in my thirty-third year. Nearly fourteen years ago I ceased to desire riches, and, if perchance they came my way, I cared for no more than a necessary livelihood, enough to support a life of culture. One book of Cicero's easily and completely persuaded me that riches were not to be sought and that, if they were acquired, they were to be used wisely and cautiously. *R.*—What about honours? *A.*—I confess that only recently, in these last few days, I have ceased to desire them. *R.*—What about marriage? Would you not like to have a wife who was beautiful, chaste, obedient, educated or at least whom you could easily teach, bringing enough dowry, though you despise wealth, at least to keep her from being a burden on your leisure, especially if you are pretty certain that she will not cause you any trouble? *A.*—Paint her virtues as you will, and heap up good qualities, nevertheless I have decided that there is nothing I must more carefully avoid than the marriage-bed. I find there is nothing which more certainly casts a man's mind out of its citadel than female blandishments and bodily contacts which are essential to marriage. So if it is part of the duty of the Sage (which I have not yet learned) to have children, anyone who has intercourse with a woman for this purpose only seems to me worthy of admiration rather than of imitation. The danger of attempting it is greater than the happiness of achieving it. Accordingly in the interests of righteousness and the liberty of my soul I have made it my rule not to desire or seek or marry a wife. *R.*—I am not now asking about your resolutions, but whether you are still struggling with lust or have already overcome it. The question has to do with the soundness of your spiritual eyes. *A.*—I am completely free from desires of this kind, and I recall them with horror and disdain. What more need I say? This virtue increases in me day by day. The more my hope increases of beholding that spiritual Beauty for which I long so eagerly, the more does all my love and pleasure turn to it. *R.*—What about the pleasures of the table? How much thought do you give to them? *A.*—Foods which I have determined not to touch attract me not at all, but I confess that those which I have not banned do indeed delight me when they are available. But I can see them removed, even when I have tasted them, without any emotion. When they are not to hand no longing for them insinuates itself to disturb my thoughts. Do not trouble to ask me any more about food or drink or baths or any other bodily pleasure. I desire only so much of them as contributes to my health.

xi, 18. *R.*—You have made good progress. But the vices which remain still greatly hinder you from seeing the light. I am attempting an argument that can apparently prove either that nothing remains for us to conquer, or that we have made no progress at all and that the corruption of our vices, which we thought to have removed, is still with us. Suppose you were persuaded that you could not live in the pursuit of wisdom with your numerous friends unless you had an ample private fortune to supply your needs, would you not desire and choose riches? *A.*—I might. *R.*—Suppose it appeared that you would persuade many to seek wisdom if your authority were increased by having honours showered upon you, and that your friends could not moderate their cupidities and turn wholly to seek God unless they themselves received honour and could do so only as a result of your having honour and dignity, would not honours be desirable, and the obtaining of them a pressing concern? *A.*—That is so. *R.*—I do not want to introduce marriage into this argument for possibly it is not so relevant. But suppose your wife had an ample income which could support all whom you wished to live with you in leisure, and that she were willing. Suppose she belonged to a noble and influential family so that through her you could easily obtain the honours you admitted might be necessary. I wonder whether you would consider yourself in duty bound to contemn all this. *A.*—When would I venture to hope so?

19. *R.*—You say that as if I were asking about your hopes. I am not asking about what gives no pleasure simply because it is beyond your reach, but about what gives pleasure when offered to you. A spent pestilence is a very different thing from one that is merely quiescent. The dictum of certain learned men is in point here. "All fools are mad just as dung stinks—you don't smell it all the time but only when you move it." There is a vast difference between smothering cupidity with despair, and driving it out of a sound mind. *A.*—Although I cannot answer you, you will never persuade me in my present state of mind to believe that I have made no progress. *R.*—I suppose the reason is that you think that, while you might conceivably desire these things, it would not be on their own account they were to be sought but on account of something else. *A.*—That is what I wanted to say. When I desired riches I desired them that I might be a rich man; and when I wanted honours, desire for which I have but recently overcome as I said, it was because I was delighted with their lustre. I never expected anything from marriage but to obtain pleasure respectably. In those days I quite simply wanted those things. Now I utterly spurn them. But if there is no other way of obtaining what I now desire, I would not seek them as things to be enjoyed. I would undergo them as things I must endure. *R.*—Quite right. I agree that cupidity is not the right name for desire for something that is wanted on account of something else.

xii, 20. But why, I ask, do you wish your friends to live and to live with you? *A.*—That with one mind we may together seek knowledge of our souls and God. For in this way, if one makes a discovery he can without trouble bring the others to see it. *R.*—But if they are unwilling to inquire? *A.*—I shall persuade them to be willing. *R.*—But if you cannot persuade them, because they think they have discovered the truth already, or that it cannot be discovered, or are hindered by other cares and longings? *A.*—We shall do the best we can. *R.*—But if their presence hinders you from inquiry, will you not wish and strive if their attitude cannot be changed, not to have them with you? *A.*—I confess that is so. *R.*—Then you desire their life and presence not for its own sake but in order to find out wisdom. *A.*—I agree at once. *R.*—If your own life was a hindrance to the obtaining of wisdom, would you want it to continue? *A.*—No; I should flee from it. *R.*—If you learned that you could reach wisdom equally by continuing in the body or by leaving it, would you greatly care whether you enjoyed what you love in this life or in another? *A.*—If I knew that I should encounter nothing that would drive me back from the point to which I have already progressed I should not care. *R.*—Your reason, then, for fearing death now is lest you be involved in some evil which would rob you of the knowledge of God. *A.*—Not only lest *I* should be robbed of such understanding as I have reached, but also lest, retaining what I myself possess, I should be precluded from the society of those whom I eagerly desire to share it. *R.*—So you do not wish for continued life on its own account but on account of wisdom? *A.*—That is so.

21. *R.*—There remains only bodily pain to distract you. *A.*—Even that I do not greatly fear except that it hinders my meditations. When, recently, I was tortured with a sharp toothache, I could only meditate upon things I had already learned and was completely prevented from learning anything new, which demands undivided attention. Still, I thought if the truth were to shine into my mind, either I should not feel the pain, or at least I could bear it. And yet, although I have never suffered anything worse, I reflected how much more grievous pains might come, and I am compelled to agree with Cornelius Celsus[1] who says that the supreme good is wisdom and the supreme evil is bodily pain. The reason he gives I think not absurd. For, he says, seeing we are composed of two parts, soul and body, of which the soul is the better and the body the inferior, the supreme good will be the best that can happen to the superior part, and the supreme evil the worst that can happen to the inferior part. Wisdom is the best the soul can have, and pain the worst thing the body can suffer. So I think we may rightly conclude that to be wise is man's supreme good and to suffer pain his supreme evil. *R.*—We shall consider that later. Perhaps Wisdom herself, towards which we struggle, will persuade us otherwise. But if she shows that it is true we shall hold this opinion about the supreme good and the supreme evil without any hesitation.

[1] A famous Roman physician, flor. A.D. 50.

xiii, 22. But now what kind of man are you to be Wisdom's lover, desirous of seeing and embracing her, as it were, without any covering garment but yet most chastely. That privilege she allows only to a very few chosen lovers. If you burned with love for some beautiful woman, she would not rightly give herself to you if she found you loved anything else besides. So that most chaste beauty, Wisdom, will not show herself to you unless you burn for her alone. *A.*—Why am I, then, kept in unhappy suspense and miserably tortured by being put off? Surely I have shown already that I love nothing else, at any rate if that is not really loved which is not loved for its own sake. Wisdom alone I love for her own sake. All else—life, leisure, friends—I wish to have or fear to lose solely on her account. What bounds can be set to love of so great a beauty, in which not only do I not envy others but also wish to have as many as possible along with me seeking her, panting after her, holding and enjoying her, in the belief that they will be my friends all the more because love for her is shared by us in common.

23. *R.*—Such should the lovers of Wisdom be. Such she seeks, with whom intercourse is truly chaste and without defilement. Not by one way is she approached.[1] Each man according to his soundness and firmness takes hold of that unique and truest Good. There is a certain ineffable and incomprehensible light of minds. Ordinary light may teach us what is its power and quality. Some eyes are so strong and vigorous that as soon as they are opened they can look at the sun without any hesitation. For them the light is in a sense their soundness. They need no teacher but only perhaps some admonition. It is sufficient for them to believe, to hope, to love. Others are smitten by the very brightness that they longed to behold, and are often glad to return without seeing it to their darkness. To such, though they may rightly be called sound, it is dangerous to show what they have not yet the power to see. They must first be exercised and their love deferred and nourished to their advantage. First, they must be shown things which do not shine by any light of their own but are rendered visible by light, such as a garment, a wall or the like. Next, they must be shown things which, though having no lustre of their own, shine more brightly in the light but not so as to hurt the eyes, such as gold, silver and the like. Then they must be made carefully to look at ordinary fire,

[1] Cf. *Retract.* I. iv. 3. "This does not sound right, as if there were another way besides Christ, who said: I am the Way. I ought to have avoided this offence to religious ears."

then at the stars, the moon, the dawn and the gradually brightening sky. So more or less speedily, following the whole course or omitting some steps in it according to his ability, a man will grow accustomed to light and will be able to look at the sun without hesitation and with great pleasure. This is what the best teachers do with students of wisdom who do not yet have sharp vision. To provide an approach to it in some kind of order is the function of good training. To reach it without order demands incredible good fortune. But we have written enough for to-day. We must be careful for your health.

xiv, 24. [One day later the conversation was resumed.] *A.*—Prescribe for me the order you mentioned. Lead me whither you wish, how you wish, by what methods you wish. Lay commands upon me as severe and arduous as you like so long as to obey them is within my power, and I gain assurance of reaching my desired goal. *R.*—There is only one prescription I can give you. I know no other. You must entirely flee from things of sense. So long as we bear this body we must beware lest our wings are hindered by their birdlime. We need sound and perfect wings if we are to fly from this darkness to yonder light, which does not deign to manifest itself to men shut up in a cave unless they can escape, leaving sensible things broken and dissolved. When you achieve the condition of finding no delight at all in earthly things, in that moment, believe me, at that point of time, you will see what you desire. *A.*—When, pray, will that be? I do not think I can ever reach complete contempt for earthly things unless I see something compared with which they become sordid.

25. *R.*—In the same way, the bodily eye might say: I shall not love darkness when I can look on the sun. There seems to be a kind of orderliness in that, though in fact there is none. The eye loves darkness because it is not strong, and unless it be strong it cannot see the sun. So the mind is often deceived, thinks itself sound and gives itself airs. Because it cannot yet see, it complains as if it had the right to do so. But the supreme beauty knows when to show itself. It performs the function of the physician, and knows who are whole better than those who are being healed. When we have emerged a little from darkness we think we see, but cannot imagine or perceive how deeply we had been sunk or how far we have progressed. Comparing our condition with graver forms of disease we believe we are healed. Do you remember how, yesterday, in complete assurance, we declared that we were free from disease, that we loved nothing

but Wisdom; all else we sought and desired only for the sake of Wisdom? How sordid, how base, how execrable, how horrible the embrace of a woman seemed to you when we were discussing the desire for marriage! But as you lay awake last night and the same question arose, you found it was very different with you than you had supposed. Imagined fondlings and bitter sweetness tickled your fancy, much less than formerly, of course, but far more than you had supposed. In that way the mysterious physician was teaching you two things; how you can evade his care, and what remains to be cured.

26. *A.*—Oh, be silent, be silent I beseech you! Why do you torture me? Why do you cut so deep? I am not too hardened for weeping. Now I promise nothing, I presume nothing. Do not ask me about these things. You say that he whom I burn to see knows when I am healed. Let him do what he pleases. Let him show himself when he pleases. I commit myself wholly to his care and clemency. Once for all I have accepted the belief that he will not cease to aid those who have set their affections on him. I shall never again say anything about my healing until I see spiritual beauty. *R.*—Do as you say, but restrain your tears and brace your mind. You have wept much, and that is not good for your chest-trouble. *A.*—You wish me to set a limit to my tears though I see no limit to my misery. You bid me consider my bodily health when I am myself consumed with wasting. But I pray you, if you do anything for me, try to lead me by some short-cut to a place near to that light where, if I have made any progress, I may be able to bear it, so that I may be reluctant to go back to the darkness which I have left—if indeed I may be said to have left it—and which soothes my blindness.

xv, 27. *R.*—Let us conclude, if you please, this first Book, so that in a second Book we may start on a suitable path if we can find one; for we must give you in your frame of mind some moderate exercise. *A.*—I shall not allow this Book to be concluded unless you give me a glimpse of what I am seeking, if it be only of something near the light. *R.*—I see the physician is treating you in his accustomed way. Some brightness touches me and invites me along a way in which I may lead you. So listen carefully. *A.*—Lead on and take me where you wish. *R.*—You say you want to know the soul and God? *A.*—That is my whole enterprise. *R.*—Nothing more? *A.*—Nothing whatever. *R.*—Well. You want to know Truth. *A.*—As if I could know anything without that. *R.*—Therefore, that must be first known by which other things are known. *A.*—I agree. *R.*—First let us ask this question. There are two words, *Veritas* and *Verum*. Do you think they signify two things, or only one? *A.*—Two things, evidently. For just as *castitas* is one thing and *castum* another, and so with many other similar pairs of words, so, I believe, Truth is one thing and that which is said to be true is another. *R.*—Which of the two do you think is more excellent? *A.*—Truth, I think. What is chaste is a particular instance of Chastity. Similarly, what is true is a particular instance of Truth.

28. *R.*—When a chaste person dies, Chastity has not died too? *A.*—By no means. *R.*—Therefore, when something that is true perishes, Truth does not perish. *A.*—I do not see how anything that is true can perish. *R.*—I am surprised at that. Don't you see thousands of things perishing before our eyes? Can you imagine that this tree is a tree but is not true, or that it cannot perish? Though you do not trust the senses and can reply that you do not know whether it is a tree, at least you will not deny, I suppose, that it is truly a tree if it is a tree. For that is a judgment not of the senses but of the intelligence. If it is a false tree it is not a tree. But if it is a tree it is true, necessarily. *A.*—I admit that. *R.*—Don't you admit also that a tree belongs to the class of things that are born and die? *A.*—I cannot deny it. *R.*—The conclusion, then, is that something that is true perishes. *A.*—I do not contradict. *R.*—You see, then, that when true things perish Truth does not perish, just as Chastity does not die when a chaste person dies. *A.*—Now I agree and expectantly await the development of your argument. *R.*—Well. Listen. *A.*—I am all agog.

29. *R.*—Do you think the statement is true: whatever is must be somewhere. *A.*—Of that I am as sure as of anything. *R.*—Truth exists. *A.*—I agree. *R.*—Then we must ask where it exists. For it cannot be in space unless you think that something which is not a material body can be in space, or that Truth itself is a corporeal thing. *A.*—I hold neither of these views. *R.*—Where, then, can it exist? For if we admit it exists, it must exist somewhere. *A.*—If I knew where it exists I should probably have no further questions to ask. *R.*—At least you can know where it does not exist. *A.*—If you tell me I might. *R.*—Certainly it does not exist in mortal things. Whatever is, cannot be permanent if that in which it exists is not permanent. A moment ago we agreed that Truth remains even when true things perish. Truth, therefore, does not exist in mortal things.

But it must exist somewhere. There are, therefore, immortal things. But nothing is true in which Truth does not exist. Therefore, only immortal things are true. A false tree is no tree; a false log is no log; false silver is not silver; universally what is false *is* not. All that is not true is false. Therefore nothing which is not immortal can be said truly to be. Consider diligently in your own mind this little piece of reasoning and see whether there is any mistake in it. If it holds we have nearly finished our job. This will perhaps become more apparent in the next Book.

30. *A.*—I am most grateful, and I shall diligently and carefully ponder these things with you in the silence of my own heart, if no darkness come upon me to charm me, as I greatly fear it may. *R.*—Believe steadfastly in God, and commit yourself wholly to him as far as you are able. Do not seek to be your own and under your own jurisdiction, but profess yourself the servant of the most clement Lord whom it is most advantageous to serve. He will not cease to lift you up to himself, and will permit nothing to happen to you that will not profit you, even when you know it not. *A.*—I understand. I believe. And to the limit of my power I shall obey. I earnestly ask him to increase my power. Do you want anything more of me? *R.*—Enough for the present. When you have seen him you will do what he prescribes.

Book II

i, 1. *Augustine.*—We have sufficiently rested from our labours. Love is impatient, and there is no limit to tears until love is given what it loves. Let us then begin the second Book. *Reason.*—Let us begin. *A.*—Let us believe in God. *R.*—Surely, if we can. *A.*—God gives us power. *R.*—Pray, then, as briefly and as perfectly as you can. *A.*—O God, who art ever the same, let me know myself and thee. That is my prayer. *R.*—You who wish to know yourself, do you know that you exist? *A.*—I do. *R.*—How do you know. *A.*—That I do not know. *R.*—Do you perceive yourself to be simple or compounded? *A.*—I do not know. *R.*—You know that you have motion? *A.*—No, I don't. *R.*—You know that you think? *A.*—I do. *R.*—Then it is true that you think. *A.*—It is true. *R.*—Do you know that you are immortal? *A.*—No. *R.*—Of all those things which you say you do not know, which would you prefer to know? *A.*—Whether I am immortal. *R.*—So you love to live? *A.*—I admit I do. *R.*—Will it satisfy you to learn that you are immortal? *A.*—It will be a great matter but not sufficient. *R.*—Though it be not sufficient, how much will you rejoice in that knowledge? *A.*—A great deal. *R.*—You will not weep any more? *A.*—No. *R.*—But if you discover that even immortal life will not enable you to know more than you already know, will you refrain from tears? *A.*—I shall weep as if that were no life at all. *R.*—So you love life not for the sake of living but for the sake of knowing. *A.*—I accept that conclusion. *R.*—But if knowledge itself made you unhappy? *A.*—I cannot believe that possible. But if it is so, no man can be happy? My unhappiness has no other source than my ignorance. If knowledge makes a man unhappy, then misery is eternal. *R.*—Now I see all that you desire. Since you believe that knowledge makes no one unhappy, it follows that probably intelligence makes a man happy. No one is happy unless he has life, and no one lives who does not exist. You want to be, to live and to know, but to be in order to live and to live in order to know. You know that you exist and live and have intelligence; but you wish to know whether you will always have being, life and intelligence, or none of them; whether some of them will endure eternally while others perish; or, if all remain, whether they will be diminished or increased. *A.*—That is so. *R.*—If we prove that we shall live eternally, it will follow that we shall exist eternally. *A.*—It will. *R.*—There will remain only the question of our knowing eternally.

ii, 2. *A.*—The order is clear and short. *R.*—Listen and answer my questions cautiously and firmly. *A.*—I am your man. *R.*—If the world is to endure for ever, it is true to say the world will endure for ever. *A.*—None can doubt it. *R.*—If it will not endure, it is similarly true that it will not endure. *A.*—I agree. *R.*—If it has perished (assuming it is to perish), it will then be true to say that the world has perished. For so long as that is not true the world has not perished. The statement "the world has perished" contradicts the statement "it is not true that the world has perished." *A.*—This too I accept. *R.*—Well, now. Do you think anything can be true if Truth ceases to exist? *A.*—By no means. *R.*—Therefore Truth will exist even if the world perishes. *A.*—I cannot deny it. *R.*—If Truth itself perishes, it will be true that Truth has perished? *A.*—Who denies it? *R.*—But nothing can be true if there is no Truth. *A.*—I have admitted that a moment ago. *R.*—Truth, therefore, can never perish. *A.*—Go on as you have begun, for nothing is more true than that conclusion.

iii, 3. *R.*—I should like you to tell me whether you think the senses belong to the soul or to the body. *A.*—To the soul, I think. *R.*—And intelligence belongs to the soul? *A.*—Certainly. *R.*—To the soul alone, or to anything else? *A.*—I see nothing besides the soul, except God, where intelligence may be supposed to reside. *R.*—Now let us look into that. If anyone said to you that that object is not a wall but a tree, what would you think? *A.*—Either that his sight or mine was at fault, or that "tree" was his word for "wall." *R.*—Suppose to him there appeared to be a tree and to you a wall. Could not both be true? *A.*—By no means, for one and the same thing cannot be both a tree and a wall. If each of us sees differently, one or other of us must have a false image. *R.*—If there was neither a tree nor a wall both of you would be wrong. *A.*—That is possible. *R.*—That possibility you neglected just now. *A.*—I confess I did. *R.*—If you recognize that a thing appears to you other than it is, are you deceived? *A.*—No. *R.*—It is possible, then, for an appearance to be false while he to whom it appears is not deceived. *A.*—It is possible. *R.*—We must confess, therefore, that a man is deceived not when he sees falsely but when he assents to what is false. *A.*—Clearly we must. *R.*—How would you define falsehood? *A.*—That is false which is other than it seems. *R.*—If, then, there is no one to be taken in, there is no falsehood. *A.*—It follows. *R.*—There is, then, no falsity in things but only in our senses. But no one is deceived who does not assent to what is false. Our conclusion is that we must make a distinction between ourselves and our senses, if indeed our senses may be deceived while we can be free from deception. *A.*—I have nothing to urge to the contrary. *R.*—But if your soul is deceived you will not venture to deny that you are false? *A.*—How could I? *R.*—But there are no senses without a soul, and no falsity without senses. Hence either the soul works alone or co-operates with falsity. *A.*—The argument compels assent.

4. *R.*—Now tell me whether you think there can ever be a time when falsity is no more? *A.*—How could I think so, when there is such difficulty in finding the truth. It would be more absurd to say that falsity can cease to be than that truth should cease. *R.*—Do you think that a man who does not live can use the senses? *A.*—It cannot be. *R.*—Then it is proved that the soul is immortal. *A.*—You make my heart glad too quickly. Step by step, I beseech you! *R.*—And yet if the argument has been correct I see no reason to doubt the conclusion. *A.*—You go too quickly, I say. I should be more readily induced to judge that I have been rash in my admissions than to be sure of the

immortality of the soul. Elucidate your conclusion and show me how it has been reached. *R.*—You said that falsity cannot be without the senses, and that it cannot cease to be. Therefore the senses are eternal. But there are no senses without a soul. Hence the soul is eternal. Moreover there are no senses without life. Therefore the soul lives eternally.

iv, 5. *A.*—A blunt weapon! You could as soon conclude that man is immortal if I agreed that the world could not exist without man, and that the world is eternal. *R.*—You are very watchful. Yet it is no small result to have ascertained that the world cannot be without the soul, if we cannot admit the possibility of there being no falsity in the world. *A.*—That follows, I agree. But I think we must consider more fully whether some of our earlier admissions are not shaky. I see that a considerable step has been taken towards proving the immortality of the soul. *R.*—Are you satisfied that you have conceded nothing rashly? *A.*—Yes. I see no reason to accuse myself of rashness. *R.*—Then it is proved that the world cannot exist without the living soul. *A.*—That may mean only that when some die others are born. *R.*—If falsity is banished from the universe, that means that all things become true. *A.*—I see it follows. *R.*—Tell me how you think that wall is a true wall. *A.*—Because I am not mistaken when I look at it. *R.*—Because it is what it seems. *A.*—For that reason too. *R.*—If a thing is false because it seems different from what it is, and true because it is what it seems, take away the percipient and it is neither true nor false. But if there is no falsity in the universe, all things are true. And nothing can be perceived except by a living soul. The soul is therefore eternal, whether falsity can be abolished or not. *A.*—I see that our conclusion was pretty strong, and we have not moved forward by this additional argument. Nevertheless, my chief difficulty remains. Souls are born and die, and the fact that there are always souls in the world is due not to their immortality but to their succession.

6. *R.*—Do you think that any corporeal things, i.e., objects of the senses, can be comprehended by the intellect? *A.*—I do not. *R.*—Do you think God uses senses to know things? *A.*—I do not venture to make any rash assertion in such a matter, but, so far as I may guess, God does not make use of senses. *R.*—We draw the conclusion, therefore, that the soul alone has senses. *A.*—Provisionally, that is probable. *R.*—Well, now. You agree that if that wall is not a true wall it is not a wall? *A.*—That is quite simple. *R.*—Nor is anything a corporeal object unless it is

truly such? *A.*—Equally simple. *R.*—Now, if nothing is true unless it is what it seems; and no bodily object can be seen except by the senses; and the soul alone has senses; and there is no corporeal object unless it is truly such; it follows that there cannot be a corporeal object unless there is a soul. *A.*—You press me hard and I cannot resist your argument.

v, 7. *R.*—Give your closest attention to this. *A.*—I am ready. *R.*—Here is a stone; truly a stone if it is what it seems. It is not a stone if it is not a true stone. And it cannot be seen except by the senses. *A.*—Well? *R.*—There are, therefore, no stones hidden deep in the earth where there is no one to see them. That would not be a stone unless we were looking at it; nor will it be a stone when we depart and there is no one else here to see it. If you completely seal up a room containing many objects, there will be nothing there. That log will not be composed of wood throughout. For the inside of an opaque body escapes the senses, and therefore cannot exist. If it existed it would be true; what is true is what it appears to be. But this does not appear to any one. Therefore it is not true. Have you any reply to this? *A.*—The conclusion seems to spring from what I have admitted. But it is equally absurd to deny anything I have said as to concede that the conclusion is correct. *R.*—I do not dispute it. But what would you prefer to say: bodily objects can be seen apart from the senses; or there can be sense apart from the soul; or a stone or any other object can exist without being true; or we must find another definition of what is true? *A.*—Let us examine the last alternative.

8. *R.*—Give a definition of truth. *A.*—Truth is that which is as it seems to him who knows it, if he will and can know it. *R.*—Then that will not be true which no one can know? If that is false which seems otherwise than it is, what happens if this seems to one man to be a stone and to another a piece of wood? Can the same thing be both false and true? *A.*—What interests me more is how a thing that cannot be known can yet be not true. I do not so much care whether one thing can be at the same time both true and false. For I see that one thing may be compared with several things and may be both greater and smaller at the same time. So it happens that nothing in itself is either greater or smaller. These words apply when comparisons are made. *R.*—But if you say that nothing is true in itself, are you not afraid of the consequence that nothing *is* in itself? The existence of this piece of wood and the truth about it come from the same source. It can neither be nor be true by itself without

someone to know it. *A.*—That is why I define in this way, and do not fear that my definition should be disapproved because it is too short. For that which is seems to me to be true. *R.*—Then, if whatever is is true there will be nothing false. *A.*—You have put me into great difficulty, and I do not know what to answer. So, though I do not wish to learn by any other method than this of question and answer, nevertheless I am afraid to be questioned.

vi, 9. *R.*—God to whom we have committed ourselves will doubtless lend his aid and deliver us from these difficulties. Only let us believe and ask him with the greatest devotion. *A.*—Certainly I would do nothing more willingly at this point, for nowhere have I experienced such darkness. God, our Father, who dost bid us pray, and givest what we ask of thee if only we are better and live better lives as we pray. Hear me as I grope in this darkness and stretch out to me thy right hand. Cause thy light to shine upon me. Recall me from error. Led by thee may I return to myself and to thee. Amen. *R.*—Give me your utmost attention. Listen and watch. *A.*—Has anything occurred to you which can save us? *R.*—Listen. *A.*—I am doing nothing else.

10. *R.*—First, let us ventilate the problem of falsity. *A.*—I wonder if falsity will be found to be anything else than what is not as it seems. *R.*—Listen rather, and let us first interrogate our senses. What the eyes see is not said to be false unless it has some resemblance to the truth. For example, a man seen in a dream is not a true man but a false one, just because there is resemblance to the truth. No one would say of a dog seen in a dream that it was a man. It is a false dog because it resembles a real dog. *A.*—It is as you say. *R.*—If any one in his waking hours saw a horse and thought he saw a man, he would be deceived because he seemed to see something resembling a man. For if nothing appeared to him but the shape of a horse he could not suppose that he had seen a man. *A.*—Quite so. *R.*—A painted tree, a face in a mirror, the motion of towers as seen by navigators, the broken oar in water—all these things we say are false for no other reason than that they have some resemblance to truth. *A.*—I agree. *R.*—So we are deceived about twins, about eggs, about different seals stamped with one signet-ring, and about other similar things. *A.*—I follow you and agree entirely. *R.*—As regards visible things it is resemblance that is the mother of falsity. *A.*—I cannot deny it.

11. *R.*—Unless I am mistaken, this whole thicket can be divided into two classes. In the one the resemblance is between

equals; in the other not so. In the first class are those cases where we can say of both equally that the one resembles the other; in the case of twins for example, or the impressions of a signet-ring. In the other class are those cases where we can say that an inferior thing resembles a better. Who, on seeing his face in a mirror, would say that he resembled that image and not rather that it resembled him? Again this class is divided into two: cases which belong to the soul's experience, and those which belong to objects seen. Those which belong to the experience of the soul are due either to the senses, as for example the false movement of a tower, or to what has been originally received from the senses, like the visions of dreamers and possibly of madmen. Furthermore, of resemblances in visible things some are brought about by nature, others by living creatures. Nature causes inferior resemblances by begetting or by reflection: by begetting, as when parents have children who resemble them; by reflecting, as from any kind of mirror. No doubt men make mirrors, but they do not make the images which mirrors reflect. Living creatures make pictures and similar works of imagination. And here may be included the figments of demons if such exist. Shadows of bodies which closely resemble bodies, and may be called false bodies—it is not the function of the eyes to decide—these may be put in the class of resemblances naturally caused by reflection. In any case, every body exposed to light throws a shadow on the side opposite to the light. Have you anything to say against all this? *A.*—Nothing. But I am eagerly waiting to hear whither all this tends.

12. *R.*—We must be patient until the other senses report also that falsity resides in verisimilitude. Take hearing. There again there are almost as many classes of resemblance. For example, we hear a voice but do not see the speaker, and think it is someone else whose voice resembles the one we hear. Of the inferior type of resemblance the echo is a witness, or a ringing in the ears, or the imitation of the merle or the raven that we hear in clocks, or even those sounds which dreamers and madmen seem to hear. It is incredible how false soft notes, of which musicians speak, correspond to the truth, as will appear later; it is sufficient to point out now how closely they resemble true notes. You follow me? *A.*—Yes, most willingly. I have no difficulty in understanding. *R.*—To cut the matter short. Do you think it is easy to distinguish one lily from another by smelling, or honey from different hives by taste, or the softness of the plumage of the swan and the goose by touch? *A.*—I do not. *R.*—When we

dream that we smell or taste or touch such things, are we not deceived because these images resemble the real things though in an inferior and vain way? *A.*—True. *R.*—So it appears that resemblances, whether among equal things or unequal, wheedle all our senses and deceive us. Or, if we are not deceived because we refuse to be wheedled or because we recognize the difference, we call these resemblances false just because we notice that they somehow resemble the truth. *A.*—I cannot doubt it.

vii, 13. *R.*—Now listen while I repeat all this, so as to make still more clear what I am trying to show you. *A.*—Speak as you will, for I am determined to endure your circuitous course and not to weary in it, so great is my hope of reaching the end of the journey. *R.*—Well done. Do you think that when we see two similar eggs we can say that one of them is false? *A.*—By no means. If they are eggs, both of them are true eggs. *R.*—When we see an image reflected from a mirror, how do we know that it is false? *A.*—Because it cannot be grasped; it makes no sound; it does not move of itself; it is not alive. And there are other innumerable signs which it would take too long to mention. *R.*—I see you wish for no delay and I must adapt myself to your haste. Not to repeat everything; if the men we see in dreams could live and speak and be grasped by us when we awake, and there was no difference between them and those whom we see and address when we are awake and of a sound mind, would we say that they were false? *A.*—We could not correctly say so. *R.*—Then, if they were true so far as they were very like the truth and there was no difference at all between them and real men, but were also false so far as they were proved to be unlike real men by the tests you have mentioned or by other tests, must we not admit that similitude is the mother of truth and dissimilitude the mother of falsity? *A.*—I have nothing I can say, and I am ashamed of the rash admission I have just made.

14. *R.*—It is absurd to be ashamed, as if it were not for this very reason that we chose this kind of conversation. As we alone take part, I wish the work to be called and entitled "Soliloquies," a new and harsh name perhaps, but quite suitable to describe what we are doing. There is no better way of seeking truth than by the method of question and answer. But hardly anyone can be found who is not ashamed to be proved wrong; and so it nearly always happens that a good discussion is spoiled by some outburst of obstinacy, with fraying of tempers generally concealed but sometimes apparent. Now our plan was, I believe,

to proceed peaceably and agreeably in our search for truth, with God's help. I was to ask the questions and you were to answer. There is no need to fear, if you get tied up in knots, to go back and try again. There is no other way out of our present difficulty.

viii, 15. *A.*—You are right. But I do not see clearly where I went wrong. Perhaps it was when I said that a thing is false when it has some likeness to the true. Nothing else deserving to be so called occurred to me. But now I am compelled to admit that false things are so called because they differ from the true. Accordingly, unlikeness is itself the cause of falsity. I am confused for I cannot easily think of anything which has two contrary causes. *R.*—Perhaps this is the solitary and unique instance in the whole world. Don't you know that if you consider the innumerable species of animals, the crocodile alone moves the upper jaw in eating? Indeed, hardly can two things be found identically alike. *A.*—Yes, I see that. But when I consider what we call "false" and how it is both like and unlike the true, I cannot make out whether its falseness is due to the likeness or the unlikeness. If to the latter, there will be nothing which cannot be called false. For there is nothing which is not unlike something we call true. If I say "to the former" those eggs will refute me, because they are true just because they are alike. Besides, I shall not escape being compelled to confess that everything is false, because I cannot deny that all things have a certain similarity. But suppose I am not afraid to reply that both likeness and unlikeness together entitle a thing to be called false, what way out will you give me? I shall be compelled to say that all things are false, because all things are partly like and partly unlike each other. I should have to say that the false is simply that which is not other than it seems, did I not dread those many monsters which I thought I had outdistanced. Again; I dare not repeat that that is true which is as it seems, remembering my unexpected giddiness caused by the inference that nothing can be true without someone to know it. I dread shipwreck on hidden rocks which are real even if they are unknown. If I say that is true which is, the conclusion will be drawn that there is no falsity anywhere, deny it who will. And so the storms return, and I see I have made no advance with all your unhurried patience.

ix, 16. *R.*—Now listen. I can never be induced to believe that we have implored divine aid in vain. After all our inquiry I see that nothing remains that we may justly term false except that which feigns itself to be what it is not, or pretends to be when it does not exist. The former kind is either fallacious or mendacious. Fallacious, strictly speaking, is that which has a certain desire to deceive and this cannot be understood apart from the soul. But deceit is practised partly by reason and partly by nature; by reason in rational beings like men, by nature in beasts like foxes. What I call lying is done by liars. The difference between the fallacious and the mendacious is that the former all wish to deceive while the latter do not all wish to do so. Mimes and comedies and many poems are full of lies, but the aim is to delight rather than to deceive. Nearly all who make jokes lie. But the fallacious person, strictly speaking, is he whose design is to deceive. Those who feign without intent to deceive are mendacious, or at least no one hesitates to call them liars. Have you any objection to urge against this?

17. *A.*—Please go on. Perhaps you have begun to teach me the truth about falsity. But I am waiting to hear what you have to say about the other kind that pretends it is and is not. *R.*—What do you expect? I have given you many examples already. Don't you think that your image in a mirror wants to be you but is false because it is not? *A.*—Yes, I do. *R.*—And every picture, statue, or similar work of art tries to be that on which it is modelled. *A.*—I must agree. *R.*—You will agree that the things which deceive dreamers and madmen are in the same class? *A.*—Yes, these above all. More than anything else these pretend to be what men see when they are awake and sane. And they are false just because they pretend to be what they cannot be. *R.*—Why need I say more about the apparent movement of towers, or the oar plunged in water, or the shadows of bodies? It is clear, I think, that they all come under this rule. *A.*—Most clear. *R.*—I say nothing of the other senses. For no one who considers the matter will fail to discover that in the realm of the senses that is called false which pretends to be something and is not.

x, 18. *A.*—You are right. But I wonder why you think poems and jests and other fallacious things are to be kept separate from this class. *R.*—It is one thing to will to be false and another not to be able to be true. We can classify comedies, tragedies, mimes and the like with the works of painters and sculptors. The picture of a man, though it tries to be like him, cannot be a true man any more than a character in the books of the comedians. These things are false not from any will or desire of their own, but from the necessity of following the will of their authors. On the stage, Roscius wants to be a false Hecuba, but by nature he is a true man. By so wanting, he is also a true tragedian, so far as he fulfils the part. But he would be a false Priam if he gave himself out as Priam and was not. But here emerges a strange fact which nobody doubts. *A.*—What is that? *R.*—In all such matters truth and falsehood are inevitably intertwined; indeed, if there is to be truth in one respect there must be falsehood in another. How could Roscius be truly a tragic actor if he refused to be a false Hector, Andromache, Hercules or the like? How could a picture of a horse be truly a picture if the horse were not false? How could there be a man's face in a glass, true as such, though not truly a man? So if a certain kind of falsity is necessary in order that there should be truth, why do we dread falsity and seek truth as a great boon? *A.*—I don't know, unless it is because there is in these examples nothing worthy of our imitation. After all, unlike actors, reflections in mirrors, or Myron's brass cow, we ought not to be both true and false: true in our proper garb but false as dressed up to represent something else. We ought to seek the absolute truth, not that double-faced thing that is partly true and partly false. *R.*—You are asking something great, nay divine. If we find that, we shall agree that we have found Truth itself, from which everything that is called true derives its quality. *A.*—I agree most heartily.

xi, 19. *R.*—Well now, do you think the art of dialectic is true or false? *A.*—Clearly true, and so is the art of literary studies [*grammatica*]. *R.*—Are both equally true? *A.*—I don't see that there can be degrees of truth. *R.*—Yet there may be a truth that has no falsehood in it. You have just said that you objected to things that cannot be true without an element of falsehood in them. You know that literary studies include fables and obvious falsehoods. *A.*—Yes. But the study of literature is not responsible for the falsehood. It demonstrates their nature. A fable is a falsehood composed for use and pleasure; while literary study is the art which guards and controls composition. By its very profession it must handle all the products of human speech, whether transmitted orally or in writing. It does not originate these falsehoods, but gives us scientific knowledge about them. *R.*—Quite right. But I am not concerned at the moment as to whether your definition is correct. I want to know whether this is properly the function of literary studies or of dialectic. *A.*—I do not deny that the power and skill to define and distinguish, as I did just now, belong to dialectic.

20. *R.*—Literary study is true inasmuch as it is a school discipline. Discipline derives its name from *discere* [to learn]. No one who has learnt and who retains what he has learnt can be said not to know, and no one can know what is false. Therefore, every school discipline is true. *A.*—I see no rashness in accepting that reasoning. I do, however, wonder whether any one will think that the fables are true, for we learn and memorize them. *R.*—Surely our teacher did not want us to believe what he taught us as well as to know it? *A.*—Oh no. What he insisted on was that we should know it. *R.*—He never insisted that we should believe the tale of Daedalus flying? *A.*—Never. But if we did not hold the tale in memory he made our hands unable to hold anything! *R.*—You do agree that there is such a fable and that such is reported of Daedalus? *A.*—Certainly that is true. *R.*—Then you learned a truth when you learned that fable. If on the contrary it were true that Daedalus *had* wings, and boys accepted and repeated it as merely a fictitious fable, their conception of the tale would be false for the very reason that the story they were repeating was true. Here is an example of what astonished us a moment ago. There could not truly be a fable about the flight of Daedalus unless it were false that Daedalus had actually flown in the air. *A.*—Now I understand. But where are we to go from that point? *R.*—We have shown that the reasoning was not false by which we proved that a school discipline can be such only if it teach what is true. *A.*—What has that got to do with our problem? *R.*—Tell me, please, why literature is a school discipline, for that will be the answer to the question why it is true. *A.*—I do not know the answer. *R.*—Don't you think it could not be a discipline if there were no definitions in it, no distinctions and distributions into classes and parts? *A.*—Now I know what you mean. I cannot imagine a discipline in which there are no definitions, divisions and reasonings, where the nature of each thing is not set forth, where each part does not receive its due attention without confusion, where anything relevant is omitted and anything irrelevant is admitted. All this is the function of a so-called discipline. *R.*—And because it performs all these functions it is said to be true. *A.*—I see that follows.

21. *R.*—Now to what discipline belongs a reasoned account of definitions, divisions and distinctions of parts? *A.*—As was said before, all that is contained in the rules of dialectic. *R.*—Therefore, literature as a true discipline is created by the same art as you have just defended against the charge of falsehood.

And I may draw this conclusion not only in the case of literature but of all the disciplines. For you truly said that you could think of no discipline which did not exercise the function of definition and distribution, for this function was the essence of a discipline. But if the disciplines are true by their very nature, will anyone deny that it is by truth itself that all disciplines are true? *A.*—You have almost my entire assent. But I have this difficulty. We have counted dialectic among the disciplines. Now I think, rather, that it is itself the Truth whence reason derives truth. *R.*—Most excellently said and most acutely. But you do not deny, I suppose, that as a discipline it is true? *A.*—Oh no; that is my point. I know that it is a discipline and therefore true. *R.*—It could not be a discipline unless there were definition and distribution of its subject matter? *A.*—Exactly. *R.*—But if, besides, to it belongs the task of defining and distributing universally it would be the souce of truth in all the disciplines. Who will think it surprising if that by which all things are true is in and by itself the very Truth? *A.*—I have no difficulty in immediately accepting that statement.

xii, 22. *R.*—Then little remains to be said, so listen. *A.*—Go on, and provided I can understand, I shall gladly agree. *R.*—We quite understand that one thing can be said to be in another in two ways: first, in such a way that it can be separated and put elsewhere, e.g., this piece of wood in this place, or the sun in the East; and second, in such a way that it cannot be separated, e.g., the form and appearance which we see in this piece of wood, or light in the sun, or heat in fire, or learning in a mind and such like. Do you agree? *A.*—That is an old old story to me. I had it drilled into me at the beginning of my adolescence. So I can agree without a moment's deliberation. *R.*—Then that which exists inseparably in a subject cannot continue to exist if the subject itself is destroyed? *A.*—That must be true; for anyone who diligently considers the matter knows that even when the subject remains, that which is in it may not remain. The colour of the body may be changed by reason of ill-health or age though the body itself has not perished. This is not equally true in all cases, but only in those cases in which the quality is not essential to the existence of the subject. That wall is not a wall by reason of the colour we see now. It would remain a wall even if by any chance it became black or white or otherwise changed its colour. On the other hand, if fire ceased to be hot, it would not be fire, and we cannot think of snow without whiteness.

xiii, 23. But to go back to your question. Who could allow or admit as a possibility that what exists in a subject could continue to exist when the subject itself has ceased to exist? It is quite absurd and quite untrue that a thing, A, which can only exist in another thing, B, can continue to exist when B has ceased to exist. *R.*—Then we have found what we were seeking. *A.*—What is that you tell me? *R.*—Exactly as you heard. *A.*—Is it, then, crystal-clear that the soul is immortal? *R.*—Absolutely clear, if all that you have admitted is true. Unless, of course, you can say that the soul exists after it is dead. *A.*—I could not say that. I should say that by the very fact of its dying the soul has ceased to exist. Nor is my opinion weakened by the statement of certain great philosophers that that which confers life by its presence cannot admit of death. No doubt a light causes light wherever it shines and cannot admit of darkness, according to the celebrated principle of contraries. Nevertheless, it can be extinguished and, thereby, the place becomes dark. That which resists darkness, and can in no way admit of darkness, nevertheless gives place to darkness by being extinguished or removed. My fear is lest in the same way death comes to the body by the removal or extinguishing of the soul. So I cannot be quite sure about every kind of death. There might be a preferable kind, in which the soul was safely removed from the body and brought to a place, if there is such a place, where it would not be extinguished. If this is not possible, and the soul is like a light kindled in the body and cannot continue anywhere else, and death is the extinction of soul and life in the body, then a man must choose as far as he may to live his present life in security and tranquillity; and yet I do not know how that is to be done if the soul is mortal. Happy are those who know by themselves or from some other source that death is not to be feared even if the soul too dies. Unhappily no reasons or books have availed to persuade me of this.

24. *R.*—Don't lament. The human soul is immortal. *A.*—How do you prove it? *R.*—From what you have already admitted after most careful consideration. *A.*—I certainly do not remember admitting anything carelessly. But, pray, sum it all up now and let us see where we have arrived by all these roundabout ways. I don't want to be asked any more questions. If you will now briefly outline our agreements, there will be no need for me to reply. Why should you delay my rejoicing if indeed we have reached a good result? *R.*—I shall do as I see you wish, but listen diligently. *A.*—Speak now. I am listening. Why

do you torment me? *R.*—If a thing, A, existing in another thing, B, lasts for ever, B must last for ever. All scientific learning is in a subject, the mind. Therefore, if learning is eternal, the mind also must be eternal. Moreover, scholastic learning is Truth and, as reason persuaded us at the beginning of this book, Truth is eternal. Therefore the mind is eternal and cannot die. He alone will reasonably deny that the mind is immortal who proves that some of our propositions have not been correctly agreed to.

xiv, 25. *A.*—I want to break out into rejoicing straight away, but two things cause me to hesitate. In the first place, I observe that we have used a circuitous route following a lengthy chain of reasoning, when the whole problem could quite as easily have been demonstrated briefly, as it has at last been demonstrated. What makes me anxious is that our talk has wandered round and round so long, as if an ambush were being laid. And secondly, I do not see how a scholastic discipline can be in the mind eternally; especially dialectic, seeing so few know it, and these have had to be indoctrinated from their youth. We cannot say that the minds of the unlearned are not minds, or that they have learning and do not know it. That would be utterly absurd. It remains either that truth is not always in a mind, or that scholastic discipline is not truth.

26. *R.*—Not in vain has our reasoning taken these circuitous ways. Our problem was, What is Truth? and I see that not even as it is have we been able to investigate it thoroughly, though we have tried almost every path, however rough, through the thicket. What are we to do? Shall we give up the attempt and wait till some other man's book comes into our hands and gives a satisfactory answer to our question? I think that before our time many books have been written which we have not read, and, not to speak of what we do not know, many are written in verse and prose, by men whose writings cannot escape our notice, and whose genius we know to be such that we cannot despair of finding in them what we want. Especially before our eyes there is Ambrose, in whom we recognize that eloquence has perfectly come to life again, which we had mourned as dead. Will he who by his writings has taught us the true manner of living allow us to be ignorant of the nature of living? *A.*—For myself I think not, and I have great hopes from that source. But one thing I am sorry for, that I have had no opportunity to reveal to him as I wish my assiduity towards himself and towards wisdom. For assuredly he would have pity on my

thirst, and would give me drink much more speedily than I can find it myself. He is untroubled by doubt and is thoroughly persuaded as to the immortality of the soul. Perhaps he does not know that there are some made miserable by their ignorance of this, whom it is cruel not to help, especially when they seek help. My friend, Zenobius, also knows my ardour. But he is far away, and, as I am situated at present, there is hardly any chance of sending him a letter. In his leisure beyond the Alps I dare say he has finished the poem by which he hoped to charm away the fear of death, and to drive from his soul the numbness and cold induced by the perennial northern ice. Meantime, until those things come which are not at present in our power, it would be a shame to waste our leisure and let our whole mind depend on an uncertain judgment.

xv, 27. Where is that for which we have prayed and do pray to God? Not riches for ourselves, or bodily pleasures, or popular honours and applause, but that a way may be opened to us as we seek God and the soul. Will he abandon us or we him? *R.*—It is far from his way to abandon those who seek such things. So it should be far from us to forsake so great a leader. So, if you please, let us briefly repeat the arguments for these two propositions that Truth is eternal, and that the science of dialectic is Truth. These you said were shaky, so that we could not be sure of the entire edifice we have erected. Or shall we rather inquire how there can be scientific learning in an untrained mind, which we must none the less regard as a mind? For this question seemed to disturb you and make it necessary to question what you had admitted. *A.*—Let us discuss the first question to begin with, then we shall see what is to be made of the second. In this way, no controversy will remain unsettled. *R.*—So be it. But give me your most careful and undivided attention. I know that you are too eager about the conclusion and want it to be reached immediately, so that you agree to what is suggested to you without due examination. *A.*—Perhaps you are right. I shall strive with all my might against this kind of sickness. Only begin, and do not let us be delayed by superfluities.

28. *R.*—So far as I remember, we concluded that Truth could not perish, because if the whole world, nay, if Truth itself perished, it would still be true that the world and Truth had perished. But nothing is true without Truth. Hence Truth cannot perish. *A.*—I remember, and I should be much surprised if this were false. *R.*—Let us then proceed to the second question.

A.—Give me a little time to consider, in case I should have to go back again which would be a shame. *R.*—It will not be true that Truth has perished? If not, then it did not perish. If it is true, how, after the decease of Truth, can anything be true? For then there will be no Truth. *A.*—I have no need of further consideration. Go on to the other question. We shall at least do what we can, so that learned and understanding men may read these words and correct any rash utterance. For myself, I do not think that now or ever anything can be found to urge against these conclusions.

29. *R.*—Truth is that by which anything that is true is true? *A.*—Certainly. *R.*—Nothing is said to be true except what is not false? *A.*—It would be silly to doubt it. *R.*—Is not that false which has a certain likeness to something, but is not that to which it bears a resemblance? *A.*—To nothing else would I more freely give the name of false. And yet that is commonly called false which is very unlike the true. *R.*—Undeniably. But there is always some imitation of the true. *A.*—But how? When we are told that Medea joined together winged serpents and sped through the air, there is no imitation of what is true. For the tale is not true, and there can be no imitation of what does not exist. *R.*—Quite right. But observe that a thing which does not exist cannot even be said to be false. If it is false it exists. If it does not exist it is not false. *A.*—Are we not, then, to say that that monstrous story about Medea is false? *R.*—Not exactly. If it is false, how is it monstrous? *A.*—Here is a surprising thing. When I hear of "Huge winged serpents joined together by a yoke" I am not to say it is false. *R.*—Of course you are, but that implies something that exists. *A.*—What exists? *R.*—The statement expressed in that verse. *A.*—And where is there any imitation of the true in it? *R.*—Because it is stated as if Medea had really done it. A false statement is expressed exactly like a true one. If it is not intended to be believed, a false statement resembles a true one only in grammatical form. It is simply false and has no intent to deceive. If it demands belief it more obviously imitates a true statement. *A.*—Now I understand that there is a great difference between mere statements and the objects about which statements are made. Now I agree, for you have removed my only reason for doubting, that we cannot rightly call anything false unless it imitates something that is true. A man who called a stone false silver would be justly laughed at. But if he were to say that a stone was silver, we should say that what he said was false, that

is, he had uttered a false statement. But it would not be absurd to call tin or lead false silver, for there is some resemblance. The falsehood lies not in our statement but in the material objects about which it is made.

xvi, 30. *R.*—You have understood perfectly. But could we appropriately call silver by the name of false lead? *A.*—I do not think so. *R.*—Why? *A.*—I don't know. I see no reason, except that I should be most unwilling to do so. *R.*—Possibly because silver is a more precious metal, and to call it imitation lead would be insulting; while to call lead imitation silver would be doing it honour, so to speak. *A.*—You have exactly explained my feelings. I believe that men are rightly held to be infamous and incapable of bearing witness or making a will who show themselves in women's garb. I do not know whether I should rather call them false women or false men. We can without hesitation call them true actors or truly infamous. Or if they are not found out, and we cannot use the word infamous unless there is public ill fame, we can at least truthfully call them truly worthless fellows. *R.*—We can discuss that at another time. For many things that seem base to the popular eye, are clearly honourable when seen in the light of some laudable purpose. It is a big problem whether for the sake of his country's liberty a man may don a woman's dress in order to deceive the enemy. In this case, by being a false woman he might be more truly a man. And should a sage, who somehow knew that his life was necessary for the welfare of mankind, prefer to die of cold rather than be clad in female garments, if nothing else were available? But as I said, we can discuss that again. At any rate you perceive how much inquiry would be necessary as to the limits of such actions, to transgress which would involve a man in inexcusable baseness. But so far as our present problem is concerned, I think it is now clear and beyond doubt that nothing is false except by some imitation of the true.

xvii, 31. *A.*—Go on to the rest of the argument, for I entirely accept this. *R.*—I ask, then, whether in addition to the scholastic disciplines, with which must be numbered the pursuit of wisdom, we can find anything so true that, unlike the Achilles of the theatre, it is not partly true and partly false. *A.*—Indeed I think many things can be found. The disciplines have nothing to do with that stone, and yet as a true stone it imitates nothing whereby it might be said to be false. This one example will show that we need name no others, for innumerable things will spontaneously occur to any one who thinks.

R.—Quite so. But don't you think they could all be included in one category, material objects? *A.*—Yes, if I were sure that there is no such thing as the void; if I thought that the mind was to be numbered among material things, and if I believed that God too was corporeal. If all this is granted, I see that everything that exists is true, having no false imitation. *R.*—You are sending us out on a long discussion, but I shall be as brief as I can. At least what you call the void is a very different thing from the Truth. *A.*—Very different. What could be more void of sense than for me, if I think Truth is a void, to seek so earnestly what is vain? What else do I desire to find but Truth? *R.*—You will allow that nothing is true which is not made to be true by Truth. *A.*—That has been perfectly clear for a long time. *R.*—You do not doubt that there is nothing besides the void unless it be matter? *A.*—I do not. *R.*—Then it appears that you think Truth is a material thing. *A.*—Not at all. *R.*—Is it in a material body? *A.*—I do not know, but it does not matter. I am sure you know that, if there is a void, it is where there is no material body. *R.*—That is clear. *A.*—Why, then, do we delay? *R.*—Do you think that Truth has created the void, or that anything is true where there is no Truth? *A.*—I do not. *R.*—Then the void is not true. Nothing can be made void by that which is not void. And it is clear that nothing is true where Truth is not, and the void is so called because it is nothing. How, therefore, can that be true which does not exist? Indeed, how can that exist which is absolutely nothing? *A.*—Come, then, let us leave the void as being utterly void.

xviii, 32. *R.*—What about the other questions? *A.*—Which? *R.*—Those which you see are my chief interest. I mean the soul and God. If these two are true because Truth is in them, no one doubts concerning the immortality of God. Moreover, the soul is believed to be immortal if Truth, which cannot perish, is proved to be in it. Wherefore, let us look at the final question, whether material substance be not truly true, that is, whether there be in it not Truth, but only a kind of semblance of Truth. For if in the body, which certainly perishes, we find such truth as is found in the sciences, the science of dialectic will not be the Truth in virtue of which all the sciences are true. For corporeal substance is true, though it does not seem to have been formed by the rational process of dialectic. If matter is true by imitation and therefore not perfectly true, there will be nothing to prevent dialectic being claimed as the very Truth. *A.*—Meantime, let us inquire about matter. Not even when this is determined do I see that controversy settled. *R.*—How do you know the will of God? But listen. I think matter is contained in some form or outward appearance without which it would not be matter. If it had true form it would be soul. Am I wrong? *A.*—I agree with your first proposition, but about the second I am in doubt. I agree that unless it were contained in some shape it would not be matter. But I fail to understand how it would be soul if it had true form. *R.*—Don't you remember speaking about geometrical figures at the beginning of the first book? *A.*—Thanks for reminding me. Of course, I remember. *R.*—Do you find in material objects such figures as geometry employs? *A.*—Oh, no. Much inferior ones. *R.*—Which, then, of the two do you think are true? *A.*—Please do not think I need to be asked such a question. Who is so blind as not to see that the figures employed in geometry belong to the Truth, or that Truth is in them; while the figures exhibited in material objects, though indeed they seem to resemble geometrical figures, somehow imitate the truth and are to that extent false. Now I understand all you were trying to show me.

xix, 33. *R.*—There is no need, then, to inquire about dialectic. Whether geometrical figures belong to Truth, or Truth is in them, no one doubts that they are contained in our minds, so that necessarily Truth is in our minds. But if any scientific discipline is in the mind inseparably, and Truth cannot perish, why, pray, should we doubt concerning the everlasting life of the mind because of our familiarity with death? Has the geometrical line or square or circle anything else to imitate in order that it may be true? *A.*—I cannot believe it, unless a line is other than length without breadth, and a circle is other than a line drawn round a centre and always equally distant from the centre. *R.*—Why, then, do we hesitate? Is there no Truth in the mathematical line and circle? *A.*—God avert such stupidity! *R.*—Is scientific learning not in the mind? *A.*—Who could say that? *R.*—Possibly that which is in a subject may continue when the subject itself has been destroyed? *A.*—I could never be so persuaded. *R.*—Perhaps Truth may pass away? *A.*—How could that be? *R.*—Very well then, the soul is immortal. Now trust your reasonings. Trust Truth. It cries out that it dwells in you, that it is immortal, that it can never be forced to abandon its dwelling place by any kind of bodily death. Turn away from your shadow, and return to your inward self. There is no death for you unless you forget that you are of such a nature that you cannot die. *A.*—As I listen to you

I begin to understand and to grasp your meaning. But please elucidate a question which has been left over. How are science and truth to be understood to exist in a mind untrained at least if we may not call it mortal? *R.*—That question would require another volume if it were to be fully treated. I see you must think over the things we have investigated according to our powers; for if no doubt remains concerning them I think we have done a good day's work, and can go on to investigate other problems with no little sense of security.

xx, 34. *A.*—It is as you say, and I willingly obey your behests. And yet, before you bring this volume to an end, I should like to ask you briefly to explain what is the difference between a true figure, such as is grasped by the intelligence, and one such as the imagination depicts, which in Greek is called a phantasy or a phantasm. *R.*—None but the most pure can understand that, and you have had too little practice in philosophy to be able to see it. In all these circuitous arguments we have been simply exercising your powers so that you may become fit to see it. But perhaps I may briefly explain how the vast difference may be made known. Suppose you have forgotten something and your friends want you to recall it to your memory. They will say, "Is it this? Is it that?" mentioning various things of a similar kind. You do not recall what you are seeking, but you know that it is none of the things they have mentioned. Now surely what has happened is not entire oblivion? For the discernment which refuses to accept a false suggestion is itself a kind of memory. *A.*—Seemingly. *R.*—In such a case you do not yet see the truth, but you are not deceived, for you have some idea of what it is you are looking for. But if some one were to tell you that you smiled a few days after you were born, you do not venture to say it is false. If the speaker is one whom you can trust, you will not remember the fact but you will believe it. That whole period is buried for you in utter oblivion. Don't you think so? *A.*—I quite agree. *R.*—This kind of forgetfulness differs greatly from the other kind we have just spoken of, which has a sort of intermediate position between forgetfulness and remembering. It is closer to remembering and reviving a truth. A similar situation occurs when we see something and are quite certain we have seen it before. We say that we know it, but where, when, how, in whose company it came to our notice, we cannot recall without a great deal of trouble. Or we may meet a man and have to ask where we made his acquaintance. When he reminds us, the whole thing suddenly comes back to our memory as if a light had been kindled, and we have no further trouble in recalling it. Is this kind of experience unknown to you or strange? *A.*—Nothing is plainer, for nothing happens to me more frequently.

35. *R.*—Such are those who are well educated in the liberal arts. Doubtless in learning them they draw them out from the oblivion[1] that has overwhelmed them, or dig them out as it were. They are not content until they fully behold the face of Truth, whose splendour glimmers even now in these liberal arts. But from these arts, too, some false colours and shapes are reflected, as it were, on the mirror of the mind, and often deceive inquirers into thinking that that is all they can know or look for. These imaginations are to be avoided with the greatest care. They are proved fallacious because they vary as the mirror of the mind varies. The face of Truth remains one and immutable. The mind will depict a square now of this size, now of that and present it to the eye. But the inward mind which seeks to see the truth turns rather, if it has the power, to the ideal square by which all squareness is judged. *A.*—Supposing someone says that the mind judges according to what it is accustomed to see with the eyes? *R.*—How, then, does it judge, as it will do if it is well trained, that a true sphere of any size whatever will touch a true plane surface at a single point? How can the eye ever see any such thing, which cannot even be imagined by thought? Do we not prove this when we think of the smallest imaginable circle and draw lines to the centre? If we draw two lines so close together that the point of a needle can hardly penetrate between them, we cannot even in imagination draw other intermediate lines that will reach the centre without coinciding. And yet reason proclaims that innumerable intermediate lines can be drawn in that incredibly narrow space, and that they will not touch except at the centre, indeed that between any two of them a circle can be drawn. Now if phantasy cannot take this in but is even more defective than the eyes which are responsible for inflicting it on the mind, clearly phantasy is very different from truth and cannot see it.

[1] Cp. *Retract.* I, iv, 4. Referring to this passage Augustine writes, "I do not approve this. When even untrained persons, suitably questioned, are able to return correct answers, a more credible reason is that they have according to their capacity the presence of the light of the Eternal Reason. Hence they catch a glimpse of immutable truth. The reason is not that they once knew it and have forgotten, as Plato and others like him have thought." In his early writings Augustine seems to have held the Platonic doctrine of Reminiscence. It is rejected in *De Trinit.* XII, xv, 24.

36. We shall speak of these things with greater care and subtlety when we begin to discuss the intelligence, which it is our intention to do, after we have discussed and solved the problem of the life of the soul as far as we are able. I suspect that you rather fear that death, even if it do not slay the soul, nevertheless may bring oblivion of everything, even of such truth as may have been discovered. *A.*—I cannot express strongly enough how much this evil is to be feared. What kind of eternal life would that be, and what death would not be preferable, if the soul so lived as we see it in a boy newly born? Not to mention the life lived in the womb, which I suppose must be called life. *R.*—Be of good courage. God will grant us his presence as we have experienced it in our present quest. He promises us a most blessed future after this bodily life, a future full of truth without any falsehood.

Note

The work is manifestly incomplete. A third book of *Soliloquies* was projected, and material for it was collected while Augustine was at Milan after his return from Cassiciacum. This material is contained in the *De Animae Immortalitate*, which he tells us was published without his consent, and in an unfinished condition. "By reason of its brevity and the confusion of its argument it is so obscure that it is wearisome to read, and my meaning is scarcely intelligible even to myself." *Retract.* I, v, 1.

The Teacher

Augustine's Review of the De Magistro. Retractations I, xii

About the same time I wrote a book entitled *De Magistro,* in which we discuss and inquire and discover that there is no teacher who teaches man knowledge except God according to what is written in the Gospel, "One is your teacher, even Christ" (Matt. 23:10). The book begins: *Quid tibi videmur efficere velle cum loquimur?*

The Teacher

INTRODUCTION

THE *De Magistro* is briefly reviewed in the *Retractations* between the *De Musica* and the *De Vera Religione*, and is said to have been written about the same time as the former, i.e., about 389, after Augustine's return to Tagaste. It is a dialogue with his natural son Adeodatus, who was then in his sixteenth year, and who died an early death shortly after. Of Adeodatus there is an interesting notice in the *Confessions* (IX, vi. 14). Along with his father and Alypius there was baptized by Ambrose in Milan on Easter Day, 387, "the boy Adeodatus, my son after the flesh, born of my sin. He was hardly fifteen years old, but in intelligence he excelled many grave and learned men. I acknowledge thy gifts in him, O Lord, my God. . . . I had nothing to give to that boy except the sin which I transmitted to him. Thou, none else, didst inspire in us the thought of bringing him up in thy discipline. I confess thine own gifts to thee. There is a book of mine extant called *The Teacher*, in which he took part with me. Thou knowest that all the opinions there expressed by my interlocutor were actually his when he was in his sixteenth year. I experienced many other marvellous things about him. His ability made me stand in awe of him. Who save thou can be the doer of such miracles? Thou didst remove his life early from this earth, and I remember him with all the greater confidence as I have no reason to fear for him any sins of boyhood, adolescence or manhood." Adeodatus was also present at the discussion on The Happy Life, during the sojourn at Cassiciacum—"the youngest member of the company, whose ability, unless parental fondness deceives me, shows great promise." He naturally takes but a minor part in the Dialogue, but his suggestion that "having God" means "having no unclean spirit" was received with approbation by Monica and by Augustine too, who gently points out that it is equivalent to "living well."

If it is true that the *De Magistro* gives the actual contribution of Adeodatus to the discussion, his father's admiration for his ability is fully justified. As we have seen, he had been brought up as a Christian, and we may suppose that his general education had not been neglected. This dialogue between father and son may well exemplify the care taken to improve his talents, at all events it is in part an exercise in dialectic. Among its attractive features is the recurrence of the personal touch—the playfulness here and there on both sides, the father's commendation of the son's acuteness, caution, modesty, and willingness to be corrected when wrong without loss of temper; and the son's obvious respect for the father, combined with tenacity in argument.

The Dialogue is an essay in epistemology. How is knowledge of truth attained? How are ideas communicated? What part does teaching play in the process of learning? The first section (1–18) is an exercise in pure dialectic to very little purpose except as an exercise, as is admitted. Fortunately it is briefly and clearly summarized by Adeodatus in a quite masterly fashion (19–20). The important part begins at x, 29 with the discussion of the relation between words and reality. Words are but signs, important as pointing beyond themselves to reality, but not by themselves imparting knowledge. At most they stimulate inquiry. Knowledge can be gained only as a result of an internal process in the mind of the pupil. All that the teacher can do by means of words is to elicit the truth. Truth is interior to the mind and cannot be communicated from without. But this does not mean that truth is subjective. It comes from God, whose eternal Truth, Christ, dwells in minds prepared to receive him. Christ is the inward teacher of all who can or will listen to him. Of course, the things Christ teaches are held to be the universal truths of reason. Historical events, e.g., the story of the Three Youths of Daniel 3:27, are not matters of knowledge but of "useful" faith.

ANALYSIS

i, 1—iii, 6. Introduction.

(1) We use words to let others know what we are thinking, to teach or remind them of something we have in mind. (2) We also use words when we pray, though we need not tell God anything. We use them also in thinking, but only to bring to mind the things they signify. Words are simply significant signs. (3) It is well-nigh impossible to get behind signs to "things." (4) Synonyms are signs too. (5) So are gestures, e.g., pointing to a visible object. Gesture-signs may be elaborate, e.g., Deaf-and-dumb signs, and miming. (6) But actions can be demonstrated without signs by merely performing them.

iv, 7—vi, 18. Words as Signs signifying merely Signs (Synonyms).

(7) We are first to consider signs which signify signs, especially words spoken or written. (8) Distinction between signs and things signified (*significabilia*), (9) "sign": "word": "name." A word is an articulated spoken sign. A name is a particular kind of word, denoting a particular thing, e.g., river. (11) "Word" and "name" in the general sense (not in the special sense of "verb" and "noun") are nearly synonymous, (12) *verbum* suggesting the physical aspect, *nomen* the mental aspect. (13) Any word, any part of speech, may be used as a noun. Several proofs follow (13–17).

vii, 19—viii, 21. Recapitulation; Estimate of the Value of the Exercise.

viii, 22—ix, 28. Signs which signify Things.

(22) The word *homo* signifies a man but is not a man. (23) No lion has come out of the mouth of one who has pronounced the word! (24) When the word *homo* is used, simply the noun may be meant, or an actual man. (25) Things signified are

more important than their signs because (26) the end is more important than the means. So far as words are the means of communicating knowledge they are valuable, but not so precious as the knowledge itself. (28) Education is a good thing, for it supplies not merely knowledge of the words "virtue" and "vice," but also knowledge of the virtues and the vices, all of which is necessary for the good life.

x, 29–xiii, 45. Final Problem. Things known without Signs. (30) We teach by giving signs, and nothing can be taught without signs; and yet (32) many things, e.g., natural objects, can be known without signs by those who have eyes to see them. (33) In fact nothing is learnt from signs or words. If I know the meaning of a word that word teaches me nothing new. If I do not know the meaning of a word, again it teaches me nothing. (34) A word is only intelligible if I know by personal experience the thing it signifies. Otherwise it can only stimulate inquiry. (37) We may know the meaning of all the words used to describe an historical event, but the event itself cannot be known. It can only be believed. (38) Knowledge is of universals, and these we do not learn by means of words. We must consult the Eternal Wisdom of God, i.e., Christ, who dwells in the inner man, gives men to see the truth according to the ability of each. And this ability depends on the moral quality of the will. (39) Knowledge is either sense-knowledge or intellectual-knowledge. Neither is conveyed by words. The former comes by sense-perception, the latter by contemplation. Sense-knowledge of things past is stored as images in the memory, and cannot be communicated except to those who have shared the experience. When spoken of, it may or may not be believed. (40) General truths of reason are not taught, but are somehow in the mind and only require to be discovered by skilful questioning. They are not put in the mind of the pupil by the teacher. (41) The pupil judges of what the teacher says in the light of the inward truth. (42 ff.) Words need not even reveal the mind of the speaker. There may be deception or misunderstanding. (45) Even if we admit that in general words do reveal the mind of the speaker, do not these exceptions suggest that the correspondence of word and thought is never quite exact? Teachers do not profess to teach their own opinions but objective truth, of which the pupil judges. No man is really a teacher. The idea that some men are teachers arises from the fact that apprehension of truth follows without appreciable interval on the words of the teacher, but the two processes are separable.

xiv, 46. Epilogue.

Words simply put us on the alert, and make us ready to learn. Knowledge comes not from outside by external means, but from the Master who dwells within, Christ the Truth of God.

The Teacher

A Dialogue between Augustine and his son Adeodatus

THE TEXT

i, 1. *Augustine.*—What do you suppose is our purpose when we use words? *Adeodatus.*—The answer that occurs to me at the moment is, we want to let people know something, or we want to learn something. *Augustine.*—I agree at once with the former, for it is clear that when we use words we want to let somebody know something. But in what way do we show that we wish to learn? *Adeodatus.*—When we ask questions, of course. *Aug.*—Even then, as I understand it, we want to let somebody know something. Do you ask a question for any other reason than to show the person questioned what you want to know? *Ad.*—No. *Aug.*—You see, then, that when we use words we desire nothing but to let someone know something. *Ad.*—Not quite, perhaps. If speaking means using words, I see that we do so when we sing. Now we often sing when we are alone, with no one present to hear us; and then I cannot think we want to tell anyone anything. *Aug.*—And yet I think there is a kind of teaching, and a most important kind, which consists in reminding people of something. I believe this will be made clear as our conversation proceeds. If, however, you do not think that we learn by remembering, or that he who reminds us of something really teaches us, I do not press the point. I assert that there are two reasons for our using words, either to teach, or to remind others or, it may be, ourselves. And we do this also when we sing. Don't you agree?

Ad.—Well, hardly. For I very rarely sing to remind myself of anything, almost always simply to give myself pleasure. *Aug.*—I see what you mean. But don't you notice that what pleases you in singing is the melody? Now this can be added to the words or not added, so that singing is not the same thing as speaking. Flutes and harps make melody. Birds sing. Sometimes we hum a bit of music without words. All these things may be called singing but not speaking. Do you disagree? *Ad.*—No. Not at all.

2. *Aug.*—You agree, then, that there is no other reason for the use of words than either to teach or to call something to mind? *Ad.*—I would agree were I not impressed by the fact that we use words when we pray; and it is not proper to believe that we teach God anything or remind him of anything. *Aug.*—I dare say you do not know that we have been commanded to pray in closed chambers, by which is meant our inmost mind, for no other reason than that God does not seek to be reminded or taught by our speech in order that he may give us what we desire. He who speaks gives by articulate sounds an external sign of what he wants. But God is to be sought and prayed to in the secret place of the rational soul, which is called "the inner man." This he wants to be his temple. Have you not read in the Apostle: "Know ye not that ye are the temple of God, and the Spirit of God dwelleth in you?" (1 Cor. 3:16) and "that Christ may dwell in the inner man" (Eph. 3:17)? Have you not observed in the Prophet: "Commune with your own hearts and be stricken on your beds. Offer the sacrifice of righteousness and hope in the Lord" (Ps. 4:4–5)? Where do you think the sacrifice of righteousness is offered save in the temple of the mind and on the bed of the heart? Where sacrifice is to be offered, there is prayer to be made. Wherefore when we pray there is no need of speech, that is of articulate words, except perhaps as priests use words to give a sign of what is in their minds, not that God may hear, but that men may hear and, being put in remembrance, may with some consent be brought into dependence on God. What do you think? *Ad.*—I entirely agree. *Aug.*—And you are not disturbed by the fact that our great Master, in teaching his disciples to pray, taught them certain words, so that it looks as if he had taught them actually what words to use in prayer? *Ad.*—No. That does not disturb me. For he did not teach them words merely, but by words, by means of which they could keep themselves in constant remembrance, he taught them realities—what they should pray for, and from whom, when they prayed in their inmost mind, as we said. *Aug.*—You have correctly understood the point. And I believe you have also noticed a further point. It might be contended that, though we utter no sound, we nevertheless use words in thinking and therefore use speech within our minds.

But such speech is nothing but a calling to remembrance of the realities of which the words are but the signs, for the memory, which retains the words and turns them over and over, causes the realities to come to mind. *Ad.*—I understand and follow.

ii, 3. *Aug.*—We agree, then, that words are signs. *Ad.*—We do. *Aug.*—That alone can be a sign which signifies something? *Ad.*—Certainly. *Aug.*—How many words are there in this verse?

> *Si nihil ex tanta superis placet urbe relinqui*
> [If it pleases the gods that nothing be left of so great a city]

Ad.—Eight. *Aug.*—Then there are eight signs? *Ad.*—There are. *Aug.*—I suppose you understand the meaning of the verse. *Ad.*—Yes, I think so. *Aug.*—Tell me what each word signifies. *Ad.*—I know what *si* signifies, but I can think of no other word to explain it. *Aug.*—At least you can explain the state of mind signified by that word. *Ad.*—It seems to me to signify doubt, and doubt is found in the mind. *Aug.*—I accept that in the meantime. Go on to the next word. *Ad.*—*Nihil* signifies simply what is not. *Aug.*—Perhaps you are right. But I am prevented from giving my assent by what you admitted a moment ago. You agreed that only that can be a sign which signifies something. Now, what is not cannot be something. So the second word in the verse is not a sign, because it does not signify something. We were wrong, therefore, in laying it down that all words are signs, or that all signs must signify something. *Ad.*—You press me sore. But surely it is utterly foolish to use a word if we have no meaning to attach to it. When you are speaking with me I believe that you do not utter any merely empty sound, but that in everything that proceeds from your mouth you are giving me a sign by which I may understand something. So you ought not in speaking to pronounce these two syllables unless by them you mean something. If you see that they are necessary to set forth some idea and to teach and remind us of something when they sound in our ears, you assuredly also see what I wish to say but cannot clearly explain. *Aug.*—What then are we to do? Shall we say that the word, *nihil*, signifies a state of mind rather than a thing which is nothing; the state of a mind, I mean, which does not see an object, and discovers or thinks it has discovered nonentity? *Ad.*—Perhaps that was what I was trying to explain. *Aug.*—However it may be, let us go on to the next point lest something most absurd happen to us. *Ad.*—What do you mean? *Aug.*—If "nothing" should detain us, and yet we should suffer delay. *Ad.*—It is indeed ridiculous, and yet somehow I see it can happen and indeed has happened.

4. *Aug.*—At the proper time we shall understand more clearly this kind of difficulty, if God will. Now go back to the verse and do your best to unfold what the other words signify. *Ad.*—The third word is the preposition *ex* for which I think we can substitute *de*. *Aug.*—But I am not asking you to substitute for one well-known word another equally well-known word which you say means the same thing, if indeed it does mean the same thing. But let that pass meantime. If the poet had written not *ex tanta urbe* but *de tanta urbe*, and I asked what *de* signified, you would say *ex*, since these two words, that is, signs, signify, you think, one and the same thing. But I am looking for the one thing which is signified by these two signs. *Ad.*—I think they mean a separation of a thing A, from a thing, B, in which it had formerly existed. A is said to be "of" or "out of" B. And this in one or other of two ways. Either B does not remain, as in this verse. For Troy has been destroyed but some Trojans could still exist. Or B remains, as when we say that business-men of the City of Rome are in Africa. *Aug.*—I shall concede your point, and not seek to enumerate the many exceptions that can be found to your rule. But you can at least observe that you have been explaining words by means of words, that is, signs by means of signs, well-known words and signs by words and signs also well-known. But I want you to show me, if you can, what are the things of which these are the signs.

iii, 5. *Ad.*—I am surprised that you do not know, or rather that you pretend not to know, that what you ask cannot be done in conversation, where we cannot answer questions except by means of words. You ask for things which, whatever they may be, are certainly not words, and yet you too use words in asking me. First put your questions without using words, and I shall reply on the same terms. *Aug.*—I admit your challenge is just. But if I were to ask what was signified when these three syllables, *par-i-es*, are pronounced couldn't you point with your finger, so that I should immediately see the thing itself of which that trisyllabic word is the sign? You would be pointing it out without using any words. *Ad.*—I agree that is possible, but only in the case of names signifying corporeal objects, if these objects were at hand. *Aug.*—But surely we do not call a colour a corporeal object? Is it not rather a quality of a corporeal object? *Ad.*—It is so. *Aug.*—Why then can it, too, be pointed out with the finger? Do you include the qualities of corporeal objects among corporeal objects, at least so far as they can be brought to knowledge without words? *Ad.*—When I said corporeal objects I meant all corporeal things to be understood, that is, all the qualities of bodies which are susceptible to sense-perception. *Aug.*—Consider, however, whether some exceptions are to be made. *Ad.*—You do well to warn me. I should have said not all corporeal objects but all visible objects. For I admit that sound, smell, taste, weight, heat, etc., which belong to the other senses, though they cannot be perceived apart from bodies and are therefore corporeal, cannot, nevertheless, be pointed out with the finger. *Aug.*—Have you never seen how men carry on conversation, as it were, with deaf people by means of gesture, and how deaf people, similarly by gesture, ask questions and reply, teach and indicate all their wishes, or at least most of them? Thus not only visible things are pointed out without the use of words, but also sounds, tastes and other such things. Actors, too, in the theatres often unfold and set forth whole stories by dancing simply and without using a single word. *Ad.*—I have no adverse comment to make except that neither I nor your dancing actor will ever be able to point out to you what the preposition, *ex*, signifies without using words.

6. *Aug.*—Perhaps you are right. But suppose he could. You would, I imagine, have no hesitation in saying that whatever movement of his body he used in trying to show me the thing signified by that word, it would still be a sign and not the thing itself. Therefore, though he indeed would not explain a word by a word, he would, none the less, explain a sign by a sign. So that both the monosyllable, *ex*, and his gesture would signify one thing, which I was asking to have pointed out to me without a sign, directly. *Ad.*—Pray, how can that possibly be done? *Aug.*—The way a wall does it. *Ad.*—But even a wall, as our reasoning showed, cannot be shown without a pointing finger. The holding out of the finger is not the wall but the sign by means of which the wall is pointed out. So far as I can see there is nothing which can be shown without signs. *Aug.*—Suppose I were to ask you what walking is, and you were to get up and do it, wouldn't you be using the thing itself to show me, not words or any other signs? *Ad.*—Yes, of course. I am ashamed that I did not notice so obvious a fact. Now thousands of examples come to my mind of things which can be demonstrated immediately and without signs, such as eating, drinking, sitting, standing, shouting and other things innumerable. *Aug.*—Well then, tell me this. Supposing I had no idea of the meaning of

the word "walking," and I were to ask you when you were walking what "walking" means, how would you teach me? *Ad.*—I should walk a little more quickly. The change in speed would give notice that I was replying to your question, and I should still be doing what I was asked to demonstrate. *Aug.*—But you know there is a difference between walking and hastening. He who walks does not suddenly hasten, and he who hastens does not necessarily walk. We speak of hastening in writing, reading and very many other things. Consequently, if, after my query, you did what you had been doing, only a little more quickly, I should conclude that walking was the same thing as hastening, for the acceleration was the new feature of your behaviour. So I should be misled. *Ad.*—I admit that a thing cannot be demonstrated without a sign, at any rate if the thing is an action in which we are engaged when we are questioned. If we add nothing new to what we are doing, our questioner will think that we don't want to show him, but are continuing in what we were doing without paying any attention to him. But if his inquiry is about actions which we can perform, and if we are not doing them when he inquires, by doing it after he has inquired we can demonstrate what he asks by the actual thing and not merely by a sign. A special case would arise if, while I was speaking, someone asked me what "speaking" was. In order to let him know I must speak, whatever I actually may say. And I shall continue to show him until I make plain to him what he wants to know, not departing from the actual thing which he wished to have demonstrated to him, and yet not seeking signs apart from the thing itself wherewith to demonstrate it.

iv, 7. *Aug.*—Most acutely stated. Are we, now, agreed that there are two classes of things that can be demonstrated without signs; those which we are not engaged in doing when we are asked and can immediately start doing, and those in which the action consists in simply giving signs? For when we speak we make signs, whence is derived the verb, *to signify*. *Ad.*—Agreed. *Aug.*—When the question concerns signs merely, signs can be demonstrated by signs. But when the question is about things which are not signs, they can be demonstrated by carrying out the action, if possible, after the question has been asked, or by giving signs by means of which the things can be brought to mind. *Ad.*—That is so. *Aug.*—Here, then, we have a threefold classification. Let us first consider, if you please, the case of signs being demonstrated by signs. Words are not the only signs? *Ad.*—No. *Aug.*—It seems to me that in speaking we use words to signify words or other signs, as when we say "gesture" or "letter"; for these two words also signify signs. Or we may express in words something which is not a sign, as for example when we say the word "stone." The word is a sign for it signifies something, but what it signifies is not a sign. But this kind of case where words signify things that are not signs does not concern our present discussion. For we undertook to consider those cases where signs are demonstrated by signs, and we found that they fall into two classes; those in which we teach or call to remembrance by signs similar signs, and those in which we teach or call to remembrance different signs. Do you agree? *Ad.*—Clearly.

8. *Aug.*—Tell me, to what sense do verbal signs pertain? *Ad.*—To the sense of hearing. *Aug.*—And gesture? *Ad.*—To sight. *Aug.*—What about written words? Surely they are words? Or are they better understood as signs of words? A word is a meaningful articulate sound, and sound is perceived by no other sense than hearing. When a word is written, a sign is given to the eyes whereby something that properly belongs to the ears is brought to mind. *Ad.*—I agree entirely. *Aug.*—You will also agree, I imagine, that when we pronounce the word, *nomen* [name], we signify something. *Ad.*—True. *Aug.*—What, then? *Ad.*—That by which something or somebody is called; for example, Romulus, Rome, Virtue, a River, etc., etc. *Aug.*—These four names signify something. *Ad.*—Indeed they do. *Aug.*—Is there a difference between these names and the things they signify? *Ad.*—A great difference. *Aug.*—I should like you to tell me what is the difference. *Ad.*—In the first place, the names are signs; the things are not. *Aug.*—Shall we call things which can be signified by signs but are not signs "significables," as we call things that can be seen visible? It will simplify our discussion of them. *Ad.*—Very well. *Aug.*—Can these four signs you have just mentioned be signified by no other sign? *Ad.*—I am surprised that you should think I have already forgotten that we found that written words are signs of spoken words, signs, therefore, of signs. *Aug.*—What is the difference? *Ad.*—Written words are visible. Spoken words are audible. Why should we not use the word, audible, if we allow "significable"? *Aug.*—I allow it at once, and am grateful for your suggestion. But I ask again whether these four signs cannot be signified by any other audible sign as well as by the visible signs you have called to mind. *Ad.*—I recall that this too was

said recently in our discussion. I said that a name signified some thing and I gave these four examples. I recognize that the word "name" and these four names are all audible when spoken. *Aug.*—What, then, is the difference between an audible sign and other audible signs signified by it? *Ad.*—So far as I can see the difference between the word "name" and the four examples is this; it is the audible sign of audible signs; they are the audible signs not of signs but of things, partly visible, like Romulus, Rome, River, partly intelligible, like Virtue.

9. *Aug.*—I understand and approve. But you know that every articulate sound pronounced with some meaning is called a word. *Ad.*—I do. *Aug.*—A name, therefore, is a word when it is pronounced articulately with a meaning. When we say of a fluent man that he uses good words, we mean also that he uses names. When the slave in Terence said to his aged master, "Good words, I pray you," he used many names. *Ad.*—I agree. *Aug.*—So when we pronounce these two syllables, *ver-bum*, we also signify a name, and the one word is the sign of the other. *Ad.*—I agree. *Aug.*—Here is another question I should like you to answer. You have said that "word" is a sign pointing to "name," and "name" is a sign pointing to "river," and "river" is the sign of a thing which can be seen. Also you have explained the difference between this "thing" and "river," which is its sign, and between "river" and "name," which is the sign of a sign. What do you think is the difference between the sign of a name, that is a word, and the name itself of which it is the sign? *Ad.*—I understand the difference to be this. What is signified by "name" is also signified by "word." A name is a word, and "river" is a word. But everything that has a verbal sign does not have a nominal sign. For *si* at the beginning of the verse you quoted, and *ex*, where this long course of reasoning started, are words but they are not names. And there are many other such words. All names are words, but all words are not names. So the difference between a word and a name is, I think, clear, that is, between the sign of a sign which signifies no other signs, and the sign of a sign that points to other signs. *Aug.*—Every horse is an animal, but every animal is not a horse? *Ad.*—Indubitably. *Aug.*—There is the same difference between "name" and "word" as between horse and animal. Unless perhaps you are prevented from assenting by the fact that we use the word "verb" in a special sense to signify those things which have tenses—I write, I wrote; I read, I have read. Clearly these are not names. *Ad.*—You have mentioned exactly what caused me

to hesitate. *Aug.*—Don't let that trouble you. In all cases where words are employed and something is signified we speak of signs universally and without qualification. On the other hand, we speak of military signs which are properly called signs because words are not used. If I were to say to you that just as every horse is an animal but every animal is not a horse, so every word is a sign but every sign is not a word, you would not hesitate, I believe. *Ad.*—Now I understand and agree that there is the same difference between a word, universally, and a name as between animal and horse.

10. *Aug.*—You know that when we say "animal," that trisyllabic name pronounced by the voice is a different thing from that which it signifies? *Ad.*— We have admitted that is true for all signs and "significables." *Aug.*—Do you think that all signs signify something different from themselves, just as the three syllables of the word animal cannot signify the word itself. *Ad.*—Not altogether. For when we say the word "sign" it signifies not only all other signs but also itself. For it is a word, and all words are signs. *Aug.*—Does not the same thing happen when we say the word *verbum*? If that word signifies every meaningful articulate sound, it is itself included in that category. *Ad.*—It is. *Aug.*—Isn't it the same with the word "name"? It signifies names of all categories, and is itself the name of no category. If I were to ask you what part of speech is a name, could you answer correctly except by saying it is a noun? *Ad.*—No, indeed. *Aug.*—There are therefore signs which signify themselves as well as other signs. *Ad.*—There are. *Aug.*—Do you think that the same is true with the quadrisyllabic sign "conjunction" when spoken? *Ad.*—By no means. It is a name, but the things it signifies are not names.

v, 11. *Aug.*—You have been most attentive. Now consider whether there are signs which signify each other mutually, the one being signified by the other. This is not the case with the word "conjunction" and the words signified by it, such as, if, or, for, unless, therefore, since, and the like. All these are signified by that one word, but by none of them is that word signified. *Ad.*—I see. And I should like to learn what signs signify one another mutually. *Aug.*—When we say "name" and "word" we use two words. *Ad.*—Yes. *Aug.*—And when we use these two words we at the same time use two names. *Ad.*—Yes. *Aug.*—So that "name" signifies "word" just as "word" signifies "name." *Ad.*—I agree. *Aug.*—Can you say how they differ except that they sound differently and are spelt differently?

Ad.—Perhaps I can, remembering what I said a little while ago. By "words" we mean everything articulately spoken and with some meaning. So every name, including the word "name," is a word; but every word is not a name, though the word "word" is itself a name.

12. *Aug.*—If someone were to affirm and prove that, just as every name is a word, so every word is a name, could you point out the difference except in sound and spelling? *Ad.*—I could not. And I do not think there is a difference. *Aug.*—If all articulate and meaningful sounds are both words and names, but for one reason they are called words and for another names, will there be no difference? *Ad.*—I don't understand how that could be. *Aug.*—You understand at any rate that every coloured thing is visible, and that every visible thing is coloured, though these two words have quite different meanings. *Ad.*—I do. *Aug.*—What if similarly every word is a name and every name a word, though these two words, viz., "name" and "word," have different meanings? *Ad.*—I now see it might be so, but I wait for you to show me how. *Aug.*—You are aware, I suppose, that every articulate significant sound smites the ear in order that it may be perceived, remembered and known? *Ad.*—I am aware of that. *Aug.*—Therefore, whenever we speak, two things happen. *Ad.*—That is so. *Aug.*—What if words are so called from one of these two things, and names from the other? That is to say, if *verbum* derives from *verberare*, *nomen* from *noscere*, the former would receive its due appellation from something that happens to the ear, the latter from something that happens in the mind.

13. *Ad.*—I shall agree when you show me how we can correctly say that all words are names. *Aug.*—That is easy. I suppose you once learned and still remember that a pronoun is so-called because it can stand for a noun (name), though it characterizes its object less fully than the noun it has replaced. I believe this is the definition which you used to repeat to your grammar teacher: A pronoun is a part of speech which, when put in place of a noun, designates the same object but less fully. *Ad.*—I remember and I approve. *Aug.*—You see, then, that, according to this definition, pronouns can serve only in place of nouns, and can be put only in the place of nouns. For example, we say, "this man," "the king himself," "the same woman," "this gold," "that silver." "This," "that," "himself," "the same" are pronouns. "Man," "king," "woman," "gold," "silver" are nouns, by means of which the things are more fully

described than by the pronouns. *Ad.*—I see and agree. *Aug.*—Now name a few conjunctions, whichever you like. *Ad.*—"And," "but," "also." *Aug.*—Don't you think that all these you have mentioned are names (nouns)? *Ad.*—Not at all. *Aug.*—Do you think that I have used correct language in saying "all these you have mentioned"? *Ad.*—Quite correct. And now I understand that you have been showing me in a wonderful way that these were nouns which I mentioned, for otherwise it would not be correct to refer to them as "these." But I have still a suspicion that I judged your language to be correct because these conjunctions are undeniably words. Therefore we can correctly refer to them as "all these," viz., "all these words." If you ask me what part of speech is "words" I can only answer "a noun." So that your expression was correct perhaps because the pronoun was implicitly attached to this noun.

14. *Aug.*—An acute observation. But you are wrong. To correct your error listen attentively to what I say, if I can manage to express myself as I wish. To use words to treat of words is as complicated as to rub fingers together and expect someone else to distinguish which fingers tingle with warmth and which help others to tingle. *Ad.*—I give you all my attention, for your similitude has aroused my interest. *Aug.*—Words are a compound of sound and letters. *Ad.*—That is right. *Aug.*—Let us use a citation from an authority, dearest of all to us. When the Apostle Paul says: "In Christ there was not Yea [*est*] and Nay, but in him was Yea [*est*]" we are not to think, I suppose, that these three letters, e-s-t, were in Christ, but rather that which is signified by them. *Ad.*—Quite true. *Aug.*—When he says: "In him was *Est*," he is to be understood as meaning, "In him was what we call *Est* [being]." If he had said: "In him was virtue," he would have to be understood to mean: "In him was what we call virtue." We should not have to think that these two syllables which we use when we speak of virtue were in him, but rather that the quality denoted by the word "virtue" was in him. *Ad.*—I follow you. *Aug.*—You understand that there is no difference between "is called virtue" and "is named virtue"? *Ad.*—That is clear. *Aug.*—It is equally clear that there is no difference between, "in him was what is called *Est*," and, "in him was what is named *Est*." *Ad.*—I see there is no difference. *Aug.*—Do you see now what I am trying to point out to you? *Ad.*—Not quite. *Aug.*—You see that a name is that by which a thing is named. *Ad.*—Nothing is clearer. *Aug.*—Then you see that *Est* is a name [noun] if that which was in him is named *Est*

[being]. *Ad.*—Undeniably. *Aug.*—But if I were to ask you what part of speech is *Est*, you would, I suppose, say it was not a noun but a verb, though our reasoning has taught us that it is also a noun. *Ad.*—It is just as you say. *Aug.*—Do you still hesitate to regard as names the other parts of speech—names in the sense we have demonstrated? *Ad.*—I do not hesitate, now that I have to confess that they may be signs of something. But if you ask what the specific things signified are called or named, I cannot answer. I can refer only to those parts of speech which we do not usually call names, but which I see we are now constrained so to call.

15. *Aug.*—Are you not disturbed by the possibility that there may be someone who would weaken our argument by saying that we must attribute to the Apostle authority in the matter of realities but not in the use of words? The ground of our argument would not be so sure as we had assumed. It is possible that, though Paul lived and taught with absolute rectitude, his language was less correct when he wrote: "In him was *Est*," especially when he himself confesses that he was unskilled in speech. How do you think we ought to refute such a man? *Ad.*—I have nothing to urge against him. I pray you, find someone among the acknowledged masters of words by whose authority you can effect what you desire. *Aug.*—You think that without authorities reason itself is hardly sufficient. But reason itself demonstrates that all the parts of speech may signify some thing, that consequently they may be names or nouns. This can be most easily seen by comparing different languages. Obviously if you ask what is the Greek name for our *quis*, the answer is *tis*; for *volo*, *thelo*; for *bene*, *kalôs*; for *scriptum*, *to gegrammenon*; for *et*, *kai*; for *ab*, *apo*; for *heu*, *oi*. The question can thus be correctly asked about all the parts of speech as I have enumerated them. This could not be done unless they were names. When we can by this process of reasoning, apart from the authority of all the eloquent men, prove that the Apostle Paul spoke correctly, what need is there to seek anyone to buttress our argument with his personal authority?

16. But possibly some man, from greater stupidity or impudence, may not agree, but on the contrary may assert that he will give way only to those authorities who with universal consent are allowed to lay down the law in regard to words. What in the Latin tongue can be found more excellent than Cicero? And yet he, in his noblest orations, called the Verrine orations, calls *coram* a noun. Now *coram* is a preposition, or possibly an

adverb in that particular passage. It may be that I do not correctly understand the passage, and others may explain it differently. But there is one point to which I think there is no possible answer. The best masters of dialectic tell us that a complete sentence, whether affirmative or negative (what Tullius somewhere also calls a pronouncement), consists of a noun and a verb; and when the verb is in the third person, the noun, they say, and rightly, must be in the nominative case. Now consider this point. When we say "the man sits" and "the horse runs" you observe there are two pronouncements. *Ad.*—I do. *Aug.*—In each of them there is one noun, in the one case, "man," in the other, "horse." There is likewise one verb, "sits" in the one case, "runs" in the other. *Ad.*—So I observe. *Aug.* If I said simply "sits" or "runs," you would very properly ask me "who or what?" I should have to reply, "the man," "the horse," "the animal" or some other noun which, when added to the verb, completes the pronouncement or affirmative or negative sentence. *Ad.*—I understand. *Aug.*—Now listen. Suppose we see some object rather far away and are uncertain whether it is an animal or a stone or something else. Suppose I say to you: "Because it is a man it is an animal." Shouldn't I be speaking rashly? *Ad.*—You would indeed, but not if you said: "If it is a man it is an animal." *Aug.*—You are right. So in your sentence "if" satisfies us both, and in mine "because" is felt to be wrong. *Ad.*—I agree. *Aug.*—Now are these two pronouncements complete sentences: "'if' satisfies," and, "'because' is wrong"? *Ad.*—Yes. They are complete. *Aug.*—Now tell me which are the verbs and which the nouns. *Ad.*—The verbs are "satisfies" and "is wrong"; and the nouns must be "if" and "because." *Aug.*—It is therefore sufficiently proved that these two conjunctions can also be nouns. *Ad.*—Quite sufficiently. *Aug.*—Can you by yourself prove that the other parts of speech can be brought under the same rule? *Ad.*—I can.

vi, 17. *Aug.*—Let us, then, pass on. Tell me whether you think that, just as we have found that all words are names and all names are words, so all names are substantives and all substantives are names. *Ad.*—I see no difference between them except their sounds. *Aug.*—I make no objection provisionally. There are some who see a distinction between them in meaning too, but we need not consider their opinion just now. But at least you observe that we have reached signs which signify one another mutually, differing in nothing but sound, and which signify themselves together with all the other parts of speech.

Ad.—I don't understand. *Aug.*—Don't you understand that "substantive" signifies "name" and "name" "substantive," and that there is no difference between them except in sound, so far as concerns the general concept, "name." For of course we use the concept, "name" (or noun), in a special sense, when we use it to denote one of the eight parts of speech over against the other seven. *Ad.*—That I understand. *Aug.*—That is what I meant when I said that substantive and name signify one another mutually.

18. *Ad.*—I understand that, but I wonder what you meant by saying they signify themselves together with the other parts of speech. *Aug.*—Didn't our previous argument teach us that all parts of speech can be used as names and substantives, that is, may be signified by the signs, "name" and "substantive"? *Ad.*—That is so. *Aug.*—If I ask you the meaning of *no-men*—I mean that disyllabic sound—wouldn't you correctly reply *nomen*? *Ad.*—Yes. *Aug.*—But it is not surely the same with the sign we give when we pronounce the four syllables, *con-junc-ti-o*? This name cannot be enumerated among the conjunctions which it signifies. *Ad.*—That I accept as right. *Aug.*—So you see what I meant by saying, a name which signifies itself and all the other things it signifies. You can work this out for yourself if you like in the case of the word, "substantive." *Ad.*—Easily enough. But it occurs to me that "name" is used in both a general and a special sense. "Substantive" is not accepted among the eight parts of speech. So there must be a difference in meaning besides the difference in sound. *Aug.*—What difference is there between *nomen* and *onoma* except a difference of sound, the difference between the Latin and the Greek languages? *Ad.*—In this case I see no difference save one of sound. *Aug.*—So we have discovered signs which signify themselves, and one another mutually. Whatever is signified by the one is also signified by the other, and they differ only in sound. We have just found out this fourth characteristic. The three former ones we learned in connection with names and words. *Ad.*—Yes. That is what we have discovered.

vii, 19. *Aug.*—I should like you to recall what we have learned as a result of our conversation. *Ad.*—I shall do the best I can. To begin with I recall that we spent some time in inquiring why we use speech, and we saw that we did so in order to teach or to call to mind. Even when we ask questions our motive is simply to let the person questioned know what we want to hear. We seem to sing for the pleasure it gives us, but the pleasure derives from the melody and not properly from the words sung. In prayer, we cannot hold that God needs to be taught or reminded, so that when we use words we do so to remind ourselves or to admonish and teach others. Then we decided that words were simply signs. Things which do not signify something beyond themselves cannot be signs. Then you quoted the verse,

Si nihil ex tanta superis placet urbe relinqui

and I tried to show what each word signified. We could not discover what the second word signifies though it is a well-known obvious word. I thought it was not an empty word but did express something, perhaps the state of mind of one who discovers that the object of his search does not exist, or at least thinks he has made that discovery. You made some reply, jestingly avoiding the profundity of the question, and putting it off for another time. Don't think I have forgotten the explanation you owe me. Then I tried to explain the third word in the verse and you urged me not to explain it by means of a synonym, but to show the reality which the word signified. I said it was impossible to do this in conversation, so we came to things which can be pointed out with the finger. I thought all corporeal objects were of this kind, but we found that only visible things were. Then somehow we spoke of deaf people and actors who without words and by gestures alone signify not only visible things but much else besides, indeed nearly everything we speak about. And we decided that these gestures also were signs. Then we began again to inquire how we could without signs point out actual things, since a wall, a colour, all visible things are indicated by pointing with the finger, which is itself a sign. When I wrongly said that nothing could be found which could be shown without a sign, we agreed that it was possible in the case of actions, provided we were not performing them when we were questioned, if we could perform them when questioned. But speaking was not among such actions for even if we were asked while we were speaking what speaking is, it would clearly be easy to demonstrate the action by performing the action itself.

20. Hence we learned that signs are demonstrated by signs, also other things which are not signs. Likewise, without a sign, actions can be demonstrated which we can perform on being questioned. Of these three statements we undertook to consider diligently and to discuss the first. The discussion showed

that, on the one hand, there are signs which cannot be signified by the signs they themselves signify, for example the word "conjunction." On the other hand some can. For example, the word "sign" signifies a word, and the word "word" signifies a sign; so that "sign" and "word" are both signs and words. In the class of signs which are mutually significant it was shown that there are degrees of correspondence. The sound, *sig-num*, signifies everything by which anything is signified, but *ver-bum* is not a sign of all signs, but only of those which are articulately pronounced. Hence it is manifest that while *sig-num* signifies *ver-bum* and vice-versa, *signum* applies more widely than *verbum*. But in a general sense *verbum* and *nomen* have the same range of application. Our argument showed us that all the parts of speech can be names, because pronouns can be substituted for or added to them. Of all of them it can be said that they "name" something, and there is none of them which cannot be made the subject of a verb to form a complete sentence. But though "name" and "word" have the same range of applicability, since all words are names, yet they are not identical in meaning. We gave a probable reason for the distinction between "word" and "name," viz., *verbum* is derived from *verberare*, to strike the ear, *nomen* from the mental process of reminding. When we want to memorize something we rightly say, "What is its name?" but we do not usually say, "What is its word?" Of absolute synonyms, differing in nothing save in sound and spelling, the only example we found was *nomen* and *onoma*, a Latin word and its Greek equivalent. In the class of mutually significant signs, it escaped me that we had found no sign which does not signify itself among the other signs it signifies. There! I have recalled as much as I am able. I am sure that in our conversation you have said nothing without conscious design, and you will know whether I have summarized our talk properly and in order.

viii, 21. *Aug.*—You have indeed repeated from memory all I wanted; and I must confess these distinctions now seem to me to be much clearer than they did when our discussion forced them out from obscurity. But it is hard to say at this point what goal we are striving to reach by all these round-about paths. Probably you think we have just been playing a game and diverting the mind from serious things by these apparently puerile questionings, or, perhaps, that a very small gain has been made, if any. Or, if you suspect that some great advantage is to arise from our debate, you want to know it now or, at all events, to be told what it is. I want you to believe that I have not been trifling in this conversation, though perhaps we have been amusing ourselves. But the game is not to be regarded as merely puerile, nor is it to be thought that only small or moderate advantages have been gained. And yet, if I say that there is a life eternally blessed, and that my desire is that God, who is very truth, should bring us thither by steps suited to our poor abilities, I am afraid I shall appear ridiculous, because I set out on so long a journey with the consideration of signs and not of the realities they signify. You will pardon me, therefore, if I play with you to begin with, not for the sake of playing, but in order to exercise and sharpen our mental powers so that we may be able not merely to endure the heat and light of the region where lies the blessed life, but also to love them. *Ad.*—Go on as you have begun, for I shall never think unworthy of attention anything you may think it necessary to say or to do.

22. *Aug.*—Let us then consider the other side of the problem, where signs signify not other signs but what we have agreed to call "significables." And first tell me whether man is man. *Ad.*—Now I am not sure whether you are joking. *Aug.*—Why? *Ad.*—Because you think it necessary to ask me that question. *Aug.*—I dare say you would also suppose I was joking if I were to ask you whether the first syllable of that noun is *ho* and the second *mo*. *Ad.*—I certainly should. *Aug.*—But these two syllables together make *homo*. Do you agree? *Ad.*—Who could deny it? *Aug.*—Now I ask; do these two syllables together make you? *Ad.*—Of course not. But now I see your point. *Aug.*—You state it, then, so that I may not seem to be abusive. *Ad.*—You think the conclusion is that I am not a man. *Aug.*—Don't you agree, seeing you have agreed that all the premises are true from which this conclusion is reached? *Ad.*—I shall not tell you what I think until you tell me whether, in asking whether man is man, you meant these two syllables *homo*, or the thing they signify. *Aug.*—You tell me, rather, in what sense you understood my question. For if it is ambiguous you should have been careful and should not have replied until you were quite sure of the meaning of the question. *Ad.*—The ambiguity would not prevent me from answering that "*homo*" is "*homo*" in both senses. For these two syllables are nothing but these two syllables; and what they signify is exactly what is signified by them. *Aug.*—All right. But why don't you understand in two senses not only the word "*homo*" but all the other words we have used? *Ad.*—Have I not done so? *Aug.*—Take my first question. If you had understood it to be nothing but a series of

syllables, you would have made no answer for I should apparently have asked no question. When I asked, *utrum homo homo sit*, I used three words, repeating one of them twice. It is clear that you took the first and last words not as mere syllables but as significant words, and so you thought you could reply with certainty and confidence. *Ad.*—That is true. *Aug.*—Why did you wish to take the middle word only in two senses, according to its sound and according to its sense? *Ad.*—Now I take the whole sentence according to the sense of the words. I agree with you that we cannot carry on a conversation at all unless the words we hear carry the mind to the things of which they are the signs. Show me, now, the fallacy of the reasoning which proved that I am not a man. *Aug.*—I shall put the questions again so that you may yourself detect your mistake. *Ad.*—That is better.

23. *Aug.*—I shall not repeat the first question, for that has been agreed. But now think. The syllable *ho* is *ho*, and *mo* is *mo*. *Ad.*—Obviously. *Aug.*—Together they form *homo*. *Ad.*—There I went wrong. I thought, rightly, that when a sign is given one should look to what it signified, and, with that in view, should answer yes or no. But I allowed significance to separate syllables when of course they have none. *Aug.*—You are quite certain, then, that no answer should be given to questions except in terms of the things signified by the words. *Ad.*—Why not, if words are used? *Aug.*—I should like to hear how you would reply to the man in the amusing story who drew the conclusion that a lion had come out of the mouth of his fellow-disputant. He first asked whether what we say comes out of our mouth. That was, of course, undeniable. Then he had no difficulty in getting the other, in the course of the discussion, to mention a lion. Whereupon he made fun of him, and insisted that, since he had confessed that what we say comes out of our mouth, and since he could not deny that he had said "lion," therefore with the best intentions he had let out a horrid beast from his mouth. *Ad.*—It would not be difficult to answer that clever jester. I should not concede that whatever we say comes out of our mouth. For our words are signs merely of things. It is the sign and not the thing signified which comes out of the mouth of the speaker. In some cases it may be simply the sign of another sign, as we have said earlier in our discussion.

24. *Aug.*—I see you are well armed against that adversary. But if I ask whether *homo* is a noun, what answer will you give me? *Ad.*—What else could it be? *Aug.*—When I see you, do I see a noun? *Ad.*—No. *Aug.*—Shall I point out what follows from

your reply? *Ad.*—Please don't. I see for myself that it must be that I am not a man because, when you asked whether *homo* was a noun I replied that it was, though I had decided to look to the significance of words in giving an affirmative or a negative answer. *Aug.*—Still I think there was some advantage gained by your slipping into that reply. The very law of reason stamped on our minds has awakened your vigilance. If I were to ask simply what is *homo*, you would probably reply, an animal. But if I were to ask what part of speech is *homo*, the only correct answer is, a noun. So *homo* is both a noun and an animal. It is a noun when it is regarded as a sign, and an animal when regard is had to the thing signified by the sign. If anyone asks me whether *homo* is a noun I shall reply that it is, for the form of the question indicates sufficiently in what sense the word is to be taken—the sense in which it is a sign. If he asks whether *homo* is an animal I shall assent even more readily. But if he asks simply what *homo* is without mentioning either noun or animal, my mind, following the rule laid down for our discourse, would at once turn to the thing signified by these two syllables, and would give no other answer but "animal," unless it gave the whole definition, which is "a rational and mortal animal." Don't you think so? *Ad.*—I do. But if we have admitted that *homo* is a noun how shall we avoid the insulting conclusion that we are not men? *Aug.*—How else than by explaining that the conclusion is inferred by importing into the word a different sense from that which we had understood in giving our assent. And if he says that was the sense he intended, the conclusion is not to be feared in any way; for why should I fear to confess that I am not a man (*hominem*), that is, I am not these three syllables? *Ad.*—Very true. Why indeed should one be offended when one is said not to be a man in that sense? According to our argument nothing could be more true. *Aug.*—The rule, which naturally carries the greatest weight, is that, as soon as signs are heard, the attention is directed to the things they signify. So, when the rule is stated, it becomes impossible not to suppose that the conclusion refers to what is signified by the two syllables, *ho-mo*. *Ad.*—I understand and agree with what you say.

ix, 25. *Aug.*—I want you now to understand that things signified are of greater importance than their signs. Whatever exists on account of something else must necessarily be of less value than that on account of which it exists. Do you agree? *Ad.*—It seems to me we must not rashly agree to that statement.

The word *caenum* (filth) for example is, I think, far preferable to the thing it signifies. What offends us when it is mentioned has nothing to do with the sound of the word. Change one letter and *caenum* becomes *caelum* (heaven), but what a difference there is between the things signified by these two words! I should not, therefore, attribute to the sign the quality I loathe in the thing signified. We prefer to hear the word to being brought into contact with the thing with our other senses. Accordingly I prefer the sign to the thing signified. *Aug.*—You are most observant. It is false, therefore, that things universally are to be preferred to their signs. *Ad.*—So it seems. *Aug.*—Tell me, then, what you think people wanted to achieve when they bestowed that name on an object so nasty and revolting. Do you approve of what they did or not? *Ad.*—I do not venture to approve or to disapprove, nor do I know what they were trying to do. *Aug.*—But you can know what you intend to do when you mention the word? *Ad.*—Certainly. I want to give a sign to the man with whom I am speaking, by means of which I may let him know what I think he ought to know. *Aug.*—The knowledge, then, conveyed by this word from you to him or from him to you, is more valuable than the word itself? *Ad.*—I agree that the knowledge conveyed by the sign is more important than the sign itself. But this does not mean that the thing signified is better than its sign.

26. *Aug.*—Therefore, though it is false that things universally are to be preferred to their signs, it is nevertheless true that whatever exists on account of something else is inferior to that on account of which it exists. Knowledge of filth, for example, to convey which knowledge the name was invented, is more important than the name, while the name is also to be preferred to the thing it designates, as we have discovered. The knowledge is superior to the sign simply because it is the end towards which the latter is the means. If some gluttonous man, a worshipper of his belly, as the Apostle says, were to say that he lived to eat, a temperate man, hearing him, and unable to bear with him, might say: "How much better it would be if you ate to live." This judgment would proceed from the same rule. What displeased him would be that the other valued his life so little that he thought less of it than of the pleasures of gluttony, saying that he lived for banqueting. The advice to eat in order to live rather than to live in order to eat, is justly praised simply because it shows understanding of what is means and what is end, that is to say, of what should be subordinate to what. Similarly

you or another man of discernment, hearing some loquacious lover of verbiage say: "I teach for the sake of talking," would reply: "My man, why don't you rather talk for the sake of teaching." Now if this is right, as you know it is, you see at once how much less value we are to attribute to words than to the things on account of which we use words. The use to which words are put is superior to the words; for words exist to be used, and used to teach. Just as it is better to teach than to talk, so speech is better than words. And knowledge is much better than words. I want to hear if you have any objection to offer.

27. *Ad.*—I agree that knowledge is better than words. But I am not sure that no objection can be urged against the general rule that everything which is means to an end is inferior to the end it serves. *Aug.*—We shall have a better opportunity at another time to discuss that problem more carefully. Meantime what you have admitted is sufficient for what I am desirous of establishing now. You grant that the knowledge of things is better than the signs of things. So knowledge of the things signified by signs is preferable to knowledge of their signs. Is it not? *Ad.*—Surely I have not granted that the knowledge of things is superior to the knowledge of signs, but not superior to the signs themselves. I am afraid to give my assent to what you have said. If the word filth is better than the thing it signifies, knowledge of the word would be preferable to knowledge of the thing. And yet the name itself is inferior to the knowledge. There are four terms here: the name, the thing, knowledge of the name, knowledge of the thing. Why is not the third better than the fourth, just as the first is better than the second? And yet surely it is not to be subordinated?

28. *Aug.*—I see you have a wonderful memory for retaining your admissions and an excellent way of expounding your views. But take the word "vice" (*vitium*). When we pronounce the word *vi-ti-um* you know that it is better than the thing it signifies. And yet mere knowledge of the word is much inferior to knowledge of the vices. Let us consider your four terms: the name, the thing, knowledge of the name, knowledge of the thing. We rightly prefer the first to the second. When Persius used the name in his poem—"This man is stupefied by vice"—he committed no fault of versification, indeed he added an ornament. And yet the thing signified by the word makes the man in whom it is found necessarily vicious. But there is not the same relation between your third and fourth terms. The fourth is obviously better than the third. Knowledge of the word vice

is inferior to knowledge of the vices. *Ad.*—Do you think that knowledge is preferable even when it makes us more miserable? For above all the penalties thought of by the cruelty of tyrants or calculated by their greed, Persius sets this one penalty which tortures men who are compelled to acknowledge vices which they cannot avoid. *Aug.*—In the same way you could deny that knowledge of the virtues is preferable to knowledge of the word "virtue," for to see and not to possess virtue was the punishment which the satirist wished tyrants to suffer. *Ad.*—May God avert such madness! Now I understand that the knowledge imparted to the mind by a good education is not to be blamed, but those are to be judged most miserable of all who are affected by a disease which no medicine can cure. This, I think, was Persius' view too. *Aug.*—Quite right. But it does not matter to us what Persius thought. In such matters we are not subject to the authority of such as he. It is not easy to explain how one kind of knowledge is preferable to another. It is enough for my present purpose that we agree that knowledge of things signified is better than the signs even if not better than knowledge of the signs. Now let us discuss the greater problem. What kind of things, as we said, can be pointed out by themselves without signs such as speaking, walking, lying, and suchlike? *Ad.*—I remember the problem.

x, 29. *Aug.*—Do you think that all actions which we can perform on being interrogated can be demonstrated without a sign? Or is there any exception? *Ad.*—Considering this whole class of things I find none which can be shown without a sign, except perhaps speaking or possibly teaching. For whatever I do by way of demonstration when someone has asked a question, I see that he cannot learn immediately from the action which he wants to have demonstrated to him. Even if I am doing nothing, or am doing something else, when I am asked what walking is, and if I immediately set about walking, and try to give an answer to the question without a sign, how am I to make sure that "walking" is not taken to mean walking the exact distance that I actually walked. In that case my questioner would be deceived, and would imagine that anyone who walked further or less far than I had walked, had not in fact walked at all. And what I have said of this one action applies to all those which I thought could be demonstrated without a sign, except the two I have mentioned.

30. *Aug.*—I grant that. But now, don't you think speaking and teaching are different things? *Ad.*—Certainly. If they were

the same, no one could teach without speaking. Who can doubt there is a difference, seeing that, in fact, we can teach many things with other signs besides words? *Aug.*—Is there any difference between teaching and giving signs? *Ad.*—I think they are the same thing. *Aug.*—So it is correct to say that we give signs in order to teach? *Ad.*—Quite correct. *Aug.*—If anyone says that we teach in order to give signs, he can easily be refuted by the previous sentence? *Ad.*—That is so. *Aug.*—If we give signs in order that we may teach, and do not teach in order that we may give signs, teaching and giving signs are different things. *Ad.*—You are right, and I was wrong when I said they were the same. *Aug.*—Now does he who shows us what teaching is do it by giving signs or otherwise? *Ad.*—I do not see how he can do it otherwise. *Aug.*—So you were wrong in saying a moment ago that, when the question is what teaching is, the true answer can be given without signs. Even this, we see, cannot be done without signs, and you have agreed that giving signs is a different thing from teaching. If, as now appears, they are different, teaching cannot be demonstrated without signs and by itself alone, as you thought. So up to this point we have discovered nothing that can be demonstrated by simply performing the action except speaking, which consists in giving signs. But even speaking is itself a sign, so that it seems there is absolutely nothing which can be taught without signs. *Ad.*—I have no reason for refusing my assent.

31. *Aug.*—It is established then that: (*a*) nothing is taught without signs, (*b*) knowledge should be more precious to us than the signs by means of which we acquire it; though (*c*) possibly not all things which are signified are better than the signs which indicate them. *Ad.*—So it seems. *Aug.*—Just think what a tiny result has been reached by so long and circuitous a path. Since we began our conversation which has now continued for a long time, we have laboured to find answers to three questions: (*a*) whether anything can be taught without signs, (*b*) whether some signs are to be preferred to the things which they signify, (*c*) whether the knowledge of things is better than the knowledge of their signs. But there is a fourth question to which I should like to hear your answer. Do you think our results now stand beyond all doubt? *Ad.*—I should dearly like to think that after all these turnings and twistings we have indeed reached certainty. But your question makes me anxious, and deters me from answering in the affirmative. For it seems to me that you would not have asked the question unless you

had some difficulty in mind. The complexity of our problems does not allow me to examine the whole field or to answer with complete confidence. I am afraid there is something hidden in these complexities, to penetrate to which my mind is not sharp enough. *Aug.*—I am not at all unhappy about your hesitation, for it indicates a cautious mind. And caution is the best guard of tranquillity. It is the most difficult thing in the world not to be upset when opinions which we hold, and to which we have given a too ready and too wilful approval, are shattered by contrary arguments and are, as it were, weapons torn from our hands. It is a good thing to give in calmly to arguments that are well considered and grasped, just as it is dangerous to hold as known what in fact we do not know. We should be on our guard lest, when things are frequently undermined which we assumed would stand firm and abide, we fall into such hatred or fear of reason that we think we cannot trust even the most clearly manifest truth.

32. But come, let us consider expeditiously whether you do right to hesitate about our conclusions. Suppose someone ignorant of how birds are deceived by twigs and birdlime should meet a birdcatcher equipped with his instruments but merely travelling and not actually engaged in his work. Suppose he followed the birdcatcher step by step and wonderingly thought and inquired what could be the purpose of the man's equipment. Suppose the birdcatcher, seeing him all attention, and eager to display his skill, got ready his twigs and tubes and hawk and caught a bird, would he not teach the spectator what he wanted to know by the action itself and without any signs? *Ad.*—I suspect the same trouble would arise as I described in the case of the man who asked what "walking" was. So far as I see the whole art of birdcatching has not been demonstrated. *Aug.*—That trouble can easily be removed by adding a further supposition. Suppose the spectator were sufficiently intelligent to learn the whole art from what he saw. It is sufficient for our present purpose that some men can be taught some, not all, things without a sign. *Ad.*—I can make the same additional supposition in the other case. A man who is sufficiently intelligent will learn the exact meaning of "walking" when the action has been shown by taking a few paces. *Aug.*—I have no objection to your doing so, and indeed I approve. Both of us have now shown that some men can be taught some things without signs, and that our previous view was wrong, that nothing at all can be shown without signs. Hence not one or

two things but thousands of things occur to my mind which can be shown by themselves and without any sign. Why should we doubt it? I need not mention the innumerable spectacles which men exhibit in the theatres, showing them without any sign and just as they are. Think of the sun, the light that suffuses and clothes all things, the moon and the stars, earth and sea, and the innumerable things they bear. Does not God exhibit them in themselves to those who behold them?

33. If we consider this a little more closely, perhaps you will find that nothing is learned even by its appropriate sign. If I am given a sign and I do not know the thing of which it is the sign, it can teach me nothing. If I know the thing, what do I learn from the sign? When I read (Dan. 3:27: LXX Dan. 3:94): "Their *saraballae* were not changed," the word, *saraballae*, does not indicate what it means. If I am told that some covering of the head is so called, would I know what a head is, or a covering, unless I knew already? Knowledge of such things comes to me not when they are named by others but when I actually see them. When these two syllables first struck my ear, *ca-put*, I was as ignorant of what they meant as I was of the meaning of *saraballae* when I first heard or read it. But when the word, *caput*, was frequently repeated, observing when it was said, I discovered it was the name of a thing well known to me from my having seen it. Before I made that discovery the word was merely a sound to me. It became a sign when I had learned the thing of which it was the sign. And this I had learned not from signs but from seeing the actual object. So the sign is learned from knowing the thing, rather than vice versa.

34. To understand this better, suppose we hear the sound, *caput*, for the first time, not knowing whether it is merely a sound or whether it has some meaning. We ask what *caput* is. Remember we want to know not the thing signified but the sign, although we cannot have that knowledge so long as we do not know what it is a sign of. If, then, in answer to our question the thing is pointed out with a finger, we look at it and learn that that was a sign which we had heard but had not known before. In a sign there are two things, sound and meaning. We perceive the sound when it strikes our ear, while the meaning becomes clear when we look at the thing signified. The pointing with the finger can indicate nothing but the object pointed out, and it points not to a sign but to a part of the body which we call *caput*. In that way, accordingly, I cannot learn the thing, because I knew it already, nor can I learn the sign because it is

not pointed to. I am not greatly interested in the act of pointing. As a gesture it is a sign of something being pointed out rather than of the object pointed out. It is as when we say, "Lo"; for we are accustomed to use that adverb when we point with the finger in case one sign is not sufficient. What I am really trying to convince you of, if I can, is this. We learn nothing by means of these signs we call words. On the contrary, as I said, we learn the force of the word, that is the meaning which lies in the sound of the word, when we come to know the object signified by the word. Then only do we perceive that the word was a sign conveying that meaning.

35. The same is true of the word "coverings," and all the rest. But even when I have come to know them all, I still do not know what *saraballae* are. If someone points them out, or makes a drawing of them, or shows me something like them, I shall not say that he did not teach me what they were, though I could easily prove that that is true with a little more argument. I content myself with saying what is obvious; he did not teach me by words. If he saw them when I was present and called my attention to them by saying: "Lo, there are *saraballae*," I should learn something I did not know, not from any words spoken but by looking at the object pointed out to me. In this way I should learn and remember the thing that gives meaning to the word. In learning the thing I did not trust the words of another but my own eyes. I trusted the words simply so far as to direct my attention to what was pointed out, that is, to find my answer by looking at a visible object.

xi, 36. The utmost value I can attribute to words is this. They bid us look for things, but they do not show them to us so that we may know them. He alone teaches me anything who sets before my eyes, or one of my other bodily senses, or my mind, the things which I desire to know. From words we can learn only words. Indeed we can learn only their sound and noise. Even if words, in order to be words really, must also be signs, I do not know that any sound I may hear is a word until I know what it means. Knowledge of words is completed by knowledge of things, and by the hearing of words not even words are learned. We learn nothing new when we know the words already, and when we don't know them we cannot say we have learned anything unless we also learn their meaning. And their meaning we learn not from hearing their sound when they are uttered, but from getting to know the things they signify. It is sound reasoning and truly said that when words are spoken we either know or do not know what they mean. If we know, we do not learn, but are rather reminded of what we know. If we do not know, we are not even reminded, but are perhaps urged to inquire.

37. But you may say: granted we cannot know those head-coverings, the sound of whose name we remember, unless we see them, and that we cannot fully know the name until we know the thing. But what about those young men of whom we have heard (Dan. 3) how they vanquished King Nebuchadnezzar and his fiery furnace by their faithfulness and religion, how they sang praises to God, and won honours from their enemy? Have we learned about them otherwise than by means of words? I reply, Yes. But we already knew the meaning of all these words. I already knew the meaning of "three youths," "furnace," "fire," "king," "unhurt by fire" and so on. But the names, Ananias, Azarias and Misael, are as unknown to me as *saraballae*, and the names did not help me to know them and could not help me. All that we read of in that story happened at that time and was written down, so that I have to confess I must believe rather than know. And the writers whom we believe were not ignorant of the difference. For the prophet says: "Unless ye believe ye shall not know" (Isa. 7:9: LXX). This he would not have said if he had thought there was no difference. What I know I also believe, but I do not know everything that I believe. All that I understand I know, but I do not know all that I believe. And I know how useful it is to believe many things which I do not know, among them this story about the three youths. I know how useful it is to believe many things of which knowledge is not possible.

38. Concerning universals of which we can have knowledge, we do not listen to anyone speaking and making sounds outside ourselves. We listen to Truth which presides over our minds within us, though of course we may be bidden to listen by someone using words. Our real Teacher is he who is so listened to, who is said to dwell in the inner man, namely Christ, that is, the unchangeable power and eternal wisdom of God. To this wisdom every rational soul gives heed, but to each is given only so much as he is able to receive, according to his own good or evil will. If anyone is ever deceived it is not the fault of Truth, any more than it is the fault of the common light of day that the bodily eyes are often deceived. Confessedly we must pay heed to the light that it may let us discern visible things so far as we are able.

xii, 39. On the one hand we need light that we may see colours, and the elements of this world and sentient bodies that we may perceive things of sense, and the senses themselves which the mind uses as interpreters in its search for sense-knowledge. On the other hand, to know intelligible things with our reason we pay attention to the interior truth. How, then, can it be shown that words teach us anything besides the sound that strikes the ear? Everything we perceive we perceive either by bodily sense or by the mind. The former we call "sensible things," the latter "intelligible things"; or, to use the terminology of our Christian authors, the former we call "carnal things," the latter "spiritual things." When we are asked about the former we reply if they are present to our senses, for example, if we are looking at the new moon and someone asks what it is or where. If our questioner does not see it he believes our words, or perhaps often does not believe them, but he learns nothing unless he himself sees what he is asking about. When he sees he learns not from words uttered but from the objects seen and his sense of sight. Words would have the same sound whether he saw or not. When the question concerns not things which are present to our senses but which once were, we do not speak of the things themselves, but of images derived from them and imprinted on the memory. I do not know how we can call these things true, since what we have in view are only false images, unless it is because we speak of them not as things we see and feel but as things we have seen and felt. So in the halls of memory we bear the images of things once perceived as memorials which we can contemplate mentally and can speak of with a good conscience and without lying. But these memorials belong to us privately. If anyone hears me speak of them, provided he has seen them himself, he does not learn from my words, but recognizes the truth of what I say by the images which he has in his own memory. But if he has not had these sensations, obviously he believes my words rather than learns from them.

40. But when we have to do with things which we behold with the mind, that is, with the intelligence and with reason, we speak of things which we look upon directly in the inner light of truth which illumines the inner man and is inwardly enjoyed. There again if my hearer sees these things himself with his inward eye, he comes to know what I say, not as a result of my words but as a result of his own contemplation. Even when I speak what is true and he sees what is true, it is not I who teach him. He is taught not by my words but by the things

themselves which inwardly God has made manifest to him. Accordingly, if asked he can make answer regarding these things. What could be more absurd than that he should suppose that by my speaking I have taught him, when, if asked, he could himself have explained these things before I spoke? It often happens that a man, when asked a question, gives a negative answer, but by further questioning can be brought to answer in the affirmative. The reason lies in his own weakness. He is unable to let the light illumine the whole problem. Though he cannot behold the whole all at once, yet when he is questioned about the parts which compose the whole, he is induced to bring them one by one into the light. He is so induced by the words of his questioner, words, mark you, which do not make statements, but merely ask such questions as put him who is questioned in a position to learn inwardly. For example, if I were to ask you the question I am at present discussing: "Can nothing be taught by means of words?" it might at first seem to you to be absurd because you cannot visualize the whole problem. So I must put my question in a way suited to your ability to hear the inward Teacher. Then, when you have admitted that what I said was true, that you are certain of it, and assuredly know it, I should say: "Where did you learn that?" You might reply that I had taught you. Then I should say: "If I were to tell you that I had seen a man flying, would my words render you as certain of their truth as if I had said, 'Wise men are better than fools'?" You would certainly say: "No, I don't believe your first statement, or, if I believe it, I certainly do not *know* that it is true; but your second statement I know most certainly to be true." In this way you would realize that neither in the case of your not knowing what I affirmed, nor in the case of your knowing quite well, had you learned anything from my words, because in answer to each question you were able to answer confidently that you did not know this and that you did know that. When you realize that all the parts which constitute the whole are clear and certain, you will then admit what you had denied. You will agree that a man who has heard what we have said must either not know whether it is true, or know that it is false, or know that it is true. In the first case he must either believe it, or suppose it, or doubt it. In the second case he must oppose it and deny it. In the third case he must testify to its truth. In no case, therefore, will he learn. When my words have been spoken both he who does not know whether my words are true, and he who knows they are false, and he who could have given the same answers when asked are proved to have learned nothing from my words.

xiii, 41. Wherefore in matters which are discerned by the mind, whoever cannot discern them for himself listens vainly to the words of him who can, except that it is useful to believe such things so long as ignorance lasts. Whoever can discern them for himself is inwardly a disciple of the truth, and outwardly a judge of the speaker, or rather of what he says. For often enough the hearer knows what is said even when the speaker does not. For example, suppose some believer in the Epicureans, who held that the soul is mortal, should expound the arguments used by wiser men in favour of the soul's immortality in the hearing of one who can behold spiritual things. The latter judges that the former has spoken the truth, though the speaker does not know whether his words are true, and indeed believes them to be utterly false. Are we to think that he can teach what he does not know? Yet he uses the same words as he might use who does know.

42. Hence words do not even have the function of indicating the mind of the speaker, if it is uncertain whether he knows what he is saying. There are liars too and deceivers, so that you can easily understand that words not only do not reveal the mind, but even serve to conceal it. I do not of course in any way doubt that the words of truthful people are endeavouring to reveal the mind of the speaker and make some claim to do so, and would do so, all would agree, if only liars were not allowed to speak. And yet we have often experienced in ourselves and others that words do not correctly convey thoughts. This can happen in one or other of two ways. A speech committed to memory and frequently conned may be spoken when we are thinking of something else entirely. This often happens when we are singing a hymn. Or by a slip of the tongue some words will get substituted for others against our will, so that those which are heard are not signs of what is in our minds. Liars, too, think of the the things they speak about, so that even if we do not know whether they speak the truth, at least we know that they intend what they say, unless either of the two accidents occur which I have mentioned. If anyone contends that this sometimes occurs and can be noticed when it occurs, I make no objection, though it often is hidden and has often escaped my notice when I have been listening.

43. There is the other kind of accident, very wide-spread and the seed of innumerable dissensions and strifes. The speaker in-

deed expresses his thoughts but is understood only by himself and by some others. What he says does not convey the same meaning to those who hear him. For example, someone might say in our hearing that some wild beasts surpass man in virtue. Our impulse would be not to endure it, but to use every effort to refute such a false and pestilential opinion. But possibly he is giving the name of virtue to bodily strength, and has correctly expressed his mind. He is not lying. He is not substantially wrong. He is not uttering words committed to memory while he he has something else in mind. He has not spoken the wrong word by a slip of the tongue. He has simply called the thing he has in mind by a different name from the one we are accustomed to use. We should at once agree with him if we could see into his thought, which he had not made clear by the words he used in expressing his opinion. It is said that definition is the remedy for this mistake. If in this question he would define virtue, it would be apparent, they say, that the controversy was not about the substance of his statement but about a word. I should agree that that is so, but how often is a man to be found who is good at definition? Many things, too, are urged against the discipline of definition, but this is not the opportune place to deal with them, and I do not approve of them.

44. I need not mention the fact that often we do not rightly hear what is said, and enter into lengthy arguments over things we wrongly thought we heard. For example, recently, when I said that a certain Punic word meant mercy, you said that you had heard from those who knew the language better that it meant piety. I objected, insisting that you had quite misunderstood what you had been told, for I thought you said not piety but faith. Now you were sitting quite close to me, and these two words are not so alike in sound as to deceive the ear. For a long time I thought you did not know what had been told you, while all the time I did not know what you had said. If I had heard you aright I should not have thought it absurd that piety and mercy should be expressed by one word in Punic. Such misunderstandings often occur, but, as I said, let us omit them lest I should put upon words the blame that is due to the negligence of listeners, or seem to be troubled by human deafness. My chief troubles are those I have mentioned, where by means of words clearly heard, Latin words when Latin is our mother-tongue, we are yet unable to learn the thoughts of those who speak to us.

xiv, 45. Putting aside all these exceptions, I agree that

when words are heard by one who knows them, he can also know that the speaker has thought the things which the words signify. Now the question is, does he also learn that the words spoken are true? Do teachers profess that it is their thoughts that are learned and retained, and not the disciplines which they imagine they transmit by their speaking? Who is so foolishly curious as to send his son to school to learn what the teacher thinks? When the teachers have expounded by means of words all the disciplines which they profess to teach, the disciplines also of virtue and wisdom, then their pupils take thought within themselves whether what they have been told is true, looking to the inward truth, that is to say, so far as they are able. In this way they learn. And when they find inwardly that what they have been told is true they praise their teachers, not knowing that they really praise not teachers but learned men, if the teachers really know what they express in words. Men are wrong when they call those teachers who are not. But because very often there is no interval between the moment of speaking and the moment of knowing, and because they inwardly learn immediately after the speaker has given his admonition, they suppose that they have been taught in an external fashion by him who gave the admonition.

46. At another time, if God permit, we shall inquire into the whole problem of the usefulness of words, for their usefulness properly considered is not slight. Now I have warned you that we must not attribute to them a greater importance than they ought to have, so that now we should not only believe but also begin to understand how truly it is written by divine authority that we are to call no one on earth our teacher, for One is our teacher who is in heaven (cf. Matt. 23:10). What is meant by "in heaven" he will teach us, by whom we are admonished through human agency and by external signs to be inwardly converted to him and so to be instructed. To know and to love him is the blessed life, which all proclaim that they are seeking but few have the joy of really finding. But I should like you to tell me what you think of my whole discourse. If you know that what I have said is true, and if you had been interrogated at every point, you would have answered that you knew it to be true. You see, then, who taught you; certainly not I, for you would of your own accord have given the right answer each time I asked. If, on the other hand, you do not know that what I have said is true, neither I nor the inward teacher has taught you. Not I, because I have never the power to teach anyone;

and not he, because you have not yet the power to learn. *Ad.*—I have learned by your warning words, that by means of words a man is simply put on the alert in order that he may learn; also that very little of the thought of a speaker is made evident by his speaking. I have also learned that in order to know the truth of what is spoken, I must be taught by him who dwells within and gives me counsel about words spoken externally in the ear. By his favour I shall love him the more ardently the more I advance in learning. And I am specially grateful that latterly you have spoken without the interruption of questions and answers, because you have taken up and resolved all the difficulties I was prepared to urge against you. You omitted nothing at all that caused me to doubt; and in every case the Secret Oracle of which you have spoken has answered me exactly according to your words.

On Free Will

Augustine's Review of the "De Libero Arbitrio." *Retractations, I, ix*

1. While we were still delayed at Rome we determined to discuss the question of the origin of evil. The principle on which the discussion was to proceed was this. We were to try if possible to let rational argument, so far as we could with God's help in our discussion, demonstrate to our intellects what we already believed about the matter on divine authority. After careful reasoning we agreed that evil has no other origin than in the free choice of the will. So the three books which the discussion produced are called *Of Free Will*. Of these I completed Books II and III in Africa after I had been ordained presbyter at Hippo-regius, using such opportunity as I then could command.

2. In these books many things are discussed. Several questions arose which I could not solve or which required lengthy treatment. They were so broadly handled in their pros and cons that, either way, even when it was not quite clear where the truth lay, our reasoning led to this conclusion: Whatever be true in these difficult matters, it is to be believed, or indeed it is demonstrated, that God is to be praised. The disputation was undertaken on account of those who deny that evil derives its origin from the free choice of the will and who contend accordingly that God the Creator of all things is to be blamed. In this way, following their impious error (for they are Manichees), they seek to introduce an evil nature, unchangeable and co-eternal with God. Because this was the subject we proposed to debate, there is no discussion in these books of the grace of God whereby he has predestined his elect and himself prepares the wills of those among them who make use of their freedom of choice. But wherever an occasion occurs to make mention of this grace it is mentioned in passing, not laboriously defended

as if it were in question. It is one thing to inquire into the origin of evil, and another to seek the means of returning to man's original good estate or even to a better one.

3. Wherefore, do not let the Pelagians exult as if I had been pleading their cause, because in these books I said much in favour of free will, which was necessary for the purpose I had in view in that discussion. For the Pelagians are a new brand of heretics who assert the freedom of the will in such a way as to leave no room for the grace of God, since they say it is given to us according to our merits. I have said, it is true, in the First Book, that evil-doing is punished by God. And I added; "It would not be justly punished unless it were done voluntarily." Again when I was showing that a good will is so great a good that it should deservedly be preferred to all material and external goods, I said: "You see now, I believe, that it lies with our will whether we enjoy or lack so great and so true a good. For what is more in the power of the will than the will itself?" [He quotes a large number of similar passages to the effect that man can live aright if he will, concluding with this from Book III. xviii. 50] "Who commits sin by an act which he could by no means avoid? If sin has been committed, therefore it could have been avoided." Pelagius has made use of this quotation in one of his books; and when I had written a book in reply to his I chose as its title *De Natura et Gratia*.

4. In these and similar words of mine no mention is made of the grace of God, because it was not under discussion. Hence the Pelagians think, or may think, that I once held their opinion. But that is a vain thought. Certainly, will is that by which a man sins or lives righteously, as I argued in these words. But mortals cannot live righteously and piously unless the will itself is liberated by the grace of God from the servitude to sin into which it has fallen, and is aided to overcome its vices. Unless this divine liberating gift preceded the good will, it would be the reward of its merits and would not be grace, which is grace precisely because it is freely given. This point I have sufficiently urged in other works of mine in refutation of these recent heretics who are enemies of this grace. And yet even in these books *On Free Will* which were written not at all against them, for they did not yet exist, but against the Manichees, I have not been completely silent about the grace of God, which in their horrible impiety they are endeavouring to abolish. In the Second Book I said that not only great goods but even the least goods cannot be had save from him from whom are all

good things, namely God. [He quotes at length II. xix. 50.] Again I said: "Believe with unshakable piety that you have no good which does not come from God." And again, "Since man cannot rise of his own accord as he fell by his own accord, let us with strong faith hold fast the right hand of God stretched to us from above, even our Lord Jesus Christ."

5. In the Third Book, after the words which as I mentioned Pelagius made use of from my book—"Who commits sin by an act which he could by no means avoid? Sin has been committed, therefore it could have been avoided"—I immediately add: "And yet some things are done in ignorance which are disapproved . . ." [III. xviii. 51 is quoted at length.] At the close of the next paragraph I say: "To approve falsehood instead of truth, so as to err in spite of himself, and not to be able to refrain from the works of lust, because of the pain involved in breaking away from earthly bonds; these do not belong to the nature of man as he was created. They are the penalty of man as condemned. When we speak of the freedom of the will to do right we are speaking of the freedom wherein man was created."

6. You see that long before the Pelagian heresy emerged, I disputed as if I were already arguing against it. All good things, great, medium and small, were said to come from God. Free will was put among the medium goods, because we can make a bad as well as a good use of it, and yet it is good because we cannot live righteously without it. To make a good use of it is virtue, and virtue is found among the greater goods, of which no one can make a bad use. Because all good things, as I said, great, medium and small, come from God, it follows that from God also comes the good use of free will, which is virtue, and which is numbered among the greater goods. Then I go on to say that the grace of God liberates men from the misery inflicted on sinners, because man was able to fall of his own accord, that is, by free will, but was not able to rise of his own accord. To the misery due to just condemnation belong the ignorance and inability which every man suffers from his birth. From that evil no man is delivered save by the grace of God. The Pelagians will not have it that misery springs from man's just condemnation, for they deny original sin. But even if ignorance and inability did belong to man's primordial nature, still God should not be blamed but praised, as I argued in that same Third Book. This thesis is to be maintained against the Manichees who do not accept the Holy Scriptures of the Old Testament, in which

original sin is recorded; and what is said about it in the apostolic writings they contend with detestable impudence has been interpolated by corrupters of the Scriptures, as if the apostles had not said it. But against the Pelagians we must defend what is maintained in both Testaments, for they profess to accept both.

On Free Will

INTRODUCTION

IT IS DOUBTFUL WHETHER THE *De Libero Arbitrio*, at all events in its entirety, is to be included among the works known to Paulinus of Nola in 394 and called by him Augustine's "Pentateuch against the Manichees," for we find Augustine sending the three books to Paulinus in 395/6 (*Epist.* 31). In any case it was written against the Manichees, though not simply as a piece of negative polemic. It is an attempt to give a reasoned answer to the question which the Manichees, like the Gnostics, sought to solve by means of an absolute dualism: Whence is evil? The subject is, in fact, the nature and origin of evil, but because its origin is found in the free will of the rational creation, the whole work received the title it bears.

Augustine began to write it during his short sojourn in Rome on his way home to Africa, but he completed the Second and Third Books after his ordination as presbyter, possibly as late as 396. Books I and II, which are in dialogue form, appear to be properly finished. In the Third Book the dialogue ceases abruptly at section 10, and the interlocutor seems to be quite forgotten except for a brief intervention in section 47. This fact, together with the difficulty of discerning a clear and coherent plan of composition, has given rise to the suggestion that this Book is rather a collection of materials put together at different times. It is noteworthy that, particularly towards the end, specifically Christian doctrines are handled albeit tentatively, e.g., the work of Christ (29–31); the effect of the sin of Adam (51–54); theories of the origin of the soul (55–59), none of which is to be held obligatory. Occasionally, too, recourse is had to Scripture quotation in the writer's later manner. On the whole the *De Libero Arbitrio* may be regarded as the high-water mark of his earlier works, and the best and fullest exposition of what may be called the peculiarly Augustinian brand of Neoplatonism.

In controverting the Manichees with largely Platonist weapons Augustine had exposed his flank to the Pelagians. Pelagius himself was happy to be able to quote from the *De Libero Arbitrio* in support of his own views. Augustine's defence is not altogether convincing, viz., that Pelagianism had not yet emerged when he wrote, and that the purpose of the work gave no occasion to speak of grace. It is true enough that at the very beginning of Book I he tells us that he received divine aid to enable him to escape from Manichaean error, and that throughout free will is assumed to be a gift of God. Pelagius made a point of that too. But the passages quoted in the *Retractations* as showing that the *De Libero Arbitrio* is virtually anti-pelagian all come from what must certainly be regarded as the later parts of the work.

ANALYSIS

Book I

i, 1—ii, 5. God is believed to be both good and just. Can this be rationally demonstrated?

(1) Evil means wrong-doing. Suffering is the just punishment of wrong-doing, therefore is not evil. If punishment is just, the wrong-doing must be voluntary. Therefore God is not the author of evil. (2) Evil cannot be taught. Only how to avoid it is taught. (4–5) In this inquiry we begin with faith: God is omnipotent creator of all things. Being the absolute good God cannot be the cause of evil. We seek to demonstrate our faith by reason.

iii, 6—vi, 15. The Essence of Wrong-doing.

(6–7) What is the essence of evil in various deeds reputed evil? Not that they are condemned by law or public opinion; not even that they transgress the rule not to do to others what you would not have done to yourself. (9) It is something internal, cupidity, i.e., (10) love of things one may lose unwillingly. (11) What of killing, judicially or in war, which is permissible and even commanded? (13) Positive law reflects imperfectly a higher law. (14) Temporal laws are changed according to circumstances, but (15) reflect in this life the eternal law of reason. All things must be in perfect order.

vii, 16—xi, 23. Perfect Order in Man.

(16) Man is superior to the beasts in possessing reason. (17) Rational life is better than life without reason. (18) Order means that the worse is subordinated to the better, that reason rules the emotions. (19) All men have reason, though the majority may be fools. When reason rules, a man is wise. (20) No vicious soul can overcome a virtuous soul. Indeed nothing can do so. Hence sin is voluntary and (22) man's present state of ignorance and inability is the just penalty of voluntary sin.

xii, 24—xiv, 30. The Good Will.

(24) We accept the story of the Fall in faith, but how can we maintain by reason the justice of man's present plight? (25) All men wish to live rightly and to reach wisdom, i.e., have a good will. (27) This implies possession of prudence, fortitude, temperance and justice and (28) happiness. (29) Hence the happy life is attained by simply willing to have it. (30) All men wish to be happy, but not all succeed. This is in accordance with the eternal law that happiness is the reward of goodness and unhappiness is the punishment of wickedness.

xv, 31—xvi, 35. Temporal and Eternal Law.

(31) Good men love the eternal law and obey it with pleasure. Bad men hate it but are subject to it, and on them the temporal law is imposed. (32) Temporal law regulates worldly desires so that peace and social life may be preserved. It regulates temporal relationships, life, property, kinship and citizenship. It inflicts punishments which are felt as evil by men who love material things. It does not punish the desire for these things but only infringements of the rights of others. (33) Worldly things are not evil in themselves, but are not necessary for the good life. (34) Evil-doing is neglect of eternal things and love of temporal things to the extent of becoming subject to them. This is done by the free choice of the will.

Book II

i, 1—ii, 6. Ought God to have given Man Free Will?

(1) Free will makes sin possible but it was given that man might live righteously. If he uses it badly he is justly punished. (4) We believe that God exists and is good, and that all his gifts are good. (5) This is proved by the authority of

Scripture, but we seek rational demonstration. (6) Scripture encourages this endeavour. It demands faith to begin with but promises understanding. Three questions to be discussed (i) Does God exist? (ii) Are all good things from him? (iii) Is free will a good thing?

iii, 7—xv, 39. Proof of the Existence of God.

(7) Existence, life, intelligence form an ascending scale of being. Man excels animals in having all three. (8 ff.) Living creatures have senses wherewith they perceive corporeal objects. They have also an interior sense which co-ordinates the work of the senses, and is superior to them because it is their ruler and judge. (13) Man alone has reason, which in turn is superior to the senses and the interior sense, because it judges them all. (14) If there be something eternal and unchangeable which is superior to reason, that will be God. (15–19) The senses belong to individuals, but the world perceived by them is common to all who perceive it. (20–24) So the science of number, which has nothing to do with the senses, is common to all reasoning beings who are capable of mastering it. (25–27) Is wisdom also common to all, or are there as many "wisdoms" as there are wise men? For men vary in their views as to what wisdom is. But all agree that wisdom is a combination of truth and happiness, which cannot be had except in conjunction. All men seek truth and happiness. Hence both are in a sense known to all men, though they seek their supreme good in different things. (28–29) There are self-evident truths common to all minds, general judgments of value. These rules of wisdom are true and unchangeable and common to all men. (30–32) Wisdom belongs only to rational souls but number permeates all existing things. There is some relationship between wisdom and number. Both are true, and truth is the common property of all minds. (34 ff.) But truth is superior to the mind because it is unchangeable and eternal. We say of it that it *is* so, not that it *ought to be* so. Possession of truth makes men happy. Panegyric on truth. (39) Truth, being superior to our minds and having nothing superior to it, is God, the Father of Wisdom, whose only begotten Son is his equal. The existence of God has been proved; faith has become knowledge, albeit a pale and tenuous form of knowledge.

xv, 40—xvii, 46. Form and order, wisdom and number are good things. They pervade all created things. Therefore all good things come from God.

xviii, 47—xx, 54. Is Free Will a good Thing?

(48) The soul is better than the body; in both there are good qualities that may be abused. (49) Things necessary and not necessary for the good life. (50) The virtues are necessary and cannot be badly used. Bodily goods are not necessary and can be badly used. There are intermediate goods which are necessary and can be badly used, e.g. (52) Free will, which is necessary for the good life, but may be used badly. It may seek and cleave to the unchangeable common good, or it may seek its own private good. To turn from the highest good to any lower good is evil, of which unhappiness is the just penalty. This "aversion" is purely voluntary; its only cause is in the will.

Book III

i, 1—iv, 11. God's Foreknowledge and Man's Freedom.

(1) Sin is a movement of the will away from unchangeable good to mutable good. Is this caused by natural necessity? (2) Unlike the movement of a falling stone, it is voluntary and therefore culpable. (4) How is this compatible with our belief in God's foreknowledge of all things? (5) That question is often asked by way of excuse by sinners. (6–10) God foreknows what his creatures are going to do, but does not thereby rob them of the freedom of willing. Foreknowledge is not coercion. God is not the agent of all that he foreknows.

v, 12—xiii, 36. God is to be praised for all his Creatures.

(12) God has made all things good in all possible and conceivable variety, but in varying degrees of excellence. Inferior things are not to be grudged existence. (17) Mere utility from man's point of view is no standard for measuring the value of God's creatures. We may not say that he *ought* to have made any of them better than he has made them. (18–23) The miserable do not really wish to die. Existence of any kind as such is good. The suicide seeks not non-existence but rest. (24) The universe is perfect as it is; it is impious to criticize its parts. (25–26) The existence of souls justly miserable contributes to that perfection. Unless sin had its due penalty there would be lack of order. (29–31) The work of Christ in delivering man by persuasion from subjection to the devil. (32 ff.) The perfection of the universe redounds to the praise of its Creator.

xiii, 37—xvi, 46. Sin is Defect.

(38) Sin is defect in an otherwise perfect nature. (41) To find fault with the defect is to praise the nature in its true state. (42) Transience is no defect in temporal things; without it the whole beauty of the temporal sequence would not be able to display itself. (44) Sin inevitably brings its own penalty according to God's law, and so is compensated for in the universe as a whole. (46) To attribute man's sin to his Creator is a contradiction. If his sin is not his own doing it is not sin.

xvii, 47—xxi, 62. The Cause of the Evil Will. The Effects of the Fall.

(48) To ask for the cause of the evil will is to start an infinite regress. (50) There can never have been compulsion, else the deed was not sin. But (51) there are sins due to ignorance and inability. (52) Man's state of ignorance and inability is itself penal. Only as originally created, i.e., before the Fall, had man freedom to will and to do right. (53) In addition to original sin, men contract personal sins by refusing humbly to confess sin and to accept God's proffered help. (54) Strictly speaking, human nature means that nature as created, but we also use the expression of man's vitiated nature in its present penal condition. (55–60) Transmission of original sin. Four theories of the origin of the soul but none is obligatory for Christian faith. (61) The origin of the soul is a fit subject for inquiry, but knowledge of it is not necessary for salvation. More important than the past is the goal ahead. (63) No cause of sin need be looked for other than the individual will.

xxii, 64—xxiii, 70. Man's Advantage even in his Penal State.

(64) Man may rise above his ignorance and inability to wisdom and righteousness. To neglect to do so is sin. (65) He has both the capacity and the aid of God. Against this optimism various objections are urged. (66 f.) Infants often die before they acquire any merit, even if they are baptized—but their parents' faith may be imputed to them. (68 ff.) There are the grievous sufferings of children and animals. But suffering has its proper uses. All elements in our experience point to the goodness of the Creator.

xxiv, 71—xxv, 77. The Origin of Sin.

(71 ff.) Man as created was neither wise nor foolish, but he was rational, i.e., capable of receiving and understanding God's commandment. According as he obeyed or disobeyed the commandment he would become wise or foolish. He

became foolish by willingly making himself his own good, instead of seeking his good in God. (74 ff.) But the will is moved by something external to itself and outwith its own power. In the case of Adam there was the commandment of God on the one hand, and the suggestion of the devil on the other. But what enticed the devil to sin? Simply the will perversely to imitate God. He thus began to be proud, then became envious and finally malevolent. His eternal punishment is a warning to men.

On Free Will

THE TEXT

Book I

i, 1. *Evodius.*—Tell me, pray, whether God be not the author of evil. *Augustine.*—I shall tell you, if you will make it clear what you mean by evil in your question. For we are wont to use the word evil in two senses: the evil a man has done, and the evil he has suffered. *Evodius.*—I want to know about both kinds of evil. *Augustine.*—If you know or believe that God is good (and we may not think otherwise) he cannot do evil. Again, if we confess that God is just (and to deny that is sacrilegious) he gives rewards to the good just as he gives punishments to the wicked, but of course these punishments are evil to those who suffer them. Hence if no one is penalized unjustly—and this we must believe, seeing we believe that the universe is governed by divine providence—God is not the author of the evil a man does though he is the author of the evil a man suffers. *Ev.*—Is there then some other author of the kind of evil which we do not attribute to the action of God? *Aug.*—There certainly is, for we cannot say that it happens without an author. But if you ask who that is I cannot tell you. For there is no one single author. Every evil man is the author of his evil deeds. If you wonder how that is, consider what we have just said: evil deeds are punished by the justice of God. They would not be justly punished unless they were done voluntarily.

2. *Ev.*—I do not know whether anyone sins without being taught to do evil. If that is true I ask from whom have we learned to do wrong. *Aug.*—Is learning a good thing? *Ev.*—Who would venture to say it was a bad thing? *Aug.*—Perhaps it is neither good nor bad? *Ev.*—I think it is a good thing. *Aug.*—Quite right, at any rate if learning gives and stirs up knowledge, and if it is the only path to knowledge. Don't you agree that

this is so? *Ev.*—I think that nothing but good is learned by education. *Aug.*—Yet possibly evil is also learned in this way, for learning [*disciplina*] is derived from the verb "to learn" [*discere*]. *Ev.*—How, then, are evils committed by a man if they are not learned? *Aug.*—Possibly because he turns away from learning and stands apart from it. However that may be, it is at least manifest that, since learning is good, evil cannot be learned. If it is learned, it must be a part of education, and education will not be good. But, as you yourself admit, it is good. Evil, therefore, is not learned, and it is vain to ask from whom we have learned to do evil. Or, if indeed evil is learned, that can only be in the sense that we learn to avoid deeds which ought not to be done. Hence to do evil is nothing but to stray away from education.

3. *Ev.*—I think there must be two kinds of education, one by which we learn to do well and one by which we learn to do evil. When you asked whether education was a good thing I replied that it was, because my enthusiasm for the good made me think of the education that teaches to do good. Now I have a suspicion that there is another kind, which I have no doubt is a bad thing. *Aug.*—At any rate you regard intelligence as entirely a good thing? *Ev.*—So good indeed that a man can have nothing better. I should never say that intelligence can possibly be evil. *Aug.*—If a man has been taught something but does not understand it, could you regard him as learned? *Ev.*—Certainly not. *Aug.*—If intelligence is entirely good and is the necessary result of learning, every one who learns does well and also arrives at intelligence, and so again does well. Whoever asks for the cause of our learning anything simply asks for the cause of our doing well. So do not look for any teacher of evil. If he is evil he is not a teacher. If he is a teacher he is not evil.

ii, 4. *Ev.*—Since you force me to agree that we are not taught to do evil, tell me the cause why we do evil. *Aug.*—That is a question that gave me great trouble when I was a young man. It wearied me and drove me into the arms of heretics. By that accident I was so afflicted and overwhelmed with such masses of vain fables that, had not my love of finding the truth obtained divine aid, I could never have found my way out or breathed the pure air of free inquiry. But I took the greatest pains to find deliverance from that quandary, so in discoursing with you I shall follow the order which led to my own deliverance. May God grant his aid, and give us to understand what we have first believed. The steps are laid down by the prophet who says: "Unless ye believe ye shall not understand" (Isa. 7:9 LXX). We know well that we must hold fast to that. We believe that all things which exist are from one God; and yet God is not the author of sins. The difficulty for the mind is this. If sins originate with souls which God has created, and which therefore have their origin from God, how are sins not to be charged against God at least mediately?

5. *Ev.*—Now you have plainly stated the problem that was troubling my mind, and which impelled me to ask my question. *Aug.*—Have courage, and hold to your faith. You cannot do better than believe even when you do not know the reason for your faith. To think the best of God is the truest foundation of piety. And to think the best of God means to believe that he is omnipotent and absolutely unchangeable, that he is the Creator of all good things, being himself more excellent than them all; that he is the most just ruler of all that he has created; that he had no assistance in creating as if he were not sufficient in himself. Hence he created all things of nothing. One, however, he did not create, but begat, One equal to himself, whom we call the only Son of God, whom we endeavour to describe more fully when we call him the Power and Wisdom of God. By him he made all things which are made of nothing. Having stated these articles of our faith let us strive with God's help to reach understanding of the problem which you have raised, and in this fashion.

iii, 6. You ask for the cause of our doing evil. First we must discuss what doing evil is. Tell me what you think about this. If you cannot put the whole thing briefly in a few words, at least indicate your opinion by naming some evil deeds one by one. *Ev.*—Adultery, homicide, sacrilege. I need mention no more. To enumerate all the others neither time nor my memory would be sufficient. But no one doubts that those I have mentioned are examples of evil deeds. *Aug.*—Tell me now why you think adultery is evil. Is it because it is forbidden by law? *Ev.*—It is not evil because it is forbidden by law. It is forbidden by law because it is evil. *Aug.*—Suppose someone were to press us, stressing the delights of adultery and asking why it is evil and why we think it worthy of condemnation. Do you think that people who wanted not only to believe that adultery is evil but also to know the reason why it is so, would be driven to appeal to the authority of the law? You and I believe without the slightest hesitation that adultery is evil, and I declare that all peoples and nations must believe that too. But our present endeavour is to obtain intelligent knowledge and assurance of what we have accepted in faith. Give this matter your best consideration and tell me the reason why you know that adultery is evil. *Ev.*—I know it is evil because I should not wish it to be committed with my own wife. Whoever does to another what he would not have done to himself does evil. *Aug.*—Suppose someone offered his wife to another, being willing that she should be corrupted by him in return for a similar licence allowed him with the other's wife. Would he have done no evil? *Ev.*—Far from that. He would have done great evil. *Aug.*—And yet his sin does not come under your general rule, for he does not do what he would not have done to him. You must find another reason to prove that adultery is evil.

7. *Ev.*—I think it evil because I have often seen men condemned on this charge. *Aug.*—But are not men frequently condemned for righteous deeds? Without going to other books, think of scripture history which excels all other books because it has divine authority. If we decide that condemnation is a certain indication of evil-doing, what an evil opinion we must adopt of the apostles and martyrs, for they were all thought worthy of condemnation for their faith. If whatever is condemned is evil, it was evil in those days to believe in Christ and to confess the Christian faith. But if everything is not evil which is condemned you must find another reason for teaching that adultery is evil. *Ev.*—I have no reply to make.

8. *Aug.*—Possibly the evil thing in adultery is lust. So long as you look for the evil in the outward act you discover difficulties. But when you understand that the evil lies in lust it becomes clear that even if a man finds no opportunity to lie with the wife of another but shows that he desires to do so and would do it if he got the chance, he is no less guilty than if he were caught in the act. *Ev.*—Nothing is more manifest; and I now see that there is no need of lengthy argument to persuade me that the same is true of homicide, sacrilege and all other sins. For it is clear that lust alone dominates the whole realm of evil-doing.

iv, 9. *Aug.*—You know that lust is also called cupidity? *Ev.*—I do. *Aug.*—Do you think there is or is not a difference between cupidity and fear? *Ev.*—Indeed there is a great difference between them. *Aug.*—I suppose you think so because cupidity longs for its object while fear avoids its object. *Ev.*—That is so. *Aug.*—What if some one kills a man from no desire to get possession of anything but from fear of suffering some evil at his hands? In that case he will not be a homicide? *Ev.*—He will indeed. Even such a deed is not without a trace of cupidity. He who kills a man from fear desires to live without fear. *Aug.*—And it is no small good to live without fear? *Ev.*—It is a great good, but the homicide cannot attain it by his crime. *Aug.*—I am not seeking what he can attain, but what he desires. Certainly he desires a good thing who desires a life free from fear, and so far his desire is not to be blamed. Otherwise we shall be blaming all lovers of good things. So we are compelled to admit that there can be homicide in which the dominance of evil cupidity is not to be found; and it will consequently be false to say that it is the dominance of lust which makes all sins evil. In other words there can be homicide which is not a sin. *Ev.*—If to kill a man is homicide it can sometimes be done without sin. When a soldier kills an enemy, or when a judge or an officer of the law puts a criminal to death, or when a weapon slips out of someone's hand without his will or knowledge, the killing of a man does not seem to me to be a sin. *Aug.*—I agree, but these are not usually called homicides. But tell me this. A slave kills his master because he feared he would be terribly tortured by him. Do you think he would have to be regarded as one of those who are not to be classed as homicides because they have killed a man? *Ev.*—His is a very different case from theirs. They act in accordance with the laws, or not contrary to the laws, but no law approves his deed.

10. *Aug.*—You are reverting again to authority. You must remember that we have undertaken to try to understand what we believe. We believe the laws and must accordingly try if we can to understand whether the law which punishes this deed does not wrongly punish. *Ev.*—It does not punish wrongly when it punishes a man who willingly and knowingly slays his master. None of these other cases we have mentioned is similar. *Aug.*—You remember you recently said that in every evil deed lust prevailed, and that for that very reason it was evil? *Ev.*—Certainly I remember. *Aug.*—Did you not also admit that he who desires to live without fear has no evil cupidity? *Ev.*—That too I remember. *Aug.*—When our slave kills his master from that motive he does so without any culpable cupidity. So we have not discovered why the deed was evil. We have agreed that all evil deeds are evil for no other reason than that they are committed from lust, that is, wrongful cupidity. *Ev.*—Now it seems I must admit that he is unjustly condemned. But I should not dare to say so if I had any other answer to give. *Aug.*—You are persuaded that so great a crime ought to go unpunished before

you consider whether the slave desired to be free of fear of his master in order to satisfy his own lusts? To desire to live without fear is characteristic of all men, not only of the good but also of the bad. But there is this difference. The good seek it by diverting their love from things which cannot be had without the risk of losing them. The bad are anxious to enjoy these things with security and try to remove hindrances so as to live a wicked and criminal life which is better called death. *Ev.*—I am recovering my wits. Now I am glad to have learned what culpable cupidity is, which we also call lust. Evidently it is love of things which one may lose against one's will.

v, 11. Let us now inquire, if you please, whether lust prevails in sacrilegious acts, many of which we see committed through superstition. *Aug.*—Perhaps that would be too hasty. I think we ought first to discuss whether an attacking enemy or an armed lier-in-wait can be slain in defence of life or liberty or chastity, without any lust. *Ev.*—How can I possibly think that men are void of lust who fight for things which they can lose against their will? If they cannot lose them, what need is there to go so far as to kill a man on their account? *Aug.*—Then the law is not just which gives the traveller authority to kill a brigand lest he should himself be killed by him. Or the law that allows any man or woman to slay, if he can, any one who comes with intent to ravish, even before the crime has been committed. The law also bids the soldier to slay the enemy. If he abstains from killing he is punished by the general. Shall we dare to say that these laws are unjust or rather null and void? For a law that is unjust does not seem to me to be a law at all.

12. *Ev.*—It is, however, evident that this law is well prepared against such an accusation, for in the state where it is in force it allows lesser evil deeds to prevent worse being committed. It is much more suitable that the man who attacks the life of another should be slain than he who defends his own life; and it is much more cruel that a man should suffer violation than that the violator should be slain by his intended victim. In killing an enemy the soldier is a servant of the law and can easily avoid lust in performing his duty. Further, a law passed to guard the people cannot be accused of lust. The proposer of the law, if he did so at the command of God, that is, at the command of eternal justice, could do it without the slightest trace of lust. If, however, he did act from some motive of lust it does not follow that his law is obeyed from lust. A good law can be passed by one who is not himself good. For the sake of argument, suppose

a man has obtained tyrannical power and is prepared to make money by it. Suppose he accepts a bribe to bring in a law making it unlawful for anyone to force a woman to become his wife. The law will not be a bad law simply because the man who laid it down was unjust and corrupt. So the law which demands that hostile force be repelled by force for the purpose of protecting the citizens can be obeyed without lust. And the same may be said of all officials who are lawfully and in an orderly fashion subject to the powers that be. And yet I do not quite see how, even if the law is blameless, those who obey it can be blameless. For the law does not compel them to kill but leaves the decision to do so in their discretion. They are free not to kill anyone for the sake of things which they can lose against their will, and therefore ought not to love. In matters affecting life it may be doubtful whether the soul is or is not destroyed when the body is slain. If it can be destroyed, it is a thing of no consequence. If it cannot be destroyed there is no occasion for fear. In the matter of chastity, who doubts that virtue has its seat in the soul itself, and cannot be snatched away by any violent violator? All that he would have robbed us of, had he not been slain, was outwith our jurisdiction, so that I cannot see how it can be said to have been ours. Therefore I do not find fault with the law which permits such to be slain, but I do not know how to defend those who use the permissive power to kill.

13. *Aug.*—Much less do I know why you should seek a defence for men whom no law charges with guilt. *Ev.*—None of the actual laws, perhaps, which are found in human statute-books. But I am not sure whether men are not bound by some more strict and secret law, at any rate if divine providence administers all things without exception. How before that law are those free from sin who are polluted by human bloodshed on account of things which they ought to despise? Mind you, I think that positive law, designed to rule a people, rightly permits these things and vindicates divine providence. The law of the state takes upon itself to vindicate all that conduces to peaceful relations between simple folk as far as it can be regulated by man. Beyond that, sins have other suitable penalties from which, it seems to me, wisdom alone can set us free. *Aug.*—I approve and applaud your distinction. No doubt it is incomplete and far from perfect, and yet it shows faith and high idealism. You think that positive law which is passed to rule states makes many concessions and leaves many things unpunished which divine providence punishes. And this is right,

for what it does is not to be disapproved simply on the ground that it does not accomplish everything.

vi, 14. But let us examine closely, if you please, how far evil deeds are to be punished by the law which governs states in this life. Then we shall consider what remains to be inevitably and secretly punished by divine providence. *Ev.*—That is my wish, if only it is possible to reach the end of so vast a theme. I think it is infinite. *Aug.*—Be brave and enter on the path of reason trusting in piety. There is nothing so hard and difficult which with God's help will not become plain and easy. Depending on God and praying for his help, let us persevere in our inquiry. And first tell me whether the law that is promulgated in writing brings aid to men while they live this life. *Ev.*—Manifestly, for states and nations are composed of these men. *Aug.*—Do men and peoples belong to the class of things which cannot perish or change but are altogether eternal? Or are they mutable and subject to time's changes? *Ev.*—Who can doubt that this class of things is mutable and liable to the changes of time? *Aug.*—If a people, then, is well balanced and serious-minded, a careful guardian of the common good; if everyone in it thinks less of his private interests than of the public interest, it would be right to pass a law allowing that people to appoint its own magistrates to administer its affairs, that is, its public affairs? *Ev.*—Quite right. *Aug.*—Now if that same people degenerated little by little, put private interests before the public interest, sold its votes and, corrupted by men who love honours, committed rule over itself to wicked and criminal men, in such a case, if there existed some good and powerful man, would he not be right to strip that people of the power to bestow honours, and to give that power into the hands of a few good men or even of one man? *Ev.*—Again entirely right. *Aug.*—These two laws are exactly contrary the one to the other. The one gives to the people the power to bestow honours; the other takes it away. The second was passed under such conditions that both could not exist simultaneously in one state. Shall we say, then, that one of them is unjust and ought not to have been passed? *Ev.*—By no means. *Aug.*—Let us, then, if you please, call that a temporal law, which, though it be just, may be justly changed to suit altered circumstances. *Ev.*—Let us so call it.

15. *Aug.*—What about that law which is called supreme reason, which must always be obeyed, by which the evil deserve an unhappy life and the good a blessed life, by which the

law we have agreed to call temporal is rightly laid down and rightly changed? Can any intelligent person not see that it is unchangeable and eternal? Can it ever be unjust that the evil should be unhappy and the good happy? Or that a good and serious-minded people should appoint its own magistrates, and that a dissolute and worthless people should be deprived of that liberty. *Ev.*—I see that that is an eternal and unchangeable law. *Aug.*—I am sure you see also that there is nothing just or legitimate in temporal law save what men have derived from the eternal law. For if the people we have been speaking of at one time bestowed honours justly and at another time unjustly, the change in question belongs to the temporal sphere, but the judgment as to justice or injustice is derived from the eternal sphere in which it is abidingly just that a serious-minded people should bestow honours, and a fickle people should not. Don't you agree? *Ev.*—I do. *Aug.*—Briefly to express in words as best I can the idea of eternal law as it is stamped upon our minds I should say this: it is just that all things should be in perfect order. If you have any other view, tell me. *Ev.*—What you say is true and I have nothing to urge against it. *Aug.*—Since, then, there is one law, of which all temporal laws by which men are ruled are variants, that one law surely cannot vary in the least degree? *Ev.*—I know that is absolutely impossible. No force, no accident, no corruption of things can ever bring it about that justice ceases to mean that all things should be in perfect order.

vii, 16. *Aug.*—Now let us see what it means to say of a man that he is perfectly in order, for a people is composed of men associated under one law, a temporal law, as we have said. Tell me whether you are quite certain that you are alive. *Ev.*—To no question can I give a more unhesitating reply in the affirmative. *Aug.*—Can you distinguish living from knowing that you live? *Ev.*—I know that no one can know he is alive unless he is alive. But I do not know whether everyone who is alive knows it. *Aug.*—How I wish you would believe it. Then you would know that beasts lack reason, and our disputation would speedily pass on from that question. But since you say you do not know, you necessitate a long disquisition. So important is the question and so closely knit the argument required, that we cannot leave it aside and go on to our goal. We often see beasts tamed by men, not only their bodies but also their souls, so that they are subject to men's wills at a touch and by force of custom. Do you think that any beast however fierce or huge or keen of sense could ever try in the same way to subjugate a man to its service, though many beasts could destroy man's body by violence or in some secret way? *Ev.*—I agree, that could not happen. *Aug.*—Very well. Since it is obvious that man is far surpassed by many beasts in strength and in other bodily functions, tell me how it is that man excels so that no beast can order him about as he orders many of them. Is it because he has what we usually call reason or intelligence? *Ev.*—I can think of nothing else. That whereby we excel the beasts must be something in the soul, since to have a living soul would make us excel dead beasts. They too are living creatures (animals), but there is something lacking in their souls which allows them to be subjected by us, and there is something in our souls that makes us better than they. Now no one can imagine that that is a trifle, and I know no more correct word for it than reason. *Aug.*—You see how easy a problem becomes if God grant his aid, even a problem which men think most difficult. I confess I thought that the question which we have settled, as I understand, would have kept us as long, perhaps, as all the other questions we have handled since our conversation began. Now notice how relevant reason is to our argument. I am sure you know that when we say: "we know," we mean simply that we have grasped something by reason. *Ev.*—That is so. *Aug.*—So he who knows he is alive has reason. *Ev.*—That follows. *Aug.*—Beasts are alive, but, as we have shown, have no part in reason. *Ev.*—Clearly. *Aug.*—So now you know what you said you did not know. Not everything which lives knows that it lives, although everything that knows it lives is necessarily a living thing.

17. *Ev.*—I have no further doubts. Go on as you have proposed. I have clearly learned that to live is one thing, and to know that one lives another thing altogether. *Aug.*—Which of the two do you think is the better? *Ev.*—Why of course to know that one lives. *Aug.*—Do you think it is better to know that one lives than to have life? But perhaps you understand knowledge to be a superior and purer form of life which none can know unless he has intelligence. For what is to have intelligence but to live more intensely and more perfectly in the very light of the mind? So, unless I am mistaken, you have not preferred something else to life, but have preferred a better life to any kind of commonplace life. *Ev.*—You have exactly understood and expounded my views, that is, if knowledge can never be a bad thing. *Aug.*—It never can, unless by knowledge we mean

knowledge gained by experience. Experience is not always a good thing, for we can experience punishments. But knowledge strictly and purely so called, because it is gained by reason and intelligence, cannot be evil. *Ev.*—I grasp that difference too. Go on to the next subject.

viii, 18. *Aug.*—This is what I want to say. Whatever it is that puts man above the beasts, mind or spirit (perhaps it is best called by both names, for we find both in the divine Scriptures), whatever it is called, if it dominates and rules the other parts of which man is composed, then a man is most perfectly ordered. We see that we have many things in common not only with the beasts but also with plants and trees. For we see that trees also have power to take nourishment, to grow, to reproduce themselves, to flourish, and yet they have the lowest form of life. And we observe that animals can see, hear, smell, taste and feel corporeal objects, many of them more keenly than we can. Add strength, vigour and firmness of limb, speed and easy motion of the body. In all these things we surpass some of them, are the equals of others, and are surpassed by not a few. We also have with the animals a common attitude to external things. To seek bodily pleasures and to avoid pain is the whole endeavour of animal life. There are some things which do not seem to occur in animals yet they do not belong to the higher part of human nature, such as jesting and laughing. Whoever judges rightly of human nature will hold these to be human qualities certainly, but to belong to the lower part of man. Then there is love of praise and glory, and ambition to dominate. These are not characteristic of beasts, and yet we must not think we are better than the beasts because we have these desires. For when such desires are not subject to reason they make us miserable. No man has ever thought that his superiority consists in a capacity for greater unhappiness. When reason rules these emotions, a man must be said to be well ordered. There is no right order, indeed there is no order at all, where the better is subordinated to the worse. Don't you agree? *Ev.*—Undoubtedly. *Aug.*—When reason or mind or spirit rules the irrational emotions, then the part dominates in a man which ought to dominate according to what we have discovered to be eternal law. *Ev.*—I see and I follow.

ix, 19. *Aug.*—When a man is so constituted and ordered, don't you think he is wise? *Ev.*—I know of no other whom I could think wise if not such a man. *Aug.*—I suppose you know that most men are foolish. *Ev.*—That, too, I know well. *Aug.*—

If the fool is the opposite of the wise man, now that we know who the wise man is, you also know who the fool is. *Ev.*—Evidently he is the man in whom mind has not the chief power. *Aug.*—What are we to say, then, when a man is in that condition? Does he lack mind? or does the mind he has fail to control? *Ev.*—The latter rather, I think. *Aug.*—I should very much like to know what signs indicate that a man has mind even when it does not exercise its leadership. *Ev.*—I wish you would answer your own question for it is not easy for me to play the part you are forcing on me. *Aug.*—At least it is easy for you to remember what you said a moment ago. Beasts are made tame and gentle by men and so come to serve them. Men might suffer this in their turn, as the argument showed, if they were not somehow superior to beasts. That superiority we did not find in their bodies. Because it was something evidently to do with their souls, we found no other name for it than reason, recognizing that it might also be called mind or spirit. If reason and mind are different things we at least agree that only mind can make use of reason. Hence it is concluded that he who has reason cannot lack mind. *Ev.*—Yes I remember that. *Aug.*—Do you believe that the tamers of beasts must be wise men? I mean by wise men those whom truth bids us call such, that is, those in whom mind rules and all lust is subdued, and who therefore are at peace with themselves. *Ev.*—It is ridiculous to give that name to men who are vulgarly known as beast-tamers or shepherds or ploughmen or charioteers, whose work it is to tame wild animals and to make use of them when they are tamed. *Aug.*—There, then, you have a clear indication of the presence of mind in a man even when it does not rule. There is mind in the men you have mentioned, for they do things that could not be done without mind. But mind does not rule, for they are still fools; and we know that there is no reign of mind except in wise men. *Ev.*—It is surprising that we had proved this so easily, and yet I could not think what to answer.

x, 20. But now let us go on to a further stage in the discussion. We have now found that human wisdom is the rule of the human mind, but that there may be mind where it does not rule. *Aug.*—Do you think that lust is more powerful than mind, though we know that, by the eternal law, to mind is given rule over the lusts? I cannot believe it in the least. For it is not consistent with good order that the weaker should rule the stronger. I think that mind must necessarily be more powerful than cupidity simply because it is right and just that cupidity should be subject. *Ev.*—I think so too. *Aug.*—Are we to be in any doubt that virtue is absolutely superior to vice, in the sense that it is as much superior in strength and power as it is in goodness and sublimity? *Ev.*—Who could entertain any doubt? *Aug.*—Then no vicious soul can overcome a soul armed with virtue? *Ev.*—Most true. *Aug.*—I do not think you will deny that any kind of soul is better and more powerful than every body. *Ev.*—No one would deny it who sees, as one easily may, that a living being is to be preferred to what is not living, and that that which gives life is to be preferred to that which receives life. *Aug.*—Much less does a body, whatever its quality, surpass a soul endowed with virtue. *Ev.*—It is self-evident. *Aug.*—Surely a just soul, or a mind that keeps its proper jurisdiction and rule, cannot cast down and subject to lust another mind that rules with equal justice and virtue? *Ev.*—By no means, not only because there is the same excellence in each, but also because it must first have fallen away from justice and become a vitiated mind if it attempts to make another mind vicious. For that very reason it will be weaker.

21. *Aug.*—You have perfectly understood the point. It remains for you to tell me if you can, whether you think there is anything more excellent than a wise and rational mind. *Ev.*—Nothing I think, save God. *Aug.*—That is also my opinion. But seeing that that is a difficult question and cannot now be suitably discussed so that we may understand it though we hold it most firmly by faith, let us complete a diligent and careful treatment of the question we have on hand just now.

xi. At present we can be sure that whatever it be that may rightly excel a mind strong in virtue, it cannot be unjust in any way. So that not even it, though it have the power, will compel a mind to serve lust. *Ev.*—There is no one who will not admit that without any hesitation. *Aug.*—So we are left with the conclusion that whatever is equal or superior to a ruling mind possessing virtue cannot make it serve lust because of its just character. And whatever is inferior cannot do it by reason of its weakness. So our argument teaches us: Nothing makes the mind a companion of cupidity, except its own will and free choice. *Ev.*—I see that is our necessary conclusion.

22. *Aug.*—The next step is that you must come to see that the soul justly pays the penalty for its sin. *Ev.*—I cannot deny that. *Aug.*—What then? Is it to be regarded as in itself a small penalty that the soul is dominated by lust, spoiled of its resources of virtue, drawn hither and thither in abject poverty, now approving

falsehood as if it were truth, now acting on the defensive, now rejecting what it had formerly approved but none the less falling into other falsehoods, now holding its assent back, and often fearing the most obvious reasonings, now despairing of ever finding the truth and sticking in the dark pit of folly, now attempting to reach the light of intelligence, and again falling back in sheer weariness? Meantime the cupidities exercise their dominion tyrannically and disturb the man's whole mind and life with varying and contrary tempests, fear on one side, longing on the other; here anxiety, there vain and false rejoicing; here torture because something loved has been lost, there eagerness to obtain what it does not possess; here grief for injury suffered, there incitements to seek revenge. Wherever it turns it can be restricted by avarice, wasted by luxury, bound by ambition, inflated by pride, tortured by envy, enveloped in sloth, excited by wantonness, afflicted by subjection, suffering all the other countless emotions which inhabit and trouble the realm of lust. Can we think that a condition like that is not penal, when we see that it must be undergone by all who do not cleave to wisdom?

23. *Ev.*—I think it is indeed a terrible penalty and an altogether just one, if anybody placed on the height of wisdom should choose to descend and become a servant to lust. But I am not sure whether it is actually within the power of any one who wants or is determined to do it. We believe that man has been created perfect by God and has been allotted a happy life so that it is by his own will that he has fallen to the miserable condition of this mortal life. But, though I firmly believe this, I have not yet grasped it with the intelligence. If you think that diligent inquiry into this question must be postponed, you do so against my will.

xii, 24. But what worries me most is why we have to suffer such bitter penalties, we who certainly are foolish and were never wise. How can we be said to deserve to suffer these things as if we had deserted the fortress of virtue and chosen servitude to lust? I should never consent to your postponing the attempt to discuss and solve this problem as far as you can. *Aug.*—You say that as if it were crystal-clear that we never have been wise. You are thinking only of the time since we were born into this life. Wisdom is a thing which exists in the soul, but whether the soul lived some kind of life before its association with the body, and whether it then lived with wisdom is a big question, a great mystery, to be considered in the proper place. But the question we now have on hand does not prevent us from seeking an answer to it as far as that is possible.

25. Let me ask you: have we a will? *Ev.*—I do not know. *Aug.*—Do you want to know? *Ev.*—Again I do not know. *Aug.*—Then do not ask me any more questions. *Ev.*—Why? *Aug.*—Because I ought not to answer your questions unless you want to know what you ask. Furthermore, if you do not wish to reach wisdom I ought not to hold conversation with you on matters of this kind. Finally you cannot be my friend unless you desire my good. So far as you are concerned yourself, you will have to see whether you have a will to the happy life for yourself. *Ev.*—I agree it is impossible to deny that we have will. Go on and let us see what conclusion you draw from this. *Aug.*—So I shall. But first tell me whether you are conscious of having a good will. *Ev.*—What is a good will? *Aug.*—A will to live rightly and honourably and to reach the highest wisdom. Just see whether you do not desire to live a right and honourable life, whether you do not eagerly desire to be wise, or whether at least you would venture to deny that when we wish such things we have a good will. *Ev.*—I deny none of these things, and accordingly admit that I have not only a will but also a good will. *Aug.*—What value, pray, do you set on such a will? Could you think that riches or honours or bodily pleasures or all these together are to be compared with it? *Ev.*—God avert such wicked madness! *Aug.*—Are we, then, to rejoice a little in having something in our souls, I mean a good will, by comparison with which all those things we have mentioned are worthless, although we see that the mass of men refuse no toils and no dangers in order to obtain them? *Ev.*—We should rejoice exceedingly. *Aug.*—Do you think that those who do not have the joy of possessing so great a good suffer only a small loss? *Ev.*—Nay, a great loss.

26. *Aug.*—You see, then, I imagine, that it is in the power of our will to enjoy or to be without so great and so true a good. For what is so completely within the power of the will as the will itself? Whoever has a good will has something which is far better than all earthly realms and all bodily pleasures. Whoever does not have it, lacks that which is more excellent than all the goods which are not in our power, and yet he can have it by willing it simply. He will probably judge himself to be most miserable if he loses glory, fame or immense riches, or other bodily goods. But won't you think him most miserable even if he have abundance of all these things, if he cleaves to things which

he can easily lose and cannot have simply by willing, and lacks the good will which is incomparably better than these things, and, though it is so great a good, can yet be had simply by willing? *Ev.*—Quite true. *Aug.*—Rightly, therefore, and deservedly foolish men, though they never were wise—and this is doubtful and quite beyond our knowing—suffer this kind of misery. *Ev.*—I agree.

xiii, 27. *Aug.*—Now consider whether you think prudence is the knowledge of what is to be sought and avoided. *Ev.*—I do. *Aug.*—And fortitude is the disposition of soul which enables us to despise all inconveniences and the loss of things not in our power? *Ev.*—That is my opinion. *Aug.*—And temperance is a disposition that restrains our desires for things which it is base to desire. Don't you agree? *Ev.*—I think exactly as you say. *Aug.*—And what shall we say justice is? Is it not the virtue that gives to each his own? *Ev.*—I have no other notion of justice. *Aug.*—We have spoken much of the excellence of the good will. Whoever has the good will, and embraces it with all the love he is capable of, delights himself in it, enjoys it and rejoices in it, knowing how great a good it is, and that it can never be snatched or stolen from him against his will—can we doubt that such a man will resist all that is inimical to this one good? *Ev.*—He will offer all resistance. *Aug.*—Can we think that a man has not prudence who sees that this good is to be sought and those things avoided which are inimical to it? *Ev.*—No one, I think could do so without prudence. *Aug.*—Quite right. But why should we not also attribute fortitude to him? He cannot love and set great store by things which are not in his power. The evil will loves these things, and he must necessarily resist it as the enemy of his dearest good. He does not love them nor grieve when he loses them but contemns them all; and this we have agreed is the function of fortitude. *Ev.*—Let us indeed attribute this virtue to him. I know of no one to whom I may more truly attribute courage than the man who can with a calm and tranquil mind bear the loss of things which it is not in his power either to obtain or to keep. This we have found he necessarily does. *Aug.*—Can we refuse to allow that he has temperance, since that is the virtue which restrains lusts? What is more hostile to the good will than lust? Hence you can understand that the lover of the good will resists and opposes lusts in every way, and so is rightly called temperate. *Ev.*—Go on, for I agree. *Aug.*—There remains justice, but I do not see how it can be lacking in such a man. He who has and loves the good will, and resists what is hostile to it, cannot will any evil to anybody. It follows that he injures nobody, which must mean simply that he gives to everyone his due. This, I said, was the function of justice, and I dare say you remember you agreed. *Ev.*—I remember. And I agree that we have shown that the four virtues which you described with my consent are found in the man who loves his good will and values it highly.

28. *Aug.*—Is there any reason why we should not allow that such a man's life is laudable? *Ev.*—No reason at all. Everything encourages us or even compels us to do so. *Aug.*—Can you by any means suppose that the unhappy life is not to be avoided? *Ev.*—Most certainly it must be avoided. That I hold to be our first duty. *Aug.*—And, of course, what is laudable is not to be avoided. *Ev.*—No indeed. It is to be most carefully sought after. *Aug.*—The laudable life therefore is not unhappy. *Ev.*—That follows. *Aug.*—You will have no difficulty now in admitting that a life which is not unhappy is the happy life. *Ev.*—Clearly. *Aug.*—We agree, then, that the man is happy who loves the will and in comparison with it scorns everything else that is called good, which can be lost even when the will to retain it remains. *Ev.*—We must agree since this is the necessary conclusion from our argument. *Aug.*—You are perfectly right. But tell me, to love the good will and to hold it in high esteem, is that not simply to have a good will? *Ev.*—True. *Aug.*—If we are right in judging this man happy, must we not rightly judge him unhappy who has a different kind of will? *Ev.*—Quite correct. *Aug.*—Why, then should we think it doubtful, even if we have never been wise formerly, that by the exercise of will we deserve and live either a laudable and happy life or a base and unhappy one? *Ev.*—I agree that we have reached this result by arguments that are certain and undeniable.

29. *Aug.*—Take this further question. I believe you remember how we defined the good will. It was the power by which we seek to live rightly and honourably. *Ev.*—I remember. *Aug.*—If we love and embrace this good will and prefer it to all the things which we cannot retain by willing, those virtues, as we have learned by our argument, which together constitute right and honourable living, dwell in our souls. Hence it follows that whoever wishes to live rightly and honourably, if he prefers that before all fugitive and transient goods, attains his object with perfect ease. In order to attain it he has to do nothing but to will it. *Ev.*—Truly I can hardly refrain from shouting for joy, when I find I can so quickly and so easily obtain so great a good.

Aug.—This very joy which comes from attaining this good, especially when it keeps the mind calm and tranquil and stable, is what we call the happy life—unless you think that to live happily is something else than to rejoice in good things that are both true and certain. *Ev.*—That is what I think.

xiv, 30. *Aug.*—Very well. But do you think there is a single man who does not in every possible way will and choose the happy life? *Ev.*—Who doubts that that is what every man wishes? *Aug.*—Why, then, do not all obtain it? We agreed that men by the use they make of their wills deserve either a happy or an unhappy life, and receive what they deserve. But now some opposition has arisen which, unless we examine it closely, threatens to throw our previous argument into confusion, though we thought it strong and carefully constructed. How has anyone to endure an unhappy life because of the use he has made of his will, when no one at all wills to live unhappily? Or how does any man attain by the use of his will a happy life, seeing that all wish to be happy and so many are unhappy? Is it because there are two different kinds of willing, a good and a bad? Or is there a difference between deserving by using a good will and deserving by using a bad will? For those who are happy —and they must also be good—are not happy simply because they wish to live happily. The bad also have the same wish. They are happy because they live rightly, which the bad do not wish to do. It is not surprising that unhappy men do not obtain what they wish, that is, a happy life. For they do not at the same time wish its accompaniment, without which no one is worthy of it, and no one obtains it, that is to say a righteous life. The eternal law, to the consideration of which we must now return, has established firmly and unchangeably that merit accrues from willing, and that happiness is the reward of goodness and unhappiness the punishment of badness. So when we say that men are unhappy voluntarily, we do not mean that they want to be unhappy, but that their wills are in such a state that unhappiness must follow even against their will. So it is not inconsistent with our previous reasoning that all men wish to be happy but cannot be; for all do not wish to live aright, and it is that wish that merits the happy life. Have you anything to say against that? *Ev.*—I have nothing.

xv, 31. But let us see how all this applies to the question raised concerning the two laws. *Aug.*—Let us do so. But first tell me whether he who loves to live aright and delights in it so that he finds it not merely right but also sweet and pleasant so to live, will love and cherish the law which he knows awards the happy life to the good will, and an unhappy life to the evil will? *Ev.*—He will be entirely devoted to it for he directs his life according to its terms. *Aug.*—In loving it, does he love something changeable and temporal or something stable and eternal? *Ev.*—Something certainly eternal and unchangeable. *Aug.*—Those who continue in an evil will no less desire to be happy. But can they love the law which deservedly allots unhappiness to such people? *Ev.*—I should think not at all. *Aug.*—Do they love anything else? *Ev.*—Yes indeed, many other things. They love the things which the evil will steadfastly seeks to obtain and keep. *Aug.*—I suppose you mean wealth, honours, pleasures, bodily beauty, and all the other things which it is possible not to obtain though they are desired, and which may be lost against one's will. *Ev.*—These are the things I mean. *Aug.*—You do not imagine these things are eternal since you see they are involved in the flux of time. *Ev.*—It would be utter madness to imagine that. *Aug.*—It is, therefore, manifest that some men are lovers of eternal things, others of temporal things, and we have agreed that there are two laws, one eternal and the other temporal. Now assuming that you have a sense of justice, which of these two classes of men would you hold was obedient to the eternal law, and which to the temporal law? *Ev.*—The answer is obvious, I think. Those who are happy on account of their love of eternal things I hold act under obedience to the eternal law, while on unhappy men the temporal law is imposed. *Aug.*—You are perfectly right, so long as you hold firmly what reason has clearly demonstrated, that those who serve the temporal law cannot be set free from subjection to the eternal law. For from the eternal law are derived all just laws even when they are variable according to circumstances, as we have said. But those who with a good will cleave to the eternal law do not need the temporal law, as apparently you well understand. *Ev.*—I see your point.

32. *Aug.*—The eternal law bids us turn our love away from temporal things, to cleanse it and turn it towards eternal things. *Ev.*—It does. *Aug.*—What, then, does the temporal law bid us do? Is it not that men may possess the things which may be called "ours" for a season and which they eagerly covet, on condition that peace and human society be preserved so far as they can be preserved in earthly things? These are, first, the body and bodily goods, such as good health, keenness of the senses, strength, beauty, and anything else that may be necessary

for the good arts of life, which are to be more highly valued than those which are of less value and importance. Next comes liberty. Of course there is no true liberty except the liberty of the happy who cleave to the eternal law. But for the moment I mean the liberty which people think they enjoy when they have no human masters, and which slaves desire who wish to be manumitted by their human masters. Then, parents, brothers, wife, children, kinsfolk near and remote, friends, and any others who may be attached to us by any bond. Then our citizenship, which is usually reckoned from the home of our parents, together with honours and praise and popular glory, as it is called. Finally there is money, which in one word covers all that we lawfully possess and which we have the right to dispose of by sale or gift. To explain how in all these matters the law distributes to each his due would be difficult and would take a long time, but clearly it is not necessary to our purpose. It is sufficient to see that the authority of this law in punishing does not go beyond depriving him who is punished of these things or of some of them. It employs fear as an instrument of coercion, and bends to its own ends the minds of the unhappy people to rule whom it is adapted. So long as they fear to lose these earthly goods they observe in using them a certain moderation suited to maintain in being a city such as can be composed of such men. The sin of loving these things is not punished; what is punished is the wrong done to others when their rights are infringed. Have we not accomplished a task which you thought would be infinite? For we set out to inquire how far the law which governs earthly peoples and cities may rightly punish. *Ev.*—I see we have accomplished our task.

33. *Aug.*—You see also that there would be no punishment inflicted on men either by injury done them or by legal sentence if they did not love the things that can be taken from them against their will. *Ev.*—I see that. *Aug.*—Some use these things badly, some use them well. He who uses them badly is he who lovingly cleaves to them and is completely involved in them. He subjects himself to things which he ought to make subject to himself, and sets before himself as his chief goods those things which he ought to subordinate and handle properly and so become good himself. He who uses them aright shows that they are good but not in themselves. They do not make him good or better, but are made good by the use he puts them to. He is not attached to them by love, making them parts of his soul, as is done by loving them, lest when they begin to be taken from

him he suffer torture and decay. He wholly transcends them, and is prepared to possess and regulate them when necessary, but is even better prepared to lose them and be without them. Since this is so, you will not blame gold and silver because there are avaricious people, or food because there are gluttons, or wine because there are drunkards, or female beauty because there are fornicators and adulterers, and so on. After all you can see that a doctor may make a good use of fire, and a poisoner may make a wicked use of bread. *Ev.*—Very true. The things are not to be blamed, but the men who make a bad use of them.

xvi, 34. *Aug.*—Quite right. We begin to see now, I think, the force of the eternal law; and how far the temporal law can go in punishing we have also discovered. We have made a sufficiently clear distinction between two classes of things, the eternal and the temporal, and between two classes of men, those who love and pursue eternal things and those who pursue temporal things. What each one chooses to pursue and embrace is within the power of his will to determine. Will alone can drive the mind from its seat of authority and from the right course. And it is manifest that when anyone uses anything badly it is not the thing but the man who uses it badly that is to be blamed. Now if you please, let us refer back to the question proposed at the beginning of this conversation, and see whether it has been answered. We set out to inquire what doing evil means, and all we have subsequently said has a bearing on this. Now we may give our minds to consider whether doing evil is anything else than to neglect eternal things which the mind itself perceives and enjoys and loves and cannot lose, and to pursue, as if they were great and wonderful, temporal things which are perceived by the body, the lowest part of human nature, and can never be possessed with complete certainty. For in this class, it seems to me, all evil deeds, that is sins, are to be included. I am waiting for you to tell me what you think.

35. *Ev.*—It is as you say. I agree that all sins are included in this one class, viz. turning away from things which are divine and truly abiding, and turning to things which are changeable and uncertain. They are right enough in their own place, and have a certain beauty of their own. But it is the mark of a perverse and disordered mind to pursue them to the point of becoming subject to them. For rightly by divine ordinance the mind is set over them and ought to bear absolute rule over them. At the same time, it seems to me, our other question has been fully answered. For after asking what doing evil means, we set out to

inquire what was the cause of evil-doing. Unless I am mistaken, reason has demonstrated that we do it by the free choice of our will. But I ask now whether our Maker ought to have given us free will seeing it is proved to be the source of our capacity to sin. If we had not had it, apparently we should not have sinned. It is to be feared that in this way God may be held to be the author of our ill-doing. *Aug.*—Have no fear of that. But another time must be found to go into the question thoroughly. An end must now be put to this conversation in which I hope you realize that we have knocked at the door of some important and recondite matters of inquiry. When we begin to enter their inmost chambers, with God's aid, you will certainly be able to judge how great a difference there is between this disputation and those which are to follow, and how much superior they are, not only in the sagacity required for their investigation, but also in the majesty of the subjects and the bright light of truth. Only let piety attend us, that by divine providence we may be permitted to hold to and complete the course on which we have set out. *Ev.*—I accept your decision, and to it and to your prayer I most willingly add my own.

Book II

i, 1. *Evodius.*—Now explain to me, if it can be done, why God has given man free choice in willing, for if he had not received that freedom he would not have been able to sin. *Augustine.*—You hold it to be certainly known that it is God who has given man this power which you think ought not to have been given. *Ev.*—My impression is that we learned in the earlier book both that we have free will, and that our sinning is due to it. *Aug.*—I too remember that that became manifest to us. But now my question was whether you know that God gave us this power which we clearly have and which is the cause of our sinning. *Ev.*—No one else could have done so, I think. For we derive our origin from him, and from him we merit punishment or reward according as we sin or act rightly. *Aug.*—Here is another thing I desire to know. Do you know this quite distinctly, or do you merely believe it, without knowing it, because you allow yourself to be influenced by authority? *Ev.*—Undoubtedly I was first brought to believe this on the ground of authority. But what can be more true than to say that every good thing is from God, that justice is entirely good, and that it is just that sinners should be punished and well-doers rewarded. Hence it follows that it is by God that sinners are made unhappy and well-doers happy.

2. *Aug.*—I am not objecting; but I ask the question: how do you know that we derive our origin from God? You have not explained this though you have explained how we merit punishment or reward at his hand. *Ev.*—If it is accepted that God punishes sins, as it must be if it is true that all justice has its source in him, this alone would prove that we derive our origin from him. No doubt it is the characteristic of goodness to confer benefits on strangers, but it is not similarly the mark of justice to punish sins in those who are not under its immediate jurisdiction. Hence it is clear that we belong to him because he is not only most kind in conferring benefits upon us, but also most just in his punishments. Moreover, from the statement I made and you accepted, that every good thing comes from God, it can be known that man also comes from God. For man, in so far as he is man, is good because he can live aright if he chooses to do so.

3. *Aug.*—Clearly if this is so, the problem you have posed is solved. If man is good, and if he would not be able to act rightly except by willing to do so, he ought to have free will because without it he would not be able to act rightly. Because he also sins through having free will, we are not to believe that God gave it to him for that purpose. It is, therefore, a sufficient reason why he ought to have been given it, that without it man could not live aright. That it was given for this purpose can be understood from this fact. If anyone uses his free will in order to sin, God punishes him. That would be unjust unless the will was free not only to live aright but also to sin. How could he be justly punished who uses his will for the purpose for which it was given? Now when God punishes a sinner what else do you suppose he will say to him than "Why did you not use your free will for the purpose for which I gave it to you, that is, in order to do right?" Justice is praised as a good thing because it condemns sins and honours righteous actions. How could that be done if man had not free will? An action would be neither sinful nor righteous unless it were done voluntarily. For the same reason both punishment and reward would be unjust, if man did not have free will. But in punishing and in rewarding there must have been justice since justice is one of the good things which come from God. God, therefore, must have given and ought to have given man free will.

ii, 4. *Ev.*—I admit now that God has given us free will. But don't you think, pray, that, if it was given for the purpose of well-doing, it ought not to have been possible to convert it to sinful uses? Justice itself was given to man so that he might live rightly, and it is not possible for anyone to live an evil life by means of justice. So no one ought to be able to sin voluntarily if free will was given that we might live aright. *Aug.*—God will, I hope, give me ability to answer you, or rather will give you the ability to answer your own question. Truth, which is the best master of all, will inwardly teach us both alike. But I wish you would tell me this: I asked you whether you know with perfect certainty that God has given us free will and you replied that you did. Now if we allow that God gave it, ought we to say that he ought not to have given it? If it is uncertain whether he gave it, we rightly ask whether it was good that it was given. If then we find that it was good, we find also that it was given by him who bestows all good things on men. If, however, we find that it was not a good thing we know that it was not given by him whom it is impious to accuse. If it is certain that he has given it, we ought to confess that, however it was given, it was rightly given. We may not say that it ought not to have been given or that it ought to have been given in some other way. If he has given it his action cannot in any way be rightly blamed.

5. *Ev.*—I believe all that unshakably. Nevertheless, because I do not know it, let us inquire as if it were all uncertain. I see that because it is uncertain whether free will was given that men might do right since by it we can also sin, another uncertainty arises, namely whether free will ought to have been given to us. If it is uncertain that it was given that we should act righteously, it is also uncertain that it ought to have been given at all. Hence it will also be uncertain whether it was God who gave it. If it is uncertain that it ought to have been given, it is uncertain that it was given by him whom it is impious to believe has given anything which ought not to have been given. *Aug.*—At any rate you are quite certain that God exists. *Ev.*—I firmly believe it, but I do not know it. *Aug.*—We read in Scripture: "The fool hath said in his heart: there is no God" (Ps. 52:18). If such a fool were to say to you there is no God, and would not believe as you do, but wanted to know whether what you believe is true, would you simply go away and leave him, or would you think it your duty somehow to try to persuade him that what you believe is true, especially if he were really eager to know and not merely to argue obstinately? *Ev.*—Your last proviso tells me what I ought to reply to him. However absurd he might

be he would assuredly agree that one ought not to dispute with an insidious and obstinate opponent about anything at all, least of all about a matter so important. He would admit that, and try to get me to believe that his inquiry was made in all good faith, and that in this matter there was neither guile nor obstinacy in him. Then I would use an argument that ought to carry great weight with any fair-minded person. I should show him that, just as he wants his neighbour to believe him when he tells of the thoughts of his mind, which he of course knows, but which are quite concealed from his neighbour, so he ought to believe that God exists because that is taught in the books of great men who have left their testimony in writing that they lived with the Son of God, and because they have written that they saw things which could not have happened if there were no God. I should urge that he would be very foolish to blame me for believing them, when he wanted me to believe himself. And when he saw that he had no good ground for finding fault with me, he would find no reason for refusing to imitate my faith. *Aug.*—If you think the existence of God is sufficiently proved by the fact that we judge it not to be rash to believe the Scripture-writers, why don't you think we should similarly trust their authority in the matters we have begun to investigate as if they were uncertain or quite beyond our knowledge? So we should be spared much labour in investigation. *Ev.*—Yes. But we want to know and to understand what we believe.

6. *Aug.*—You remember the position we adopted at the beginning of our former discussion. We cannot deny that believing and knowing are different things, and that in matters of great importance, pertaining to divinity, we must first believe before we seek to know. Otherwise the words of the prophet would be vain, where he says: "Except ye believe ye shall not understand" (Isa. 7:9. LXX). Our Lord himself, both in his words and by his deeds, exhorted those whom he called to salvation first of all to believe. When he afterwards spoke of the gift that was to be given to believers he said, not: "This is life eternal that they may believe"; but: "This is life eternal that they may know thee, the only true God, and Jesus Christ whom thou hast sent" (John 17:3). To those who already believed he said: "Seek and ye shall find" (Matt. 7:7). He cannot be said to have found, who merely believes what he does not know. And no one is fit to find God, who does not first believe what he will afterwards learn to know. Wherefore, in obedience to the precepts of the Lord, let us press on in our inquiry. What we seek at his

bidding we shall find, as far as that can be done in this life, and by people such as we are. And he himself will demonstrate it to us. We must believe that these things are perceived and possessed by people of superior character even while they dwell on earth, and certainly, more clearly and perfectly, by all the good and pious after this life. So we must hope it will be with us, and, despising earthly and human things, we must in every way desire and love heavenly things.

iii, 7. Let us discuss these three questions, if you please, and in this order. First, how it is manifest that God exists. Secondly, whether all good things, in so far as they are good, are from him. Lastly, whether free will is to be counted among the good things. When these questions have been answered it will, I think, be evident whether free will has been rightly given to man. First, then, to begin with what is most obvious, I ask you: "Do you exist?" Are you perhaps afraid to be deceived by that question? But if you did not exist it would be impossible for you to be deceived. *Ev.*—Proceed to your other questions. *Aug.*—Since it is manifest that you exist and that you could not know it unless you were living, it is also manifest that you live. You know these two things are absolutely true. *Ev.*—I do. *Aug.*—Therefore this third fact is likewise manifest, namely, that you have intelligence. *Ev.*—Clearly. *Aug.*—Of these three things which is most excellent? *Ev.*—Intelligence. *Aug.*—Why do you think so? *Ev.*—To exist, to live and to know are three things. A stone exists but does not live. An animal lives but has not intelligence. But he who has intelligence most certainly both exists and lives. Hence I do not hesitate to judge that that is more excellent, which has all these qualities, than that in which one or both of them is absent. That which lives, thereby exists, but it does not follow that it has also intelligence. That is a life like that of an animal. That which exists does not necessarily have either life or intelligence. Dead bodies must be said to exist but cannot be said to live. Much less can that which has not life have intelligence. *Aug.*—We gather, therefore, that of these three things a dead body lacks two, an animal one, and man none. *Ev.*—That is true. *Aug.*—And of these three things that is most excellent which man has along with the other two, that is intelligence. Having that, it follows that he has both being and life. *Ev.*—I am sure of that.

8. *Aug.*—Tell me now whether you know that you have these common bodily senses—seeing, hearing, smelling, taste, touch. *Ev.*—Yes I know. *Aug.*—What do you think belongs to the sense

of sight, that is, what do we sense by seeing? *Ev.*—Corporeal objects. *Aug.*—Do we perceive hardness and softness by seeing? *Ev.*—No. *Aug.*—What then belongs properly to the function of the eyes to perceive? *Ev.*—Colour. *Aug.*—And to the ears? *Ev.*—Sound. *Aug.*—And to the sense of smell? *Ev.*—Odour. *Aug.*—To the sense of taste? *Ev.*—Taste. *Aug.*—To the sense of touch? *Ev.*—The soft and the hard, the smooth and the rough, and many such things. *Aug.*—The forms of corporeal objects, great and small, square and round, and such like qualities we perceive both by sight and touch, and so they cannot be ascribed solely to either sight or touch, but to both. *Ev.*—I understand. *Aug.*—You understand, then, that some things belong to one particular sense whose function it is to convey information about them, while other things belong in this way to several senses? *Ev.*—That also I understand. *Aug.*—Can we by any of the senses decide what belongs to any particular sense, or what belongs to all or several of them together? *Ev.*—By no means. That has to be decided by something else within us. *Aug.*—Perhaps that would be reason, which the beasts lack? For, I suppose, it is by reason that we comprehend sense-data and know that they are as they are. *Ev.*—Rather I think that by reason we comprehend that there is a kind of interior sense to which the ordinary senses refer everything. For in the case of the beast the sense of sight is a different thing from the sense to shun or to seek the things it sees. The former belongs to the eyes, the latter is within the soul itself. For of the things they see or hear or perceive with the other bodily senses, some the animals seek with pleasure and accept, others they avoid as displeasing, and refuse to take. This sense can be called neither sight nor hearing nor smell nor taste nor touch, but must be some other sense which presides over all the others alike. While we comprehend this by reason, as I said, still we cannot call it reason, since clearly the beasts have it too.

9. *Aug.*—I recognize that there is that faculty and I do not hesitate to call it the interior sense. But unless the information conveyed to us by the bodily senses goes beyond that sense it cannot become knowledge. What we know we comprehend by reason. We know that colours are not perceived by hearing nor voices by seeing, to mention these only. When we know this it is not by means of the eyes or the ears or by that interior sense which the beasts also possess. We cannot believe that they know that light is not perceived by the ears nor voices by the eyes, for we do not discern these things without rational observation

and thought. *Ev.*—I cannot say that I quite see that. Suppose they do distinguish by the interior sense which you admit the animals have, and realize that colours cannot be perceived by hearing nor voices by seeing? *Aug.*—You do not suppose that they can distinguish between the colour that is seen, the sense that is in the eyes, the interior sense that is in the soul, and the reason by which all these things are defined and enumerated? *Ev.*—Not at all. *Aug.*—Could reason distinguish these four things and define their limits unless the notion of colour were conveyed to it in these various stages. First the sense of sight in the eyes would report to the interior sense which presides over all the external senses, and it would then report direct to reason, that is to say, if there is no intermediate stage. *Ev.*—I see no other way. *Aug.*—The sense of sight perceives colour but is itself perceived by no other sense. Do you see that? You do not see sight with the same sense as you see colour. *Ev.*—Certainly not. *Aug.*—Try to distinguish these two things; for I suppose you do not deny that colour is one thing, and to see colour is another entirely different thing. Moreover, it is another different thing to have the sense that enables us to see colour as if it were before us, even when in actual fact there is no colour before us. *Ev.*—I distinguish these things and admit that they are all different. *Aug.*—Well take these three things. Do you see anything with the eyes except colour? *Ev.*—Nothing else. *Aug.*—Tell me, then, how you see the other two things, for you cannot distinguish between them if you have not seen them. *Ev.*—I know no way. I know it is so, that is all. *Aug.*—So you do not know whether it is by reason or by what we call the interior sense which presides over the bodily senses, or by something else? *Ev.*—I do not know. *Aug.*—And yet you know that they can be defined only by reason, and that reason could not do this unless sense-data were offered for its examination. *Ev.*—That is certain. *Aug.*—Then all in the act of knowing which does not come from sense-perception is provided by reason, to which are reported and referred all external circumstances. And so sense-data can be accepted, but strictly within their own limits, and can be comprehended not by sense only but also by knowledge. *Ev.*—That is so. *Aug.*—Reason distinguishes the senses which are its servants from the data they collect. Likewise it knows the difference between the senses and itself, and is sure that it is much more powerful than they. Does reason comprehend reason by any other means than by reason itself? Would you know that you possess reason otherwise than by reason? *Ev.*—Surely not.

Aug.—When we see a colour we do not, with the sense of sight, see that we see; when we hear a sound, we do not hear our hearing; when we smell a rose we do not smell our smelling; when we taste anything we do not taste taste in our mouths; and when we touch anything we cannot touch the sense of touch. It is clear, therefore, that none of the five senses can perceive itself, though all in their several ways perceive corporeal objects. *Ev.*—That is quite clear.

iv, 10. *Aug.*—I think it is also clear that the interior sense perceives not only the data passed on to it by the five senses, but also perceives the senses too. A beast would not make the movement necessary for seeking or avoiding anything unless it was conscious of perceiving, which of course it could not be by using the five senses only. I do not suggest that this consciousness in the beast is a step towards knowledge, for that belongs to reason, simply that it is a prerequisite of movement. If there is still some obscurity here an example will elucidate the point. It will be enough to consider the case of one of the senses, say sight. A beast would be quite unable to open its eyes and direct them towards an object it desired to see unless it perceived that it could not see the object so long as its eyes were closed and not directed to the object. If it is conscious of not seeing when it does not see, it must also be conscious of seeing when it does see. The fact that when it sees an object it does not make the movement that would be necessary to bring it into view indicates that it perceives that it sees or does not see. But it is not so clear whether a beast has self-consciousness, as well as consciousness, of perceiving corporeal objects. Possibly it has an inward feeling that every living thing shuns death which is the opposite of life. If so, every living thing which shuns the opposite of life must be conscious of itself as living. But if that is not clear let us omit it, and not strive to establish our position with proofs that are not both certain and self-evident. What is evident is this: corporeal objects are perceived by bodily sense; no bodily sense can perceive itself; the interior sense can perceive both corporeal objects perceived by a bodily sense, and also that bodily sense itself; but reason knows all these things and knows itself, and therefore has knowledge in the strict sense of the term. Don't you think so? *Ev.*—I do indeed. *Aug.*—Come, then, what about the question the answer to which we desired to reach? To reach that answer we have taken all this time and trouble in preparing the way.

v, 11. *Ev.*—So far as I remember, of the three questions we formulated to give the discussion some order, we are now engaged with the first, namely, How is it to be made evident that God exists, a proposition which is most firmly to be accepted in faith. *Aug.*—You are quite right. But I want you to keep firm hold of this too. When I asked you whether you know that you exist, it appeared that you know not only this but two other things as well. *Ev.*—I remember that too. *Aug.*—Now to which of the three do you understand all that impinges on the bodily senses to pertain? I mean, in which class of things would you put all that we perceive by means of the eyes or any other bodily organ? Would you say that all this belongs to the class that merely exists, or to that which also has life, or to that which has intelligence as well? *Ev.*—In that which merely exists. *Aug.*—And where would you put the senses? *Ev.*—In that which has life. *Aug.*—And which do you judge to be superior, the senses or their objects? *Ev.*—The senses surely. *Aug.*—Why? *Ev.*—Because that which has life is superior to what merely exists.

12. *Aug.*—What about the interior sense, which we have discovered to be inferior to reason, and possessed by us in common with the beasts? Do you have any hesitation in putting it higher than the senses by means of which we come into contact with corporeal objects, and which you have said are to be reckoned superior to corporeal objects? *Ev.*—I should have no hesitation. *Aug.*—I should like to know why not. You cannot say that the interior sense is to be placed in the category of intelligent things, for it is found in beasts which have no intelligence. This being so, I ask why you put the interior sense higher than the senses which perceive corporeal objects, since both belong to the class of things that have life. You put the bodily senses above corporeal objects just because they belong to the kind of things which merely exist, while it belongs to the kind which also live. So also does the interior sense. Tell me, then, why you think it superior. If you say it is because the interior sense perceives the other senses, I do not believe you will be able to find a rule by which we can establish that every perceiving thing is superior to what it perceives. That would mean that we should be compelled to say that every intelligence is superior to that which it knows. But that is false; for man knows wisdom but is not superior to wisdom. Wherefore consider for what reason you think that the interior sense is superior to the senses by which we perceive corporeal objects. *Ev.*—It is because I recognize that it is in some kind of way a ruler and judge among the other senses. If they failed in their duty it

would be like a master demanding a debt from a servant, as we just recently were saying. The eye cannot see whether it has vision or not and therefore it cannot judge where it is defective or where it is sufficient. That is what the interior sense does, as when it teaches a beast to open its eyes and supply what it perceives is lacking. No one doubts that he who judges is superior to that over which he exercises judgment. *Aug.*—You observe, then, that a bodily sense also judges in a manner corporeal objects? Pleasure and pain fall within its jurisdiction, when the body is affected gently or harshly. Just as the interior sense judges whether the sight of the eyes is defective or adequate, so sight judges what is defective or adequate in colours. Just as the interior sense judges of our hearing whether it is sufficient or defective, so the sense of hearing judges voices, whether they flow smoothly or are noisily harsh. We need not go over the other senses. You observe already, I think, what I wish to say. The interior sense judges the bodily senses, approving their integrity and demanding that they do their duty, just as the bodily senses judge corporeal objects approving of gentleness and reproving the opposite. *Ev.*—I see that and agree that it is true.

vi, 13. *Aug.*—Now consider whether reason also judges of the interior sense. I am not asking whether you have any doubts as to its superiority, for I have no doubt that you judge it to be superior. Nor perhaps is it worth inquiring whether reason judges of the interior sense. For about those things which are inferior to reason, that is, about corporeal objects, bodily senses and the interior sense, reason alone tells us how one is superior to another and how reason is more excellent than them all. How could it do so if it were not a judge over them? *Ev.*—That is obvious. *Aug.*—A nature which not only exists but also lives, like that of the beast, though it have not intelligence, is higher than a nature which merely exists and has no life, like an inanimate object. And higher still is a nature which exists and lives and has intelligence, like the rational mind in man. Surely you do not think that in us, that is, in a complete human nature, anything can be found more excellent than that which we have put third among these three levels of being? Obviously we have a body, and life which animates the body. These two things we recognize that beasts also have. But there is a third thing, the head, as it were, or the eye of our soul, or whatever else more fitly describes reason and intelligence, which beasts do not have. Can you, I pray, find anything in human nature higher than reason? *Ev.*—I see nothing at all that could be superior.

14. *Aug.*—If, now, we could find something which you could unhesitatingly recognize not only as existing but also as superior to our reason, would you have any hesitation in calling it, whatever it may be, God? *Ev.*—Well, I should not without hesitation give the name, God, to anything that I might find better than the best element in my natural composition. I do not wish to say simply that God is that to which my reason is inferior, but that above which there is no superior. *Aug.*—Clearly so, for it is God who has given to your reason to have these true and pious views of him. But, I ask, supposing you find nothing superior to our reason save what is eternal and unchangeable, will you hesitate to call that God? You realize that bodies are mutable; and it is evident that life which animates the body is not without mutability by reason of its varying affections. Even reason is proved to be mutable, for sometimes it strives to reach the truth and sometimes it does not so strive. Sometimes it reaches the truth and sometimes it does not. If without the aid of any bodily organ, neither by touch nor by taste nor by smell, neither by the ears nor the eyes, but by itself alone reason catches sight of that which is eternal and unchangeable, it must confess its own inferiority, and that the eternal and unchangeable is its God. *Ev.*—This I will certainly confess to be God than whom there is nothing superior. *Aug.*—Very well. It will be enough for me to show that there is something of this nature which you will be ready to confess to be God; or if there be something higher still that at least you will allow to be God. However that may be, it will be evident that God exists when with his aid I have demonstrated to you, as I promised, that there is something above reason. *Ev.*—Then proceed with your demonstration as you promise.

vii, 15. *Aug.*—I shall do so. But I first ask you this. Is my bodily sense identical with yours, or is mine mine and yours yours only? If the latter were not the case I should not be able to see anything with my eyes which you also would not see. *Ev.*—I admit that at once, though while each of us has severally the senses of sight, hearing and the rest, your senses and mine belong to the same class of things. For one man can both see and hear what another does not see or hear, and with any of the other senses can perceive what another does not perceive. Hence it is evident that your sense is yours alone and mine mine alone. *Aug.*—Will you make the same reply about the interior sense? *Ev.*—Exactly. My interior sense perceives my perceiving, and yours perceives yours. Often someone who sees something will ask me whether I also see it. The reason for asking simply is that I know whether I see or not, and the questioner does not know. *Aug.*—Has each of us, then, his own particular reason? For it can often happen that I know something when you do not know it, and I know that I know it, but you cannot know that. *Ev.*—Apparently each of us has his own private rational mind.

16. *Aug.*—But you cannot say that each of us has his own private sun or moon or stars or the like, though each of us sees these things with his own particular sense of sight? *Ev.*—No, of course I would not say that. *Aug.*—So, many of us can see one thing simultaneously, though our senses, by which we perceive the object we all see together, are our own. In spite of the fact that my sense and yours are two different things, what we actually see need not be two different things, one of which I see, while you see the other. There is one object for both of us, and both of us see it simultaneously. *Ev.*—Obviously. *Aug.*—We can also hear one voice simultaneously, so that, though my hearing is not your hearing, there are not two voices of which you hear one and I another. It is not as if my hearing caught one part of the sound and yours another. The one sound, and the whole of it, is heard by both of us simultaneously. *Ev.*—That, too, is obvious.

17. *Aug.*—But notice, please, what is to be said about the other senses. It is pertinent to the present discussion to observe that the case with them is not quite the same as with sight and hearing, though it is not entirely different. You and I can breathe the same air and feel its effects by smelling. Likewise we can both partake of one piece of honey, or some other food or drink, and feel its effects by tasting. That is to say, there is one object, but we each have our own senses. You have yours and I have mine. So while we both sense one odour and one taste, you do not sense it with my sense nor I with yours, nor with any sense that we can have in common. My sense is entirely mine and yours yours, even though both of us sense the same odour or the same taste. In this way these senses somewhat resemble sight and hearing. But there is this dissimilarity, which is pertinent to the present problem. We both breathe the same air with our nostrils, and taste one food. And yet I do not breathe in the same particles of air as you do, and I consume a different portion of food from that consumed by you. When I breathe I draw in as much air as is sufficient for me, and when you breathe you draw in as much as is sufficient for you, but both of us use different parts of air. If between us we consume

one food, the whole of it is not consumed either by you or by me, as we both hear the whole sound of a word spoken, or see the whole object offered to our sight simultaneously. One part of a drink must pass into your mouth and another into mine. Do you understand? *Ev.*—I admit that is all clear and certain.

18. *Aug.*—Do you think the sense of touch is comparable to the senses of sight and hearing in the fashion we are now discussing? Not only can we both feel one body by touching it, but we can both feel not only the same body but the same part of it. It is not as in the case of food where both of us cannot consume the whole of it when we both eat it. You can touch what I touch and touch the whole of it. We do not touch each one a different part but each of us touches the whole. *Ev.*—So far, I admit that the sense of touch resembles the first two senses, sight and hearing. But I see there is this difference. We can both simultaneously at one and the same time see or hear the whole of what is seen or heard. No doubt we can both touch simultaneously the whole of one object, but in any one moment we can only touch different parts. The same part we can only touch at different times. I cannot touch the part you are touching unless you move away your hand.

19. *Aug.*—You are most vigilant. But here is another thing you ought to notice, since there are some things which both of us can feel, and others which we must feel severally. Our own senses, for example, we must feel each for himself. I cannot feel your sense nor you mine. But in the case of corporeal things, that is, things we perceive with the bodily senses, when we cannot both perceive them together but must do so severally, it is due to the fact that we make them completely ours by consuming them and making them part of ourselves, like food and drink of which you cannot consume the same part as I do. It is true that nurses give infants food which they have chewed, but the part which has been squeezed out and been swallowed, cannot be recalled and used to feed the child. When the palate tastes something pleasant it claims a part, even if only a small part, which it cannot give up, and does with it what is consonant with corporeal nature. Were this not so no taste would remain in the mouth when what had been chewed was put out. The same can be said of the part of the air which we draw into our nostrils. You may breathe in some of the air which I breathe out, but you cannot breathe that part which has gone to nourish me, for I cannot breathe it out. Physicians sometimes bid us take medicine through our nostrils. I alone feel it when I

breathe it in and I cannot put it back again by breathing out, so that you may breathe it in and feel it. All sensible things, which we do not destroy and take into our systems when we sense them, we can perceive, both of us, either at the same time or at different times, one after the other, in such a way that the whole or the part which I perceive can also be perceived by you. I mean such things as light or sound or bodily objects which we do not destroy when we use and perceive them. *Ev.*—I understand. *Aug.*—It is therefore evident that things which we perceive with the bodily senses without causing them to change are by nature quite different from our senses, and consequently are common to us both, because they are not converted and changed into something which is our peculiar and almost private property. *Ev.*—I agree. *Aug.*—By "our peculiar and private property" I mean that which belongs to each of us alone, which each of us perceives by himself alone, which is part of the natural being of each of us severally. By "common and almost public property" I mean that which is perceived by all sentient beings without its being thereby affected and changed. *Ev.*—That is so.

viii, 20. *Aug.*—Now consider carefully, and tell me whether anything can be found which all reasoning beings can see in common, each with his own mind and reason; something which is present for all to see but which is not transformed like food and drink for the use of those for whom it is present; something which remains complete and unchanged, whether they see it or do not see it. Do you perhaps think there is nothing of that kind? *Ev.*—Indeed, I see many such, but it will be sufficient to mention one. The science of numbers is there for all reasoning persons, so that all calculators may try to learn it, each with his own reason and intelligence. One can do it easily, another with difficulty, another cannot do it at all. But the science itself remains the same for everybody who can learn it, nor is it converted into something consumed like food by him who learns it. If anyone makes a mistake in numbers the science itself is not at fault. It remains true and entire. The error of the poor arithmetician is all the greater, the less he knows of the science.

21. *Aug.*—Quite right. I see you are not untaught in these matters, and so have quickly found a reply. But suppose someone said that numbers make their impression on our minds not in their own right but rather as images of visible things, springing from our contacts by bodily sense with corporeal objects, what would you reply? Would you agree? *Ev.*—I could never agree

to that. Even if I did perceive numbers with the bodily senses I could not in the same way perceive their divisions and relations. By referring to these mental operations I show anyone to be wrong in his counting who gives a wrong answer when he adds or subtracts. Moreover, all that I contact with a bodily sense, such as this sky and this earth and whatever I perceive to be in them, I do not know how long it will last. But seven and three make ten not only now but always. In no circumstances have seven and three ever made anything else than ten, and they never will. So I maintain that the unchanging science of numbers is common to me and to every reasoning being.

22. *Aug.*—I do not deny that your reply is certainly most true. But you will easily see that numbers are not conveyed to us by our bodily senses if you consider that the value of every number is calculated according to the number of times it contains the number one. For example, twice one is called two; thrice one is called three; ten times one is called ten, and every number receives its name and its value according to the number of times it contains the number one. Whoever thinks with exactitude of unity will certainly discover that it cannot be perceived by the senses. Whatever comes into contact with a bodily sense is proved to be not one but many, for it is corporeal and therefore has innumerable parts. I am not going to speak of parts so minute as to be almost unrealizable; but, however small the object may be, it has at least a right-hand part and a left-hand part, an upper and a lower part, a further and a nearer part, one part at the end and another at the middle. We must admit that these parts exist in any body however small, and accordingly we must agree that no corporeal object is a true and absolute unity. And yet all these parts could not be counted unless we had some notion of unity. When I am seeking unity in the corporeal realm and am at the same time certain that I have not found it, nevertheless I know what I am seeking and failing to find, and I know that I cannot find it, or rather that it does not exist among corporeal things. When I know that no body is a unity, I know what unity is. If I did not know what unity is, I could not count the plurality of parts in a body. However I have come to know unity, I have not learned it from the bodily senses, for by them I can know only corporeal objects, and none of them, as we have proved, is a true unity. Moreover, if we do not perceive unity with any bodily sense, neither do we perceive any number, of the kind at any rate which we discern with the intellect. For there is none of them which is not a

multiple of unity, and unity cannot be perceived by the bodily senses. The half of any body, however small, requires the other half to complete the whole, and it itself can be halved. A body can be divided into two parts but they are not simply two. [They may in turn be further sub-divided.] But the number two consists of twice simple unity, so that the half of two, that is, simple unity, cannot be sub-divided by two or three or any other number whatever, because it is true and simple unity.

23. Following the order of the numbers we see that two comes next to one, and is found to be the double of one. The double of two does not immediately follow. Three comes first and then four, which is the double of two. Throughout the numerical series this order extends by a fixed and unchangeable law. After one, which is the first of all numbers, two follows immediately, which is the double of one. After the second number, that is, two, in the second place in order comes the double of two. In the first place after two comes three and in the second place four, the double of two. After the third number, three, in the third place comes its double, for after three four comes first, five second, and in the third place six, which is the double of three. Similarly the fourth number after the fourth is its double; five, six, seven, and in the fourth place eight, which is the double of four. And throughout the numerical series you will find the same rule holds good from first to last. The double of any number is found to be exactly as far from that number as it is from the beginning of the series. How do we find this changeless, firm and unbroken rule persisting throughout the numerical series? No bodily sense makes contact with all numbers, for they are innumerable. How do we know that this rule holds throughout? How can any phantasy or phantasm yield such certain truth about numbers which are innumerable? We must know this by the inner light, of which bodily sense knows nothing.

24. By many such evidences all disputants to whom God has given ability and who are not clouded by obstinacy, are driven to admit that the science of numbers does not pertain to bodily sense, but stands sure and unchangeable, the common possession of all reasoning beings. Many other things might occur to one that belong to thinkers as their common and, as it were, public property, things which each beholder sees with his own mind and reason, and which abide inviolate and unchangeable. But I am glad that the science of numbers most readily occurred to you when you had to answer my question. For it is not in vain that the holy books conjoin number and wisdom, where it

is written, "I turned and [inclined] my heart to know and consider and seek wisdom and number" (Eccl. 7:25).

ix, 25. Now, I ask, what are we to think of wisdom itself? Do you think that individual men have wisdoms of their own? Or is there one wisdom common to all, so that a man is wiser the more he participates in it? *Ev.*—I do not yet know what you mean by wisdom. I observe that men judge variously of what deeds or words are wise. Soldiers think they are acting wisely in following their profession. Those who despise military service and give all their care and labour to agriculture think themselves wise. Those who leave all these things aside or reject all such temporal concerns and devote all their zeal to the search for truth, how they can know themselves and God, judge that this is the chief task of wisdom. Those who are unwilling to give themselves to the life of leisure for the purpose of seeking and contemplating truth, but prefer to accept laborious cares and duties in the service of their fellows and to take part in justly ruling and governing human affairs, they too think themselves to be wise. Moreover, those who do both of these things, who live partly in the contemplation of truth and partly in laborious duties, which they think they owe to human society, those think they hold the palm of wisdom. I do not mention the sects innumerable, of which there is none which does not put its own members above all others and claim that they alone are wise. Since we are now carrying on this discussion on the understanding that we are not to state what we merely believe but what we clearly understand, I can make no answer to your question, unless in addition to believing I also know by contemplation and reason what wisdom is.

26. *Aug.*—Surely you do not suppose that wisdom is anything but the truth in which the chief good is beheld and possessed? All those people whom you have mentioned as following diverse pursuits seek good and shun evil, but they follow different pursuits because they differ as to what they think to be good. Whoever seeks that which ought not to be sought, even though he would not seek it unless it seemed to him to be good, is nevertheless in error. There can be no error when nothing is sought, or when that is sought which ought to be sought. In so far as all men seek the happy life they do not err. But in so far as anyone does not keep to the way that leads to the happy life, even though he professes to desire only to reach happiness, he is in error. Error arises when we follow something which does not lead to that which we wish to reach. The more a man errs in

his way of life, the less is he wise, the further he is from the truth in which the chief good is beheld and possessed. Everyone is happy who attains the chief good, which indisputably is the end which we all desire. Just as it is universally agreed that we wish to be happy, it is similarly agreed that we wish to be wise, because no one is happy without wisdom. For no one is happy except by the possession of the chief good which is beheld and possessed in the truth which we call wisdom. Before we are happy the notion of happiness is stamped upon our minds; that is why we know and can say confidently without any hesitation that we want to be happy. Likewise, even before we are wise we have the notion of wisdom stamped upon our minds. For that reason each of us, if asked whether he wants to be wise, will, without any groping in the dark, answer that, of course, he does.

27. Perhaps we are now agreed as to what wisdom is. You may not be able to express it in words, but if you had no notion in your mind of what it is you would not know that you want to be wise, and that you ought to want to be wise. That, I am sure you will not deny. Suppose, then, that we are agreed as to what wisdom is, please tell me whether you think that wisdom too, like the science of numbers, is common to all reasoning beings. Or, seeing that there are as many minds as there are men, and I cannot observe anything that goes on in your mind, nor you what goes on in mine, do you suppose that there are as many wisdoms as there can be wise men? *Ev.*—If the chief good is one for all men, the truth in which it is seen and possessed, that is, wisdom, must be one and common to all. *Aug.*—Have you any doubt that the chief good, whatever it may be, is one for all men? *Ev.*—I certainly have, because I see that different men rejoice in different things as if they were their chief good. *Aug.*—I wish there were no more doubt about the nature of the chief good than there is about the fact that without it, whatever it may be, no one can become happy. But that is a big question and demands a long discourse, so let us suppose that there are just as many "chief goods" as there are different things sought by different people under the impression that they are "chief goods." Surely it does not follow that wisdom is not one and common to all because the good things which men see in it and choose are manifold and diverse? If you think it does, you might as well doubt whether the light of the sun is one light because there are many diverse things which we see by means of it. Of these each one chooses at will something to enjoy looking at. One man likes to behold a high mountain and

rejoices to look at it. Another prefers the plain, another a hollow valley, or green woods, or the wavy expanse of the sea. Some one may like all these or some of them whose united beauty contributes to the pleasure of looking at them. The things which men see by the light of the sun and choose for enjoyment are many and various, but the light is one in which each man sees what he enjoys looking at. So, although there are many diverse good things from among which each may choose what he likes, and seeing and possessing it and enjoying it, may rightly and truly constitute it his own chief good, nevertheless it may be that the light of wisdom in which these things can be seen and possessed is one light common to all wise men. *Ev.*—I admit it may be so, and that there is nothing to prevent there being one wisdom common to all, though there are many various chief goods. But I should like to know whether it is so. To admit that something may be is not exactly the same as to admit that it is. *Aug.*—Meantime we have established that there is such a thing as wisdom, but we have not yet determined whether it is one and common to all, or whether individual wise men have their particular wisdoms just as they have their particular souls or minds. *Ev.*—That is so.

x, 28. *Aug.*—We hold it as settled that there is such a thing as wisdom, or at least that there are wise men, and also that all men want to be happy. But where do we see this? For I have no doubt at all that you see this and that it is true. Do you see this truth in such a way that I cannot know it unless you tell me what you think? Or could I see this truth, just as you understand it, even if you did not tell me? *Ev.*—I do not doubt that you too could see it even if I did not want you to. *Aug.*—Is not one truth which we both see with our different minds common to both of us? *Ev.*—Clearly. *Aug.*—Again, I believe you do not deny that men should strive after wisdom. You admit that that is true? *Ev.*—I have no doubt about that. *Aug.*—Here is another truth which is one and common to all who know it, though each one sees it with his own mind and not with mine or yours or any other man's. Can we deny that, since what is seen can be seen in common by all who see it? *Ev.*—We cannot deny it. *Aug.*—Again, take such propositions as these: Man ought to live justly; the worse ought to be subjected to the better; like is to be compared with like; each man should be given his due. Don't you admit that these statements are absolutely true and stable, to be shared by you and me and all who see them? *Ev.*—I agree. *Aug.*—The same would be true of these statements: The incorrupt is better than the corrupt, the eternal than the temporal, the inviolable than the violable? *Ev.*—Undeniably. *Aug.*—Could anyone claim truths of that kind as his own private truths, seeing they are unchangeably present for all to contemplate who have the capacity to contemplate them? *Ev.*—No one could claim any one of them as his own, for not only are they true but they are equally common property to all. *Aug.*—And again, who denies that the soul ought to be turned from corruption and converted to incorruption, in other words not corruption but incorruption ought to be loved? Who, confessing that that is true, does not also understand that it is unchangeably true and can be understood in common by all minds which have the capacity to understand it? *Ev.*—Most true. *Aug.*—Will anyone doubt that a life which no adversity can drive from a certain and honourable opinion is better than one which is easily broken and overwhelmed by temporal disadvantages? *Ev.*—Who can doubt it?

29. *Aug.*—I shall ask no more questions of that kind. It is sufficient that you see as I do that these rules and guiding lights of the virtues, as we may call them, are true and unchangeable, and singly or all together they stand open for the common contemplation of those who have the capacity to behold them, each with his own mind and reason. This you admit is quite certain. But I do ask whether you think these truths belong to wisdom. For I am sure you think that he who has acquired wisdom is wise. *Ev.*—I most certainly do. *Aug.*—Could the man who lives justly so live unless he saw how to apply the principles of subordinating the inferior to the superior, joining like to like, and giving to each his due? *Ev.*—He could not. *Aug.*—Would you deny that he who sees this sees wisely? *Ev.*—I would not. *Aug.*—Does not he who lives prudently choose incorruption and perceive that it is preferable to corruption? *Ev.*—Clearly. *Aug.*—If he makes what no one doubts is the right choice as to the goal towards which he should direct his mind, can it be denied that he has made a wise choice? *Ev.*—I could not deny it. *Aug.*—When he directs his mind to what he has wisely chosen, again he does it wisely? *Ev.*—Most certainly. *Aug.*—And if by no terrors or penalties can he be driven from what he has wisely chosen and towards which he has wisely directed his mind, again there is no doubt that he acts wisely? *Ev.*—There is no doubt. *Aug.*—It is therefore abundantly evident that these rules and guiding lights of virtue, as we have called them, belong to wisdom. The more a man uses them in living his life, and the

more closely he follows them, the more wisely does he live and act. Everything that is wisely done cannot rightly be said to be done apart from wisdom. *Ev.*—That is perfectly true. *Aug.*—Just as the rules of numbers are true and unchangeable, and the science of numbers is unchangeably available for all who can learn it, and is common to them all, so the rules of wisdom are true and unchangeable. When you were asked about them one by one you replied that they were true and evident and open to the common contemplation of all who have the capacity to examine them.

xi, 30. *Ev.*—I cannot doubt it. But I should very much like to know whether wisdom and numbers are contained within one class of things. You mentioned that they were linked together in the Holy Scriptures. Or is one of them derived from the other or contained within the other? For example, is number derived from wisdom or is it contained in wisdom? I should not dare to suggest that wisdom is derived from number or is contained in it. For I know many arithmeticians or accountants, or whatever they are to be called, who count perfectly and indeed marvellously, but somehow very few of them have wisdom, perhaps none. So wisdom strikes me as being far more worthy of respect than arithmetic. *Aug.*—You mention a matter which has often made me wonder, too. When I consider in my mind the unchangeable science of numbers and the recondite sanctuary or region, or whatever other name we are to give to the realm and abode of numbers, I find myself far removed from the corporeal sphere. I find possibly some vague idea but no words adequate to express it, and so in order to say something I return wearily to these numbers which are set before our eyes and call them by their wonted names. The same thing happens when I am thinking as carefully and intently as I can about wisdom. And so I greatly marvel that though wisdom and number are alike in being mysteriously and certainly true, and are linked together by the testimony of Scripture which I have quoted, I say I marvel greatly that number is so contemptible to the majority of men, while wisdom is precious. To be sure it may be because they are one and the same thing. On the other hand it is also written in Scripture of Wisdom that "she reaches from one end of the world to the other with full strength and ordereth things graciously" (Wisdom 8:1). Perhaps it is called number from its potency to reach with strength from end to end, and is properly called wisdom because it graciously ordereth all things. For both are functions of wisdom alone.

31. Wisdom has given numbers even to the smallest and most remote of things, and all bodies have their own numbers. But it has not given to bodies the power to be wise, nor even to all souls, but only to rational souls, in which, as it were, it has taken up its abode from whence it ordereth all things, even the smallest to which it has given numbers. Now we have no difficulty in judging corporeal things as things which belong to a lower order, and the numbers they bear stamped upon them we see are also lower than we are. Therefore we hold them in contempt. But when we begin to consider them from another angle we discover that they transcend our minds and abide unchangeably in the truth. And because few can be wise and many fools can count, men admire wisdom and despise numbers. But learned and studious men, the further they are removed from earthly corruption, behold the more clearly in the light of truth both numbers and wisdom, and hold both to be precious. By comparison with truth they prize neither gold nor silver nor the other things over which men strive, indeed they even come to think of themselves as of little account.

32. There is no need to be surprised that men think little of numbers and value wisdom highly, because counting is easier than being wise. You see how they set a higher value on gold than on the light of a candle, compared with which gold is a ridiculous thing. But a vastly inferior thing is more highly honoured because any beggar can light himself a candle, and only a few possess gold. Far be it from me to suggest that compared with numbers wisdom is inferior. Both are the same thing, but wisdom requires an eye fit to see it. From one fire light and heat are felt as if they were "consubstantial," so to speak. They cannot be separated one from the other. And yet the heat reaches those things which are brought near to the fire, while the light is diffused far and wide. So the potency of intellect which indwells wisdom causes things nearer to it to be warm, such as rational souls. Things further away, such as bodies, it does not affect with the warmth of wisdom, but it pours over them the light of numbers. Probably you will find that obscure, but no similitude drawn from visible things can be completely adapted to explain an invisible thing so as to be understood by everybody. Only take note of this which is sufficient for the problem we have in hand, and is clear enough to humbler kinds of mind such as ours. Though it cannot be made crystal-clear to us whether number is part of wisdom or is derived from wisdom or vice versa, or whether both names can

be shown to designate one thing, it is at least evident that both are true and unchangeably true.

xii, 33. Accordingly, you will never deny that there is an unchangeable truth which contains everything that is unchangeably true. You will never be able to say that it belongs particularly to you or to me or to any man, for it is available and offers itself to be shared by all who discern things immutably true, as if it were some strange mysterious and yet public light. Who would say that what is available to be shared by all reasoning and intelligent persons can be the private property of any of them? You remember, I dare say, our recent discussion about the bodily senses. Those things with which we both make contact by means of our eyes or ears, colours and sounds which you and I see or hear together, do not belong to our actual eyes or ears, but are common to both of us so that we may alike perceive them. So you would never say that those things which you and I behold in common, each with his own mind, belong to the actual mind of either of us. You would not say that what the eyes of two persons see belongs to the eyes of one or the other of them. It is a third thing towards which both direct their regard. *Ev.*—That is most clear and true.

34. *Aug.*—Do you, then, think that this truth of which we have already spoken so much and in which we behold so many things, is more excellent than our minds, or equal to our minds, or inferior? If it were inferior we should not use it as a standard of judgment, but should rather pass judgment on it, as we do on bodies which are inferior to our minds. For of them we often say not only that it *is* so or is not so, but that it *ought to be* so or not so. Similarly with our minds we know not only that it *is* thus or thus, but often also that it *ought to be* thus or thus. We judge of bodies when we say this is not so white as it ought to be, or not so square and so on. Of minds we say this one is not so capable as it ought to be, or it is not gentle enough or eager enough, according to our moral standard. All these judgments we make according to those inward rules of truth, which we discern in common. But no man passes any judgment on these rules. One may say the eternal *is* superior to the temporal, or seven and three *are* ten, but no one says these things *ought to be* so. Knowing simply that they are so one does not examine them with a view to their correction but rejoices to have discovered them. If, then, truth were the equal of our minds, it too would be mutable. Our minds sometimes see more sometimes less, and so confess their mutability. But truth abiding steadfast in itself

neither advances when we see more, nor falls short when we see less. Abiding whole and uncorrupt it rejoices with its light those who turn to it, and punishes with blindness those who turn from it. We pass judgment on our minds in accordance with truth as our standard, while we cannot in any way pass judgment on truth. For we say of our mind it understands less than it ought, or it understands exactly as it ought; and a mind approaches the proper standard of intelligence as it is brought nearer to unchangeable truth, and becomes able to cleave to it. Hence if truth is neither inferior to nor equal to our mind it must be superior and more excellent.

xiii, 35. I promised, if you remember, to show you something superior to the human mind and reason. There it is, truth itself. Embrace it if you can. Enjoy it. Delight in the Lord and he will grant you the petitions of your heart. What do you ask for more than to be happy? And what is more happy than to enjoy unshakable, unchangeable truth which is excellent above all things? Men exclaim that they are happy when they embrace the beautiful bodies, deeply longed for, of their wives or even of harlots, and shall we doubt that we are happy in the embrace of truth? Men exclaim that they are happy when with throats parched with heat they find a fountain flowing with pure water, or being hungry, find a copious meal all ready prepared, and shall we deny that we are happy when truth is our meat and drink? We are wont to hear the voices of people proclaiming that they are happy if they lie among roses or other flowers and enjoy scented ointments, and shall we hesitate to call ourselves happy when we are inspired by truth? Many place happiness in music, vocal and instrumental, flutes and strings. When they are without music they consider themselves unhappy; when they have it, they are transported with joy. Shall we, when the harmonious and creative silence of truth steals, so to speak, noiselessly over our minds, seek the happy life elsewhere, and fail to enjoy that which is ours now and securely. Men delight in the sheen of gold and silver, gems and colours. They delight in the brightness and pleasantness of visible light as it appears in fire or in the sun, moon and stars. When no trouble or want comes to rob them of that pleasure they think themselves happy, and therefore wish to live for ever. Shall we fear to place the happy life in the light of truth?

36. Nay, since the chief good is recognized to be truth and is possessed when truth is possessed, and truth is wisdom, in wisdom let us discern the chief good and possess it and enjoy it.

He is happy indeed who enjoys the chief good. Truth points out all the things that are truly good, and intelligent men, according to their capacity, choose one or more of them in order to enjoy them. People, for example, find pleasure in looking at some object which they are glad to behold in the light of the sun. Those among them who are endowed with strong healthy eyes love to look at nothing better than at the sun itself, which sheds its light upon the other things which delight weaker eyes. So a strong and vigorous mental vision may behold many true and changeless things with certain reason, but directs its regard to the truth itself whereby all things are made clear, and, cleaving to the truth and forgetting, as it were, all other things, it enjoys them all together in the truth. Whatever is pleasant in other true things is pleasant also in truth itself.

37. Herein is our liberty, when we are subject to truth. And Truth is our God who liberates us from death, that is, from the condition of sin. For the Truth itself, speaking as Man to men, says to those who believe in him: "If ye abide in my word ye are truly my disciples, and ye shall know the truth and the truth shall make you free" (John 8:31–32). No soul enjoys a thing with liberty unless it also enjoys it with security.

xiv. But no one is secure in the possession of goods which he can lose against his will. Truth and wisdom no one can lose unwillingly. From them there can be no spatial separation. What is called separation from truth and wisdom is a perverse will which loves lower things. No one wills anything involuntarily. Here is something which we can all enjoy equally and in common. Here there is no straitness, no deficiency. She receives all her lovers, being grudging to none, shared by all in common but chaste to each. None says to another: "Stand back that I too may approach," or "Remove your hand that I too may touch." All cleave to the same wisdom. All are brought into contact with it. Nothing is consumed as in the case of food, and you cannot drink so as to prevent me from drinking too. From that common store you can convert nothing into your private possession. What you take remains unharmed for me to take also. I do not have to wait for you to breathe out what you have breathed in that I may then breathe it in. Nothing ever belongs to one man or to any group of men as a private possession. The whole is common to all at one and the same time.

38. Truth, therefore, is less like the things we touch or taste or smell, and more like the things we hear and see. For every word is heard as a whole by all who hear it and by each one at the same

time. And every sight offered to the eyes is exactly the same for all who see it, and is seen by all at the same time. But though there is similarity there is also a great difference. A whole word is not spoken all at once. It is extended over a period of time, one syllable being pronounced first and another after it. Every visible sight varies with the place from which it is seen, and is nowhere seen in its totality. And certainly all these things can be taken from us whether we will or no, and there are difficulties in the way of our enjoying them. Even supposing someone could sing sweetly for ever, those who were eager to hear him would come as rivals. They would get packed closely together, and the more there were of them they would strive for seats, each one anxious to get nearer to the singer. And when they heard him no one would be able to retain permanently what was heard. They would hear nothing but transient fugitive sounds. If I wanted to look at the sun and had the power to do so without being dazzled, nevertheless it would forsake me when it set, or it might be veiled in cloud, and for many other causes I might unwillingly lose my pleasure in seeing the sun. And supposing I had the power and pleasure of eternally seeing the light and hearing music, what great advantage would I have, seeing that even beasts could share it with me? But the beauty of truth and wisdom, so long as there is a persevering will to enjoy it, does not exclude those who come by any packed crowd of hearers. It does not pass with time or change with locality. It is not interrupted by night or shut off by shadow, and is not subject to the bodily senses. To all who turn to it from the whole world, and love it, it is close at hand, everlasting, bound to no particular spot, never deficient. Externally it suggests, internally it teaches. All who behold it, it changes for the better, and by none is it changed for the worse. No one judges it, and no one without it judges aright. Hence it is evident beyond a doubt that wisdom is better than our minds, for by it alone they are made individually wise, and are made judges, not of it, but by it of all other things whatever.

xv, 39. You admitted for your part that if I could show you something superior to our minds you would confess that it was God, provided nothing existed that was higher still. I accepted your admission and said it would be sufficient if I demonstrated that. If there is anything more excellent than wisdom, doubtless it, rather, is God. But if there is nothing more excellent, then truth itself is God. Whether there is or is not such a higher thing, you cannot deny that God exists, and this was the question set for our discussion. If you are influenced by what we have received in faith from the holy discipline of Christ, that there is the Father of Wisdom, remember that we also received in faith that there is one equal to the eternal Father, namely Wisdom who is begotten of him. Hence there should be no further question, but we should accept it with unshakable faith. God exists and is the truest and fullest being. This I suppose we hold with undoubting faith. Now we attain it with a certain if tenuous form of knowledge. This is sufficient for the question in hand, so that we can go on to explain other pertinent questions; unless you have any opposition to offer. *Ev.*—I accept what you have said with incredible and inexpressible joy, and I declare it to be absolutely certain. I declare it in my mind where I hope to be heard by the truth itself, and where I hope to cleave to truth. For I confess that it is not only good, but the chief good and the beatific good.

40. *Aug.*—Indeed you are right, and I too am very glad. But are we already wise and happy, or are we still merely making for the source of wisdom and happiness? *Ev.*—I think we are rather making for the source. *Aug.*—Whence then do you derive your comprehension of the certain truths which have made you shout for joy? Has your comprehension got some connection with wisdom? Or can a foolish person know wisdom? *Ev.*—So long as he remains foolish he cannot. *Aug.*—Are you then wise already, or do you not yet know wisdom? *Ev.*—Indeed I am not yet wise, and yet I should not say that I am foolish, for I have some inkling of wisdom. I cannot deny that, since these things which I know are certain, and they belong to wisdom. *Aug.*—Tell me, pray, wouldn't you admit that he who is not just is unjust; and he who is not prudent is imprudent; and he who is not temperate is intemperate? Is there any doubt about that? *Ev.*—I admit that *when* a man is not just he is unjust; and I should reply similarly with regard to prudence and temperance. *Aug.*—Why, then, shouldn't a man be foolish *when* he is not wise? *Ev.*—I allow that too. *When* anyone is not wise he is foolish. *Aug.*—Now to which class do you belong? *Ev.*—Whichever of these epithets you care to apply to me, I do not venture yet to call myself wise. I see that the consequence of my admissions is that I must not hesitate to call myself foolish. *Aug.*—Then a foolish person knows wisdom. For as we said, no one would be certain that he wanted to be wise, and that he ought to be wise, unless the notion of wisdom were implanted in his mind. Think how you were able to reply to one question after another in

matters which belong to wisdom, and how you rejoiced to know them. *Ev.*—Yes. That is so.

xvi, 41. *Aug.*—What do we do when we are eager to be wise? Don't we with all possible keenness give our whole soul, so to speak, to what is mentally discerned, and keep it steadfastly fixed on that, so that it may not rejoice in any private possession of its own which will implicate it in transient things, but, having put off all affections for things temporal and spatial, it may apprehend what remains ever one and the same? For as the soul is the whole life of the body, so is God the happy life of the soul. While we do as I have just described, so long as we continue, we are in the way [*in via*]. If it is given us to rejoice in these true and certain blessings as they glimmer for us even now on our still darkly shadowed way, perhaps this is what Scripture means when it describes how wisdom deals with the lovers who come to her. For it is written: "In their paths she appeareth unto them graciously, and in every purpose she meeteth them" (Wisdom 6:16). Wherever you turn she speaks to you through certain traces of her operations. When you are falling away to external things she recalls you to return within by the very forms of external things. Whatever delights you in corporeal objects and entices you by appeal to the bodily senses, you may see is governed by number, and when you ask how that is so, you will return to your mind within, and know that you could neither approve nor disapprove things of sense unless you had within you, as it were, laws of beauty by which you judge all beautiful things which you perceive in the world.

42. Behold the heaven, the earth, the sea; all that is bright in them or above them; all that creep or fly or swim; all have forms because all have number. Take away number and they will be nothing. From whom have they their being if not from him who has made number? For they exist only in so far as they have number. The artificers of all corporeal forms work by number and regulate their operations thereby. In working they move their hands and tools until that which is fashioned in the outer world, being referred to the inward light of number, receives such perfection as is possible, and, being reported on by the senses, pleases the internal judge who beholds the supernal ideal numbers. Do you ask who moves the limbs of the artificer? It will be number, for they, too, move by number. Suppose there is no actual work in hand and no intention to make anything, but the motions of the limbs are done for pleasure, that will be dancing. Ask what delights you in dancing

and number will reply: "Lo, here am I." Examine the beauty of bodily form, and you will find that everything is in its place by number. Examine the beauty of bodily motion and you will find everything in its due time by number. Examine the art which produces all these things and you never anywhere find in it either space or time, but it is alive with number. It has neither place in space nor length of days. And yet those who want to become artificers, while they accustom themselves to learning their art, move their bodies in space and time, and their minds at least in time. They become more skilled, I mean, with the passing of time. But rise above even the mind of the artificer to behold the eternal realm of number. Then wisdom will shine upon you from its inward seat, from the secret place of truth. If truth repels you still because you look for it somewhat languidly, direct your mental vision to that path in which "she shows herself graciously." Remember that you have postponed a vision that you will seek again when you have become stronger and sounder.

43. Woe to those who abandon thy leading and wander among things which are but signs of thy working, who love thy nod rather than thyself and are oblivious to what thou teachest thereby, O Wisdom, sweetest light of the purified mind. For thou ceasest not to suggest to us what and how great thou art. Thy pleasure is the whole glory of created beings. An artificer somehow suggests to the spectator of his work, through the very beauty of the work itself, not to be wholly content with that beauty alone, but to let his eye so scan the form of the material thing made that he may remember with affection him who made it. Those who love thy creatures in place of thee are like men who, listening to an eloquent sage, pay too much attention to the sweetness of his voice and the aptness of his verbal style and miss the meaning of his sentences, of which the words are but the sound-signals, as it were. Woe to those who turn away from thy light and are happy enough to remain in their own obscurity. It is as if they turned their backs on thee and went on with their carnal labours in their own shadows; yet even so what pleases them is theirs because of thy light shining all round them. But so long as the shadow is loved the mind's eye is made languid and becomes less able to bear to behold thee. So a man becomes more and more shrouded in darkness so long as he pursues willingly what he finds in his weakness is more easy to receive. Then he begins not to be able to see what supremely is, and to consider that to be evil which deceives him because

of his lack of foresight, or tempts him because he is in need, or tortures him because he is a slave. All these things he deservedly suffers because he has turned away from truth, and whatever is just cannot be evil.

44. Neither by bodily sense nor by the thinking mind can you find any mutable thing which is not contained in some numerical form. Take away the form and it sinks to nothingness. Nevertheless do not doubt that there is an eternal and immutable form which prevents these mutable things from being reduced to nothingness, and preserves them through their appointed periods of existence in their measured motions and with their distinct varieties of form. That eternal form is neither contained in nor diffused through space, nor does it extend through or vary with changing times. Yet by it all other things can be formed, and, each in its own kind, can occupy spaces and times in which number rules.

xvii, 45. Every mutable thing must also be capable of receiving form. We call that mutable which can be changed, and similarly we call that "formable" which is capable of receiving form. Nothing can "form" itself, because nothing can give itself what it does not have. To be "formed" means precisely to have form. Hence if a thing has form, it does not need to receive what it has. If it has not form it cannot give itself form. So, as we said, nothing can form itself. What more shall we say about the mutability of the body and the mind? We have said enough before. The conclusion is that both body and mind receive form from a form that is unchangeable and eternal. Of this form it is written: "Thou shalt change them and they shall be changed, but thou art the same, and thy years have no end" (Ps. 102:26–27). The prophetic word says "years without end," meaning eternity. Again of this form it is written: "She, remaining in herself, reneweth all things" (Wisdom 7:27). Hence we understand that all things are ruled by providence. If all existing things would cease to be if form were taken from them, the unchangeable form by which all mutable things exist and fulfil their functions in the realm of number is to them a providence. If it were not, they would not be. Therefore he who journeys towards wisdom, beholding and considering the whole created universe, finds wisdom appearing unto him graciously on his way and meeting him in every purpose or providence; and his eagerness to press along that way is all the greater because he sees that the way is rendered beautiful by the wisdom he longs to reach.

46. If you can find any other kind of creature besides these three—that which is but has not life, that which is and has life but not intelligence, and that which is and has life and intelligence—you may then dare to say that there is some good thing which does not owe its existence to God. Now instead of speaking of three kinds of things, we may speak simply of two, body and life. For the life of beasts, which live but have not intelligence, and the life of men, who have intelligence too, are both alike correctly called life. Of course we also speak of the life of the Creator but that is life in a supreme sense. When I speak now about body and life I am thinking only of created things. Well, these two created things, body and life, being "formable" as we said and returning to nothingness when form is completely taken from them, clearly show that they owe their existence to the form which remains always the same. There can be no good things, whether great or small, which do not owe their existence to God. Among created things, what can be greater than intelligent life, and what can be smaller than body? However defective they may become, thereby tending to nothingness, still some form remains in them so that they have some kind of existence. Whatever of form remains in any defective thing derives from that form which cannot be defective, and which does not allow the movement of things up or down the scale of being to transgress the laws of their being. Whatever, therefore, in nature is observed to be praiseworthy, whether it is thought worthy of great or small praise, should point to the exceeding and ineffable praise of the Creator. Have you anything to say to that?

xviii, 47. *Ev.*—I confess I am entirely convinced; and I see also how it can be demonstrated, so far as that is possible in this life and among people like us, that God exists and that all good things come from him. For all things which exist, whether they merely exist or have in addition life and intelligence, all are from God. Now let us look at the third question, which is this. Can it be shown that free will is to be numbered among the things which are good? When this has been demonstrated I shall not hesitate to concede that God has given us free will and has rightly given it to us. *Aug.*—You do well to recall the questions we proposed for our discussion; and you have shown your vigilance in observing that the second of them has been answered. But you ought to have seen that the third also has been solved. You said you thought that we ought not to have been given free will because by it men commit sin. When I urged against your statement that without free choice men could not act rightly, and asserted instead that God gave it to that end, you replied that we should have been given free will just as we have been given justice which can only be used rightly. Your reply compelled us to travel the long circuitous route of discussion in order to prove that all good things, great and small, come from God alone. For that could not be clearly shown unless in the first place our poor reason, such as it is, should, with God's aid on our perilous journey, hit upon some evident answer in so great a matter to the opinions of impious folly such as the fool shows who says in his heart there is no God. These two propositions—that God exists, and that all good things come from him—we already held firmly by faith. But we have so thoroughly discussed them that the third proposition too—that free will is to be numbered among the things which are good—has been made clear.

48. In our previous discussion it was made obvious, and was agreed by us both, that body occupies by nature a lower rank in the scale of being than does soul; and that therefore soul is a greater good than body. If, then, we find among the good things of the body some that a man can abuse, and yet cannot on that account say that they ought not to have been given, since we admit that they are good, it should not be matter for surprise if in the soul too there are some good things which may be abused, but which, because they are good, could only have been given by him from whom all good things come. You see of how much good a body is deprived if it has no hands, and yet a man makes a bad use of his hands who uses them to do cruel or base deeds. If you see a man without feet you will admit that, from the point of view of the wholeness of his body, a very great good is wanting. And yet you would not deny that a man makes a bad use of his feet who uses them to hurt another or to dishonour himself. With the eyes we see the light and distinguish the forms of bodies. Sight is the most splendid possession our bodies have, and for that reason the eyes are set in a place of great dignity. By the use of them we look after our safety and enjoy many other advantages in life. Yet many people use their eyes for many base purposes, compelling them to serve the interests of lust. You see how much good is lost to the human face if it has no eyes. Now who has given us eyes if not God, the bountiful giver of all good things? Just as you approve these good things which the body enjoys, and praise him who has given them, paying no attention to those who make a bad use

of them; even so ought you to confess that free will, without which no one can live aright, is a good thing divinely bestowed, and that those are to be condemned who make a bad use of it, rather than to suggest that he who gave it ought not to have done so.

49. *Ev.*—I should like you first to prove to me that free will is a good thing. Then I shall agree that God gave it, because I admit that all good things come from God. *Aug.*—Have I not proved this to your satisfaction after all the labour of our previous discussion? You admitted that every corporeal form derives its existence from the supreme form of all, that is, from the truth. And you agreed that every form was good. Truth himself, in the Gospel, tells us that even the hairs of our heads are numbered. Have you forgotten what we said about the supremacy of number, and its power which extends from one end to the other? What perversity it is to number our hairs among the good things though they are small and utterly contemptible, and to attribute their creation to God, the Creator of all good things because all good things, the greatest and the least, come from him from whom is all good; and yet to hesitate to ascribe free will to him, seeing that without it no one can live aright even on the testimony of those who live evil lives. Now tell me, pray, what in us seems to be superior, that without which we *can* live aright, or that without which we *cannot* live aright. *Ev.*—Now please spare me. I am ashamed of my blindness. Who can doubt that that is far superior without which there can be no right living? *Aug.*—Will you deny that a one-eyed man can live rightly? *Ev.*—Away with such shocking madness. *Aug.*—You agree that an eye is a good thing, and yet the loss of it does not prevent right living. Can you imagine that free will, without which no one can live aright, is no good thing?

50. Look at justice, of which no one can make a bad use. It is numbered among the best good things which a man can have. So are all the virtues of the soul which constitute the righteous and honourable life. No one makes a bad use of prudence or fortitude or temperance. In all of these, as in justice which you have chosen to mention, right reason prevails, without which there can be no virtues. And no one can make a bad use of right reason. [xix.] These are therefore great good things. But you must remember that there can be no good things, great or small, save from him from whom all good things come, that is, God. So we were persuaded by our previous discussion, in

the course of which you so often and so gladly expressed your assent. The virtues then, whereby life is rightly lived, are great goods. But the forms of bodies, without which life can be rightly lived, are the least of good things. And the powers of the soul, without which there can be no righteous life, are intermediate goods. No one makes a bad use of the virtues. But of the other goods, the intermediate and the small, anyone can make not only a good but also a bad use. No one makes a bad use of virtue, just because the function of virtue is the good use of the things of which we can also make a bad use. No one makes a bad use of anything when he uses it well. Wherefore God in his great and lavish goodness affords us not only great goods, but small ones too, and some intermediate between great and small. His goodness is more to be praised for the great goods than for the intermediate ones, and for the intermediate ones more than for the small ones. But for all, his goodness is to be praised more than if he had given only the great goods and not the lesser as well.

51. *Ev.*—I agree, but I still have this difficulty. We see that free will makes use of other things either well or ill. How, then, is it to be numbered among the things we use? *Aug.*—Everything we know scientifically we know by means of reason, and yet reason itself is numbered among the things we know by reason. Have you forgotten that when we were inquiring as to the things we know by reason, you admitted that reason was known by reason? Do not marvel, therefore, if we use other things by free will, and can also use free will by itself. Will, which uses other things, somehow also uses itself, just as reason which knows other things knows itself also. Memory, too, contains not only all the other things which it remembers; but because we do not forget that we have memory, somehow memory remembers itself as well as other things. Or rather by memory we remember other things and memory too.

52. Will is therefore an intermediate good when it cleaves to the unchangeable good as something that is common property and not its own private preserve; of the same nature, that is to say, as truth of which we have spoken a great deal, but nothing worthy of so great a theme; when will cleaves to this good, man attains the happy life. And the happy life, that is, the disposition of soul cleaving to the unchangeable good, is the proper and first good of man. All the virtues are there which no one can use badly. However great and important the virtues may be, we know well enough that they are not common property, but

are the property of each individual man. Truth and wisdom are common to all, and all wise men are also happy by cleaving to truth. But one man does not become happy by another's happiness. If one man seeks to attain happiness by imitating another, he seeks his happiness where he sees the other found his, that is to say in unchangeable and common truth. No one is made prudent by the prudence of another, or courageous by his courage, or temperate by his temperance, or just by his justice. A man is made virtuous by regulating his soul according to the rules and guiding lights of the virtues which dwell indestructibly in the truth and wisdom that are the common property of all. For so the virtuous man whom he set before him for imitation has regulated his soul, giving it a fixed objective.

53. The will, therefore, which cleaves to the unchangeable good that is common to all, obtains man's first and best good things though it is itself only an intermediate good. But the will which turns from the unchangeable and common good and turns to its own private good or to anything exterior or inferior, sins. It turns to its private good, when it wills to be governed by its own authority; to what is exterior, when it is eager to know what belongs to others and not to itself; to inferior things, when it loves bodily pleasure. In these ways a man becomes proud, inquisitive, licentious, and is taken captive by another kind of life which, when compared with the life we have just described, is really death. And yet it is still governed and disposed by divine providence, which appoints for all things their proper places, and distributes to each man his due according to his deserts. So it happens that the good things sought by sinners cannot in any way be bad, nor can free will be bad, for we found that it was to be numbered among the intermediate goods. What is bad is its turning away from the unchangeable good and its turning to changeable goods. That "aversion" and "conversion" is voluntary and is not coerced. Therefore it is followed by the deserved and just penalty of unhappiness.

xx, 54. But perhaps you are going to ask what is the cause of the movement of the will when it turns from the immutable to the mutable good. That movement is certainly evil, although free will must be numbered among good things since without it no one can live aright. We cannot doubt that that movement of the will, that turning away from the Lord God, is sin; but surely we cannot say that God is the author of sin? God, then, will not be the cause of that movement; but what will be its cause? If you ask this, and I answer that I do not know, probably you will be saddened. And yet that would be a true answer. That which is nothing cannot be known. Only hold fast to your pious opinion that no good thing can happen to you, to your senses or to your intelligence or to your thought, which does not come from God. Nothing of any kind can happen which is not of God. Do not hesitate to attribute to God as its maker every thing which you see has measure, number and order. When you take these things completely away nothing at all will remain. Wherever measure, number and order are found, there is perfect form. If there is some kind of inchoate form, wanting measure, number and order, you must remove it too, for inchoate form is a kind of material lying to the hand of the artificer to use for perfecting his work. For if the perfection of form is good, the beginning of form is not without some grain of good. Take away all good, and absolutely nothing will remain. All good is from God. Hence there is no natural existence which is not from God. Now that movement of "aversion," which we admit is sin, is a defective movement; and all defect comes from nothing. Observe where it belongs and you will have no doubt that it does not belong to God. Because that defective movement is voluntary, it is placed within our power. If you fear it, all you have to do is simply not to will it. If you do not will it, it will not exist. What can be more secure than to live a life where nothing can happen to you which you do not will. But since man cannot rise of his own free will as he fell by his own will spontaneously, let us hold with steadfast faith the right hand of God stretched out to us from above, even our Lord Jesus Christ. Let us wait for him with certain hope, and long for him with burning charity. If you think that we must still make diligent inquiry for the origin of sin—I myself think that there is no need at all for such inquiry—but if you think so, we must put it off till another discussion. *Ev.*—I bow to your will, but only so far as to postpone to another time the question you have raised. But I will not allow you to imagine that our inquiry has already gone far enough.

Book III

i, 1. *Evodius.*—It is sufficiently evident to me that free will is to be numbered among the good things, and, indeed, not among the least of our good things. We are, therefore, compelled to confess that it has been given us by God, and that he has rightly given it to us. But now, if you think a suitable time has come, I want to learn from you whence arises the movement by which the will itself turns from the unchangeable good, which is the common property of all, to its own interests or to the interests of others or to things beneath it, and so turns to mutable goods. *Augustine.*—Why must you know this? *Ev.*—Because if free will is so given that it has that movement by nature, it turns of necessity to mutable goods; and no blame attaches where nature and necessity prevail. *Aug.*—Do you like or dislike that movement? *Ev.*—I dislike it. *Aug.*—So you find fault with it? *Ev.*—I do. *Aug.*—Then you find fault with a movement of the mind though it is faultless. *Ev.*—No, I do not. But I do not know whether there is any fault in abandoning the unchangeable good and turning towards the mutable goods. *Aug.*—Then you are finding fault with something which you do not know. *Ev.*—Don't insist on a verbal point. I said that I did not know whether there was any fault, but I meant to be understood really as having no doubt about it. Certainly I said I do not know, but obviously I was being ironical in suggesting that there could be any doubt about so clear a matter. *Aug.*—Just consider what is that truth you hold to be so certain that it has caused you so soon to forget what you said a moment ago. If that movement of the will exists by nature or necessity, it is in no way culpable. And yet you are so firmly convinced that it is culpable that you think fit to wax ironical about hesitation over a matter so certain. Why did you think it right to affirm, or at least to say with some hesitation, what you yourself show to be obviously false? You said: "If free will has been given in such fashion that it has that movement by nature, then it turns to mutable things of necessity, and no fault can be found where nature and necessity rule." But you ought to have had no doubt that it was not given in that fashion, since you do not doubt that that movement is culpable. *Ev.*—I said that the movement is culpable, and that therefore it displeases me, and that I cannot doubt that it is reprehensible. But I hold that a soul which is thereby drawn from the unchangeable good to mutable goods is not to be blamed if its nature is such that it is so moved by necessity.

2. *Aug.*—To whom belongs the movement which you admit is blameworthy? *Ev.*—I see that it is in the soul, but to whom it belongs I know not. *Aug.*—You do not deny that the soul is moved by that motion? *Ev.*—No. *Aug.*—Do you then deny that the motion by which a stone is moved is the motion of the stone? I don't mean the motion that we give to it, or that is given to it by some other force, when it is thrown upwards, but

that by which of its own accord it falls back to earth. *Ev.*—I do not deny that the motion you refer to, by which it turns and falls downwards, is the motion of the stone, but it is its natural motion. If the motion of the soul is like that, it too is natural, and it cannot rightly be blamed for a motion that is natural. Even if it moves to its own destruction, it is compelled by the necessity of its own nature. Moreover because we have no doubt that the soul's motion is culpable we must absolutely deny that it is natural, and therefore not like the motion of the stone, which is natural motion. *Aug.*—Did we achieve anything in our two previous discussions? *Ev.*—I am sure we did. *Aug.*—No doubt you remember that in the first discussion we discovered that the mind can become the slave of lust only by its own will. No superior thing and no equal thing compels it to such dishonour, because that would be unjust. And no inferior thing has the power. It remains that that must be the mind's own motion when it turns its will away from enjoyment of the Creator to enjoyment of the creature. If that motion is accounted blameworthy—and you thought anyone who doubted that deserved to be treated ironically—it is not natural but voluntary. It is like the motion of the falling stone, in so far as it is a motion of the soul as the former is the motion of the stone. But it is dissimilar in this, that it is not in the power of a stone to arrest its downward motion, while if the soul is not willing it cannot be moved to abandon what is higher and to love what is lower. Thus the stone's motion is natural, the soul's voluntary. Hence anyone who says that a stone sins when it is carried downwards by its own weight is, I will not say more senseless than the stone but, completely mad. But we charge the soul with sin when we show that it has abandoned the higher things and prefers to enjoy lower things. What need is there, therefore, to seek the origin of the movement whereby the will turns from the unchangeable to the changeable good? We acknowledge that it is a movement of the soul, that it is voluntary and therefore culpable. And all useful learning in this matter has its object and value in teaching us to condemn and restrain that movement, and to convert our wills from falling into temporal delights to the enjoyment of the eternal good.

3. *Ev.*—I see, and in a sense grasp that what you say is true. There is nothing that I feel more certainly and more personally than that I have a will, and that it moves me to enjoy this or that. I know nothing I could call my own if the will by which I will "yea" or "nay" is not my own. If I use it to do evil, to

whom is the evil to be attributed if not to myself? Since a good God has made me, and I can do nothing right except by willing, it is clearly evident that it was to this end that the will has been given to me by God who is good. Moreover, unless the movement of the will towards this or that object is voluntary and within our power, a man would not be praiseworthy when he turns to the higher objects nor blameworthy when he turns to lower objects, using his will like a hinge. There would be no use at all in warning him to pay no attention to temporal things and to will to obtain the eternal things, or to will to live aright and to be unwilling to live an evil life. But whoever thinks that man is not to be so warned ought to be cut off from membership in the human race.

ii, 4. That being so, I have a deep desire to know how it can be that God knows all things beforehand and that, nevertheless, we do not sin by necessity. Whoever says that anything can happen otherwise than as God has foreknown it, is attempting to destroy the divine foreknowledge with the most insensate impiety. If God foreknew that the first man would sin—and that anyone must concede who acknowledges with me that God has foreknowledge of all future events—I do not say that God did not make him, for he made him good, nor that the sin of the creature whom he made good could be prejudicial to God. On the contrary, God showed his goodness in making man, his justice in punishing his sin, and his mercy in delivering him. I do not say, therefore, that God did not make man. But this I say. Since God foreknew that man would sin, that which God foreknew must necessarily come to pass. How then is the will free when there is apparently this unavoidable necessity?

5. *Aug.*—You have knocked vigorously. May God in his mercy grant us his presence and open the door to those who knock. But I verily believe that the vast majority of men are troubled by that question for no other reason than that they do not ask it in a pious fashion. They are swifter to make excuses for their sins than to make confession of them. Some are glad to hold the opinion that there is no divine providence presiding over human affairs. They commit themselves, body and soul, to fortuitous circumstances, and deliver themselves to be carried about and tormented by lusts. They deny that there is any divine judgment, and deceive human judges when they are accused. They imagine that they are driven on by the favour of fortune. In sculpture or painting they are wont to represent Fortune as blind, either because they are better than the god-

dess by whom they think they are ruled, or because they confess that in their sentiments they are afflicted with that same blindness. In the case of such people it is not absurd to admit that they do everything by chance, seeing that they stumble in all that they do. But against this opinion, so full of foolish and senseless error, we have, I think, sufficiently spoken in our second disputation. Others do not venture to deny that the providence of God presides over human affairs, but they would rather indulge in the wicked error of believing that providence is weak or unjust or evil than confess their sins with suppliant piety. If all these would suffer themselves to be persuaded to believe that the goodness, justice and power of God are greater far, and far superior to any thought they can have of goodness, justice or might, if they would but take thought to themselves, they would know that they owe thanks to God, even if he had willed them to be somewhat lower in the scale of being than they actually are, and with all that is within them they would exclaim with the Psalmist: "I have spoken: Lord have mercy upon me; heal my soul for I have sinned against thee" (Ps. 41:5). So by stages the divine mercy would bring them to wisdom. They would be neither inflated by what they discover, nor rebellious when they fail to find the truth; by learning they would become better prepared to see the truth, and by recognizing their ignorance they would become more patient in seeking it. I am quite sure that these are your views too. Now first answer a few questions I am going to put to you, and you will see how easily I can find a solution to your tremendous problem.

iii, 6. Your trouble is this. You wonder how it can be that these two propositions are not contradictory and incompatible, namely that God has foreknowledge of all future events, and that we sin voluntarily and not by necessity. For if, you say, God foreknows that a man will sin, he must necessarily sin. But if there is necessity there is no voluntary choice in sinning, but rather fixed and unavoidable necessity. You are afraid that by that reasoning the conclusion may be reached either that God's foreknowledge of all future events must be impiously denied, or, if that cannot be denied, that sin is committed not voluntarily but by necessity. Isn't that your difficulty? *Ev.*—Exactly that. *Aug.*—You think, therefore, that all things of which God has foreknowledge happen by necessity and not voluntarily. *Ev.*—Yes. Absolutely. *Aug.*—Try an experiment, and examine yourself a little, and tell me what kind of will you are going to have to-morrow. Will you want to sin or to do right? *Ev.*—I do not know. *Aug.*—Do you think God also does not know? *Ev.*—I could in no wise think that. *Aug.*—If God knows what you are going to will to-morrow, and foresees what all men are going to will in the future, not only those who are at present alive but all who will ever be, much more will he foresee what he is going to do with the just and the impious? *Ev.*—Certainly if I say that God has foreknowledge of my deeds, I should say with even greater confidence that he has foreknowledge of his own acts, and foresees with complete certainty what he is going to do. *Aug.*—Don't you see that you will have to be careful lest someone say to you that, if all things of which God has foreknowledge are done by necessity and not voluntarily, his own future acts will be done not voluntarily but by necessity? *Ev.*—When I said that all future events of which God has foreknowledge happen by necessity, I was having regard only to things which happen within his creation, and not to things which happen in God himself. Indeed, in God nothing happens. Everything is eternal. *Aug.*—God, then, is not active within his creation? *Ev.*—He determined once for all how the order of the universe he created was to go on, and he never changes his mind. *Aug.*—Does he never make anyone happy? *Ev.*—Indeed he does. *Aug.*—He does it precisely at the time when the man in question actually becomes happy. *Ev.*—That is so. *Aug.*—If, then, for example, you yourself are happy one year from now, you will be made happy at that time. *Ev.*—Exactly. *Aug.*—God knows to-day what he is going to do a year hence? *Ev.*—He eternally had that foreknowledge, but I agree that he has it now, if indeed it is to happen so.

7. *Aug.*—Now tell me, are you not God's creature? And will not your becoming happy take place within your experience? *Ev.*—Certainly I am God's creature, and if I become happy it will be within my experience. *Aug.*—If God, then, makes you happy, your happiness will come by necessity and not by the exercise of your will? *Ev.*—God's will is my necessity. *Aug.*—Will you then be happy against your will? *Ev.*—If I had the power to be happy, I should be so at once. For I wish to be happy but am not, because not I but God makes me happy. *Aug.*—The truth simply cries out against you. You could not imagine that "having in our power" means anything else than "being able to do what we will." Therefore there is nothing so much in our power as is the will itself. For as soon as we will [*volumus*] immediately will [*voluntas*] is there. We can say rightly that we do not grow old voluntarily but necessarily, or that we do not die

voluntarily but from necessity, and so with other similar things. But who but a raving fool would say that it is not voluntarily that we will? Therefore though God knows how we are going to will in the future, it is not proved that we do not voluntarily will anything. When you said that you did not make yourself happy, you said it as if I had denied it. What I say is that when you become happy in the future it will take place not against your will but in accordance with your willing. Therefore, though God has foreknowledge of your happiness in the future, and though nothing can happen otherwise than as he has fore-known it (for that would mean that there is no foreknowledge) we are not thereby compelled to think that you will not be happy voluntarily. That would be absurd and far from true. God's foreknowledge, which is even to-day quite certain that you are to be happy at a future date, does not rob you of your will to happiness when you actually attain happiness. Similarly if ever in the future you have a culpable will, it will be none the less your will because God had foreknowledge of it.

8. Observe, pray, how blind are those who say that if God has foreknowledge of what I am going to will, since nothing can happen otherwise than as he has foreknown it, therefore I must necessarily will what he has foreknown. If so, it must be admitted that I will, not voluntarily but from necessity. Strange folly! Is there, then, no difference between things that happen according to God's foreknowledge where there is no intervention of man's will at all, and things that happen because of a will of which he has foreknowledge? I omit the equally monstrous assertion of the man I mentioned a moment ago, who says I must necessarily so will. By assuming necessity he strives to do away with will altogether. If I must necessarily will, why need I speak of willing at all? But if he puts it in another way, and says that, because he must necessarily so will, his will is not in his own power, he can be countered by the answer you gave me when I asked whether you could become happy against your will. You replied that you would be happy now if the matter were in your power, for you willed to be happy but could not achieve it. And I added that the truth cries out against you; for we cannot say we do not have the power unless we do not have what we will. If we do not have the will, we may think we will but in fact we do not. If we cannot will without willing, those who will have will, and all that is in our power we have by willing. Our will would not be will unless it were in our power. Because it is in our power, it is free. We have

nothing that is free which is not in our power, and if we have something it cannot be nothing. Hence it is not necessary to deny that God has foreknowledge of all things, while at the same time our wills are our own. God has foreknowledge of our will, so that of which he has foreknowledge must come to pass. In other words, we shall exercise our wills in the future because he has foreknowledge that we shall do so; and there can be no will or voluntary action unless it be in our power. Hence God has also foreknowledge of our power to will. My power is not taken from me by God's foreknowledge. Indeed I shall be more certainly in possession of my power because he whose foreknowledge is never mistaken, foreknows that I shall have the power. *Ev.*—Now I no longer deny that whatever God has foreknown must necessarily come to pass, nor that he has foreknowledge of our sins, but in such a way that our wills remain free and within our power.

iv, 9. *Aug.*—What further difficulty do you have? Perhaps you have forgotten what we established in our first disputation, and now wish to deny that we sin voluntarily and under no compulsion from anything superior, inferior or equal to us. *Ev.*—I do not venture to deny that at all. But I must confess I do not yet see how God's foreknowledge of our sins and our freedom of will in sinning can be other than mutually contradictory. We must confess that God is just and knows all things beforehand. But I should like to know with what justice he punishes sins which must necessarily be committed; or how they are not necessarily committed when he knows that they will be committed; or how the Creator is to escape having imputed to him anything that happens necessarily in his creature.

10. *Aug.*—Why do you think our free will is opposed to God's foreknowledge? Is it because it is foreknowledge simply, or because it is God's foreknowledge? *Ev.*—In the main because it is God's foreknowledge. *Aug.*—If you knew in advance that such and such a man would sin, there would be no necessity for him to sin. *Ev.*—Indeed there would, for I should have no real foreknowledge unless I knew for certain what was going to happen. *Aug.*—So it is foreknowledge generally and not God's foreknowledge specially that causes the events foreknown to happen by necessity? There would be no such thing as foreknowledge unless there was certain foreknowledge. *Ev.*—I agree. But why these questions? *Aug.*—Unless I am mistaken, you would not directly compel the man to sin, though you knew beforehand that he was going to sin. Nor does your prescience

in itself compel him to sin even though he was certainly going to sin, as we must assume if you have real prescience. So there is no contradiction here. Simply you know beforehand what another is going to do with his own will. Similarly God compels no man to sin, though he sees beforehand those who are going to sin by their own will.

11. Why then should he not justly punish sins which, though he had foreknowledge of them, he did not compel the sinner to commit? Just as you apply no compulsion to past events by having them in your memory, so God by his foreknowledge does not use compulsion in the case of future events. Just as you remember your past actions, though all that you remember were not actions of your own, so God has foreknowledge of all his own actions, but is not the agent of all that he foreknows. Of evil actions he is not the agent but the just punisher. From this you may understand with what justice God punishes sins, for he has no responsibility for the future actions of men though he knows them beforehand. If he ought not to award punishment to sinners because he knew beforehand that they would sin, he ought not to reward the righteous, because he knew equally that they would be righteous. Let us confess that it belongs to his foreknowledge to allow no future event to escape his knowledge, and that it belongs to his justice to see that no sin goes unpunished by his judgment. For sin is committed voluntarily and not by any compulsion from his foreknowledge.

v, 12. As to your third question how the Creator is to escape having imputed to him anything that happens necessarily in his creature, it is fitting for us to remember the rule of piety which says that we owe thanks to our Creator. That will provide us with the answer. His lavish goodness should be most justly praised even if he had made us with some lower rank in his creation. Though our soul be soiled with sins it is nevertheless loftier and better than if it were changed into visible light. And yet light is an eminent part of creation, as you can see by considering how much God is praised for it, even by souls wholly given over to bodily sense. Wherefore, though sinful souls are censured, do not let that provoke you to say in your heart that it would have been better if they did not exist. They are censured because they are compared with what they might have been if they had not willed to sin. God, their Maker, is to be gloriously praised for the human faculties with which he has endowed them, not only because he justly subjects them to his order when they sin, but also because he made them such that, even when soiled with sin, they are not surpassed in dignity by corporeal light, for which also God is rightly praised.

13. Possibly you would not go so far as to say that it would have been better if sinful souls did not exist, but take care also not to say that they should have been other than they are. Whatever better argument true reason may suggest to you, know at least that God made them, and that he is author of all good things. For it is not true reason but envious weakness that bids you think that anything ought to have been made better than it is, and that nothing inferior should have been made at all. That is as if you looked at the heavens and concluded that the earth ought not to have been made. That is all wrong. You would be quite right to find fault if you saw that the earth had been made, and no heavens, for then you might say the earth ought to have been made according to your ideal conception of the heavens. But now you see that your ideal earth has been made, only it is called not earth but heaven. I believe that since you have not been defrauded of the better creation you ought not to grudge that there is an inferior creation which we call the earth. In the earth again there is such a variety among its parts that you can think of nothing of an earthly nature which God has not made somewhere in the totality of his work. For the earth contains land of all kinds, passing by gradual stages from the most fruitful and pleasant to the most deceitful and infertile tracts, so that you can only find fault with one kind of land by comparing it with a better kind. So you ascend through all the grades of land with their varying praiseworthy qualities, and when you find the very best land you are glad that there are the other kinds as well. And yet what a difference there is between earth, in all its variety, and heaven! Water and air are interposed. Of these four elements various other forms and species of things are made, innumerable to us but all numbered by God. There may be things in the natural realm which you would never have thought of yourself, but the wholly and purely rational cannot but be. You can think of nothing better in the creation which the Creator did not think of. When the human soul says: "This is better than that," and if it says so truly, it will say so because of its relation to the divine reasons on which it depends. If it understands what it says, it does so likewise because of its relation to these reasons. Let it therefore believe that God has made what true reason knows he must have made, even if it is not evident in created things. If the heavens were invisible, but true reason led to the conclusion

that such a thing must have been created, we ought to believe that it has been created though it do not appear to the eye. For thought would have no idea that it ought to have been created if it did not have some relation to the reasons through which all things were created. What does not exist can no more be thought than have true existence.

14. Many err because, beholding the better things with their minds, they look for them also with their eyes in the wrong places. That would be as if someone, who by reason understood perfect rotundity, should be annoyed that he did not observe it in a nut, assuming that he never saw any other round object besides that fruit. So when some people see with true reason that there are better creatures who, though they have free will, have ever adhered to God and have never sinned, they look at the sins of men and lament not that they may cease from sin but simply that men have been created at all. They say: "He did not create us such that we should will ever to enjoy his unchangeable truth and never to sin." Do not let them cry out or be annoyed. He did not compel them to sin by the mere fact that he created them and gave them power to choose good or evil as they would. He made them so far like those angels who never sinned and never will sin. If you delight in a creature which by voluntary perseverance never sins, there is no doubt you rightly prefer it to a sinful creature. Just as you give it the preference in your thought, so God gives it the preference in his universal order. You may believe that there are such creatures in the loftier regions of the heavens. For if God showed his goodness in creating creatures whom he knew beforehand would sin, he would show his goodness no less in creating creatures whom he knew beforehand would never sin.

15. Those sublime creatures have their happiness perpetually in the eternal enjoyment of their Creator; and their happiness they merit by their perpetual will to hold fast to righteousness. Below them sinful creatures have their proper order. By their sins they have lost happiness, but they have not lost the capacity to recover it. Herein they are superior to those creatures whose will is to remain perpetually in sin. Between these two extremes —those who continue in the will to righteousness and those who continue in the will to sin—there is this middle class who by the humility of repentance recover their exalted rank. But God did not withhold the lavishness of his bounty even from his creatures who he knew beforehand would not only sin but would continue in the will to sin; for he showed it in creating them. An

errant horse is better than a stone that cannot err because it has neither motion nor feeling of its own. So a creature which sins by its own free will is more excellent than one which cannot sin because it has no free will. I would praise wine that was good of its kind, and would censure the man who drank it to excess. And yet I would hold the man whom I had censured, even while he was drunk, to be superior to the wine which made him drunk, even though I had praised it. So the corporeal creature is rightly to be praised in its own order, though those are to be censured who use it to excess and are thereby turned away from perception of the truth. And those perverse people, drunkards or the like, are to be preferred to the thing, laudible in its own order, greediness for which made them vain; not indeed because of their vices but because of the dignity of their nature which still remains.

16. Soul is universally superior to body. No soul can fall so far in sinfulness as to be changed into body. Its quality as soul cannot be taken from it, and it cannot in any way lose that which makes it superior to body. Now among corporeal objects light holds the first place. Consequently the worst soul is superior to the first of corporeal things. It is of course possible that some body may be preferable to the body in which a soul resides, but it cannot be preferred to the soul itself. Why, then, should not God be praised with all possible praise, who made souls that were to abide in the laws of righteousness, even if he also made other souls which he knew beforehand would sin or even persevere in sin? For even these are better than things that cannot sin because they have not reason or free choice of will. They are even better than the most splendid brilliance of bodies of any kind, though some people [the Manichees], greatly erring, venerate light as if it were the substance of God most high. In the order of corporeal creatures, from the sidereal choir down to the number of our hairs, the beauty of good things is so perfectly graded that it is a sign of lack of understanding to ask: "What is this?" or "To what purpose is that?" All things are created each in its own order. How much more does it show lack of understanding to ask such questions about any soul whatever? No matter how great a diminution of its glory it may suffer or what defects it may exhibit, nevertheless it will always and without any doubt surpass in dignity every kind of body.

17. Reason has a different standard of judgment from that of utility. Reason judges by the light of truth, and correctly subordinates lesser things to those that are greater. Utility, guided

by experience of convenience, often attributes a higher value to things which reason convinces us are of lesser rank. Reason sets a vast difference in value between celestial and terrestrial bodies, but what carnal man would not prefer that several stars should be wanting in the heavens, than that one shrub should be lacking in his field or one cow from his herd? Older men pay no attention to, or at least are prepared patiently to correct, the judgments of children, who prefer the death of a man (except one of those bound to them by the ties of happy affection), to the death of a favourite sparrow, especially if the man was an object of terror to them, and the sparrow was tuneful and beautiful. So, if there are people, unskilled in judging the values of things, who praise God for his lesser creatures, finding them more easily appreciated by their carnal senses, and do not praise him for his better and superior creatures, or praise him less than they ought, or try to find fault with his creatures and to point out how they might have been better, or even do not believe that he created them, those who have advanced some way towards wisdom either entirely scorn such judgments or hear them with good-natured patience if they cannot correct them or until they are corrected.

vi, 18. Such being the case, it is far from the truth that the sins of the creature must be attributed to the Creator, even though those things must necessarily happen which he has foreknown. So much so that when you say you can find no reason why whatever necessarily happens in the creature should not be attributed to him, I on the contrary find no way, and I assert that none exists or can be found, of attributing to him what is done, necessarily no doubt, but also by the will of the sinner. If anyone says, I should prefer not to exist than to exist in unhappiness, I shall reply: That is a lie; for you are miserable now, and yet you do not wish to die, simply because you wish to exist. You don't want to be miserable but you want to continue in life all the same. Give thanks, therefore, because you exist, as you wish to do, so that the misery you do not wish may be taken from you. You exist as you wish to do, but you are unhappy against your will. If you are ungrateful for your existence you are rightly compelled to be unhappy, which you do not wish. I praise the goodness of the Creator because, even when you are ungrateful, you have what you wish. And I praise the justice of the Orderer of things because for your ingratitude you suffer what you do not wish.

19. If he says: I don't want to die, not because I prefer to live

in misery rather than not to live at all, but lest I should be still more miserable after death, my reply will be: You will not be miserable if that would be unjust. But if it would be just, let us praise him by whose laws you are dealt with justly. If he says: How shall I know that I shall not be miserable unless misery be my just reward? I shall reply: If you are in your own power either you will not be miserable, or you will be justly miserable because you rule yourself unjustly. If you wish to rule yourself justly and cannot, you will not be in your own power. You will then be in the power of no one or in the power of another. If you are in no one's power you will act willingly or unwillingly. It cannot be unwillingly, unless some superior force overpowers you. But he who is in the power of no one cannot be overpowered by any force; if willingly, you are in no one's power, and you must be in your own power, and either you will be miserable by ruling yourself unjustly, or, seeing you can be what you wish, you have cause to give thanks for the goodness of your Creator. If you are not in your own power, then someone must have you in his power who is either more powerful or less powerful than yourself. If he is less powerful the fault is your own and the misery just. But if someone, more powerful than you are, hold you in his power you will not rightly think so rightful an order to be unjust. It is true, therefore, that you will not be miserable if it is unjust, and if it is just, let us praise him whose laws bring it to pass.

vii, 20. If my opponent says: I prefer to be miserable rather than not to be at all, because I already exist. If I could have been consulted before I began to be, I should have chosen not to be rather than to be miserable. The fact that, being miserable, I fear to become non-existent is part of my misery. I ought to wish not to be rather than to be miserable, but I do not. I confess that I do now actually prefer to be miserable than not to be; but the folly of this preference is in proportion to my misery. The more clearly I see how true it is that I should not have this preference, the greater is my misery. My reply will be this: Take all the greater care not to err when you think you see the truth. If you were happy you would prefer to be rather than not to be. Now when you are miserable you nevertheless prefer a miserable existence to non-existence, though you do not wish to be miserable. Consider, then, how great a boon existence is, seeing that both the happy and the miserable desire it. If you consider this carefully you will see that your misery is in proportion to your failure to draw near to that which supremely exists. You will see that the opinion that non-existence is better than miserable existence depends on the extent to which you ignore what supremely exists; and that you wish to be because you derive your origin from him who supremely is.

21. If, therefore, you wish to escape misery, love the very desire you have to exist. For if you wish more and more to exist, you will draw near to him who exists supremely. And give thanks now that you exist. You may be inferior to the blessed, but you are superior to things which have not even the will to beatitude, though many of these things are praised by miserable men. All things are to be praised for the reason that they exist; for what exists is for that reason alone good. The more fully you love to have being the more fully will you desire eternal life, and choose to be formed so that your affections will not be set on temporal things. Emotions kindled by love for temporal things are unjust and uncontrolled. And temporal things, before they come to be, are not; while they are in existence, they are fleeting; and when gone, will not be. When they come into being in the future, they are not yet. When they are past, they already are not. How can things be possessed abidingly, if the beginning of their existence is a step towards their end? He who loves existence approves them so far as they have existence, but loves what has eternal existence. If, loving temporal things, he was weak and variable, loving eternal things he will be made strong. If he was distracted by love of transient things, by love of that which abides he will be made stable. He will remain, and possess being, which he wished, inasmuch as he feared non-existence. He could not stand fast when he was snared by love of fleeting things. Do not therefore let it displease you, rather let it give you the greatest pleasure, that you prefer even miserable existence to non-existence, even if thereby you hope to escape misery. If you begin by wishing to exist, and add a desire for fuller and fuller existence, you rise in the scale, and are furnished for life that supremely is. So also you will keep yourself from every fall whereby lowest existence passes into non-existence and undermines the strength of him who loves it. Hence he who prefers non-existence to miserable existence, cannot attain non-existence, and therefore must remain miserable. He who loves existence more than he hates misery can, by seeking an ever fuller existence, exclude the misery he hates. When he has attained perfect existence after his kind, he will not be miserable.

viii, 22. See how absurd and stupid it is to say: I should

prefer non-existence to miserable existence. He who says, I prefer this to that, chooses something. Non-existence is not something; it is nothing. There can be no real choice when what you choose is nothing. You say you want to be, though you are miserable, but ought not to do so. What ought you to want? Not to be, you say. If you ought so to want, not-being must be better than being. But not-being cannot be better than being. Therefore you ought not to wish it. The common sense which keeps you from really wishing non-existence is more truthful than the opinion that bids you affirm that you ought to wish it. Every man should seek the right object of choice, for when he obtains it he must necessarily become better. But he cannot become better if he ceases to exist. No one therefore can rightly choose non-existence. We ought not to be influenced by the views of those who have committed suicide because misery pressed sore upon them. Either they fled for refuge to a place which they thought would be better for them—in which case there is nothing contrary to our argument, whether they were right or wrong in their thinking. Or they believed that they would not exist at all; in this case the false choice of those who choose nothing will affect us much less. How shall I follow one who when asked what his choice is answers, "Nothing"? Whoever chooses non-existence is immediately convicted of choosing nothing, whether he is willing to admit it or not.

23. I shall tell you my opinion, if I can, about this whole matter. It seems to me that no one, when he commits suicide or attempts somehow to put himself to death, really feels that he will not exist after he is dead, though he may have some kind of opinion to that effect. Opinion has to do with truth or error in the mind of the thinker or believer; but feeling draws its force from custom or nature. That we can hold an opinion and yet feel quite differently about a matter is easily known from the fact that often we believe that something should be done, but find pleasure in doing something else. Sometimes feeling is more truthful than opinion, if the latter is in error, and the former is dictated by nature, for example when a sick man finds both pleasure and advantage in drinking cold water, though he wrongly believes that it will hurt him if he drink it. Sometimes opinion is more truthful than feeling, as when a man believes his physician's word that cold water will harm him (assuming it will be hurtful) and nevertheless finds pleasure in drinking it. Sometimes both are equally truthful, as when that which is advantageous is not only believed to be so, but is also felt to be

pleasurable. Sometimes both are wrong, as when that which is hurtful is believed to be advantageous and also gives pleasure. Right opinion is wont to correct wrong custom, and wrong opinion to pervert nature even when it is right. Such is the power of reason when it leads and rules. When a man who believes that he will not exist after death is driven by intolerable evils to desire death with all his heart, and snatches at death, his opinion that he will be rid of all being is false, but so far as feeling is concerned he has merely a natural desire for rest. But what is at rest is not nothing. Indeed it has fuller being than what is restless. Restlessness sets the emotions one against the other, so that they destroy one another. But rest has a certain constancy, highly suggestive of what we mean when we say of a thing simply that it exists. The whole object of wanting to die is not non-existence but rest. So while such a man erroneously believes that he will no longer exist, his nature longs to be at rest, that is, to have fuller being. So, just as no one can find pleasure in non-existence, no one ought to be ungrateful to the goodness of his Creator for the fact that he has existence.

ix, 24. If it is said: It would not have been difficult or laborious for Almighty God to have seen to it that all his creatures should have observed their proper order so that none of them should have come to misery. If he is omnipotent that would not have been beyond his power; and if he is good he would not have grudged it; this is my answer. The order of creatures proceeds from top to bottom by just grades, so that it is the remark of envy to say: That creatures should not exist, and equally so to say: *That* one should be different. It is wrong to wish that anything should be like another thing higher in the scale, for it has its being, perfect in its degree, and nothing ought to be added to it. He who says that a thing ought to be different from what it is, either wants to add something to a higher creature already perfect, in which case he lacks moderation and justice; or he wants to destroy the lower creature, and is thereby wicked and grudging. Whoever says that any creature ought not to be is no less wicked and grudging, for he wants an inferior creature not to exist, which he really ought to praise. For example the moon is certainly far inferior to the sun in the brightness of its light, but in its own way it is beautiful, adorns earthly darkness, and is suited to nocturnal uses. For all these things he should admit that it is worthy of all praise in its own order. If he denies that, he is foolish and contentious. Anyone who said that there should be no light would feel that he deserved to be laughed at.

How then will he dare to say there should not be a moon? If instead of saying that the moon should not exist he said that the moon ought to be like the sun, what he is really saying without knowing it is, not that there should be no moon, but that there should be two suns. In this there is a double error. He wants to add something to the perfection of the universe, seeing he desires another sun. But he also wants to take something from that perfection, seeing he wants to do away with the moon.

25. Perhaps he will reply that he is not complaining about the moon, because though its light is less, it is not unhappy; his trouble does not concern the lack of lustre in souls but their misery. Let him carefully consider that so far as concerns the brightness of the moon and the sun there is no question of happiness or unhappiness. Though these are celestial bodies, they are none the less bodies so far as their light is concerned. For it is perceived by the corporeal eyes. Corporeal things in themselves, as such, cannot be happy or unhappy, although they can be the bodies of happy or unhappy creatures. But the analogy suggested from the celestial luminaries teaches us this lesson. When you contemplate the differences between bodies and observe that some are brighter than others, it is wrong to ask that the dimmer ones should be done away or made equal to the brighter ones. All must be contemplated in the light of the perfection of the universe; and you will see that all differences in brightness contribute to the perfection of the whole. You will not be able to imagine a perfect universe unless it contains some greater things and some smaller in perfect relation one to the other. Similarly you must consider the differences between souls. In them also you will discover that the misery you lament has this advantage. The fact that there are souls which ought to be miserable because they willed to be sinful contributes to the perfection of the universe. So far is it from being the case that God ought not to have made such souls, that he ought to be praised for having made other creatures far inferior to miserable souls.

26. But one who does not quite understand what has been said may have this to urge against our argument: If our being miserable completes the perfection of the universe, it will lose something of its perfection if we should become eternally happy. If the soul does not come to misery save by sinning, our sins also are necessary to the perfection of the universe which God has made. How then does he justly punish sins without which his creation could be neither complete nor perfect? The answer

is: Neither the sins nor the misery are necessary to the perfection of the universe, but souls as such are necessary which have power to sin if they so will, and become miserable if they sin. If misery persisted after their sins had been abolished, or if there were misery before there were sins, then it might be right to say that the order and government of the universe were at fault. Again, if there were sins and no consequent misery, that order is equally dishonoured by lack of equity. But since there is happiness for those who do not sin, the universe is perfect; and it is no less perfect because there is misery for sinners. Because there are souls whose sins are followed by misery and whose righteous conduct is followed by happiness—because it contains all kinds of natures—the universe is always complete and perfect. Sin and its punishment are not natural objects but states of natural objects, the one voluntary, the other penal. The voluntary state of being sinful is dishonourable. Hence the penal state is imposed to bring it into order, and is therefore in itself not dishonourable. Indeed it compels the dishonourable state to become harmonized with the honour of the universe, so that the penalty of sin corrects the dishonour of sin.

27. Hence it comes that the sinful creature, though superior, is punished through the instrumentality of inferior creatures. These latter are inferior but in such a way that they can be honoured by dishonourable souls, and so be brought into harmony with the honour of the universe. There is nothing greater in a house than a man, and nothing lower and less honourable than a drain. Yet a slave who is found so sinful as to be held worthy of cleaning out a drain, nevertheless, dishonourable though he may be, does honour to the drain. The slave's dishonour and the cleansed drain together form one whole. Both together are adapted to the proper management of the house, and both contribute honourably and in perfect order to the good of the whole house. If the slave had not sinned by his own will the household management would have provided some other way to accomplish the necessary work of cleansing. What holds a lower place in the scale of being than the earthly body? But even a sinful soul can adorn corruptible flesh, so as to provide it with a comely appearance and vital motion. Such a soul, because of its sin, does not harmonize with a celestial habitation, but it harmonizes with a terrestrial habitation, because of its punishment. So, whatever a soul may choose, ever beautiful and well-ordered in all its parts is the universe whose Maker and Governor is God. Good souls which inhabit earthly bodies adorn

them by making a good use of them, and not by being associated with them through any misery of their own, for they have none. But if sinful souls were allowed to inhabit celestial regions, it would be wrong, for they are not suited to things of which they cannot make a good use, and on which they can confer no honour.

28. Although this earthly globe must be accounted among corruptible things, yet it preserves, so far as it can, the image of higher things, and ceases not to show us examples and traces of higher things. If we see some good and great man burned by fire, so far as his body is concerned, in obedience to the command of duty, we do not call that the penalty of sin, but the evidence of courage and endurance. Though the basest corruption consumes his bodily members, we love him more for it than we should if he suffered nothing of that kind. We marvel that his mind did not share the mutability of his body. If we see the members of a cruel brigand consumed by a like punishment, we approve the legal order. Both throw a certain glory upon their torments, but the one by the merit of his virtue, the other by the demerit of his sin. But suppose after or even before the burning we saw the good man changed in a manner agreeable to the celestial habitation and carried up to the stars, we should be glad. But who would not be offended if we saw the criminal brigand, either before or after his punishment but continuing to serve the cause of willing crime, carried to the eternal seat of glory in heaven? So both of them can adorn inferior creatures, but only one of them can adorn superior creatures. So are we bidden to take note that the first man adorned the mortality of our flesh inasmuch as his punishment befitted his sin; and that our Lord Jesus did so likewise, inasmuch as his mercy set us free from sin. The just man, abiding in justice, could have a mortal body. But the wicked man, while he continues in iniquity, cannot in the same way reach the immortality of the saints, that is, sublime and angelic immortality. I do not mean the immortality of those angels of whom the apostle wrote: "Know ye not that we shall judge angels" (I Cor. 6:3). But of those of whom the Lord spoke: "They shall be equal to the angels of God" (Luke 20:36). Those who desire equality with angels for their own vain glory do not really want to be themselves equal with the angels but to have the angels equal with them. If they persist in so willing, they will be made equal in punishment with the apostate angels who loved their own power rather than the power of Almighty

God. To such, placed upon his left hand because they did not seek God by way of the door of humility which the Lord Jesus Christ showed us in his own Person, and because they lived proudly and without mercy, he will say: "Depart into eternal fire prepared for the devil and his angels" (Matt. 25:41).

x, 29. There are two sources of sin, a man's own spontaneous thought, and the persuasion of a neighbour. That is what the prophet meant when he said: "Cleanse me from my secret sins, O Lord, and keep thy servant from the sins of others" (Ps. 19:12–13). Both, however, are voluntary. The man who sins by his own thought does not sin unwillingly, and if he consents to one who persuades him to evil, he does not consent without his own will. It is more serious to sin by one's own will with none persuading, and in addition by envy and guile to persuade another to sin, than to be brought to sin by the persuasion of another. But in both kinds of sin the justice of the Lord in punishing is preserved. In weighing the case equitably it was found just not to keep man from falling into the power even of the devil, who by evil persuasion had subjected man to himself. It would have been inequitable that he should not have had dominion over his captive. But it cannot be that the justice of God, most high and most true, which extends everywhere, should take no part in preserving order even after the downfall of sinners. Because man had sinned less than the devil, he was aided in the recovery of salvation by the very fact that he had been given over until death to the prince of this world, that is, the lowest and mortal part of the universe, to the prince of all sin and the lord of death. Timid, as a result of his consciousness of his mortality, fearing sufferings and death from the vilest, most abject, even the most minute of beasts, and uncertain of the future, man accustomed himself to restrain unlawful pleasures, and especially to curb pride which had persuaded him to his fall, a vice which alone refuses the medicine of mercy. Who needs mercy more than the miserable man; and who is less worthy of it than he who is at once both proud and miserable?

30. Hence it happened that the Word of God, by whom all things were made and whom all the happy angels enjoy, stretched forth his clemency to our misery. "The Word became flesh and dwelt among us." So man could eat the bread of angels. But man was not yet made equal to the angels, even if the Bread of angels did think fit to make himself the equal of men. But by coming down to us he did not abandon the angels. Remaining at the same time one with them and one with us, he nourishes

them inwardly by his divinity, and outwardly by his humanity he admonishes us and fits us by faith to be nourished sacramentally like the angels. The rational creature feeds upon the Word as its own best food. But the human soul is rational. It was held in penalty for its sin in mortal bonds, and was so brought low that by surmising from visible things it might strive to understand invisible things. The Food of the rational creature became visible, not by changing his own nature but by adapting it to ours, in order that he might recall those who follow visible things to embrace him who is invisible. So the soul, which in its inward pride had forsaken him, finds him again in humble guise in the outward world. By imitating his visible humility it will return to its invisible position of superiority.

31. The Word of God, God's only Son, assuming human nature, brought the devil, whom he has always had and will have under his own laws, under subjection to man. He extorted nothing from him by violence, but overcame him by the law of justice. For the devil, having deceived the woman, and by her having caused her husband to fall, claimed the entire offspring of the first man as subject to the law of death inasmuch as it was sinful. This he did with a malicious desire to do harm, but at the same time with absolute right, so long as his power prevailed, that is, until he slew the Just Man, in whom he could point out nothing worthy of death. Not only was he slain without fault, but he was also born without lust. And to lust, the devil had subjugated his captives, so that he might keep possession of all born of them, as fruits of his own tree, through a wicked desire to hold them, but also by a just right of possession. Most justly, therefore, is the devil compelled to give up those who believe in him whom he unjustly slew. In that they suffer temporal death, they pay what they owe. In that they live eternally, they live in him who paid on their behalf what he did not owe. But those whom the devil has persuaded to persist in unbelief, he is justly allowed to keep as his companions in eternal damnation. So man was not snatched from the devil by force, seeing that the devil had taken him captive not by force but by persuasion. And man, who was justly brought low so as to serve him to whose evil persuasion he had consented, was justly set free by him to whose good persuasion he had consented. All this is in accordance with justice because man sinned less in consenting than the devil sinned by persuading him to sin.

xi, 32. God, therefore, made all natures, not only those

which were to abide in virtue and justice, but also those that were to sin. He did not make them in order that they might sin, but that whether they willed to sin or not to sin they might be ornaments of his universe. If there were no souls occupying the highest rank in the universe, such as would have power to shake and weaken the universe if they should choose to fall into sin, that would be a great defect in creation. That would be lacking which secures the stability and unity of the universe. Such are the good and holy and sublime souls of the powers celestial and super-celestial, over whom God alone rules, and to whom the whole world is subject. Without their just and perfect offices there can be no universe. Again if there were no souls who, whether by sinning or not sinning, make no difference to the order of the universe, again there would be a grave defect. These are rational souls like in nature to those that are better but unlike in office. Besides these, there are many inferior but praiseworthy degrees of creatures all made by God most high.

33. This is the nature of those who hold the highest rank. The order of the universe would suffer loss if they did not exist and also if they sinned. In the case of those who hold a lower rank the loss would be caused by their non-existence, not by their sinning. To the former is given the potency to keep all things in their proper order, and without that the order of things cannot continue. But they do not continue in the good will because they received that office. Rather they received the office because he who gave it foresaw that they would so continue. Nor do they keep all things in the proper order by their own majesty, but because they cleave to the majesty and devotedly obey the commands of him by whom, through whom and in whom all things are made. To the latter also, if they do not sin, is given the potent office of keeping things in order, but it is not given to them as their own. They must fulfil it in alliance with the higher beings, because God knows beforehand that they will sin. Spiritual natures can be joined together without being increased in mass, and separated without being decreased. The higher beings do not have their action made any easier by the assistance of the lower beings, nor does their action become more difficult if the lower beings desert their duty by sinning. For they are not joined together by space or bodily mass but by similarity of affection. And spiritual creatures can be separated by lack of likeness one to another though each possesses its own body.

34. When sin has been committed the soul, which has its

abode by God's order in an inferior and a mortal body, rules its own body not according to its own whim, but as the laws of the universe allow. But such a soul is not inferior to a celestial body, though earthly bodies are inferior to celestial bodies. The ragged garment of a condemned slave is much inferior to the garment of a slave who has deserved well and is held in high honour by his master. But the slave is better than any garment however precious, because he is a man. The soul of higher nature inhabiting a celestial body and enjoying angelic power adheres to God and adorns and rules even an earthly body according to the commands of him whose nod it ineffably observes. But the soul that is burdened with mortal members has difficulty in ruling the body that oppresses it, and yet it adorns it as far as it is able. Other things by which it is surrounded it can affect, as it has the power, but its power is vastly weaker.

xii, 35. The conclusion is that even the lowest corporeal creature would not have lacked a fitting ornament, even if no soul had willed to sin. That which can rule the whole also rules the part; but that which has less power certainly cannot exercise more abundant power. The perfect physician can efficaciously cure the scab. But one who can give useful advice in a case of the scab cannot forthwith heal every disease of mankind. If there is any certain reason why there ought to have been creatures which have never sinned nor ever will, it will also make clear that they refrained from sin by their own free will. They were not compelled not to sin. They remained sinless by choice. But even if they had sinned (but that was impossible because God knew beforehand that they would not) . . . even if they had sinned, God's ineffable power would have been sufficient to rule the universe, to render to all what was right and fitting, and to permit nothing base or dishonourable throughout his whole dominion. Even if all the powers he created to help him failed him, even if angelic nature had sinned and rebelled against his commandments, he would still by his own majesty rule all things honourably and perfectly. He would not grudge existence to spiritual creatures, who has made corporeal creatures though they are far inferior even to sinful spiritual creatures. So great is his goodness that no one can reasonably view the heaven and the earth, and all visible natures in their kinds, measured, formed, ordered, and believe that there is any other creator of all these things but God, or refuse to confess that he is to be ineffably praised. There is no better way of ordering the universe than that angelic nature should have pre-eminence by reason of the excellence of its nature and the goodness of its will. But even if all the angels had sinned the Creator of angels would not have lacked resources for the government of his dominion. No weariness would have prevented his goodness, and no difficulty his omnipotence, from creating others to set in the places of those who by sinning abandoned them. And no multitude of spiritual creatures condemned for their demerits could throw into confusion an order which has a proper and suitable place for as many as are damned. In whatever direction we turn our attention we find that God is to be ineffably praised who is the best Creator of all natures, and their most just Ruler.

xiii, 36. In conclusion, let us leave the contemplation of the beauty of things to those who have the divine gift of seeing it. Do not let us try with words to induce those who have not the power to behold ineffable things. And yet because there are loquacious, weak or guileful men, let us briefly summarize our answer to this great problem. Any nature that can become less good, must be good. A nature becomes less good when it is corrupted. Either corruption does it no hurt and it is not corrupted; or, if it is corrupted, corruption hurts it. If it hurts it, it takes away some of its good and makes it less good. If it entirely deprives it of good, what remains will not be able to be corrupted, for there will be no good left which corruption can take away so as to do hurt. Nothing is corrupted if corruption can do it no hurt. A nature which is not corrupted is incorruptible. So there will be a nature which by corruption is rendered incorruptible; which is utterly absurd. Therefore, it is true to say that any nature, so far as it is such, is good. If it is incorruptible it is better than what is corruptible. But if it is corruptible it is doubtless good since it becomes less good as the process of corruption goes on. Every nature is corruptible or incorruptible. Therefore every nature is good. And by "a nature" I mean what is also usually called a substance. Every substance is either God or comes from God, because every good thing is either God or from God.

37. These principles being established at the beginning of our discourse, listen to what I am going to say. Every rational nature endowed with free will is indubitably to be praised if it abide in the enjoyment of the chief and changeless good. Everyone that seeks so to abide is also to be praised. But every one that does not abide in the chief good and does not will so to act that it may abide in it, is so far and on that account to be

blamed. If a created rational nature is to be praised, no one can doubt that its creator is also to be praised. If it is to be blamed, no doubt even by blaming it its creator is praised. If we blame it because it will not enjoy the highest and unchanging good, that is, its creator, clearly we are praising him. How great is that chief good! And how ineffably by every tongue and every thought is God the Creator of all things to be honoured and praised! For we can be neither praised nor blamed without praise being given to him. The only reason for blaming us for not abiding in him is that to abide in him is our first and greatest and highest good. How so, if it be not that he is ineffably good? And how can he be blamed for our sins, seeing there can be no blame for our sins which does not imply his praise?

38. In things which are blamed nothing is blamed but their fault. And nothing has a fault to be blamed if it has not a nature to be praised. Either what you blame is natural and not a fault, and you are to be taught to correct your fault-finding. Or, if it is really a fault and rightly to be blamed, it must be contrary to nature. Every fault, by the very fact that it is a fault, is contrary to nature. It is no fault if it does no damage to nature. If it does damage, it is for that reason alone a fault, and, therefore, it is a fault because it is contrary to nature. If a nature is corrupted by another's fault and not by its own, it is unjust to blame it, and we must inquire whether the other nature is not corrupted by its own fault whereby it has the power to corrupt another nature. What is it to be vitiated, if not to be corrupted by vice or fault? A nature which is not vitiated has no fault. But it has a fault if another nature can be vitiated by it. Hence anything that has the power to corrupt another thing with its own fault is itself vitiated to begin with and corrupts with its own fault. Hence we conclude that all fault or vice is contrary to nature, contrary also to the nature of the thing to which the fault originally belongs. Nothing is blamed in anything except vice or fault, and vice is vice precisely because it is contrary to the nature of the thing in which it is found. Therefore a fault is not rightly blamed without at the same time praising the nature in which the fault is found. You have no right to be displeased with a fault except in so far as it vitiates a nature that pleases you.

xiv, 39. Now we must see whether a nature can be truly said to be corrupted by another's vice without any vice of its own. If one thing approaches another in order to corrupt it with its own vice, it cannot do so unless it finds something there which is capable of being corrupted. If it finds that, it can then bring about the corruption by means of its own vice. The stronger cannot be corrupted by the weaker unless it is willing to be corrupted. If it is willing, the corruption starts with its own vice and not with the vice of the other. Similarly an equal cannot be corrupted by its equal unless it is willing. A vitiated nature, attacking one that is free from vice, is not its equal, but is weaker by reason of its own vice. If the stronger corrupts the weaker, then either it is by the vice of both of them, there being base desire in both; or it is by the vice of the stronger, if its nature is so outstanding that even when vitiated it excels that of the weaker which it corrupts. How could one rightly blame the fruits of the earth because men do not make a good use of them, but, being themselves corrupt by their own fault, corrupt these fruits by abusing them in the interests of luxury? For it would be madness to doubt that man's nature, even when vitiated, is more powerful and more excellent than that of any of the fruits of the earth, even if they are without fault.

40. It may happen that a more powerful nature corrupts a less powerful one with no fault on either side, if by fault we mean that which is worthy of blame. Who would venture to blame a frugal man who sought from the fruits of the earth no more than his natural nourishment? Or who would blame these fruits for being corrupted through use as food? Correct usage does not speak of that as corruption, for the accepted meaning of corruption, generally speaking, makes it a synonym for vice. It is easy to find examples of a stronger nature corrupting a weaker one even without using it to supply its own needs. In the order of justice, for example, guilt is punished. This is the rule to which the apostle refers when he says: "If anyone corrupts the Temple of God, him will God corrupt" (I Cor. 3:17). Or, again, in the order of mutable things, one thing gives place to another according to the most fitting laws imposed upon the universe, regulating the strength of every part. If the brightness of the sun destroys anyone's eyes because they are too weak to endure the light, the sun cannot be thought to do so in order to supply any need of its own; nor does it do so through any fault of its own. Nor are the eyes to be blamed, for they obeyed their possessor when they were opened in face of the light, or they were destroyed through being too weak to bear the light. Of all kinds of corruption, that only is rightly to be blamed which is vicious. Other kinds are not even to be called by that name, or, at any rate, cannot be properly blamed

since they are not vicious. Blame is applicable, that is, right and fitting, in the case of vice alone. Hence it is supposed to derive its name (*vituperatio*) from *vitium*.

41. Now, as I said, vice is evil for no other reason than that it is hostile to the nature of the thing in which it exists as a fault. Hence clearly the thing itself is by nature praiseworthy, though the fault in it is blameworthy. So we must confess that all vituperation of vices is actually praise of the natures whose vices are blamed. Because vice is the enemy of nature, the evil of a vice is greater in proportion to the damage done to the integrity of the nature. When you blame a vice you thereby praise the thing which you would like to see undamaged. You praise the nature of the thing regarded in its integrity. Nature is perfect. Not only is it free from blame but it deserves praise in its own order. If you see anything lacking in the perfection of nature you call it a vice or fault. By the very fact that you blame its imperfection you bear witness that you would be pleased with it if only it were perfect.

xv, 42. If blame of vices is praise of the honour and dignity of the natures of which these are vices, how much more is God to be praised even though there be these vices, for he is the Maker of all natures. From him they derive their being as natures, and they are vicious in so far as they depart from his purpose in creating them. They are rightly blamed in so far as he who blames them sees the purpose in creating them and blames only that which is no longer to be seen in them. The Purpose with which they were all created, that is, the supreme and unchangeable Wisdom of God, truly and supremely is what he is. See, then, whither things tend which depart from him. But that defection would not be blameworthy if it were not voluntary. Would you be right in blaming anything which is as it ought to be? I should think not. It is to be blamed for not being as it ought. No one owes what he has not received. To whom is a debt owed, if not to him from whom something has been received? Things returned by bequest are returned to him who made the bequest. What is paid back to the legal successors of a creditor is really paid back to the original creditor in the persons of his legal successors; otherwise there would be no paying back, but a simple surrender of goods or a passing on of an inheritance, or whatever other name can be given to such a procedure. Wherefore all temporal things are so placed in this temporal order that they must come to an end if the future is to succeed to the past, allowing the whole beauty of things in their temporal sequence to be displayed. It would be most absurd to say that they should not come to an end. What they have received they traffic with and pay back to him to whom they owe their being in so far as it is being. Whoever laments that temporal things should come to an end should observe his own speaking. Take for example his lamentation, which no doubt he thinks is just and proceeds from prudence. So far as the sounds are concerned which he utters in making it, one has to come to an end and be followed by another so that the whole speech may be made. If anyone loved one particular sound and did not want it to cease and give place to the others, he would be adjudged astonishingly mad.

43. In things which come to an end because it is not given them to last any longer, so that all things may happen in their due times, no one has the right to find fault with their coming to an end. No one can say: It ought to abide, for it cannot pass its appointed bounds. In rational creatures, whether they sin or do not sin, the beauty of the universe reaches its appropriate limit. In them, either there are no sins, which is absurd (for he sins who condemns as sins what are not sins); or sins are not to be blamed, which is no less absurd, for wrong actions will begin to be praised and the whole purpose of the human mind will be thrown into confusion and human life will be subverted, or right action be blamed and execrable madness will arise, or, to use a milder expression, a miserable error. If right reason compels us, as it does, to blame sins and to blame them because they ought not to be what they are, ask yourself what debt sinful nature owes, and the answer will be: Right action. Ask yourself to whom it owes the debt, and the answer will be: God. From God it received the power to act rightly when it would. From him also it received the alternatives, misery if it acts unrighteously, happiness if it acts righteously.

44. No man can overcome the laws of the omnipotent Creator. Therefore it is not permitted to the soul to escape payment of its debt. It pays it by making a good use of what it has received, or by losing what it was unwilling to make a good use of. If it does not pay its debt by doing what it ought, it will pay it by suffering misery. In either case the word obligation is in order, so we could thus amplify what we said. If it does not pay its debt by doing what it ought, it will pay it by suffering what it ought to suffer. There is no interval of time between failure to do what ought to be done and suffering what ought to be suffered, lest for a single moment the beauty of the universe

should be defiled by having the uncomeliness of sin without the comeliness of penalty. What is now not punished openly is reserved for future judgment, that the misery imposed may become manifest and be most sharply felt. He who is not awake is asleep. In the same way, he who does not do what he ought immediately suffers what he ought. For such is the happiness of doing justly that no one can depart from it without immediately finding misery. In all deficiencies the things which are defective have not received power to last longer, if they have no guilt. Likewise there is no guilt if they are what they are because they did not receive power to have an ampler existence. Or they may be unwilling to be what they have been given power to be if they would; and because they have the power to be good there is guilt if they will not.

45. God owes nothing to any man, for he gives everything gratuitously. If anyone says God owes him something for his merits, God did not even owe him existence. Nothing could be owing to one who did not yet exist. And what merit is there in turning to him from whom you derive existence, that you may be made better by him from whom you derive existence? Why do you ask him for anything as if you were demanding repayment of a debt? If you were unwilling to turn to him, the loss would not be his but yours. For without him you would be nothing, and from him you derive such existence as you have; but on condition that, unless you turn to him, you must pay him back the existence you have from him, and become, not indeed nothing, but miserable. All things owe him, first, their existence so far as they are natural things, and secondly, that they can become better if they wish, receiving additional gifts if they wish them and being what they ought to be. No man is guilty because he has not received this or that power. But because he does not do as he ought he is justly held guilty. Obligation arises if he has received free will and sufficient power.

46. No blame attaches to the Creator if any of his creatures does not do what he ought. Indeed, that the wrong-doer suffers as he ought redounds to the praise of the Creator. In the very act of blaming anyone for not doing as he ought, he is praised to whom the debt is owed. If you are praised for seeing what you ought to do, and you only see it in him who is unchangeable truth, how much more is he to be praised who has taught you what you ought to wish, has given you the power to do it, and has not allowed you to refuse to do it with impunity? If "oughtness" depends upon what has been given, and man has been so

made that he sins by necessity, then he ought to sin. So when he sins he does what he ought. But it is wicked to speak like that. No man's nature compels him to sin, nor does any other nature. No man sins when he suffers what he does not wish. If he has to suffer justly he does not sin in suffering unwillingly. He sinned in that he did something voluntarily which involved him in suffering justly what he did not wish. If he suffers unjustly, where is the sin? There is no sin in suffering something unjustly but in doing something unjustly. So, if no one is compelled to sin either by his own nature or by another, it remains that he sins by his own will. If you want to attribute his sin to the Creator you will make the sinner guiltless because he has simply obeyed the laws of the Creator. If the sinner can be rightly defended he is not a sinner, and there is no sin to attribute to the Creator. Let us then praise the Creator whether or not the sinner can be defended. If he is justly defended he is no sinner and we can therefore praise the Creator. If he cannot be defended, he is a sinner so far as he turns away from the Creator. Therefore praise the Creator. I find, therefore, no way at all, and I assert that there is none to be found, by which our sins can be ascribed to the Creator, our God. I find that he is to be praised even for sins, not only because he punishes them, but also because sin arises only when a man departs from his truth.

Evodius.—I most gladly approve all you have said, and assent with all my heart to the truth that there is no way at all of rightly ascribing our sins to our Creator. xvii, 47. But I should like to know, if possible, why those beings do not sin whom God knew beforehand would not sin, and why those others do sin whom he foresaw would sin. I do not now think that God's foreknowledge compels the one to sin and the other not to sin. But if there were no cause rational creatures would not be divided into classes as they are: those who never sin, those who continually sin, and the intermediary class of those who sometimes sin and sometimes are turned towards well-doing. What is the reason for this division? I do not want you to reply that it is the will that does it. What I want to know is what cause lies behind willing. There must be some reason why one class never wills to sin, another never lacks the will to sin, and another sometimes wills to sin and at other times does not so will. For they are all alike in nature. I seem to see that there must be some cause for this three-fold classification of rational beings according to their wills, but what it is I do not know.

48. *Augustine.*—Since will is the cause of sin, you now ask

what is the cause of will. If I could find one, are you not going to ask for the cause of the cause I have found? What limit will there be to your quest, what end to inquiry and explanation? You ought not to push your inquiry deeper, for you must beware of imagining that anything can be more truly said than that which is written: "Avarice is the root of all evils" (I Tim. 6:10), that is, wanting more than is sufficient. That is sufficient which is demanded by the need of preserving any particular creature. Avarice, in Greek *philarguria*, derives its name from *argentum* [silver], because among the ancients coins were made of silver or more frequently with an admixture of silver. But avarice must be understood as connected not only with silver and money but with everything which is immoderately desired, in every case where a man wants more than is sufficient. Such avarice is cupidity, and cupidity is an evil will. An evil will, therefore, is the cause of all evils. If it were according to nature it would preserve nature and not be hostile to it, and so it would not be evil. The inference is that the root of all evils is not according to nature. That is sufficient answer to all who want to accuse nature. But you ask what is the cause of this root. How then will it be the root of all evils? If it has a cause, that cause will be the root of evil. And if you find a cause, as I said, you will ask for a cause of that cause, and there will be no limit to your inquiry.

49. But what cause of willing can there be which is prior to willing? Either it is a will, in which case we have not got beyond the root of evil will. Or it is not a will, and in that case there is no sin in it. Either, then, will is itself the first cause of sin, or the first cause is without sin. Now sin is rightly imputed only to that which sins, nor is it rightly imputed unless it sins voluntarily. I do not know why you should want to inquire further, but here is a further point. If there is a cause of willing it is either just or unjust. If it is just, he who obeys it will not sin, if unjust he who does not obey it will not sin either.

xviii, 50. But it may perhaps be violent, and compel him against his will? Are we to repeat our reply over and over again? Remember how much we have spoken earlier about sin and free will. Perhaps it is difficult to commit everything to memory, but hold fast to this brief statement. Whatever be the cause of willing, if it cannot be resisted no sin results from yielding to it. If it can be resisted, and it is not yielded to, no sin results. Possibly it may deceive a man when he is off his guard? Let him then take care not to be deceived. Is the deception so great that he cannot possibly avoid it? In that case no sin results? No one commits sin in doing what there was no means of avoiding? Yes, indeed, sin does result, and that means he is able to be on his guard.

51. Nevertheless, some things are done in ignorance which are held to be wrong and worthy of correction, as we read in the divinely authoritative books. The apostle says: "I obtained mercy because I did it in ignorance" (I Tim. 1:13). And the prophet says: "Remember not the sins of my youth and of my ignorance" (Ps. 25:7). Wrong things are done by necessity when a man wills to do right and has not the power. For thus it is written: "The good that I would I do not, but the evil which I would not, that I do." Again: "To will is present with me; but how to perform that which is good I find not" (Rom. 7:18–19). And again: "The flesh lusteth against the spirit, and the spirit against the flesh; for these are contrary the one to the other, so that ye cannot do the things that ye would" (Gal. 5:17). These are the words of men emerging from deadly damnation. If this were a description of man's nature and not of the penalty of sin, his situation would not be sinful. If man has not departed from the natural state in which he was created, and which could not be made better, he is doing what he ought even when he does evil. But now man might be good if he were different. Because he is what he now is, he is not good, nor is it in his power to become good, either because he does not see what he ought to be, or, seeing it, has not the power to be what he sees he ought to be. Who can doubt that his is a penal state? Every just penalty is the penalty of sin and is called punishment. If the penalty is unjust, there is no doubt that it is, in fact, penalty, but it has been imposed on man by some unjust power that lords it over him. But it is mad to have any doubt about the omnipotence or the justice of God. Therefore man's penalty is just and is recompense for sin. No unjust lord could have usurped dominion over man, as it were, without the knowledge of God. No one could have forced him in his weakness against his will either by terrorism or by actual affliction, so that man's punishment might be held to be unjust. It remains, therefore, that his punishment is just and comes to him because he is to be condemned.

52. It is not to be wondered at that man, through ignorance, has not the freedom of will to choose to do what he ought; or that he cannot see what he ought to do or fulfil it when he will, in face of carnal custom which, in a sense, has grown as strong,

almost, as nature, because of the power of mortal succession. It is the most just penalty of sin that man should lose what he was unwilling to make a good use of, when he could have done so without difficulty if he had wished. It is just that he who, knowing what is right, does not do it should lose the capacity to to know what is right, and that he who had the power to do what is right and would not should lose the power to do it when he is willing. In fact there are for every sinful soul these two penal conditions, ignorance and difficulty. From ignorance springs disgraceful error, and from difficulty comes painful effort. To approve falsehood instead of truth so as to err in spite of himself, and not to be able to refrain from the works of lust because of the pain involved in breaking away from fleshly bonds: these do not belong to the nature of man as he was created. They are the penalty of man as condemned. When we speak of the freedom of the will to do right, we are speaking of the freedom wherein man was created.

xix, 53. Here comes in the question which men, who are ready to accuse anything for their sins except themselves, are wont to cast up, murmuring amongst themselves. They say: If Adam and Eve sinned, what have we miserable creatures done to deserve to be born in the darkness of ignorance and in the toils of difficulty, that, in the first place, we should err not knowing what we ought to do, and, in the second place, that when the precepts of justice begin to be opened out to us, we should wish to obey them but by some necessity of carnal lust should not have the power? To them I reply: Keep quiet and stop murmuring against God. They might perhaps rightly complain if no man had ever been victorious over error and lust. And yet there is One present everywhere who, in many ways, by means of the creation that serves him as its Lord, calls back him who has gone astray, teaches him who believes, comforts him who has hope, exhorts the diligent, helps him who is trying and answers prayer. You are not held guilty because you are ignorant in spite of yourself, but because you neglect to seek the knowledge you do not possess. You are not held guilty because you do not use your wounded members but because you despise him who is willing to heal them. These are your own personal sins. To no man is it given to know how to seek to his advantage what to his disadvantage he does not know. He must humbly confess his weakness, so that as he seeks and makes his confession *he* may come to his aid who, in aiding, knows neither error nor difficulty.

54. All that a man does wrongfully in ignorance, and all that he cannot do rightly though he wishes, are called sins because they have their origin in the first sin of the will when it was free. These are its deserved consequences. We apply the name "tongue" not only to the member which we move in our mouth when we speak, but also to what follows from that motion, namely, words and language. Thus we speak of the Greek or the Latin tongue. So we apply the word "sin" not only to that which is properly called sin, that is, what is committed knowingly and with free will, but also to all that follows as the necessary punishment of that first sin. So we use the word "nature" in a double sense. Properly speaking, human nature means the blameless nature with which man was originally created. But we also use it in speaking of the nature with which we are born mortal, ignorant and subject to the flesh, which is really the penalty of sin. In this sense the apostle says: "We also were by nature children of wrath even as others" (Eph. 2:3).

xx, 55. As we are born from the first pair to a mortal life of ignorance and toil because they sinned and fell into a state of error, misery and death, so it most justly pleased the most high God, Governor of all things, to manifest from the beginning, from man's origin, his justice in exacting punishment, and in human history his mercy in remitting punishment. When the first man was condemned, happiness was not so completely taken from him that he lost also his fecundity. Though his offspring was carnal and mortal, yet in its own way it could contribute some glory and ornament to the earth. That he should beget children better than himself would not have been equitable. But if any of Adam's race should be willing to turn to God, and so overcome the punishment which had been merited by the original turning away from God, it was fitting not only that he should not be hindered but that he should also receive divine aid. In this way also the Creator showed how easily man might have retained, if he had so willed, the nature with which he was created, because his offspring had power to transcend that in which he was born.

56. Again, if only one soul was originally created, and the souls of all men since born derive their origin from it, who can say that he did not sin when the first man sinned? If however souls are created separately in individual men as they are born, it appears not to be unreasonable but rather most appropriate and in accordance with right order that the ill desert of an earlier soul should determine the nature of those which are

created afterwards, and that by its goodness a soul later created should deserve to regain the state which the earlier one had lost. There would be nothing unworthy about it if the Creator had determined to show in this way that the soul so far excelled in dignity every corporeal creature that one soul could start from the position to which another had fallen. The sinful soul reached an estate of ignorance and toil, which is rightly called penalty, because before the penalty it had been better. Even if a soul, before it sinned and even before it was born, was given a nature like that which another acquired after a guilty life, it has no small good for which to give thanks to its Creator, for even in its inchoate beginning it is better than any body however perfect. These are no mean advantages, not only to be a soul and so naturally to excel all bodies, but also to have the power with the aid of the Creator to cultivate itself, and with pious care to acquire all the virtues by which it may be liberated both from tormenting toil and from blinding ignorance. If that is so in the case of souls that are born, ignorance and toil will not be punishment for sin but a warning to improve themselves, and the beginning of their perfecting. It is no small thing to have been given, before there has been any merit gained by any good work, the natural power to discern that wisdom is to be preferred to error and tranquillity to toil, and to know that these good things are to be reached not simply by being born but by earnestly seeking them. But if the soul will not act in this way it will rightly be held guilty of sin for not making a good use of the power it has received. Though it is born in ignorance and toilsomeness there is no necessity for it to remain in that state. Indeed it could not exist were not Almighty God the Creator of such souls. For before he was loved he made them. In love he restores them. And being loved he perfects them. To souls which do not yet exist he gives existence; and to those who love him who gives them existence he gives happiness too.

57. If, on the other hand, souls pre-exist in some secret place and are sent out to quicken and rule the bodies of individuals when they are born, their mission is to govern well the body which is born under the penalty of the sin of the first man, that is, mortality. They are to discipline it with the virtues, and subject it to an orderly and legitimate servitude, so that in due order and in the due time men may attain the place of heavenly perfection. When they enter this life and submit to wearing mortal members these souls must also undergo forgetfulness of

their former existence and the labours of their present existence, with consequent ignorance and toil which in the first man were a punishment involving mortality and completing the misery of the soul. But for these souls ignorance and toil are opportunities for ministering to the restoration of the integrity of the body. The flesh coming from a sinful stock causes this ignorance and toil to infect the souls sent to it. Only in this sense are they to be called sins, and the blame for them is to be ascribed neither to the souls nor to their Creator. For he has given them power to do good in difficult duties, and has provided for them the way of faith where oblivion had brought blindness. Also and above all, he has given them the insight which every soul possesses; that it must seek to know what to its disadvantage it does not know, and that it must persevere in burdensome duties and strive to overcome the difficulty of well-doing, and implore the Creator's aid in its efforts. By the law without and by direct address to the heart within, he has commanded that effort be made, and he has prepared the glory of the Blessed City for those who triumph over the devil, who with wicked persuasion overcame the first man and reduced him to his state of misery. That misery these souls undergo in lively faith in order to overcome the devil. No little glory is to be gained from the campaign to overcome the devil, waged by undergoing the punishment which he glories in having brought upon his victim, man. Whoever yields to love of the present life and takes no part in that campaign can by no means justly attribute the shame of his desertion to the command of his king. Rather the Lord of all will appoint his place with the devil, because he loved the base hire wherewith he bought his desertion.

58. But if souls existing in some place are not sent by the Lord God, but come of their own accord to inhabit bodies, it is easy to see that any ignorance or toil which is the consequence of their own choice cannot in any way be ascribed as blame to the Creator. He would be entirely without blame. If we accept the view that he himself sent souls, he did not take from them even in the state of ignorance and toil their freedom to ask and seek and endeavour, and was ever ready to give to those who ask, to demonstrate to those who seek and to open to those who knock. Similarly, on this other view, he would allow conquest over ignorance and difficulty on the part of earnest and right-minded souls to count as a crown of glory. He would not lay the ignorance or the difficulty to the charge of the negligent or of those who wished to defend their sins on the ground of their

infirmity. But he would justly punish them because they would rather abide in ignorance and difficulty than reach truth and a life free from struggle by zeal in seeking and learning, and by humility in prayer and confession.

xxi, 59. Now there are these four opinions about the origin of the soul, viz., that it comes by propagation, that it is newly created with each individual who is born, that it exists somewhere beforehand and comes into the body of the newly-born either being divinely sent or gliding in of its own accord. None of these views may be rashly affirmed. Either that question, because of its obscurity and perplexity, has not been handled and illumined by catholic commentators on Holy Writ. Or, if it has been done, their writings have not come into our hands. God give us a true faith that will hold no false or unworthy opinion concerning the substance of the Creator. For by the path of piety we are wending our way towards him. If we hold any other opinion concerning him than the true one, our zeal will drive us not to beatitude but to vanity. There is no danger if we hold a wrong opinion about the creature, provided we do not hold it as if it were assured knowledge. We are not bidden to turn to the creature in order to be happy, but to the Creator himself. If we are persuaded to think otherwise of him than we ought to think or otherwise than what is true we are deceived by most deadly error. No man can reach the happy life by making for that which is not, or, if it does exist, does not make men happy.

60. That we may be able to enjoy and cleave to eternal truth in contemplation, a way out of temporalities has been prepared for our weakness, so that we may trust the past and the future so far as is sufficient for our journey towards eternal things. The discipline of faith is governed by the divine mercy, so that it may have supreme authority. Things present are perceived as transient so far as the creature is concerned. They consist in the mobility and mutability of body and soul. Of these things we cannot have any kind of knowledge unless they enter into our experience. If we are told on divine authority about the past or the future of any created thing we are to believe it without hesitation. No doubt some of this was past before we could have perceived it. Some of it has not yet reached our senses. Nevertheless we are to believe it, for it helps to strengthen our hope and call forth our love, inasmuch as it reminds us, through the ordered temporal series, that God does not neglect our liberation. If any error assumes the rôle of divine authority

it is most reasonably refuted, if it is shown to hold or to affirm that there is any mutable form that is not the creation of God, or that there is any mutability in the substance of God; or if it contends that the substance of God is more or less than a Trinity. To understand that Trinity soberly and piously occupies all the watchful care of Christians, and that is the goal of every advance. Concerning the unity of the Trinity and the equality of persons and the properties of each, this is not the place to discourse. To relate some things which pertain to saving faith and which concern the Lord our God, Author and Maker and Governor of all things, may give useful support to a child-like incipient purpose to rise from earthly to heavenly things. That is easy to do and it has already been done by many. But to handle the whole question so as to bring all human intelligence into the light of clear reason, as far as possible in this life, does not seem an easy task for any man's eloquence or even for any man's thought, much less ours. It is therefore not to be lightly attempted. Let us go on with what we have begun, so far as we have the permission and the help of God. All that we are told of past events concerning the creation, and all that is foretold concerning the future is to be believed without hesitation, because it helps to commend pure religion by stimulating in us sincere love to God and our neighbour. It is to be defended against unbelievers, either by wearing down their unbelief with the weight of authority, or by showing them, as far as possible, first, that it is not foolish to believe it, and, secondly, that it is foolish not to believe it. But false doctrine, not about past or future events so much as about the present and above all about unchangeable things, must be convincingly refuted by clear reasoning, so far as it is granted to us.

61. Of course when we are thinking of the series of temporal things, expectation of things to come is more important than research into things past. In the divine books also past events are narrated, but they carry with them the forecast or promise or attestation of things to come. In fact no one pays much attention to temporal prosperity or adversity when they are past. All anxiety and care are bestowed on what is hoped for in the future. By some intimate and natural mechanism of the mind things which have happened to us, after they are past, are accounted, in any reckoning of felicity and misery, as if they had never happened. What disadvantage is it to me not to know when I began to be, when I know that I exist now and do not cease to hope that I shall continue to exist? I am not so

interested in the past as to dread as deadly error any false opinion I may entertain as to what actually transpired. But as to my future I direct my course, guided by the mercy of my Maker. But if I have any false belief or opinion about my future, or about him with whom I am to be for ever, I must with all my might beware of that error. Otherwise I shall not make the necessary preparation, or I shall not be able to reach him who is the objective of my enterprise, because my outlook has been confused. If I were buying a garment it would be no disadvantage to me to have forgotten last winter, but it would be a disadvantage if I did not believe that cold weather was coming on. So it would be no disadvantage to my soul to forget anything that it may perhaps have endured, so long as it diligently observes and remembers all that may warn it to make preparation for the future. For example, it will do no harm to a man who is sailing to Rome to forget from what shore he set sail, so long as he knows all the time whither he is directing his course. It will do him no good to remember the shore from which he began his voyage, if he has made some false calculation about the port of Rome and runs upon rocks. So it is no disadvantage to me not to remember the beginning of my life, so long as I know the end where I am to find rest. Nor would any memory or guess concerning life's commencement be of any advantage to me if, holding unworthy opinions of God who is the sole end of the soul's labours, I should run upon the reefs of error.

62. What I have said is not to be taken to mean that I forbid those who have the ability to inquire whether, according to the divinely inspired Scriptures, soul is propagated from soul, or whether souls are created separately for all animate beings; whether they are sent at the divine behest from some place where they abide to animate and rule the body, or whether they insinuate themselves of their own accord. Such inquiries and discussions are justifiable if reason demands them in order to answer some necessary question, or if leisure from more necessary matters is available. I spoke as I did rather that no one in so great a problem should rashly become angry with another because he will not yield to his opinion, having grounds for hesitation based perhaps on a broader culture; or even that no one who has clear and certain understanding of these matters from Scripture should suppose that another has lost all hope for the future because he does not remember the soul's origin in the past.

xxii, 63. However that may be, whether that question is to

be passed over entirely or to be deferred for later consideration, there is no obstacle preventing us from answering the question with which we are dealing at present in such a way as to make clear that by the upright, just, unshaken and changeless majesty and substance of the Creator souls pay the penalty for their own sins. These sins, as we have explained at great length, are to be ascribed to nothing but to their own wills, and no further cause for sins is to be looked for.

64. If ignorance and moral difficulty are natural to man, it is from that condition that the soul begins to progress and to advance towards knowledge and tranquillity until it reaches the perfection of the happy life. If by its own will it neglects to advance by means of good studies and piety—for the capacity to do so is not denied to it—it justly falls into a still graver state of ignorance and struggle, which is now penal, and is ranked among inferior creatures according to the appropriate and fitting government of the universe. Natural ignorance and natural impotence are not reckoned to the soul as guilt. The guilt arises because it does not eagerly pursue knowledge, and does not give adequate attention to acquiring facility in doing right. It is natural for an infant not to know how to speak and not to be able to speak. But that ignorance and inability are not only blameless according to the rules of the teachers, but are also attractive and pleasing to human feeling. In this case there is no faulty failure to acquire the power of speaking, nor, if possessed, was it lost through any fault. If we supposed that happiness was to be found in eloquence and it was thought criminal to commit a fault in speaking, as it is thought criminal to commit a fault in action, no one would put the blame on our infancy, though as infants we began to acquire eloquence. But clearly one would be deservedly blamed if by perversity of will one either remained in the infantile condition or fell back into it. In the same way, if ignorance of the truth and difficulty in doing right are natural to man, and he has to begin to rise from that condition to the happiness of wisdom and tranquillity, no one rightly blames him for the natural condition from which he started. But if he refuses to progress, or voluntarily falls back from the path of progress, he will justly and deservedly pay the penalty.

65. But his Creator is to be praised on all counts. He gave him the power to rise from such beginnings to ability to attain the chief good. He renders aid as he advances. He completes and perfects his advance. And if he sins, that is, if he refuses to rise

from these beginnings to perfection or if he falls back from any progress he may have made, he imposes on him a most just condemnation according to his deserts. The soul was not created evil because it was not given all that it had power to become. All corporeal things however perfect are far inferior to the soul's beginning, though anyone who takes a sane view of things judges that they, too, are to be praised in their own kind. That the soul does not know what it should do is due to its not yet having received that gift. It will receive it if it makes a good use of what it has received. It has received the power to seek diligently and piously if it will. That it cannot instantly fulfil the duty it recognizes as duty, means that that is another gift it has not yet received. Its higher part first perceives the good it ought to do, but the slower and carnal part is not immediately brought over to that opinion. So by that very difficulty it is admonished to implore for its perfecting the aid of him whom it believes to be the author of its beginning. Hence he becomes dearer to it, because it has its existence not from its own resources but from his goodness, and by his mercy it is raised to happiness. The more it loves him from whom it derives its existence, the more surely it rests in him, and enjoys his eternity more fully. We do not rightly say of a young shoot of a tree that it is sterile, because several summers must pass before at the appointed time it reveals its fruitfulness. Why should not the Author of the soul be praised with due piety if he has given it so good a start that it may by zeal and progress reach the fruit of wisdom and justice, and has given it so much dignity as to put within its power the capacity to grow towards happiness if it will?

xxiii, 66. Against this reasoning, ignorant men are wont to repeat a calumny based upon the deaths of infants and certain bodily torments with which we often see them afflicted. They say: What need had the infant to be born if it was to die before it had acquired any merit in life? How is it to be reckoned in the future judgment, seeing that it cannot be put among the just since it performed no good works, nor among the evil because it never sinned? I reply: If you think of the all-embracing complexity of the universe, and the orderly connection of the whole creation throughout space and time, you will not believe that a man, whatsoever he may be, can be created superfluously. Why, not even the leaf of a tree is created superfluously. But it is idly superfluous to inquire about the merits of one who has done nothing to merit anything. There is no need to fear lest there be a life lived which is neither righteous nor sinful, nor that the judge will be able to pronounce sentence involving neither reward nor punishment.

67. At this point men are wont to ask what good the sacrament of Christ's Baptism can do to infants, seeing that many of them die after having been baptized but before they can know anything about it. In this case it is pious and right to believe that the infant is benefited by the faith of those who bring him to be consecrated. This is commended by the salutary authority of the Church, so that everyone may realize how beneficial to him is his faith, seeing that one man's faith can be made beneficial for another who has no faith of his own. The son of the widow of Nain could have had no advantage from any faith of his own, for, being dead, he had no faith. But his mother's faith procured him the benefit of being raised from the dead (Luke 7:11 ff.). How much more may the faith of another benefit an infant seeing that no faithlessness of its own can be imputed to it?

68. A greater complaint, and one with a show of pity about it, is often occasioned by the bodily torments which infants suffer, for by reason of their tender age they have committed no sins, at least if the souls which animate them have had no existence prior to their birth as human beings. People say: What evil have they done that they should suffer such things? As if innocence could have any merit before it has the power to do any hurt! Perhaps God is doing some good in correcting parents when their beloved children suffer pain and even death. Why should not such things happen? When they are past they will be for those who suffered them as if they never happened. And those on whose account they happened will be made better if they accept correction from temporal troubles and choose to live more righteously. Or, if they will not allow the sufferings of this life to turn their desire towards eternal life, they will be without excuse when they are punished at the last judgment. By the torments of their children parents have their hard hearts softened, their faith exercised and their tenderness proved. Who knows what good compensation God has reserved in the secrecy of his judgments for the children themselves who, though they have not had the chance of living righteously, at least have committed no sin and yet have suffered? Not for nothing does the Church commend for honour as martyrs the children who were slain by the orders of Herod when he sought to slay the Lord Jesus Christ.

69. These casuists, who ask questions of that kind not because

they want to examine them seriously but because they are loquacious and want to ventilate them, are wont also to trouble the faith of the less learned by pointing to the pains and labours of animals. What evil, they say, have the animals deserved that they suffer such woes, or what good can they hope for in having such troubles imposed on them? They say that or feel like that because they have a perverted sense of values. They are not able to see what the chief good is, and they want to have everything just as they conceive the chief good to be. They can think of no chief good except fine bodies like the celestial bodies which are not subject to corruption. And so without any sense of order they demand that the bodies of animals shall not suffer death or any corruption, as if forsooth they were not mortal, being lowly bodies, or were evil because celestial bodies are better. The pain which the animals suffer commends the vigour of the animal soul as admirable and praiseworthy after its own fashion. By animating and ruling the body of the animal it shows its desire for unity. For what is pain but a certain feeling that cannot bear division and corruption? Hence it is clearer than day that the animal soul is eager for unity in the whole body and is tenacious of unity. Neither gladly nor with indifference, but reluctantly and with obstinate resistance it meets bodily suffering which it is grieved to know destroys the unity and integrity of the body. We should never know what eagerness there is for unity in the inferior animal creation, were it not for the pain suffered by animals. And if we did not know that, we should not be made sufficiently aware that all things are framed by the supreme, sublime and ineffable unity of the Creator.

70. Indeed, if you give pious and diligent attention, every kind of creature which can come under the consideration of the human mind contributes to our instruction, speaking by its diverse movements and feelings as in so many diverse tongues, everywhere proclaiming and insisting that the Creator is to be recognized. There is no creature that feels pain or pleasure which does not by some sort of unity attain a beauty appropriate to its own kind, or some sort of stability of nature. There is no creature sensitive to pain or pleasure which does not, simply by avoiding pain and seeking pleasure, show that it avoids its own destruction and seeks unity. In rational souls all desire for knowledge, which is the delight of the rational nature, refers its acquisitions to unity, and, in avoiding error, avoids nothing so much as the confusion of incomprehensible am-

biguity. Why is ambiguity so detestable save that it has no certain unity? Hence it is clear that all things, whether they offend or are offended, whether they delight or are delighted, proclaim or suggest the unity of the Creator. But if ignorance and moral difficulty from which we must set out on the rational life are not natural to souls, they must be undertaken as a duty or imposed as a punishment. I think we have said enough about these matters now.

xxiv, 71. What sort of creature the first man was when created is a more important question than how his posterity was propagated. People seem to pose a very acute question when they say: If the first man was created wise, why has he been seduced? If he was created foolish how is God to escape being held to be the author of vice, since folly is the greatest vice of all? As if human nature might not receive some intermediate quality which can be called neither folly nor wisdom! Man begins to be either foolish or wise, and one or other of these terms must necessarily be applied to him, as soon as it becomes possible for him to have wisdom or to neglect it. Then his will is guilty, for his folly is his own fault. No one is so foolish as to call an infant foolish, though it would be even more absurd to call it wise. An infant can be called neither foolish nor wise though it is already a human being. So it appears that human nature receives an intermediate condition which cannot be rightly called either folly or wisdom. Similarly, if anyone was animated by a soul disposed as men are who lack wisdom through negligence, nobody could rightly call him foolish, because he would owe his condition not to his own fault but to the nature with which he was endowed. Folly is not any kind of ignorance of things to be sought and avoided, but ignorance which is due to a man's own fault. We do not call an irrational animal foolish, because it has not received the power to be wise. Yet we often apply terms improperly where there is some similarity. Blindness is the greatest fault that eyes can have, yet it is not a fault in puppies, and is not properly called blindness.

72. If man was created such that, although he was not yet wise, he could at least receive a commandment which he ought to obey, it is not surprising that he could be seduced. Nor is it unjust that he pays the penalty for not obeying the commandment. Nor is his Creator the author of sins, for it was not yet a sin in man not to have wisdom, if that gift were not yet given him. But he had something that would enable him to attain what he did not have, provided he was willing to make a good

use of it. It is one thing to be a rational being, another to be a wise man. Reason makes a man able to receive the precept to which he ought to be loyal, so that he may perform what is commanded. The rational nature grasps the precept, obedience to which brings wisdom. What nature contributes to the grasping of the precept, will contributes to obedience to it. As the merit of receiving the precept, so to speak, is to have a rational nature, so the merit of receiving wisdom is obedience to the precept. As soon as a man begins to have the power to receive the precept, he begins also to have the possibility of sinning. Before he becomes wise he sins in one or other of two ways. Either he does not fit himself to receive the precept, or, receiving it, he does not obey it. The wise man sins if he turns away from wisdom. The precept does not come from him on whom it is laid, but from him who gives it; so wisdom, too, comes not from him who is illumined, but from him who gives the light. Why then should not the Creator of man be praised? Man is good, and better than the cattle because he is capable of receiving the precept; better still when he has received the precept; and still better when he has obeyed it; best of all when he is made happy by the eternal light of wisdom. Sin, or evil, consists in neglect to receive the precept or to obey it, or to hold fast the contemplation of wisdom. So we learn that, even although the first man had been created wise, it was nevertheless possible for him to be seduced. Because his sin was committed with his free will, a just penalty followed by divine law. As the apostle Paul says: "Saying they are wise they have become fools" (Rom. 1:22). It is pride that turns man away from wisdom, and folly is the consequence of turning away from wisdom. Folly is a kind of blindness, as he says: "Their foolish heart was darkened." Whence came this darkness, if not from turning away from the light of wisdom? And whence came the turning away, if not from the fact that man, whose good God is, willed to be his own good and so to substitute himself for God. Accordingly the Scriptures say: "Looking to myself, my soul is cast down" (Ps. 42:6. LXX). And again: "Taste and ye shall be as gods" (Gen. 3:5).

73. Some people are troubled by this question. Did folly cause the first man to depart from God, or did he become foolish by departing from God? If you answer that folly made him depart from wisdom, it will appear that he was foolish before he did so, so that folly is the cause of his doing so. If you reply that he became foolish by departing from wisdom, they

ask whether he acted foolishly or wisely in departing. If wisely he did right and committed no sin. If foolishly there was folly already in him, they say, which made him depart from wisdom. For without folly he could do nothing foolishly. Clearly there is some middle state of transition from wisdom to folly, which cannot be called either wisdom or folly; but it is not given to men to understand this except by way of contrast with both. No mortal becomes wise unless he passes from folly to wisdom. If there is folly in the actual transition it is not a good thing, but to say that would be mad. If there is wisdom in it, there must already be wisdom in a man before he makes the transition to wisdom. But that is equally absurd. Hence we learn that there is an intermediate state which may be said to be neither folly nor wisdom. In the same way when the first man passed from the citadel of wisdom to folly, the transition in itself was neither foolish nor wise. In the matter of sleeping and waking, to be asleep is not the same thing as to fall asleep, nor is to be awake the same thing as to awake. There is a transitional state between sleeping and waking as between folly and wisdom. But there is this difference. In the former case there is no intervention of will; in the latter the transition never takes place except by the action of the will. That is why the consequence is just retribution.

xxv, 74. But the will is not enticed to do anything except by something that has been perceived. It is in a man's power to take or reject this or that, but it is not in his power to control the things which will affect him when they are perceived. We must admit, therefore, that the mind is affected by perceptions both of superior things and of inferior things. Thus the rational creature may take from either what it will, and, according to its deserts in making the choice, it obtains as a consequence either misery or happiness. In the Garden of Eden the commandment of God came to man's attention from above. From beneath came the suggestion of the serpent. Neither the commandment of God nor the suggestion of the serpent was in man's power. But if he has reached the healthy state of wisdom he is freed from all the shackles of moral difficulty, and has freedom not to yield to the enticing suggestions of inferior things. How free he is we can infer from the fact that even fools overcome them as they pass on to wisdom, though of course they have the difficulty of trying to do without the deadly sweetness of the pernicious things to which they have been accustomed.

75. Here it may be asked, if man had impressions from both

sides, from the commandment of God and from the suggestion of the serpent, whence did the devil receive the suggestion to follow impiety which brought him down from his abode on high. If there was nothing in his experience to affect him he would not have chosen to do what he did. If nothing had come into his mind he would not have directed his purpose to wickedness. Whence then did the thought come into his mind to attempt things which made of a good angel a devil? Whoever wills wills something. He cannot exercise will unless some hint comes to him from outside through bodily sense, or some thought comes into his mind in some secret way. We must distinguish two kinds of experience. One proceeds from the will of another who uses persuasion, as, for example, when man sinned by consenting to the persuasion of the devil. The other kind springs from environment, mental and spiritual, or corporeal and sensational. The environment of the mind may be said to include the unchangeable Trinity, though the Trinity rather stands high above the mind. More properly the environment of the mind is, first of all, the mind itself which enables us to know that we live, and, secondly, the body which the mind governs, moving the appropriate limb to accomplish any action that may be required. The environment of the senses is corporeal objects of all kinds.

76. The mind is not sovereign wisdom, for that is unchangeable. Yet in contemplating sovereign wisdom the mutable mind may behold itself and in a fashion come to know itself. But that cannot be unless a distinction is made. The mind is not as God is, and yet, next to God, it can give us satisfaction. It is better when it forgets itself in love for the unchangeable God, or indeed utterly contemns itself in comparison with him. But if the mind, being immediately conscious of itself, takes pleasure in itself to the extent of perversely imitating God, wanting to enjoy its own power, the greater it wants to be the less it becomes. Pride is the beginning of all sin, and the beginning of man's pride is revolt from God (Eccl. 10:12–13). To the devil's pride was added malevolent envy, so that he persuaded man to show the same pride as had proved the devil's damnation. So man had imposed on him a penalty which was corrective rather than destructive. As the devil had offered himself to man as a pattern of pride to be imitated, so the Lord, who promises us eternal life, offered himself as a pattern of humility for our imitation. Now that the blood of Christ is shed for us, after unspeakable toils and miseries, let us cleave to our Liberator with

such love, let us be so enraptured with his brightness, that nothing coming into our experience from the lower realms may rob us of our vision of the higher things. And if any suggestion springing from a desire for the inferior should deflect our purpose, the eternal damnation and torments of the devil will recall us to the true path.

77. Such is the beauty of justice, such the pleasure of the eternal light, that is, of unchangeable truth and wisdom, that, even if we could not abide in it more than the space of a single day, for that day alone innumerable years of this life full of delights and abundance of temporal goods would be rightly and deservedly despised. Deep and unfeigned is the emotion expressed in these words: "One day in thy courts is better than thousands" (Ps. 84:10). These words can be understood in another sense. Thousands of days might be understood of mutable time, and by the expression "one day" changeless eternity might be denoted. I do not know whether I have omitted any point in replying, as God has deigned to give me the power, to your questions. Even if anything else occurs to you, moderation compels us now to bring this book to an end, and to take some rest after this disputation.

Of True Religion

St. Augustine's Review of "De Vera Religione."
Retractations I, xiii

1. At that time also I wrote a book *Concerning True Religion* in which I argued at great length and in many ways that true religion means the worship of the one true God, that is, the Trinity, Father, Son and Holy Spirit. I pointed out how great was his mercy in granting to men by a temporal dispensation the Christian religion, which is true religion, and how man is to adjust his life to the worship of God. But the book is written chiefly against the two natures of the Manichees.

2. In a passage in that book (chap. x) I say, "There could have been no error in religion had not the soul worshipped in place of God either soul or body or its own phantasms." By "soul," here, I meant the whole incorporeal creation. I was not using the language of Scripture which, when it speaks of soul, under that name seems to mean nothing but that which animates living beings including men so long as they are mortal. A little later I put my meaning better and more briefly, "Let us not serve the creature rather than the Creator, nor become vain in our thoughts." By "creature" I indicated by one word both spiritual and corporeal creation. And "Let us not become vain in our thoughts" corresponds to "the phantasms of the soul."

3. Again, in the same chapter, I said, "That is the Christian religion in our times, which to know and follow is most sure and certain salvation." I was speaking of the name, here, and not of the thing so named. For what is now called the Christian religion existed of old and was never absent from the beginning of the human race until Christ came in the flesh. Then true religion which already existed began to be called Christian. After the resurrection and ascension of Christ into heaven, the apostles began to preach him and many believed, and the dis-

ciples were first called Christians in Antioch, as it is written. When I said, "This is the Christian religion in our times," I did not mean that it had not existed in former times, but that it received that name later.

4. In another place I say, "Listen to what follows as diligently and as piously as you can; for God aids such." This is not to be understood as if he aids the diligent and pious only. He aids those who are not such to be such, and to seek diligently and piously. Those who do so he aids so that they may find. Again, I say (chap. xii), "After the death of the body which we owe to the first sin, in its own time and order this body will be restored to its pristine stability." That is to be accepted as partially true. The pristine stability of the body, which by sinning we lost, had so great felicity that it would not fall into the decline of old age. To this state the body will be restored at the resurrection of the dead. But it will have more; for it will not need to be sustained by material food. It will be sufficiently animated by spirit alone when it is resurrected as a vivifying spirit. For this reason also it will be spiritual. Man's original nature, though it would not have died if man had not sinned, yet was made a living soul.

5. In another place (chap xiv) I say, "Sin is so much voluntary evil, that there would be no such thing as sin unless it were voluntary." That may appear a false definition; but if it is diligently discussed it will be found to be quite true. We are to consider as sin simply sin and not what is really the penalty of sin, as I showed above when I was dealing with passages from the third book of the *De Libero Arbitrio*. Sins which are not unjustifiably said to be non-voluntary because they are committed in ignorance or under compulsion cannot be said to be committed entirely involuntarily. He who sins in ignorance uses his will to some extent, for he thinks he should do what in fact ought not to be done. He who does not the things that he would because the flesh lusteth against the spirit, may be unwilling but he lusts all the same, and thereby does not the things he would. If he is overcome he voluntarily consents to lust, and thereby does what he wishes, being free from righteousness and the servant of sin. What we call original sin in infants, who have not yet the use of free choice, may not absurdly also be called voluntary, because it originated in man's first evil will and has become in a manner hereditary. So my statement was not false. By the grace of God not only is the guilt of past sins done away in all who are baptized in Christ, by the spirit of regeneration;

but also in grown-up people the will itself is healed and made ready by the Lord, by the spirit of faith and love.

6. In another place (chap. xvi) I said of the Lord Jesus Christ that "He did nothing by violence, but everything by persuasion and advice." I had forgotten that he used a whip to drive the buyers and sellers from the Temple. But what does this amount to? He also drove demons from men against their will, not by persuasive speech but by the might of his power. Again, I say (chap. xxv), "These are first to be followed who say that the most high true God is alone to be worshipped. If the truth does not shine out among them, then we must go elsewhere." That would seem to suggest that there is some doubt about the truth of this religion. I was adapting my words to the situation of him whom I was addressing. I had no doubt myself that the truth *would* shine out among them. The apostle says, "If Christ be not raised," never doubting that he was raised.

7. Again, I said (chap. xxv), "These miracles were not permitted to last till our times, lest the soul should always seek visible things, and the human race should grow cold by becoming accustomed to things which stirred it when they were novel." That is true. When hands are laid on in Baptism people do not receive the Holy Spirit in such a way that they speak with the tongues of all the nations. Nor are the sick now healed by the shadow of Christ's preachers as they pass by. Clearly such things which happened then have later ceased. But I should not be understood to mean that to-day no miracles are to be believed to happen in the name of Christ. For when I wrote that book I myself had just heard that a blind man in Milan had received his sight beside the bodies of the Milanese martyrs, Protasius and Gervasius. And many others happen even in these times, so that it is impossible to know them all or to enumerate those we do know.

8. In another place (chap. xli) I said, "As the apostle says, all order is of God." But the apostle does not use these very words, though his meaning seems to be the same. He actually says "the things that are are ordained of God." Again I say, "Let no one deceive us. Whatever is rightly blamed is rejected by comparison with what is better." This is said of substances and natures which were under discussion, not of good and bad actions. Again (chap. xlvi) I say, "Man is not to be loved by man, as brothers after the flesh love, or sons, spouses, relatives, citizens. That is temporal love. We should not have any such

relationships, which are contingent on birth and death, if our nature had remained in the precepts and image of God, and had not been condemned to corruption." I completely disapprove of this notion, of which I have already disapproved in reviewing the first book of my *On Genesis, against the Manichees*. It leads to the conclusion that the first pair would not have begotten offspring unless they had sinned, as if it were necessary that the offspring of intercourse between man and woman should be born to die. I had not yet seen that it was possible that children who would not die might be born of parents who would not die, if human nature had not been changed for the worse by the first great sin. In that case, if fertility and felicity remained both in parents and in children, men would have been born who were destined, not to succeed parents who die, but to reign with their parents in life, up to the fixed number of the saints which God has predetermined. If there were no sin or death, these kinships and relationships would exist.

9. In another place (chap. lv) I say, "Tending to One God, and binding our souls to him alone [*religantes*], whence religion is supposed to be derived, let us be without superstition." The account which is given in these words of the derivation of the word "religion" pleased me best. To be sure I was not unaware that authors of Latin tongue have given another derivation, from *religere* which is a composite verb from *legere*, to choose. *Religo* seems the proper Latin form, following the analogy of *eligo*.

Of True Religion

INTRODUCTION

THE *De Vera Religione* IS DEDICATED TO ROMANIANUS, and was sent to him with a brief epistle (*Epist.* 15) in 390. Romanianus, a wealthy citizen of Tagaste, had befriended the young Augustine and contributed financially to enable him to study in Carthage. During a business visit to Milan he met Augustine again, and was one of those who discussed a plan to form a quasi-monastic community for religious and philosophic inquiry (*Conf.* vi, 14). His son, Licentius, was left with Augustine as a pupil, accompanied him to Cassiciacum and took part in the early dialogues. The *Contra Academicos* is also dedicated to Romanianus, and there (II, iii, 8) reference is made to the abilities and progress of his son. There too the promise is given to discuss true religion with him, should opportunity offer. On Augustine's return to Africa Romanianus pressed for a fulfilment of the promise, and offered to put his house at Tagaste at the disposal of Augustine and his friends. The offer was gracefully refused. The *De Vera Religione* was one of the five works of Augustine sent to Paulinus of Nola in 394, which the latter delightedly hailed as his "Pentateuch against the Manichees" (*Epist.* 25). In 415, in answer to queries addressed to him by Evodius, Augustine refers to this work, as also to the *De Libero Arbitrio*, as containing in principle at least the solution to Evodius' difficulties (*Epist.* 162).

Of the *De Vera Religione* it has been said, "Scarcely any other of Augustine's works is of more value in demonstrating the greatness of his genius." At the same time it must be admitted that it is extremely diffuse, almost defying analysis. The inference Augustine wishes Evodius to draw from it, viz., that reason cannot afford compelling proof of the existence of God, hardly seems to emerge from the argument, which is that God's temporal dispensation in nature and in history is congruous with, supports and makes available for all men the Platonic teaching with regard to nature and the Good. The Christian religion, now graciously revealed by God for man's salvation, is the true religion ineffectively glimpsed by Plato and his followers, giving a true account of man's fall, present condition and way of regeneration. Those who accept this can live the good life even under earthly conditions, provided they look for blessedness to God alone, the supreme Good. One may note the seminal idea of the *De Civitate Dei* in xxvii, 50.

ANALYSIS

i, 1—vi, 11. Christ has achieved what Plato sought in vain to do.

(1) True religion is the way of the blessed life, and is incompatible with polytheism and idolatry. (2–6) Plato saw this afar off; Christ has made it generally available. (7) Platonists, unless smitten with envy, are becoming Christians. (8–11) Philosophers, Jews, heretics, schismatics, only stimulate the thought of the Catholic Church.

vii, 12—x, 20. Address to Romanianus; and Outline of the Argument.

(13) God's temporal dispensation for man's salvation rightly understood provides (14–16) a sure defence against all heresies, especially Manicheeism. (18) Root of all heresy is failure to distinguish between Creator and creature. (19) All creation, obedient to the law of God, bears witness to the eternal Creator. God has come to man's aid in giving the Christian religion. (20) Augustine's varied experience in commending it.

xi, 21—xxiii, 44. The Fall and Redemption of Man.

(21–25) The soul by disobedience is involved in material things and becomes "carnal." By God's grace it can return to God. Even the body can be renewed. (27) Sin is voluntary, and its penalty, which includes moral inability, is just. But salvation is possible. (30) Christ honoured human nature by assuming it in order to liberate it. (31–34) He taught and set the standard of the perfect life. (35 ff.) Sin is loving the lower in place of the higher good, and its cause is the mutability of the creature and disobedience to God's command. (42) Beauty even in transient things, e.g., a poem. (43) So also in history; only we are involved in history as parts of it, and cannot see it whole. (44) History is a process of purgation, making for the salvation of the righteous and the final damnation of the impious.

xxiv, 45—xxxviii, 71. God's Methods of winning men from the Temporal to the Eternal. *A.* Authority (45–51). *B.* Reason (52–71).

A. Authority. (45) Authority prior in time to reason. (46) Belongs to those who call us to worship one God, for unity is supreme. (47) Miracles necessary at the beginning of the Church but not now. (48) Five stages of the natural life of the individual. (49) Seven stages of the spiritual life, i.e., putting off "the old man" and putting on "the new man." (50) World history from Adam to the Judgment; Two classes of men, the regenerate and the impious. Their final destiny. (51) The economy of the divine education of the human race in Israel and in the Church.

B. Reason. (52) Life superior to the inanimate. (53) Reason superior to Life. (54–58) Above reason is the ideal world; Truth, the eternal law, God. (59–64) Difficulty in getting men to transcend sense-knowledge. (68–69) Hence all idolatry, and worse still, the worship of the vices. (71) The Three Temptations of Christ show how vices are to be overcome.

xxxix, 72—liv, 106. Reason sees the created universe as pointing to God. (72) Vestiges of truth everywhere, even in bodily pleasures. Things enjoyed are good; evil only as compared with what is better. (73) Even to know that one doubts, is the beginning of truth. (74) There is good in all material processes even the lowest. (76) The universe as a whole is beautiful. Even a worm has a beauty of its own. (79) Number in all things. (84) The desire to excel is good; even pride is a perverted imitation of almighty God. (85 ff.) The desire to be unconquered has good in it, especially if what is desired is to be unconquered by vice. By loving men as they ought to be loved we conquer anger, jealousy and partiality. (94) Curiosity is a perversion of the laudable desire to know the truth. Idle curiosity is sin. But the desire to know God and the meaning of Scripture is entirely good and the way of salvation. (106) The Five Talents in the parable are the five senses. When they are well used an extra talent is given, i.e., power to understand eternal things.

lv, 107–113. Final Exhortation to the Worship of the One True God.

Of True Religion

THE TEXT

i, 1. The way of the good and blessed life is to be found entirely in the true religion wherein one God is worshipped and acknowledged with purest piety to be the beginning of all existing things, originating, perfecting and containing the universe. Thus it becomes easy to detect the error of the peoples who have preferred to worship many gods rather than the true God and Lord of all things, because their wise men whom they call philosophers used to have schools in disagreement one with another, while all made common use of the temples. The peoples and the priests knew quite well how divergent were the views of the philosophers concerning the nature of the gods, for none shrank from publicly professing his opinion, and indeed each endeavoured as far as he could to persuade everybody. And yet all of them with their co-sectaries, in spite of their diverse and mutually hostile opinions, came to the common religious rites, none saying them nay. Now the question is not, Whose opinion was nearest to the truth? But one thing, so far as I can see, is abundantly clear. What the philosophers observed along with the people in the way of religious rites was something quite different from what they defended in private, or even in the hearing of the people.

ii, 2. Socrates is said to have been somewhat bolder than the others. He swore by a dog or a stone or any other object that happened to be near him or came to hand, so to speak, when he was to take an oath. I suppose he knew how many natural objects, produced and governed by divine providence, are much better than the works of human artificers, and therefore worthier of divine honours than are the images which are worshipped in the temples. Not that dogs and stones were rightly to be worshipped by wise men; but that in this way all who had intelligence might understand how sunk in superstition men are. He wanted to show that an oath of this kind did represent an advance though not a very great one. If men were ashamed to take this step, they might at least see how shameful it was to remain in the still baser condition of religious practice to which they were accustomed. At the same time those who supposed that the visible world was the supreme God were given to realize their turpitude, for they were taught that any stone might be rightly worshipped as a particle of God most high. If they saw that that was offensive, they might change their minds and seek the one God who alone is superior to our minds, and by whom clearly every soul and the whole world has been created. Plato afterwards wrote all this down, making it pleasant to read rather than potent to persuade. These men were not fit to change the minds of their fellow-citizens, and convert them from idolatrous superstition and worldly vanity to the true worship of the true God. Thus Socrates himself venerated images along with his people, and after his condemnation and death no one dared to swear by a dog or to call a stone Jupiter. These things were merely recorded and handed down to memory. Whether this was due to fear of punishment or to the influence of the times it is not for me to judge.

iii, 3. This, however, I will say with complete confidence, in spite of all who love so obstinately the books of the philosophers. In Christian times there can be no doubt at all as to which religion is to be received and held fast, and as to where is the way that leads to truth and beatitude. Suppose Plato were alive and would not spurn a question I would put to him; or rather suppose one of his own disciples, who lived at the same time as he did, had addressed him thus: "You have persuaded me that truth is seen not with the bodily eyes but by the pure mind, and that any soul that cleaves to truth is thereby made happy and perfect. Nothing hinders the perception of truth more than a life devoted to lusts, and the false images of sensible things, derived from the sensible world and impressed on us by the agency of the body, which beget various opinions and errors. Therefore the mind has to be healed so that it may behold the immutable form of things which remains ever the same, preserving its beauty unchanged and unchangeable, knowing no spatial distance or temporal variation, abiding absolutely one and the same. Men do not believe in its existence, though it alone truly and supremely exists. Other things are born, die, are dissolved or broken up. But so far as they do exist they have existence from the eternal God, being created by his truth. To the rational and intellectual soul is given to enjoy the contemplation of his eternity, and by that contemplation it is armed and equipped so that it may obtain eternal life. So long as it is weakened by love of things that come to be and pass away, or by pain at losing them, so long as it is devoted to the custom of this life and to the bodily senses, and becomes vain among vain images, it laughs at those who say that there is something which cannot be seen by the eyes, or conjured up by any phantasm, but can be beheld by the mind alone, by the intelligence. You, my master, have persuaded me to believe these things. Now, if some great and divine man should arise to persuade the peoples that such things were to be at least believed if they could not grasp them with the mind, or that those who could grasp them should not allow themselves to be implicated in the depraved opinions of the multitude or to be overborne by vulgar errors, would you not judge that such a man is worthy of divine honours?" I believe Plato's answer would be: "That could not be done by man, unless the very virtue and wisdom of God delivered him from natural environment, illumined him from his cradle not by human teaching but by personal illumination, honoured him with such grace, strengthened him with such firmness and exalted him with such majesty, that he should be able to despise all that wicked men desire, to suffer all that they dread, to do all that they marvel at, and so with the greatest love and authority to convert the human race to so sound a faith. But it is needless to ask me about the honours that would be due to such a man. It is easy to calculate what honours are due to the wisdom of God. Being the bearer and instrument of the wisdom of God on behalf of the true salvation of the human race, such a man would have earned a place all his own, a place above all humanity."

4. Now this very thing has come to pass. It is celebrated in books and documents. From one particular region of the earth in which alone the one God was worshipped and where alone such a man could be born, chosen men were sent throughout the entire world, and by their virtues and words have kindled the fires of the divine love. Their sound teaching has been confirmed and they have left to posterity a world illumined. But not to speak of ancient history, which anyone may refuse to believe, to-day throughout the nations and peoples the proclamation is made: "In the beginning was the Word, and the

Word was with God, and the Word was God. This was in the beginning with God, and all things were made by him, and without him was nothing made" (John 1:1). In order that men may receive the Word, love him, and enjoy him so that the soul may be healed and the eye of the mind receive power to use the light, to the greedy it is declared: "Lay not up for yourselves treasures upon earth where moth and rust destroy, and where thieves break through and steal. But lay up for yourselves treasures in heaven where neither moth nor rust destroys, and where thieves do not break through nor steal. For where your treasure is there will your heart be also" (Matt. 6:19). To the wanton it is said: "He who sows in the flesh shall of the flesh reap corruption. He who sows in the spirit shall of the spirit reap eternal life" (Gal. 6:8). To the proud it is said: "Whosoever exalteth himself shall be abased and whosoever humbleth himself shall be exalted" (Luke 14:11). To the wrathful it is said: "Thou hast received a blow. Turn the other cheek" (Matt. 5:39). To those who strive it is said: "Love your enemies" (Matt. 5:44). To the superstitious: "The kingdom of God is within you" (Luke 17:21). To the curious: "Look not on the things which are seen, but on the things which are not seen. For the things which are seen are temporal, but the things which are not seen are eternal" (II Cor. 4:18). Finally, to all it is said: "Love not the world nor the things which are in the world. For everything that is in the world is the lust of the flesh, the lust of the eyes and the ambition of this world" (I John 2:15).

5. These things are read to the peoples throughout all the earth and are listened to most gladly and with veneration. After all the Christian blood shed, after all the burnings and crucifixions of the martyrs, fertilized by these things churches have sprung up as far afield as among barbarian nations. That thousands of young men and maidens contemn marriage and live in chastity causes no one surprise. Plato might have suggested that, but he so dreaded the perverse opinion of his times that he is said to have given in to nature and declared continence to be no sin. Views are accepted which it was once monstrous to maintain, even as it is monstrous now to dispute them. All over the inhabited world the Christian rites are entrusted to men who are willing to make profession and to undertake the obligations required. Every day the precepts of Christianity are read in the churches and expounded by the priests. Those who try to fulfil them beat their breasts in contrition. Multitudes enter upon this way of life from every race, forsaking the riches

and honours of the present world, desirous of dedicating their whole life to the one most high God. Islands once deserted and many lands formerly left in solitude are filled with monks. In cities and towns, castles and villages, country places and private estates, there is openly preached and practised such a renunciation of earthly things and conversion to the one true God that daily throughout the entire world with almost one voice the human race makes response: Lift up your hearts to the Lord. Why, then, do we still admiringly yearn for the darkness of yesterday, and look for divine oracles in the entrails of dead cattle? Why, when it comes to disputation, are we so eager to mouth the name of Plato rather than to have the truth in our hearts?

iv, 6. Those who think it a vain or even a wicked thing to despise the world of sense, and to subject the soul to God most high that he may purge it with virtue, must be refuted with a different argument; if indeed they are worth disputing with. But those who admit that that is a good ideal to be pursued should acknowledge God and submit to him who has brought it to pass that all nations now are persuaded that these things ought to be believed. They would themselves have brought this to pass if they had had the power. Seeing they had not the power, they cannot avoid the charge of envy. Let them, then, submit to him who has brought it to pass. Let them not be prevented by inquisitiveness or by vain-glory from recognizing the gap that subsists between the timid guesses of the few and the obvious salvation and correction of whole peoples. If Plato and the rest of them, in whose names men glory, were to come to life again and find the churches full and the temples empty, and that the human race was being called away from desire for temporal and transient goods to spiritual and intelligible goods and to the hope of eternal life, and was actually giving its attention to these things, they would perhaps say (if they really were the men they are said to have been): That is what we did not dare to preach to the people. We preferred to yield to popular custom rather than to bring the people over to our way of thinking and living.

7. So if these men could live their lives again to-day, they would see by whose authority measures are best taken for man's salvation, and, with the change of a few words and sentiments, they would become Christians, as many Platonists of recent times have done. If they would not admit this or do this, but remained in their pride and envy, I know not whether it would

be possible for them, encumbered with these rags and bird-lime, to resort to the things they once said were to be sought and striven for. I do not know whether such great men would have been prevented by the other vice which prevents present-day pagans, who now concern us, from accepting the Christian salvation, for indeed it is utterly puerile. I mean, of course, their curiosity in inquiring at demons.

v, 8. However philosophers may boast, anyone can easily understand that religion is not to be sought from them. For they take part in the religious rites of their fellow-citizens, but in their schools teach divergent and contrary opinions about the nature of their gods and of the chief good, as the multitude can testify. If we could see this one great vice healed by the Christian discipline, no one should deny that that would be an achievement worthy of all possible praise. Innumerable heresies that turn aside from the rule of Christianity testify that men are not admitted to sacramental communion who think and endeavour to persuade others to think otherwise of God the Father, of his wisdom and of the divine gift [the Holy Spirit] than as the truth demands. So it is taught and believed as a chief point in man's salvation that philosophy, i.e., the pursuit of wisdom, cannot be quite divorced from religion, for those whose doctrine we do not approve do not share in *our* sacramental rites.

9. There is little to be surprised at in this in the case of men who have chosen to have different religious rites from ours such as the Ophites whoever they may be, or the Manichaeans and others. It is more noticeable in the case of those who celebrate similar religious rites but differ from us in doctrine and are more vigorous in defending their errors than careful to have them corrected. These are excluded from Catholic communion and from participation in our rites in spite of their similarity. They have deserved to have names of their own and separate meetings, being different not only in matters of words, but also because of their superstition; like the Photinians, the Arians and many others. It is another matter with those who have caused schisms. The Lord's threshing-floor might have kept them as chaff until the time of the last winnowing, had they not in their levity been carried off by the wind of pride, and separated from us of their own accord. The Jews, it is true, worship the one omnipotent God, but they expect from him only temporal and visible goods. Being too secure they were unwilling to observe in their own Scriptures the indications of a new people of God arising out of humble estate, and so they remained in "the old

man." This being so, religion is to be sought neither in the confusion of the pagans, nor in the offscourings of the heretics, nor in the insipidity of schismatics, nor in the blindness of the Jews, but only among those who are called Catholic or orthodox Christians, that is, guardians of truth and followers of right.

vi, 10. This Catholic Church, strongly and widely spread throughout the world, makes use of all who err, to correct them if they are willing to be aroused, and to assist its own progress. It makes use of the nations as material for its operations, of heretics to try its own doctrine, of schismatics to prove its stability, of the Jews as a foil to its own beauty. Some it invites, others it excludes, some it leaves behind, others it leads. To all it gives power to participate in the grace of God, whether they are as yet to be formed or reformed, admitted for the first time or gathered in anew. Its own carnal members, i.e., those whose lives or opinions are carnal, it tolerates as chaff by which the corn is protected on the floor until it is separated from its covering. On this floor everyone voluntarily makes himself either corn or chaff. Therefore every man's sin or error is tolerated until he finds an accuser or defends his wicked opinion with pertinacious animosity. Those who are excluded return by way of penitence, or in baleful liberty sink into wickedness as a warning to us to be diligent; or they cause schisms to exercise our patience; or they beget a heresy to try our intelligence or to quicken it. By such ways carnal Christians leave us, for they could neither be corrected nor endured.

11. Often, too, divine providence permits even good men to be driven from the congregation of Christ by the turbulent seditions of carnal men. When for the sake of the peace of the Church they patiently endure that insult or injury, and attempt no novelties in the way of heresy or schism, they will teach men how God is to be served with a true disposition and with great and sincere charity. The intention of such men is to return when the tumult has subsided. But if that is not permitted because the storm continues or because a fiercer one might be stirred up by their return, they hold fast to their purpose to look to the good even of those responsible for the tumults and commotions that drove them out. They form no separate conventicles of their own, but defend to the death and assist by their testimony the faith which they know is preached in the Catholic Church. These the Father who seeth in secret crowns secretly. It appears that this is a rare kind of Christian, but examples are not lacking. Indeed there are more than can be believed. So divine

providence uses all kinds of men as examples for the oversight of souls and for the building up of his spiritual people.

vii, 12. A few years ago, my dear Romanianus, I promised to write down for you my sentiments concerning true religion. I think the time has now come to do so. In view of the love wherewith I am bound to you I can no longer allow your eager questions to run on endlessly. Repudiating all who do not carry philosophy into religious observance or philosophize in a religious spirit; those also who wax proud in wicked opinions or some other cause of dissension and so deviate from the Rule of Faith and from the communion of the Catholic Church; and those who refuse to own the light of the Holy Scripture and the grace of the spiritual people of God, which we call the New Testament—all of whom I have censured as briefly as I could—we must hold fast the Christian religion and the communion of the Church which is Catholic, and is called Catholic not only by its own members but also by all its enemies. Whether they will or no, heretics and schismatics use no other name for it than the name of Catholic, when they speak of it not among themselves but with outsiders. They cannot make themselves understood unless they designate it by this name which is in universal use.

13. In following this religion our chief concern is with the prophetic history of the dispensation of divine providence in time—what God has done for the salvation of the human race, renewing and restoring it unto eternal life. When once this is believed, a way of life agreeable to the divine commandments will purge the mind and make it fit to perceive spiritual things which are neither past nor future but abide ever the same, liable to no change. There is one God; Father, Son and Holy Spirit. When this Trinity is known as far as it can be in this life, it is perceived without the slightest doubt that every creature, intellectual, animal and corporeal, derives such existence as it has from that same creative Trinity, has its own form, and is subject to the most perfect order. It is not as if the Father were understood to have made one part of creation, the Son another, and the Holy Spirit another, but the Father through the Son in the gift of the Holy Spirit together made all things and every particular thing. For every thing, substance, essence or nature, or whatever better word there may be, possesses at once these three qualities: it is a particular thing; it is distinguished from other things by its own proper form; and it does not transgress the order of nature.

viii, 14. When this is known it will be as clear as it can be to men that all things are subject by necessary, indefeasible and just laws to their Lord God. Hence all those things which to begin with we simply believed, following authority only, we come to understand. Partly we see them as certain, partly as possible and fitting, and we become sorry for those who do not believe them, and have preferred to mock at us for believing rather than to share our belief. The Holy Incarnation, the birth from a virgin, the death of the Son of God for us, his resurrection from the dead, ascension into heaven and sitting at the right hand of the Father, the forgiveness of sins, the day of judgment, the resurrection of the body are not merely believed, when the eternity of the Trinity and the mutability of created things are known. They are also judged to be part and parcel of the mercy of the most high God, which he has shown towards the human race.

15. It has been truly said: "There must be many heresies, that they which are approved may be made manifest among you" (I Cor. 11:19). Let us also make use of that gift of divine providence. Men become heretics who would have no less held wrong opinions even within the Church. Now that they are outside they do us more good, not by teaching the truth, for they do not know it, but by provoking carnal Catholics to seek the truth and spiritual Catholics to expound it. There are in the Holy Church innumerable men approved by God, but they do not become manifest among us so long as we are delighted with the darkness of our ignorance, and prefer to sleep rather than to behold the light of truth. So, many are awakened from sleep by the heretics, so that they may see God's light and be glad. Let us therefore use even heretics, not to approve their errors, but to assert the Catholic discipline against their wiles, and to become more vigilant and cautious, even if we cannot recall them to salvation.

ix, 16. I believe that God will lend us his aid so that Scripture, being read by good men inspired by piety, may avail not against one false and bad opinion only but against all. But chiefly it is set against those who think that there are two natures or substances at war with one another, each with its own principle. Some things they like and others they dislike, and they will have God to be the author of the things they like, but not of those they dislike. When they cannot overcome temptation and are snared in carnal traps, they think there are two souls in one body, one from God and sharing his nature, the other from the race of darkness which God neither begat, nor made, nor produced, nor cast from him; which has its own independent life, its territory, its offspring and living things, in short its kingdom and unbegotten principle. At a certain time it rebelled against God, and God, having no other resource and finding no other means of resisting the enemy, under dire necessity, sent the good soul hither, a particle of his substance. They fondly imagine that the enemy was subdued and the world fabricated by this soul becoming mixed up with the elements of darkness.

17. I am not now refuting their opinions, partly because I have already done so and partly because I intend to do so again, if God permit. In this work I am showing as far as I can with the arguments God deigns to supply, how secure the Catholic faith is against them, and how the things which move men to give in to their opinions need not disturb the mind. You know my mind very well, and I want you above all to believe firmly that I do not make this solemn declaration with an arrogance which ought to be avoided. I say, whatever error is to be found in this book it alone is to be attributed to me. Whatever is truly and suitably expounded I owe entirely to God, the giver of all good gifts.

x, 18. Let it be clearly understood that there could have been no error in religion had not the soul worshipped in place of its God either a soul or a body or some phantasm of its own, possibly two of these together or all of them at once. In this life the soul should have frankly accepted the temporal condition of human society but should have directed its regard to eternal things and worshipped the one God without whose changeless permanence no mutable thing could have any abiding existence. Anyone who studies his own emotions can learn that the soul is mutable, not in space certainly but in time. That body is mutable both in space and time is easy for anyone to observe. Phantasms are nothing but figments of corporeal shapes appearing to bodily sense. It is the easiest thing in the world to commit them to memory as they appear or, by thinking about them, to divide or multiply, contract or expand, set in order or disturb, or give them any kind of shape. But when truth is being sought it is difficult to be on one's guard against them and to avoid them.

19. Do not, then, let us serve the creature rather than the Creator, or become vain in our thoughts. That is the rule of perfect religion. If we cleave to the eternal Creator we must neces-

sarily be somehow affected by eternity. But because the soul, implicated in and overwhelmed by its sins, cannot by itself see and grasp this truth, if in human experience there were no intermediate stage whereby man might strive to rise above his earthly life and reach likeness to God, God in his ineffable mercy by a temporal dispensation has used the mutable creation, obedient however to his eternal laws, to remind the soul of its original and perfect nature, and so has come to the aid of individual men and indeed of the whole human race. That is the Christian religion in our times. To know and follow it is the most secure and most certain way of salvation.

20. This religion can be defended against loquacious persons and expounded to seekers in many ways. Omnipotent God may himself show the truth, or he may use good angels or men to assist men of good will to behold and grasp the truth. Everyone uses the method which he sees to be suitable to those with whom he has to do. I have given much consideration for a long time to the nature of the people I have met with either as carping critics or as genuine seekers of the truth. I have also considered my own case both when I was a critic and when I was a seeker; and I have come to the conclusion that this is the method I must use. Hold fast whatever truth you have been able to grasp, and attribute it to the Catholic Church. Reject what is false and pardon me who am but a man. What is doubtful believe until either reason teaches or authority lays down that it is to be rejected or that it is true, or that it has to be believed always. Listen to what follows as diligently and as piously as you can. For God helps men like that.

xi, 21. There is no life which is not of God, for God is supreme life and the fount of life. No life is evil as life but only as it tends to death. Life knows no death save wickedness [*nequitia*] which derives its name from nothingness [*ne quidquam*]. For this reason wicked men are called men of no worth. A life, therefore, which by voluntary defect falls away from him who made it, whose essence it enjoyed, and, contrary to the law of God, seeks to enjoy bodily objects which God made to be inferior to it, tends to nothingness. This is wickedness, but not because the body as such is nothing. A corporeal object has some concord between its parts, otherwise it could not exist at all. Therefore it was made by him who is the head of all concord. A corporeal object enjoys a certain degree of peace, due to its having form. Without that it would be nothing. Therefore he is the creator of matter, from whom all peace comes, and who is the uncreated and most perfect form. Matter participates in something belonging to the ideal world, otherwise it would not be matter. To ask, therefore, who created matter is to ask for him who is supreme in the ideal world. For every idea comes from him. Who is he, then, save the one God, the one truth, the one salvation of all, the first and highest essence from which all that exists derives existence as such? For all existence as such is good.

22. For that reason death does not come from God. "God did not create death, nor does he take pleasure in the destruction of the living" (Wisdom 1:13). The highest essence imparts existence to all that exists. That is why it is called essence. Death imparts no actual existence to anything which has died. If it is really dead it has indubitably been reduced to nothingness. For things die only in so far as they have a decreasing part in existence. That can be more briefly put in this way: things die according as they become less. Matter is less than any kind of life, since it is life that keeps even the tiniest quantity of matter together in any thing, whether it be the life that governs any particular living thing, or that which governs the entire universe of natural things. Matter is therefore subject to death, and is thereby nearer to nothingness. Life which delights in material joys and neglects God tends to nothingness and is thereby iniquity.

xii, 23. In this way life becomes earthly and carnal. So long as it is so it will not possess the kingdom of God, and what it loves will be snatched from it. It loves what, being matter, is less than life, and, on account of the sinfulness of so doing, the beloved object becomes corruptible, is dissolved and lost to its lover, even as it, in loving a material thing, has abandoned God. It neglected his precepts: Eat this and do not eat that. Therefore it is punished; for by loving inferior things it is given a place among the inferior creatures, being deprived of its pleasures and afflicted with grief. What is bodily grief but the sudden loss of integrity in something which the soul has made a bad use of, so rendering it liable to corruption? And what is spiritual grief but to lose mutable things which the soul enjoyed or hoped to be able to enjoy? This covers the whole range of evil, i.e., sin and its penalty.

24. If the soul, while it continues in the course of human life, overcomes the desires which it has fed to its own undoing by enjoying mortal things, and believes that it has the aid of God's grace enabling it to overcome them, if it serves God with the mind and a good will, it will undoubtedly be restored, and will

return from the mutable many to the immutable One. It will be re-formed by the Wisdom which is not formed but has formed all things, and will enjoy God through the spirit, which is the gift of God. It becomes "spiritual man, judging all things and judged of none," "loving the Lord its God with all its heart and all its soul and all its mind, and loving its neighbour not carnally but as itself. He loves himself spiritually who loves God with all that lives within him. On these two commandments hang the whole law and the prophets" (Matt. 22:40).

25. The consequence will be that after the death of the body, which we owe to the primal sin, in its own time and order the body will be restored to its pristine stability; but it will owe its stability not to itself but to the soul whose stability is in God. For the soul too owes its stability not to itself but to God whom it enjoys. Thus it has an ampler life than the body. For the body lives by the soul and the soul by the immutable truth, who is the only Son of God. So even the body lives by the Son of God, because all things live by him. By God's gift, given to the soul, i.e., the Holy Spirit, not only does the soul, which receives it, become sound and peaceful and holy, but the body also will be vivified and will be cleansed completely. The Master himself said: "Cleanse that which is within and that which is without shall be clean" (Matt. 23:26). And the apostle says: "He shall quicken your mortal bodies on account of the Spirit that abideth in you." (Rom. 8:11). Take away sin, and sin's penalty goes too. And where is evil? "O death, where is thy victory? O death, where is thy sting? Being overcomes nothingness, and so death is swallowed up in victory" (I Cor. 15:54–55).

xiii, 26. The evil angel, who is called the devil, will have no power over the sanctified. Even he, so far as he is angel, is not evil, but only so far as he has been perverted by his own will. We must admit that even angels are mutable if God alone is immutable. By willing to love God rather than themselves angels abide firm and stable in him and enjoy his majesty, being gladly subject to him alone. The bad angel loved himself more than God, refused to be subject to God, swelled with pride, came short of supreme being and fell. He became less than he had been, because, in wishing to enjoy his own power rather than God's, he wished to enjoy what was less. He never had supreme existence for that belongs to God alone, but he had an ampler existence than he has now, when he enjoyed that which supremely is. His present existence is not evil *quâ* existence, but so far as it is less ample than it formerly was. To that extent he tends towards extinction. It is no marvel that his loss occasioned poverty, and poverty envy, which is the truly diabolical characteristic of the devil.

xiv, 27. If the defect we call sin overtook a man against his will, like a fever, the penalty which follows the sinner and is called condemnation would rightly seem to be unjust. But in fact sin is so much a voluntary evil that it is not sin at all unless it is voluntary. This is so obvious that no one denies it, either of the handful of the learned or of the mass of the unlearned. We must either say that no sin has been committed or confess that it has been willingly committed. No one can rightly deny that a soul has sinned who admits that it can be corrected by penitence, that the penitent should be pardoned, or that he who continues in sin is condemned by the just law of God. Lastly if it is not by the exercise of will that we do wrong, no one at all is to be censured or warned. If you take away censure and warning the Christian law and the whole discipline of religion is necessarily abolished. Therefore, it is by the will that sin is committed. And since there is no doubt that sins are committed, I cannot see that it can be doubted that souls have free choice in willing. God judged that men would serve him better if they served him freely. That could not be so if they served him by necessity and not by free will.

28. The angels accordingly serve God freely. That is to their advantage, not God's. God needs no good thing from others, for all good comes from himself. What is begotten of him is equally divine, begotten not made. Things which are made need his good, i.e., the chief good, the supreme essence. They become less when by sin they are less attracted to him. But they are never entirely separated from him. Otherwise they would not exist at all. Movements of the soul are the affections, depending on the will. Bodily movements are movements in space. Man is said to have been persuaded by the wicked angel, but even so it was his will that consented. If he had consented by necessity, he would have been held guilty of no sin.

xv, 29. The human body was perfect of its kind before man sinned, but after he had sinned it became weak and mortal. Though that was the just punishment for sin, nevertheless it showed more of the clemency of the Lord than of his severity. We are thus admonished that we ought to turn our love from bodily pleasures to the eternal essence of truth. The beauty of justice is in complete accord with the grace of loving-kindness, seeing that we who were deceived by the sweetness of inferior goods should be taught by the bitterness of penalties. For divine providence has so moderated our punishment that even in this corruptible body it is permitted to us to work towards righteousness, to lay aside all pride and submit to God alone, not to trust in ourselves but to commit ourselves to be ruled and defended by him alone. So with God's guidance a man of good will can turn the troubles of this present life to the advantage of courage. Among abounding pleasures and temporal prosperity, he may prove and strengthen temperance. In temptations he may sharpen his prudence, that he may not only not be led into them, but may also become more vigilant and more eager in his love of truth which alone never deceives.

xvi, 30. To heal souls God adopts all kinds of means suitable to the times which are ordered by his marvellous wisdom. I must not speak of these, or at least they must be spoken of only among the pious and the perfect. But in no way did he show greater loving-kindness in his dealings with the human race for its good, than when the Wisdom of God, his only Son, coeternal and consubstantial with the Father, deigned to assume human nature; when the Word became flesh and dwelt among us. For thus he showed to carnal people, given over to bodily sense and unable with the mind to behold the truth, how lofty a place among creatures belonged to human nature, in that he appeared to men not merely visibly—for he could have done that in some ethereal body adapted to our weak powers of vision—but as a true man. The assuming of our nature was to be also its liberation. And that no one should perchance suppose that the creator of sex despised sex, he became a man born of a woman.

31. He did nothing by violence, but everything by persuasion and warning. The old servitude was past and the day of liberty had dawned and man was fitly and helpfully taught how he had been created with free will. By his miracles he, being God, produced faith in God, and by his passion, in the human nature he had assumed, he furthered respect for human nature. Speaking to the multitudes as God he refused to recognize his mother when her coming was announced, and yet, as the Gospel says, he was obedient to his parents (Matt. 12:48, Luke 2:51). In his doctrine the God appeared, and the Man in the various stages of his life. When, as God, he was about to turn water into wine, he said: "Woman, depart from me; what have I to do with thee? My hour is not yet come" (John 2:4). But when his hour had come when, as man, he should die, he recognized his mother

from the Cross and commended her to the disciple whom he loved more than the others (John 19:26-27). The peoples to their own destruction sought riches that minister to pleasures: He determined to be poor. They panted for honours and empires: He refused to be made a king. They thought it a great boon to have sons after the flesh. He scorned marriage and offspring. In their great pride they dreaded insults: He bore with insults of every kind. They thought injuries were not to be endured: what greater injury can there be than that a just and innocent man should be condemned. They execrated bodily pain: He was beaten and tortured. They feared to die: He was condemned to death. They thought a cross the most shameful form of death: He was crucified. All the things which men unrighteously desired to possess, he did without and so made them of no account. All the things which men sought to avoid and so deviated from the search for truth, he endured and so robbed them of their power over us. There is no sin that men can commit which is not either a seeking of what he avoided, or an avoiding of what he bore.

32. His whole life on earth as Man, in the humanity he deigned to assume, was an education in morals. His resurrection from the dead showed that nothing of human nature can perish, for all is safe with God. It showed also how all things serve the Creator either for the punishment of sin or for the liberation of man, and how the body can serve the soul when the soul is subject to God. When the body perfectly obeys the soul and the soul perfectly serves God, not only is there no evil substance, for that there can never be, but, better still, substance cannot be affected by evil, for it can be so affected only by sin or its punishment. This natural discipline is worthy of the complete faith of less intelligent Christians, and for intelligent Christians it is free from all error.

xvii, 33. This method of teaching fulfils the rule of all rational discipline. For as it teaches partly quite openly and partly by similitudes in word, deed and sacrament, it is adapted to the complete instruction and exercise of the soul. The exposition of mysteries is guided by what is clearly stated. If there was nothing that could not be understood with perfect ease, there would be no studious search for truth and no pleasure in finding it. If there were sacraments in Scripture, and if they were not signs and tokens of truth, action would not be properly related to knowledge. Piety begins with fear and is perfected in love. So in the time of servitude under the old Law the people were constrained by fear and burdened with many sacraments. That was advantageous for them in that they might desire the grace of God which the prophets foretold would come. When it came, the wisdom of God having assumed human nature and called us into liberty, few most salutary sacraments were appointed to maintain the society of the Christian people, i.e., of the multitude of those set free to serve the one God. Many things which were imposed upon the Hebrew people, i.e., a multitude bound by Law under the same God, are no longer observed in practice, but they remain valid for faith and are susceptible of (allegorical) interpretation. They do not now bind in servile bonds, but they afford the mind exercise in its freedom.

34. Whoever denies that both Testaments come from the same God for the reason that our people are not bound by the same sacraments as those by which the Jews were bound and still are bound, cannot deny that it would be perfectly just and possible for one father of a family to lay one set of commands upon those for whom he judged a harsher servitude to be useful, and a different set on those whom he deigned to adopt into the position of sons. If the trouble is that the moral precepts under the old Law are lower and in the Gospel higher, and that therefore both cannot come from the same God, whoever thinks in this way may find difficulty in explaining how a single physician prescribes one medicine to weaker patients through his assistants, and another by himself to stronger patients, all to restore health. The art of medicine remains the same and quite unchanged, but it changes its prescriptions for the sick, since the state of their health changes. So divine providence remains entirely without change, but comes to the aid of mutable creatures in various ways, and commands or forbids different things at different times according to the different stages of their disease, whether it be the vice which is the beginning of death, or the final stage when death itself is imminent. In all cases divine providence recalls to its true and essential nature whatever manifests defect, i.e., tends to nothingness, and so strengthens it.

xviii, 35. But you say, Why do they become defective? Because they are mutable. Why are they mutable? Because they have not supreme existence. And why so? Because they are inferior to him who made them. Who made them? He who supremely is. Who is he? God, the immutable Trinity, made them through his supreme wisdom and preserves them by his supreme loving-kindness. Why did he make them? In order that they might exist. Existence as such is good, and supreme existence is the chief good. From what did he make them? Out of nothing. Whatever is must have some form, and though it be but a minimal good it will be good and will be of God. The highest form is the highest good, and the lowest form is the lowest good. Every good thing is either God or derived from God. Therefore even the lowest form is of God. And the same may be said of species. We rightly praise alike that which has form and that which has species. That out of which God created all things had neither form nor species, and was simply nothing. That which by comparison with perfect things is said to be without form, but which has any form at all, however small or inchoate, is not nothing. It, too, in so far as it has any being at all, is of God.

36. Therefore, if the world was made out of some unformed matter, that matter was made out of absolutely nothing. If it was as yet unformed, still it was at least capable of receiving form. By God's goodness it is "formable." Even capacity for form is good. The author of all good things, who gives form, also gives the capacity for form. All that exists receives existence from God, and that which does not as yet exist but may do so, receives its potential existence from God. In other words, all that is formed receives its form from God, and from him all that is not yet formed receives power to be formed. Nothing has integrity of nature unless it be whole of its kind. From God comes all wholeness as every good thing comes from him.

xix, 37. He whose mental eyes are open and are not darkened or confused by zeal for vain verbal victory, understands easily that all things are good even though they become vitiated and die; whereas vice and death are evil. Vice and death do no damage to anything except by depriving it of soundness, and vice would not be vice if it did no damage. If vice is the opposite of wholeness no doubt wholeness is good. All things are good which have vice opposed to them, and vice vitiates them. Things which are vitiated are therefore good, but are vitiated because they are not supremely good. Because they are good they are of God. Because they are not supremely good they are not God. The good which cannot be vitiated is God. All other good things are of him. They can of themselves be vitiated because by themselves they are nothing. God keeps them from being wholly vitiated, or, if vitiated, makes them whole.

xx, 38. The primal vice of the rational soul is the will to do what the highest and inmost truth forbids. Thus was man driven from paradise into the present world, i.e., from eternal things to temporal, from abundance to poverty, from strength to weakness. Not, however, from substantial good to substantial evil, for there is no substantial evil; but from eternal good to temporal good, from spiritual to carnal good, from intelligible to sensible good, from the highest to the lowest good. There is therefore a good which it is sin for the rational soul to love because it belongs to a lower order of being. The sin is evil, not the substance that is sinfully loved. The tree was not evil which, we read, was planted in the midst of paradise, but the transgression of the divine command was evil, and as a consequence had its just condemnation. But from the tree which was touched contrary to the prohibition came the power to distinguish between good and evil. When the soul has become involved in its sin, it learns, by paying the penalty, the difference between the precept it refused to obey and the sin which it committed. In this way it learns by suffering to know the evil it did not learn to know by avoiding it. By making comparison between its former and its present state it loves more earnestly the good which it loved too little, as is seen from its failure to obey.

39. Vice in the soul arises from its own doing; and the moral difficulty that ensues from vice is the penalty which it suffers. That is the sum-total of evil. To do and to suffer have nothing to do with substance; hence substance is not evil. Water is not evil, nor is a creature that lives in the air. But to throw oneself voluntarily into water and be suffocated, as the drowned man is, is evil. An iron style which has one part for writing with and another part for making deletions is ingeniously manufactured and beautiful in its own way, and most useful to us. But if one wanted to write with the part intended for making deletions, or to make a deletion with the writing end, one would not cause the style to be evil. One would rightly blame one's own action. Correct the action and where will be the evil? Suppose one were suddenly to turn one's eyes to look at the mid-day sun. The eyes would be dazzled and pained; but neither the sun nor the eyes would for that reason be evil. They are substances. Careless looking at the sun and the disturbance that is its consequence is evil. And there would be no evil if the eyes had been practised and made fit to look at the light. Nor is light evil when the light we see with our eyes is worshipped instead of the light of wisdom which is seen by the mind. The superstition is evil that serves the creature rather than the Creator; and there

would be no such evil if the soul recognized its Creator, subjected itself to him alone, and understood that other things were made subject to it by him.

40. Every corporeal creature, when possessed by a soul that loves God, is a good thing of the lowest order, and beautiful in its own way, for it is held together by form and species. If it is loved by a soul that neglects God, not even so is it evil in itself. But the sin of so loving it brings a penalty to him who so loves it. It involves him in miseries, and feeds him with fallacious pleasures which neither abide nor satisfy, but beget torturing sorrows. Time in all the beauty of its changefulness holds on its appointed course, and the thing desired escapes him who loved it. It torments him by passing beyond his power to sense it, and disturbs his mind with errors. For it makes him suppose that the material object which the flesh had wrongly delighted in, and which he had known through the uncertain senses, was the primal form, when in fact it was the lowest form of all; so that, when he thinks, he believes he understands, being deluded by shadowy phantasms. If he does not hold fast to the whole discipline of divine providence but imagines he does, and tries to resist the flesh, he merely reaches the images of visible things. He vainly excogitates vast spaces of light exactly like ordinary light which he sees has fixed limits here, and promises himself a future habitation there. He does not know that he is still entangled in the lust of the eye, and that he is carrying this world with him in his endeavour to go beyond it. He thinks he has reached another world simply by falsely imagining the bright part of this world infinitely extended. One could do the same not only with light but also with water, wine, honey, gold, silver, even with the flesh, blood and bones of animals, and other like things. There is no bodily object seen singly which cannot in thought be infinitely multiplied, and there is nothing which, as we see it, occupies a small space, which cannot by the same faculty of imagination be infinitely extended. It is very easy to execrate the flesh, but very difficult not to be carnally minded.

xxi, 41. By this perversity of the soul, due to sin and punishment, the whole corporeal creation becomes, as Solomon says: "Vanity of them that are vain, all is vanity. What advantage has man in all his labour which he does under the sun?" (Eccl. 1:2). Not for nothing does he say, "of them that are vain," for if you take away vain persons who pursue that which is last as if it were first, matter will not be vanity but will show its own beauty in its own way, a low type of beauty, of course, but not deceptive. When man fell away from the unity of God the multitude of temporal forms was distributed among his carnal senses, and his sensibilities were multiplied by the changeful variety. So abundance became laborious, and his needs, if one may say so, became abundant, for he pursues one thing after another, and nothing remains permanently with him. So what with his corn and wine and oil, his needs are so multiplied that he cannot find the one thing needful, a single and unchangeable nature, seeking which he would not err, and attaining which he would cease from grief and pain. For then he would have as a consequence the redemption of his body, which no longer would be corrupted. As it is, the corruption of the body burdens the soul, and its earthly habitation forces it to think of many things; for the humble beauty of material objects is hurried along in the order in which one thing succeeds another. The reason why corporeal beauty is the lowest beauty is that its parts cannot all exist simultaneously. Some things give place and others succeed them, and all together complete the number of temporal forms and make of them a single beauty.

xxii, 42. But all this is not evil because it is transient. A line of poetry is beautiful in its own way though no two syllables can be spoken at the same time. The second cannot be spoken till the first is finished. So in due order the end of the line is reached. When the last syllable is spoken the previous ones are not heard at the same time, and yet along with the preceding ones it makes the form and metrical arrangement complete. The art of versifying is not subject to change with time as if its beauty was made up of measured quantities. It possesses, at one and the same time, all the rules for making the verse which consists of successive syllables of which the later ones follow those which had come earlier. In spite of this the verse is beautiful as exhibiting the faint traces of the beauty which the art of poetry keeps steadfastly and unchangeably.

43. Some perverse persons prefer a verse to the art of versifying, because they set more store by their ears than by their intelligence. So many love temporal things and do not look for divine providence which is the maker and governor of time. Loving temporal things they do not want the things they love to pass away. They are just as absurd as anyone would be who, when a famous poem was being recited, wanted to hear one single syllable all the time. There are no such hearers of poems, but there are multitudes of people who think in this way about historical events. There is no one who cannot easily hear a whole

verse or even a whole poem; but there is no one who can grasp the whole order of the ages. Besides, we are not involved as parts in a poem, but for our sins we are made to be parts of the secular order. The poem is read for us to judge of it. The course of history is made up of our labours. No one who is vanquished in competitive games finds pleasure in them, but they are honourable because of his dishonour. Here is a sort of parable of the truth. For no other reason are we kept from such spectacles than lest we should be deceived by the shadows of things and wander from the things themselves whereof they are shadows. So the condition and government of the universe displeases only impious and damned souls, and, in spite of their misery, it pleases many who are victorious upon earth, or who look on in heaven without any risk. Nothing that is just displeases a just man.

xxiii, 44. Every rational soul is made unhappy by its sins or happy by its well-doing. Every irrational soul yields to one that is more powerful, or obeys one that is better, or is on terms of equality with its equals, exercising rivals, or harming any it has overcome. Every body is obedient to its soul so far as permitted by the merits of the latter or the orderly arrangement of things. There is no evil in the universe, but in individuals there is evil due to their own fault. When the soul has been regenerated by the grace of God and restored to its integrity, and made subject to him alone by whom it was created, its body too will be restored to its original strength, and it will receive power to possess the world, not to be possessed by the world. Then it will have no evil. For the lowly beauty of temporal changes will not involve it, for it will have been raised above change. There will be, as it is written, a New Heaven and a New Earth, and there souls will not have to do their part in toiling, but will reign over the universe. "All things are yours," says the apostle, "and ye are Christ's and Christ is God's" (I Cor. 3:21-23). And again: "The head of the woman is the man, the head of the man is Christ, and the head of Christ is God" (I Cor. 11:3). Accordingly, since the vice of the soul is not its nature but contrary to its nature, and is nothing else than sin and sin's penalty, we understand that no nature, or, if you prefer it, no substance or essence, is evil. Nor does the universe suffer any deformity from the sins and punishments of its soul. Rational substance which is clear of all sin and subject to God dominates other things which are subject to it. But rational substance which has committed sin is appointed to be where it is fitting, so that all things should be glorious, God being the maker and ruler of the universe. The beauty of the created universe is free from all fault because of these three things—the condemnation of sinners, the proving of the just, and the perfecting of the blessed.

xxiv, 45. The treatment of the soul, which God's providence and ineffable loving-kindness administers, is most beautiful in its steps and stages. There are two different methods, authority and reason. Authority demands belief and prepares man for reason. Reason leads to understanding and knowledge. But reason is not entirely absent from authority, for we have got to consider whom we have to believe, and the highest authority belongs to truth when it is clearly known. But because we dwell among temporal things, and love of them is an obstacle to our reaching eternal things, a kind of temporal medicine, calling not those who know but those who believe back to health, has priority by the order, not of nature or its inherent excellence, but of time. Wherever a man falls there he must lie until he is raised up. So we must strive, by means of the carnal forms which detain us, to come to know those of which carnal sense can bring us no knowledge. And by carnal sense I mean eyes, ears, and other bodily senses. To carnal or corporeal forms boys must necessarily and lovingly adhere, adolescents almost necessarily. But with increasing years the necessity disappears.

xxv, 46. Divine providence not only looks after individuals as it were privately but also after the whole human race publicly. How it deals with individuals God knows, who does it, and they also know, with whom he deals. But how he deals with the human race God has willed to be handed down through history and prophecy. The trustworthiness of temporal things whether past or future can be believed rather than known by the intelligence. It is our duty to consider what men or what books we are to believe in order that we may rightly worship God, wherein lies our sole salvation. Here the first decision must be this: Are we to believe those who summon us to the worship of many gods or those who summon us to worship one God? Who can doubt that we ought rather to follow those who summon us to worship one God, especially since the worshippers of many gods agree that there is one God who rules all things? At least the numerical series begins from the number one. Those, therefore, are to be followed who say that the one most high God is the only true God and is to be worshipped alone. If the truth does not shine out brightly among them, then, but not till then, must we go elsewhere. In the realm of nature there is a presumption of greater authority when all things are brought into unity. In the human race a multitude has no power unless by consent, i.e., agreement in unity. So in religion the authority of those who summon us to unity ought to be greater and more worthy of being believed.

47. Another thing which must be considered is the dissension that has arisen among men concerning the worship of the one God. We have heard that our predecessors, at a stage in faith on the way from temporal things up to eternal things, followed visible miracles. They could do nothing else. And they did so in such a way that it should not be necessary for those who came after them. When the Catholic Church had been founded and diffused throughout the whole world, on the one hand miracles were not allowed to continue till our time, lest the mind should always seek visible things, and the human race should grow cold by becoming accustomed to things which when they were novelties kindled its faith. On the other hand we must not doubt that those are to be believed who proclaimed miracles, which only a few had actually seen, and yet were able to persuade whole peoples to follow them. At that time the problem was to get people to believe before anyone was fit to reason about divine and invisible things. No human authority is set over the reason of a purified soul, for it is able to arrive at clear truth. But pride does not lead to the perception of truth. If there were no pride there would be no heretics, no schismatics, no circumcised, no worshippers of creatures or of images. If there had not been such classes of opponents before the people was made perfect as promised, truth would be sought much less eagerly.

xxvi, 48. This is the tradition concerning God's temporal dispensation and his providential care for those who by sin had deservedly become mortal. First, consider the nature and education of any individual man who is born. His first age, infancy, is spent in receiving bodily nourishment, and it is to be entirely forgotten when he grows up. Then follows childhood when we begin to have some memories. To this, adolescence succeeds, when nature allows propagation of offspring and fatherhood. After adolescence comes young manhood, which must take part in public duties and be brought under the laws. Now sins are more strictly forbidden, and sinners have to undergo the servile coercion of penalty. In carnal souls this of itself causes more dreadful onsets of lust, and wrong-doing is redoubled. For sin has a double aspect. It is not merely wrong-doing. It is disobedience. After the labours of young manhood, a little peace is given to old age. But it is an inferior age, lacking in lustre, weak and more subject to disease, and it leads to death. This is the life of man so far as he lives in the body and is bound by desires for temporal things. This is called "the old man" and "the exterior or earthly man," even if he obtain what the vulgar call felicity in a well-ordered earthly city, whether ruled by kings or princes or laws or all of them together. For without these things no people can be well-ordered, not even a people that pursues earthly goods. Even such a people has a measure of beauty of its own.

49. I have described "the old or exterior or earthly man." He may be a moderate man after his kind, or he may transgress the measure of servile justice. Some live thus from the beginning to the end of their days. But some begin in that way, as they necessarily must, but they are reborn inwardly, and with their spiritual strength and increase of wisdom they overcome "the old man" and put him to death, and bring him into subjection to the celestial laws, until after visible death the whole is restored. This is called "the new man," "the inward and heavenly man," whose spiritual ages are marked, not according to years, but according to his spiritual advance. In the first stage he is taught by the rich stores of history which nourish by examples. In the second stage he forgets human affairs and tends towards divine things. He is no longer kept in the bosom of human authority, but step by step by the use of reason he strives to reach the highest unchangeable law. In the third stage he confidently marries carnal appetite to strong reason, and inwardly rejoices in the sweetness of the union. Soul and mind are joined together in chaste union. There is as yet no compulsion to do right, but, even though no one forbids sin, he has no pleasure in sinning. The fourth stage is similar, only now he acts much more firmly, and springs forth as the perfect man, ready to endure and overcome all the persecutions, tempests and billows of this world. In the fifth stage he has peace and tranquillity on all sides. He lives among the abundant resources of the unchangeable realm of supreme ineffable wisdom. The sixth stage is complete transformation into life eternal, a total forgetfulness of temporal life passing into the perfect form which is made according to the image and likeness of God. The seventh is eternal rest and perpetual beatitude with no distinguishable ages. As the end of "the old man" is death, so the end of "the new man" is eternal life. The "old man" is the man of sin, but the "new man" is the man of righteousness.

xxvii, 50. No one doubts that these two lives are related as follows: A man can live the whole of this life as "the old and earthly man." But no one in this life can live as "the new and heavenly man," but must associate with the "old man." For he must begin there, and must so continue till death, though the old grows weaker and the new progresses. Similarly, the entire human race, whose life, like the life of an individual from Adam to the end of the world, is so arranged by the laws of divine providence that it appears divided among two classes. In one of these is the multitude of the impious who bear the image of the earthly man from the beginning to the end of the world. In the other is the succession of the people devoted to the one God. But from Adam to John the Baptist they live the life of the earthly man under a certain form of righteousness. Their history is called the Old Testament having the promise of a kind of earthly kingdom, which is nothing but the image of the new people and the New Testament, with the promise of the kingdom of heaven. Meantime the life of this people begins with the coming of the Lord in humility and goes on till the day of judgment, when he will come in all clearness. After the judgment the "old man" will come to an end, and there will take place the change that betokens the angelic life. For we shall all be raised, but we shall not all be changed (I Cor. 15:51). The pious people will be raised as they transform the remnants of the "old man" that cling to them into the "new man." The impious people who have kept the "old man" from the beginning to the end, will be raised in order to be precipitated into the second death. Those who read diligently can make out the divisions of the ages. They have no horror of tares or chaff. For the impious lives with the pious, and the sinner with the righteous, so that, by comparing the two, men may more eagerly rise to seek perfection.

xxviii, 51. If any of the earthly people at any time had the merit of reaching the illumination of the inward man, he gave to the human race in his day his aid showing it what that age required, hinting by prophecy what it was not opportune to show clearly. Such were the patriarchs and the prophets. So those discover who do not behave like children, but who diligently and piously handle this good and great secret of the divine-human relations. In the time of the new people I see that this has been most carefully provided by great and spiritual men for the nurselings of the Catholic Church. They are not to treat publicly of what they know is not seasonable to be handled before the people. They earnestly feed the multitude of those who are weak and needy with copious supplies of milky food; and the few who are wise they feed with stronger meats. They speak wisdom among the perfect, but from the carnal and the psychics, though they be "new men," they keep some things back, because they are still children, but they never lie. They do not look to vain honours and vain praise for themselves, but to the advantage of those with whom they have deserved to be associated in this life. This is the law of divine providence that no one is to receive assistance from his superiors to know and grasp the grace of God, unless he is prepared with a pure affection to assist his inferiors to the same. So out of our sin, which our nature committed in the first sinful man, the human race is made the great glory and ornament of the world, and is so properly governed by the provisions of divine providence that the art of God's ineffable healing turns even the foulness of sin into something that has a beauty of its own.

xxix, 52. We have said enough for the present about the benefit of authority. Let us see how far reason can advance from visible to invisible things in its ascent from temporal to eternal things. We should not vainly behold the beauty of the sky, the order of the stars, the brightness of light, the alternations of day and night, the monthly courses of the moon, the fourfold seasons of the year, the meeting of the four elements, the life-force of seeds begetting forms and numbers, and all things that keep their nature and their appropriate measure each in its own kind. In considering these things there should be no exercise of vain and perishing curiosity, but a step should be taken towards immortal things that abide for ever. The first thing to notice is living nature which senses all these things. Because it gives life to the body it must necessarily excel the body. No mass of matter, however great or however bright, is to be held of much account if it is without life. Any living substance is by the law of nature to be preferred to any inanimate substance.

53. No one doubts that irrational animals also live and feel. So in the human mind the most excellent part is not that which perceives sensible objects but that which judges of sensible objects. Many animals see more sharply and have a keener sense of corporeal objects than men have. But to judge of bodies belongs not to life that is merely sentient, but to life that has also the power of reasoning. Where the animals are lacking, there is our excellence. It is easy to see that that which judges is superior to that which is judged. For living reason judges not only of sensible things but also of the senses themselves. It knows why

the oar dipped in water must appear crooked though it is really straight, and why the eyes must see it in that way. Ocular vision can only tell us that it is so but cannot judge. Wherefore it is manifest that as the life of sense excels the body the life of reason excels both.

xxx, 54. If rational life judges by itself alone, then there is nothing more excellent. But clearly it is mutable, since it can be skilled at one moment and unskilled at another. The more skilled it is the better it judges, and its skill is in proportion to its participation in some art, discipline or wisdom. Now we must ask what is the nature of an art. By an art in this context I would have you understand not something that is observed by experience but something that is found out by reason. There is nothing very remarkable in knowing that sand and lime bind stones more securely together than mud, or that he who would build elegantly, must put a feature that is to be unique in the middle of the building, and, if there are several features, they must be made to correspond, like with like. That is sense-knowledge, but it is not far from reason and truth. We must indeed inquire what is the cause of our being dissatisfied if two windows are placed not one above the other but side by side, and one of them is greater or less than the other, for they ought to have been equal; while, if they are placed one directly above the other, even though they are unlike, the inequality does not offend us in the same way. Why don't we notice very much how much the one is greater or less than the other? If there are three windows, sense itself seems to demand either that they should not be unequal, or that between the largest and the smallest there should be an intermediate one as much larger than the smallest as it is smaller than the largest. In this way we take counsel with nature, as it were, to see what she approves. And here we must observe how that which displeases us only a little when we simply look at it, is rejected when we compare it with what is better. Thus we discover that art in the popular sense is nothing but the memory of things we have experienced and which have given us pleasure, with the addition of some skilled bodily activity. If you lack the skill you can still judge of the works produced even though you cannot produce them. And the power of judging is much better.

55. In all the arts it is symmetry that gives pleasure, preserving unity and making the whole beautiful. Symmetry demands unity and equality, the similarity of like parts, or the graded arrangements of parts which are dissimilar. But who can

find absolute equality or similarity in bodily objects? Who would venture to say, after due consideration, that any body is truly and simply one? All are changed by passing from form to form or from place to place, and consist of parts each occupying its own place and extended in space. True equality and similitude, true and primal unity, are not perceived by the eye of flesh or by any bodily sense, but are known by the mind. How is equality of any kind demanded in bodies, and how are we convinced that any equality that may be seen there is far different from perfect equality, unless the mind sees that which is perfect? If indeed that which is not made [*facta*] can be called perfect [*perfecta*].

56. All things which are beautiful to the senses, whether they are produced by nature or are worked out by the arts, have a spatial or temporal beauty, as for example the body and its movements. But the equality and unity which are known only by the mind, and according to which the mind judges of corporeal beauty by the intermediary of the senses, are not extended in space or unstable in time. It would be wrong to say that a wheel can be judged to be round by this standard, while a little jar cannot, or a jar can but a penny cannot. So in the case of times and motions of corporeal things, it would be ridiculous to say that years can be judged by any standard to be of equal length but months cannot, or that months can and days cannot. Whether a proper movement occupies a larger space of time or is measured by hours or brief minutes, all are judged by one and the same standard of changeless equality. If greater and smaller movements and spatial figures are all judged according to the same standard of equality or similitude or fitness, the standard is greater than all of them in potency. But it is neither greater nor less in a spatial or a temporal sense. If it were greater we should not use the whole of it to judge things that are less. If it were smaller we could not use it to judge things that are larger. As it is, we use the absolute standard of squareness to judge the squareness of a market-place, a stone, a table or a gem. And we use the absolute standard of equality to judge the movements of the feet of a running ant and those of an elephant on the march. Who then can doubt that it is neither greater nor less in a spatial or temporal sense, but in potency surpasses all else? This standard of all the arts is absolutely unchangeable, but the human mind, which is given the power to see the standard, can suffer the mutability of error. Clearly, then, the standard which is called truth is higher than our minds.

xxxi, 57. We must not have any doubt that the unchangeable substance which is above the rational mind, is God. The primal life and primal essence is where the primal wisdom is. This is unchangeable truth which is the law of all the arts and the art of the omnipotent artificer. In perceiving that it cannot judge by itself the form and movement of bodies, the soul ought at the same time to realize that its nature excels the nature of what it judges, but also that it is excelled by the nature according to which it judges and concerning which it cannot judge. I can say why the corresponding members of a single body, one on the one side and the other on the other, ought to be alike, because I delight in absolute equality which I behold not with the bodily eyes but with the mind. And therefore I judge that things seen with the eyes are better the nearer they are in their own kind to the things which I know with my mind. No one can say why these intelligible things should be as they are; and no one in his sober senses should say that they ought to be as they are, as if they could be otherwise.

58. No one, if he rightly understands the matter, will venture to say why intelligible things please us, and why when we are wise we earnestly love them. As we and all rational souls rightly judge of inferior creatures when we judge according to truth, so truth alone judges of us when we cleave to it. Not even the Father judges of truth, for it is not less than he is. What the Father judges he judges by means of the truth. All things which seek unity have this rule or form or example, or whatever it is to be called. For unity alone bears the whole similitude of him from whom it has received existence, if it is not incongruous to say "it has received existence" in view of the significance which attaches to the word Son. In any case it derives its existence not from itself but from the first and highest principle which is called the Father: "from whom the whole family in heaven and on earth is named" (Eph. 3:15). "The Father therefore judgeth no man, but hath given all judgment to the Son" (John 5:22). "The spiritual man judgeth all things and is himself judged of none" (I Cor. 2:15), that is by no man, but only by the law according to which he judges all things. Wherefore it is most truly said "we must all appear before the judgment throne of Christ" (II Cor. 5:10). He judges all things because he is above all when he is with God. He is with God when he knows most purely and loves what he knows with all charity. Accordingly, the law is that according to which he judges all things and concerning which no man can judge. In the case of temporal laws,

men have instituted them and judge by them, and when they have been instituted and confirmed no judge may judge them but must judge according to them. He who draws up temporal laws, if he is a good and wise man, takes eternal life into account, and that no soul may judge. He determines for the time being what is to be commanded and forbidden according to the immutable rules of eternal life. Pure souls may rightly know the eternal law but may not judge it. The difference is that, for knowing, it is enough to see that a thing is *so* and not *so*. For judging, it is necessary in addition to see that a thing can be thus or not thus; as when we say it ought to be thus, or to have been thus, or to be thus in the future, as workmen do with their works.

xxxii, 59. But many stop with what delights men and are unwilling to rise to higher things, so that they may judge why visible things give pleasure. If I ask a workman why, after constructing one arch, he builds another like it over against it, he will reply, I dare say, that in a building like parts must correspond to like. If I go further and ask why he thinks so, he will say that it is fitting, or beautiful, or that it gives pleasure to those who behold it. But he will venture no further. He will bow and direct his eyes downward and not understand the cause for all this. But if I have to do with a man with inward eyes who can see the invisible, I shall not cease to press the query why these things give pleasure, so that he may dare to be the judge of human pleasure. He transcends it and escapes from its control in judging pleasure and not according to pleasure. First I shall ask him whether things are beautiful because they give pleasure, or give pleasure because they are beautiful. Then I shall ask him why they are beautiful, and if he is perplexed, I shall add the question whether it is because its parts correspond and are so joined together as to form one harmonious whole.

60. When he sees that that is so, I shall ask whether they completely achieve the unity they aim at, or fall far short of it, and in a measure misrepresent it. No one who is put on his guard can fail to see that there is no form or material thing which does not have some trace of unity, or that no material thing however beautiful can possibly achieve the unity it aims at, since it must necessarily have its parts separated by intervals of space. If this is so, I shall ask him to tell me where he sees that unity, and what is its source; and if he cannot see it, how does he know what it is that material things imitate but cannot completely achieve. If he says of material things: You would not

exist unless some kind of unity held you together, but on the other hand if you were unity itself you would not be material things? the correct reply would be: Whence have you acquired the knowledge of unity according to which you judge material things. Unless you had seen it you would not be able to judge that they come short of it. You would not be right to say that you see it with your bodily eyes, although things do show traces of it, but they come nowhere near it. With the bodily eyes you see nothing but corporeal things. Therefore it is with the mind that we see true unity. But where? If it were here where our body is, it would not be visible to a man who in eastern parts judges in the same way about corporeal things. It is not, then, circumscribed by space. It is present wherever anyone judges in this way. It is nowhere present spatially, but its potency is nowhere absent.

xxxiii, 61. If corporeal things travesty unity, we must not trust things that deceive, lest we fall into the vanities of them that are vain. Since they deceive by appearing to show to the eye of flesh the unity which is seen by the mind alone, we must rather ask whether they deceive by resembling unity or in failing to achieve unity. If they achieved it they would be completely identical with what they imitate. In that case there would be no difference at all. If that were so there would be no deception. They would be exactly what unity is. In any case, if you consider the matter closely they do not actively deceive. He is a deceiver who wants to appear what he is not. He who, without willing it, is thought to be other than he is, is not a deceiver but simply causes mistakes. This is how a deceiver is distinguished from one who causes mistakes. Every deceiver has the will to deceive, whether he is believed or not. But mistakes can be caused by one who has no intention to deceive. Therefore a corporeal form, which can have no will of its own, does not deceive. Nor does it cause mistakes if it is not thought to be what it is not.

62. Even the eyes do not cause mistakes, for they can report nothing to the mind except what they actually see. If not only the eyes but also all the bodily senses report simply as they are affected, I know not what more we ought to expect of them. If there are no vain people there will be no vanity. Anyone who thinks that the oar is broken in the water and is restored when it is taken out has nothing wrong with his senses, but he is a bad judge of what they convey to him. By nature he could have seen nothing else in the water, nor ought he to have seen anything

else. Air and water differ, so it is proper that sensations should be different according as they relate to things in air and in water. So the eye does its duty correctly, for it was made simply to see. But the mind operates perversely, for it and not the eye was made to contemplate supreme beauty. Such a man as we have been speaking of wants to turn his mind to corporeal things and his eyes to God. He seeks to know carnal things and to see spiritual things. But that is impossible.

xxxiv, 63. That perversity must be corrected. Otherwise things are all out of order, up is down and down is up. Such a man will not be fit for the kingdom of heaven. Do not let us seek the highest in the lowest, nor cleave to the lowest. Let us judge these things lest we be judged along with them. Let us attribute to them no more than, as lowest forms, they deserve, lest seeking the first in the last, we be numbered with the last instead of with the first. That is no disadvantage to these lowest things but is a great disadvantage to us. The divine providential government is not on that account any less fitting because the unjust are put in their just place and the foul are fairly dealt with. If the beauty of visible things causes us to make mistakes because it consists in unity but does not completely achieve unity, let us understand if we can that the mistake arises not from what they are but from what they are not. Every corporeal thing is a true body but a false unity. For it is not supremely one and does not completely imitate unity. And yet it would not be a body either if it did not have some unity. Besides it could have no unity unless it derived it from supreme unity.

64. Obstinate souls! Give me a single man who can see without being influenced by imaginations derived from things seen in the flesh. Give me a single man who can see that there is no principle of unity but that alone from which all unity derives, whether it be complete unity or not. Point me out one who sees, not one who merely cavils, and wants to appear to see what he does not see. Give me a man who can resist the carnal senses and the impressions which they impose on the mind; one who can resist human custom and human praise, who suffers the stings of conscience on his bed and restores his soul, who loves not external vanities nor seeks lies; who can say to himself: If there is only one Rome which some Romulus is said to have founded on the Tiber, that is a false Rome which I conjure up in my thoughts. My imaginary Rome is not the real Rome, nor am I really there; otherwise I should know what was taking place

there. If there is one sun, that is a false one which I conjure up in thought, for the real sun pursues its course in its appointed place and time. The imaginary sun I place where and when I will. If my friend is one, I conjure up a false image. I do not know where the real one is, but the imaginary one is where I like to put him. I myself am one person, and I feel that my body is here, but in imagination I go where I like, and speak to whom I like. These imaginary things are false, and what is false cannot be known. When I contemplate them and believe in them, I do not have knowledge, because what I contemplate with the intelligence must be true, and not by any possibility what are commonly called phantasms. Whence, then, is my mind full of illusions? Where is the truth which the mind beholds? It can be replied to one who thinks in this way that that is the true light which enables you to know that these things are not true. By the true light you see the unity whereby you judge whatever you see to be one. But it is quite a different thing from any mutable thing you can see.

xxxv, 65. If your mind eagerly pants to behold these things, keep quiet. Do not strive except against being accustomed to material things. Conquer that habit and you are victorious over all. We seek unity, the simplest thing of all. Therefore let us seek it in simplicity of heart. "Be still and know that I am God" (Ps. 46:10). This is not the stillness of idleness but of thought, free from space and time. Swelling fleeting phantasms do not permit us to see abiding unity. Space offers us something to love, but time steals away what we love and leaves in the soul crowds of phantasms which incite desire for this or that. Thus the mind becomes restless and unhappy, vainly trying to hold that by which it is held captive. It is summoned to stillness so that it may not love the things which cannot be loved without toil. So it will master them. It will hold them and not be held by them. "My yoke," says the Lord, "is light" (Matt. 11:30). He who is subject to that yoke has everything else subject to himself. He will not labour, for what is subject does not resist. Men could be masters of this world if they were willing to be the sons of God, for God has given them the power to become his sons. But the unhappy friends of this world so fear to be separated from its embrace that nothing is more toilsome to them than to be at rest.

xxxvi, 66. Whoever clearly sees that falsehood is thinking something is what it is not, knows that truth is that which declares what is. If material things deceive us in so far as they fall short of the unity which they demonstrably imitate, we naturally approve them; for that is the principle from which all unity derives, and to resemble which all things strive. We equally disapprove all that departs from unity and tends towards its opposite. We can understand that there is something so resembling the sole unity and principle of all unity that it coincides with it and is identical with it. This is truth, the Word that was in the beginning [*in principio*], the divine Word that was with God. If falsehood springs from things which imitate unity, not in so far as they imitate it but in so far as they cannot achieve it, the truth which does achieve it, and is identical with it, is unity and manifests unity as it is in reality. Hence, it is rightly called unity's Word and Light. Other things may be said to be like unity in so far as they have being, and so far they are also true. But this is itself the complete likeness of unity, and is therefore truth. Truth makes all things true which are true, and likeness makes things like which are alike. Truth is the form of all things which are true, and likeness of all things which are alike. Since things are true in so far as they have being, and have being in so far as they resemble the source of all unity, that is, the form of all things that have being, which is the supreme likeness of the principle. It is also perfect truth because it is without any unlikeness.

67. Falsehood arises not because things deceive us, for they can show the beholder nothing but their form, and that they have received according to their position in the scale of beauty. Nor do the senses deceive us, for when they are in contact with natural objects they report to their presiding mind nothing but the impressions formed upon them. It is sin which deceives souls, when they seek something that is true but abandon or neglect truth. They love the works of the artificer more than the artificer or his art, and are punished by falling into the error of expecting to find the artificer and his art in his works, and when they cannot do so they think that the works are both the art and the artificer. God is not offered to the corporeal senses, and transcends even the mind.

xxxvii, 68. This is the origin of all impiety of sinners who have been condemned for their sins. Not only do they wish to scrutinize the creation contrary to the commandment of God, and to enjoy it rather than God's law and truth—that was the sin of the first man who misused his free will—but in their state of condemnation they also make this addition to their sin. They not only love but also serve the creature rather than the Creator, and worship the parts of the creation from the loftiest to the lowliest. Some worship the soul in place of the most high God, the first intellectual creature which the Father made by means of the truth, that it might ever behold the truth, and beholding the truth might also behold himself whom the truth resembles in every way. Next, men come to the living creature through which God eternal and unchangeable makes things visible and temporal in the realm of becoming. Then they slip further down and worship animals and even material things, among which they first choose the more beautiful, above all the heavenly bodies. Some are satisfied with the sun, the most obvious of the heavenly bodies. Others think the moon worthy of religious veneration because of its brightness. It is nearer to us, we are told, and so is felt to have a form that is closer to us. Others add the rest of the stars and the sky as a whole with its constellations. Others join the air to the ethereal sky and make their souls subordinate to these two superior corporeal elements. But those think themselves most religious who worship the whole created universe, that is, the world with all that is in it, and the life which inspires and animates it, which some believe to be corporeal, others incorporeal. The whole of this together they think to be one great God, of whom all things are parts. They have not known the author and maker of the universe. So they abandon themselves to idols, and, forsaking the works of God, they are immersed in the works of their own hands, all of them visible things.

xxxviii, 69. There is another worse and lower idolatry which worships phantasms. Whatever the erring soul in its swelling pride can imagine, they hold as an object of religious worship until at last some conclude that nothing at all should be worshipped, and that men err who allow themselves to get involved in superstition and miserable servitude. But these opinions are vain. They cannot make themselves free. There remain the vices, and they are drawn towards the notion of worshipping them. They are slaves of desire in three forms—desire of pleasure, desire of excelling, desire of novel entertainment. I say that there is no man who holds that there is nothing he ought to worship, who is not the slave of carnal pleasures, or seeks vain power, or is madly delighted by some showy spectacle. So, without knowing it, they love temporal things and hope for blessedness therefrom. Whether he will or no, a man is necessarily a slave to the things by means of which he seeks to be happy. He follows them whithersoever they lead, and fears anyone who seems to have the power to rob him of them. Now a spark of fire or a tiny animal can do that. In short, not to mention innumerable adverse possibilities, time itself must snatch away all transient things. Now since the world includes all temporal things, those who think to escape servitude by not worshipping anything are in fact the slaves of all kinds of worldly things. In their present extremity unhappy men are so placed that they allow their vices to lord it over them, and are condemned for their lust, pride or curiosity, or for two of them or all together. Nevertheless, so long as they are in this stadium of human life they may attack these vices and overcome them, if they begin by believing what they cannot yet grasp with the understanding, and thereby cease to love the world. As it is written: "All that is in the world is lust of the flesh, lust of the eyes, and ambition of this world" (I John 2:16). Three classes of men are thus distinguished; for lust of the flesh means those who love the lower pleasures, lust of the eyes means the curious, and ambition of this world denotes the proud.

71. The threefold temptation of the Man whom the truth assumed has given us an example for our warning. "Bid these stones that they become bread," says the tempter. To which our one and only teacher replies: "Man does not live by bread alone, but by every word of God" (Matt. 4:3–4). So he taught that desire for pleasure should be brought under, and that we should not yield even to hunger. But possibly some one who could not be overcome by the pleasures of the flesh could be by the pomp of temporal domination. So all the kingdoms of the world were shown, and the tempter said: "All these things will I give thee, if thou wilt fall down and worship me." To this it was replied: "Thou shalt worship the Lord thy God and him only shalt thou serve" (Matt. 4:9–10). So was pride trodden under foot. Moreover the utmost enticements of curiosity were also overcome. For the only reason for urging him to cast himself down from the pinnacle of the temple was that he might have a remarkable experience. Not even so was he overcome, but in order that we should understand that to know God there is no need to explore divine power by subjecting it to visible experiments, he replied: "Thou shalt not tempt the Lord thy God" (Matt. 4:7). Wherefore he who is inwardly fed upon the Word of God does not seek pleasure in the desert. He who is subject to the one God does not seek glory on the mountain, that is, in earthly elation. He who begins to cleave to the eternal spectacle of unchangeable truth is not thrown down by the pinnacle of the body, that is, the eyes, to seek to know inferior and temporal things.

xxix, 72. What obstacle then remains to hinder the soul from recalling the primal beauty which it abandoned, when it can make an end of its vices? The Wisdom of God extends from end to end with might. By wisdom the great Artificer knit his works together with one glorious end in view. His goodness has no grudging envy against any beauty from the highest to the lowest, for none can have being except from him alone. So that no one is utterly cast away from the truth who has in him the slightest vestige of truth. What is it about bodily pleasure that holds us fast? You will find that it is agreeableness. Disagreeable things beget grief and agreeable things beget pleasure. Seek therefore the highest agreeableness. Do not go abroad. Return within yourself. In the inward man dwells truth. If you find that you are by nature mutable, transcend yourself. But remember in doing so that you must also transcend yourself even as a reasoning soul. Make for the place where the light of reason is kindled. What does every good reasoner attain but truth? And yet truth is not reached by reasoning, but is itself the goal of all who reason. There is an agreeableness than which there can be no greater. Agree, then, with it. Confess that you are not as it is. It has to do no seeking, but you reach it by seeking, not in space, but by a disposition of mind, so that the inward man may agree with the indwelling truth in a pleasure that is not low and carnal but supremely spiritual.

73. If you do not grasp what I say and doubt whether it is true, at least make up your mind whether you have any doubt about your doubts. If it is certain that you do indeed have doubts, inquire whence comes that certainty. It will never occur to you to imagine that it comes from the light of the sun, but rather from that "true light which lighteth every man that cometh into the world." It cannot be seen with these eyes, nor with the eyes which seem to see the phantasms of the brain, but with those that can say to phantasms: You are not the thing I am seeking. Nor are you the standard by which I put you in your rightful place, disapproving of all that is base in you, and approving of all that is beautiful. The standard according to which I approve and disapprove is still more beautiful, so I approve more highly of it and prefer it not only to you but to all those bodily shapes from which you spring. Now think of the rule in this way. Everyone who knows that he has doubts knows with certainty something that is true, namely, that he doubts. He is certain, therefore, about *a* truth. Therefore everyone who doubts whether there be such a thing as *the* truth has at least *a*

truth to set a limit to his doubt; and nothing can be true except truth be in it. Accordingly, no one ought to have doubts about the existence of *the* truth, even if doubts arise for him from every possible quarter. Wherever this is seen, there is light that transcends space and time and all phantasms that spring from spatial and temporal things. Could this be in the least destroyed even if every reasoner should perish or grow old among inferior carnal things? Reasoning does not create truth but discovers it. Before it is discovered it abides in itself; and when it is discovered it renews us.

xl, 74. So the inward man is reborn, and the outward man decays day by day. The inward man regards the outward man and sees that he is base by comparison. Nevertheless, in his own kind he is beautiful and rejoices in what is convenient for the body, destroying what he converts to his own good, e.g., the nourishment he takes for the sake of his body. That which is destroyed, i.e., loses its form, passes into the workshop of his members, nourishes what needs nourishment and is transformed as is suitable. Somehow the processes of life make a selection. Some things which are suitable are assumed into the structure of the visible body and make it beautiful. Those which are not suitable are cast out by appropriate means. The most filthy part is returned to the earth to assume other forms. Something is exhaled by the whole body. Another part receives the latent numerical qualities of the living person, and is fitted to result in offspring. Prompted by the agreement of two bodies or by some like phantasm, it flows from the genital organs in basest pleasure, though not without the co-operation of the head. Within the mother over a fixed period of time it takes shape, and the members assume their proper place and function, and if they preserve their proper measure and symmetry and colour is added, a body is born which is called comely and is keenly loved by those who take delight in it. But what gives pleasure is not so much the mobile form as the life which causes the mobility. For if the child loves us it strongly attracts us. If it hates us we are angry and cannot endure it, even though its form be such as we might enjoy. All this is the realm of pleasure and of beauty of the lowest grade. It is subject to corruption, otherwise it would be mistaken for the supreme beauty.

75. Divine providence is at hand to show that the beauty of the human form is not evil, because it exhibits manifest traces of the primal numbers, though divine wisdom is not numbered

among them; but also that it is beauty of the lowest grade, for mixed up with it are griefs and diseases, distortions of limbs, darkness of colour, and conflicts and dissensions of mind. By these things we are admonished that we must seek something unchangeable. These evils providence brings about by the agency of inferior beings who find their pleasure in doing this, and whom the divine Scriptures call avengers and ministers of wrath, though they themselves do not know the good that is being done by means of them. Like these are men who rejoice in the miseries of others, and make sport and mocking spectacles by subverting others or by leading them astray. In all these things the good are admonished and exercised, and they are victorious, triumphant and regal. But the bad are deceived and tortured. They are vanquished, condemned and made to be slaves, not of the one most high Lord of all, but of his lowest servants, the bad angels who feed upon the griefs and misery of the damned, and in return for their malevolence are tortured when they see the good set free.

76. All have their offices and limits laid down so as to ensure the beauty of the universe. That which we abhor in any part of it gives us the greatest pleasure when we consider the universe as a whole. When we are judging a building we ought not to consider one angle only. So when we are judging a good-looking man we should not take account only of his hair. And with one who is making a good speech we should not merely pay attention to the motion of his hands. When we are thinking of the moon's course we should not study its phases over a period of merely three days. The very reason why some things are inferior is that though the parts may be imperfect the whole is perfect, whether its beauty is seen stationary or in movement. It must all be considered if we wish to reach a right judgment. If our judgment concerning the whole or the part is true, it is also beautiful. It is superior to the whole world, and in so far as our judgment is true we cling to no part of the world. When we are wrong, and pay exclusive attention to the part, our judgment is in itself base. The colour black in a picture may very well be beautiful if you take the picture as a whole. So the entire contest of human life is fittingly conducted by the unchanging providence of God who allots different rôles to the vanquished and the victorious, the contestants, the spectators, and the tranquil who contemplate God alone. In all these cases there is no evil except sin and sin's penalty, that is, a voluntary abandonment of highest being, and toil among inferior beings which is

not voluntary; in other words, freedom from justice and slavery under sin.

xli, 77. The outward man is destroyed either by the progress of the inward man, or by his own failure. When he is destroyed by the progress of the inward man, the whole man is reformed and made better, and is restored to his integrity "at the last trump." No longer will he corrupt or be corrupted. By his own failure he is cast down among corruptible beauties which rank as penalties. Do not be surprised if I still call them beautiful things, for everything is beautiful that is in due order. As the apostle says: "All order is of God" (Rom. 13:2). We must admit that a weeping man is better than a happy worm. And yet I could speak at great length without any falsehood in praise of the worm. I could point out the brightness of its colouring, the slender rounded shape of its body, the fitness of its parts from front to rear, and their effort to preserve unity as far as is possible in so lowly a creature. There is nothing anywhere about it that does not correspond to something else that matches it. What am I to say about its soul animating its tiny body? Even a worm's soul causes it to move with precision, to seek things suitable for it, to avoid or overcome difficulties as far as possible. Having regard always to the sense of safety, its soul hints much more clearly than its body at the unity which creates all natures. I am speaking of any kind of living worm. Many have spoken fully and truly in praise of ashes and dung. What wonder is it then if I say that a man's soul, which, wherever it is and whatever its quality, is better than any body, is beautifully ordered, and that other beauties arise even from the penalties it undergoes? For when it is unhappy it is not where it is fitting that only the happy should be, but where it is fitting that the unhappy should be.

78. Henceforth, let no one deceive us. Whatever is rightly to be blamed is spurned in comparison with what is better. Every existing thing however lowly is justly praised when it is compared with nothingness. Nothing is good if it can be better. If we can be in good case having the truth itself, our state is bad if we have only a trace of truth, and much worse if the trace is extremely slight as when we adhere to fleshly pleasures. Let us conquer the blandishments and troubles of desire. If we are men let us subdue this woman, *Cupiditas*. With our guidance she will herself become better and be called no longer Cupidity but Temperance. When she leads and we follow she is called Lust and we Rashness and Folly. Let us follow

Christ our Head, that she whose head we are may follow us. This precept can be laid upon women too, not by marital but by fraternal right. In Christ there is neither male nor female. Women too have some virile quality whereby they can subdue feminine pleasures, and serve Christ and govern desire. This is exemplified by many godly widows and virgins, and in many too who are married but who by the dispensation of the Christian people preserve conjugal rights in the bond of fraternity. God bids us dominate desire, and exhorts us and gives us the power to be restored to our own possession. If therefore by negligence or impiety a man, i.e., mind and reason, is subdued by desire he will be a base and unhappy man. His destiny in this life and his ordained place hereafter will be where the most high Ruler and Lord will apportion him. The universal creation may not be stained by any filthiness.

xlii, 79. Let us therefore walk while we have the day, i.e., while we can use reason. Let us turn to God so that we may deserve to be illumined by his Word, the true light, and that darkness may not take possession of us. Day is the presence of the "light that lighteth every man coming into the world" (John 1:9). "Every man," says Scripture, meaning everyone who can use reason, and who, when he has fallen, can earnestly seek to rise. If fleshly pleasure is loved, let it be carefully considered and vestigial traces of number will be recognized in it. We must, then, seek the realm where number exists in complete tranquillity; for there existence is, above all, unity. And if number is found in living movement, as for example in growing seeds, it will be even more wonderful than when found in corporeal things. If in seeds number could change and swell as seeds themselves do, half a tree would grow from half a fig-seed. Whole and complete animals would not be produced except from complete animal seeds (as they are in the case of the litters of certain animals); and a single tiny seed would not have the power to multiply its own kind innumerably. Obviously, from a single seed, according to the nature of each, crops can propagate crops, woods woods, herds herds, and peoples peoples throughout the ages, so that there is not a single leaf or hair in all that rhythmic succession, the reason for which did not exist in the first single seed. Again, think of the rhythmic and pleasantly beautiful sounds transmitted by the air when the nightingale sings. And yet the soul of that bird could not produce them so freely when it pleased, unless it had them incorporeally impressed upon it by the life force. This can be observed in other living creatures which lack reason but do not lack sense. There is none of them which does not in the sound of its voice or in some other movement or activity of its members show something rhythmical and in its own fashion orderly, not indeed by reason of any knowledge, but by reason of the deep ties of nature which are arranged by the unchangeable law of numbers.

xliii, 80. Let us return to ourselves and pass over the things we have in common with trees and beasts. The swallow builds its nest in one way, and every kind of bird has its own way of building its nest. What is it in us that enables us to judge all these, the plan they are following and how far they accomplish it; to judge ourselves, too, in our buildings and other activities of the body, as if we were lords of all such things? What gives us these innumerable thoughts? What is it within us that knows that these corporeal things are relatively great or small, that every body can be halved, whatever size it may have, and even then may be subdivided into innumerable parts? If a grain of millet bears the same relation to one of its parts as our body bears to the world, it is as great in respect of that part as the world is in respect of us. And the world is full of designs and is beautiful not because of its size but because of the reason that is in it. It seems great not because of its quantity but by comparison with our smallness and the smallness of the living things it contains. These again can be infinitely divided, and are small not in themselves but by comparison with other things and above all with the universe itself. Nor is it different with respect to lengths of time. As in the case of space, every length of time can be halved. However brief it may be it has a beginning, a duration and an end. So it must have a middle point, being divided at the point where it draws nearer to the end. The short syllable is short by comparison with a long syllable, and the hour is short in winter when compared with a summer hour. So the space of a single hour is short by comparison with a day. So a day is short by comparison with a month, a month with a year, a year with a lustrum, a lustrum with the larger circles of time and they with universal time. The whole rhythmic succession and gradation in space and time is judged to be beautiful not by its size or length but by its ordered fitness.

81. The mode of order lives in perpetual truth. It has no bulk or temporal process. By its potency it is greater than all space, and by its eternity it remains changeless above the flux of time. And yet without it, vast bulk can have no unity, and length of

time cannot be kept in the straight path. There could be neither matter nor motion. It is the principle of unity, having neither size nor change whether finite or infinite. It has not one quality here and another there, or one now and another afterwards; for it is supremely the unique Father of Truth and Father of Wisdom, which is like the Father in all respects. Hence it is called his similitude and image because it comes from him. It is rightly called also the Son, and from him other things proceed. But before him is the universal form perfectly identical with the unity from which it springs, so that all other things, so far as they have being and resemble unity, are made according to that form.

xliv, 82. Some things are made conformable to that first form such as rational and intellectual creatures, among whom man is rightly said to be made in the image and likeness of God. Not otherwise could he behold unchangeable truth with his mind. But other things are made through the first form but are not in its image. If the rational creature serve its creator by whom, through whom, and to whom it was made, all other things will serve it. Life, which is next in the scale below soul, will lend aid in commanding the body. And the soul will even rule over the body, that last and lowest being, for the body will yield to its will in all things and will give no trouble; because the soul will not seek its happiness from the body or by it, but will receive happiness by itself from God. So the body too will be reformed and sanctified, and the soul will rule it without loss or corruption and without any burden of difficulty. "In the resurrection they neither marry nor are given in marriage but will be like the angels in heaven" (Matt. 22:30). "Meats for the belly and the belly for meats, but God will destroy both it and them" (I Cor. 6:13). "The kingdom of God is not eating and drinking, but righteousness and peace and joy" (Rom. 14:17).

xlv, 83. Wherefore even in bodily pleasure we find something to teach us to despise it, not because the body is evil by nature, but because it is shameful for a being who can cleave to higher things and enjoy them to be the sport of love of the lowest good. When a charioteer loses control and pays the penalty for his rashness he accuses his equipment. But let him implore aid; let him take command of the situation; let him control his steeds which are making a spectacle of his downfall and bid fair to bring about his death if no help supervenes. Let him get back into his place in the chariot, and take control of the reins, and tame his horses and rule them more cautiously.

Then he will realize how well the chariot had been made with all its equipment, which by his ruinous handling brought danger upon himself and left the course of becoming moderation. So in paradise the greediness of the soul which badly used its body produced weakness. For it snatched at forbidden food against the prescription of the physician, in following which salvation is to be found.

84. If in the very weakness of visible flesh, where no happy life can be, some pointer towards happiness can be found, because the form of it reaches from the top to the bottom of the scale of existence, much more can a pointer be found in the search for rank and excellence, even in the pride and vain pomp of this world. For what else does a man seek in this case but to be if possible the sole lord of all things, perversely imitating Almighty God? If he submissively imitated him by living according to his commandments, God would put all other things under him, and he would not reach such deformity as to fear a little animal even while he wants to rule over men. Pride in a manner seeks unity and omnipotence, but in the realm of temporal things, where all things are transient like a shadow.

85. We want to be unconquered and rightly so, for the nature of our mind is unconquerable though only as we are subject to God in whose image we are made. But his commandments had to be observed, and if they were obeyed no one would overcome us. But now while the woman to whose words we basely consented is subject to the pains of childbirth, we labour on the ground and are disgracefully overcome by anything that can trouble or disturb us. We do not want to be overcome by men, but we cannot overcome anger. What more execrable baseness can there be? We admit that we are men, and even a vicious man is better than vice. How much more honourable it would be to be conquered by a man than by a vice? Who would doubt that envy is a monstrous vice which must necessarily torture and subdue anyone who is unwilling to be conquered in temporal things. It is better that a man should overcome us than that we should be overcome by envy or any other vice.

xlvi, 86. He who has overcome his vices cannot be overcome by man either. Only he is overcome who has what he loves snatched from him by his adversary. He who loves only what cannot be snatched from him is indubitably unconquerable, and is tortured by no envy. He loves what many have come to know and to love, thereby deserving to be congratulated. For he loves God with all his heart and with all his soul and with all his mind, and his neighbour as himself. God does not grudge his becoming as he is himself. Rather he even helps him as much as possible. He cannot lose his neighbour whom he loves as himself, for he does not love even in himself the things that appear to the eyes or to any other bodily sense. So he has inward fellowship with him whom he loves as himself.

87. The rule of love is that one should wish his friend to have all the good things he wants to have himself, and should not wish the evils to befall his friend which he wishes to avoid himself. He shows this benevolence towards all men. No evil must be done to any. Love of one's neighbour worketh no evil (Rom. 13:10). Let us then love even our enemies as we are commanded, if we wish to be truly unconquered. For no man is unconquerable in himself, but by the unchangeable law which makes free those who serve it and them only. What they love cannot be taken from them, and by that fact alone they are rendered unconquerable and perfect men. If a man were to love another not as himself but as a beast of burden, or as the baths, or as a gaudy or garrulous bird, that is for some temporal pleasure or advantage he hoped to derive, he must serve not a man but, what is much worse, a foul and detestable vice, in that he does not love the man as a man ought to be loved. When that vice is dominant it leads to the lowest form of life or rather to death.

88. Man is not to be loved by man even as brothers after the flesh are loved, or sons, or wives, or kinsfolk, or relatives, or fellow citizens. For such love is temporal. We should have no such connections as are contingent upon birth and death, if our nature had remained in obedience to the commandments of God and in the likeness of his image. It would not have been relegated to its present corrupt state. Accordingly, the Truth himself calls us back to our original and perfect state, bids us resist carnal custom, and teaches that no one is fit for the kingdom of God unless he hates these carnal relationships. Let no one think that is inhuman. It is more inhuman to love a man because he is your son and not because he is a man, that is, not to love that in him which belongs to God, but to love that which belongs to yourself. What marvel if he who loves his private advantage and not the commonweal does not obtain a kingdom? Someone will say he should love both, but God says he must love one. Most truly says the Truth: "No man can serve two masters" (Matt. 6:24). No one can perfectly love that *to* which we are called unless he hate that *from* which we are called.

We are called to perfect human nature as God made it before we sinned. We are recalled from love of what we have deserved by sinning. Therefore we must hate that from which we choose to be set free.

89. If we are ablaze with love for eternity we shall hate temporal relationships. Let a man love his neighbour as himself. No one is his own father or son or kinsman or anything of the kind, but is simply a man. Whoever loves another as himself ought to love that in him which is his real self. Our real selves are not bodies. So we are not to desire and set great store by a man's body. Here, too, the precept is valid: Thou shalt not covet they neighbour's property. Whoever, then, loves in his neighbour anything but his real self does not love him as himself. Human nature is to be loved whether it be perfect or in process of becoming perfect, but without any condition of carnal relationship. All are related who have one God for their Father and who love him and do his will. And all are fathers and sons to one another, fathers when they take thought for others, sons when they obey, but above all they are brothers because one Father by his Testament calls them to one inheritance.

xlvii, 90. Why should not he be unconquered who in loving man loves nothing but the man, the creature of God, made according to his image? And how can he fail to discover the perfect nature he loves, since God is perfect? For example, if anyone loves a good singer, not this or that particular one but any good singer, being himself a perfect singer, he wants all to be such, while at the same time preserving his own power to do what he loves, for he too sings well. But if he is envious of any good singer, he does not love good singing for itself but for the praise or some other advantage he wishes to obtain by singing well. But that advantage can be diminished or indeed taken away if another sings well. He who is envious of a good singer does not love him for his singing; and on the other hand, he who lacks talent does not sing well. This could be much more fitly said of one who lives rightly, because he can envy no one. For the reward of right living is the same for all, and it is not made less when many obtain it. A time may come when a good singer cannot sing properly, and requires another's voice to show what he loves. He might be at a banquet where it was wrong for him to sing, but where he might properly hear another sing. But it is never improper to live aright. Whoever does this and loves it, not only does not envy those who imitate him, but also treats them with the greatest possible kindness and good will. But he does not stand in any need of them. What he loves in them he himself completely and perfectly possesses. So when a man loves his neighbour as himself, he is not envious of him any more than he is envious of himself. He gives him such help as he can as if he were helping himself. But he does not need him any more than he needs himself. He needs God alone, by cleaving to whom he is happy. No one can take God from him. He, then, is most truly and certainly an unconquered man who cleaves to God, not indeed that he may merit any extra good thing from him, but because for him to cleave to God is itself good.

91. Such a man, so long as he is in this life, uses his friend to repay favours received, his enemy to cultivate patience, anyone at all in order to exercise beneficence, and all men as objects of benevolence. Though he does not love temporal things, he uses them rightly himself, and takes thought for men according to the lot of each, if he cannot treat them all alike. So if he is more ready to speak to one of his friends than to anyone else, it is not because he loves him more, but because he has greater confidence in addressing him, and opportunity opens the door. He treats those who are devoted to temporal concerns all the better because he is himself less bound to temporal things. If he cannot help all whom he loves equally without preferring to benefit those who are more closely related to him, he is unjust. Relationship of mind is a greater thing than relationships due to the place or time where or when we were born in the flesh. But the relationship which binds all together is the most important of all. He is not made sorrowful by the death of anyone, for he who loves God with all his mind knows that nothing can perish for him unless it perish also in the sight of God. But God is Lord of the living and the dead. He is not made unhappy by the unhappiness of another, any more than he is made just by the justice of another. As no one can take from him God and justice, so no one can take from him his happiness. If at any time he is touched with feeling for another's danger or error or grief, he lets it go so far as to help or correct or console that other, but not to subvert himself.

92. In all laborious duties he cherishes the certain expectation of rest to come, and so is not crushed. What can harm him who can make a good use even of an enemy? He does not fear enmities because he is guarded and protected by God who has given both the command and the ability to love enemies. In tribulations he feels it is a small thing not to be saddened. Rather he even rejoices, knowing that "tribulation worketh patience,

and patience experience, and experience hope, and hope maketh not ashamed, because the love of God is shed abroad in our hearts by the Holy Spirit, which is given unto us" (Rom. 5:3-5). Who can hurt such a man? Who can subdue him? In prosperity he makes moral progress, and in adversity learns to know the progress he has made. When he has abundance of mutable goods he does not put his trust in them; and when they are withdrawn he gets to know whether or not they had taken him captive. Usually when we have them we imagine that we do not love them, but when they begin to leave us we discover what manner of men we are. We have a thing without loving it when we can let it go without grieving. He who by excelling obtains what he will grieve to lose, seems to be victorious but is in reality vanquished; and he who by giving way obtains what he cannot unwillingly lose is really victorious though he seem to be vanquished.

xlviii, 93. He who delights in liberty seeks to be free from the love of mutable things. He who delights to rule should submissively cleave to God, the sole ruler of all things, loving God more than himself. This is perfect justice, to love the better things more and the lesser things less. He should love a wise and perfect soul because it has the quality of justice, and a foolish soul because it has the power to become wise and perfect. He ought not to love even himself if he is foolish; for he who loves himself when he is foolish will make no progress towards wisdom. No one will become what he desires to be unless he hates himself as he is. But until he reaches wisdom and perfection he bears with the folly of his neighbour as he would bear with his own, supposing he were foolish and at the same time a lover of wisdom. Wherefore, if even pride itself is the shadow of true liberty and true royalty, by it also divine providence reminds us what we are worth when we are stained with vice, and to what we must return when we have been corrected.

xlix, 94. All curiosity with regard to spectacles aims at nothing else than the joy of knowing things. What, then, is more wonderful and beautiful than truth? Every spectator admits that he wants to reach truth. Hence he takes great care not to be deceived, and vaunts himself if he shows more acuteness and vivacity than others in watching and learning and judging. Men carefully and closely watch a juggler who professes nothing but deceit. If his tricks elude discovery they are delighted with the cleverness of the man who hoodwinks them. If he did not know how to mislead those who were looking on, or was believed not to know, no one would applaud. But any of the people who catches him out thinks himself worthy of greater praise than the juggler for no other reason than that he could not be deceived or taken in. If many see through the trick the juggler is not praised, but the rest who cannot see it are laughed at. So the palm is always awarded to knowledge, to the comprehension of truth. But no one can reach truth who looks for it outside the mind.

95. When we are asked which is better, truth or falsehood, we answer with one voice that truth is better. And yet we are so sunk in trifles and baseness that we are much more ready to cling to jests and games in which deception, not truth, delights us, than to the precepts of the truth itself. So by our own judgment and out of our own mouth we are sentenced because we approve one thing by reason and pursue another in our vanity. So long as a thing is a matter of fun and games, we know that it arouses laughter when it counterfeits truth. But when we love such things we fall away from truth, and cannot discover what they imitate, and so we pant for them as if they were the prime objects of beauty. Getting further away from these primal objects we embrace our phantasms. When we return to seek truth phantasms meet us in the way and will not allow us to pass on, attacking us like brigands, not indeed with violence but with dangerous pitfalls, because we do not know how widely applicable is the saying: "Keep yourselves from images" (I John 5:21).

96. So some go vaguely wandering in thought through innumerable worlds. Others have thought that God cannot exist except as corporeal fire. Others have thought of God as the brightness of an immense light radiating through infinite space in all directions, except that on one side it is cloven as by a black wedge. They are of opinion that there are two realms, one over against the other, and they set up two opposing principles as fabulous as their phantasms. If I were to urge them to declare on oath whether they know that these things are true, probably they would not dare to go so far; but they might reply: *You* show us what truth is. If I were to reply simply that they should look for the light that enables them to be certain that believing is one thing and knowing another, they themselves would swear that that light cannot be seen with the eyes, nor thought of as filling any space however vast, and yet that it is everywhere present to those who seek; and that nothing can be found more certain or more serene.

97. All that I have said about the light of the mind is made

clear by that same light. By it I know that what I have said is true, and that I know that I know it. I know that that light has extension neither in space nor in time. I know that I cannot know unless I am alive, and I know more certainly that by knowing I attain a richer life. Eternal life surpasses temporal life in vivacity, and only by knowing do I get a glimpse of what eternity is. By looking at eternity with the mind's eye I remove from it all changeableness, and in eternity I see no temporal duration, for periods of time are constituted by the movements, past or future, of things. In eternity there is neither past nor future. What is past has ceased to be, and what is future has not yet begun to be. Eternity is ever the same. It never "was" in the sense that it is not now, and it never "will be" in the sense that it is not yet. Wherefore, eternity alone could have said to the human mind "I am what I am." And of eternity alone could it be truly said: "He who is hath sent me" (Ex. 3:14).

l, 98. If we cannot yet cleave to eternity, at least let us drive away our phantasms, and cast out of our mental vision trifling and deceptive games. Let us use the steps which divine providence has deigned to make for us. When we delighted over much in silly figments, and grew vain in our thoughts, and turned our whole life into vain dreams, the ineffable mercy of God did not disdain to use rational angelic creatures to teach us by means of sounds and letters, by fire and smoke and cloudy pillar, as by visible words. So with parables and similitudes in a fashion he played with us when we were children, and sought to heal our inward eyes by smearing them with clay.

99. Let us then make clear to ourselves what faith we ought to repose in history and what in intelligence; what we ought to commit to memory, not knowing that it is true but believing all the same; where is the truth that neither comes nor passes away but abides ever the same; what is the mode of interpreting allegory, believed to have been spoken in wisdom through the Holy Spirit; whether it is enough to allegorize things that have been seen in ancient days and in more recent times, or is it to be applied to the affections and nature of the soul, and to unchangeable eternity. Do some stories signify visible deeds, others movements of minds, and others the law of eternity; or are some found in which all these are to be discovered? What is stable faith, historical and temporal or spiritual and eternal, according to which all interpretation of authoritative writings is to be directed? What advantage is to be derived from believing temporal things for knowing and possessing eternal things,

which is the end of all good actions? What is the difference between allegorizing history and allegorizing facts or speeches or sacraments? How is the diction of the divine Scriptures to be received according to the idiom of various languages? Every language has its own special modes of expression which seem absurd when translated into another language. What is the advantage of such a lowly form of speech? For in the sacred books we find mention made of the anger of God, his sadness, his awaking from sleep, his remembering and forgetting, and other things which can happen to good men. Not only so, there is also mention of his repentance, his zeal, his feasting and other such things. Are God's eyes and hands and feet, and other members named in Scripture, to be held to refer to something like the visible form of the human body? Or do they signify intelligible and spiritual powers, as do such words in Scripture as helmet, shield, sword, girdle and the like? Above all we must ask how it profits the human race that the divine providence has spoken to us by human rational and corporeal creatures who have been the servants of God. When we have come to know that one truth, all puerile impudence is driven from our minds and holy religion comes into its own.

li, 100. Putting aside, therefore, all theatrical and poetic trifling, let us by the diligent study of the divine Scriptures, find food and drink for our minds; for they are weary and parched with the hunger and thirst of vain curiosity, and desire in vain to be refreshed and satisfied with silly phantasms, as unreal as painted banquets. Let us be wholesomely educated by this truly liberal and noble game. If wonderful and beautiful spectacles afford us delight, let us desire to see wisdom "which teaches from one end to the other with might, and pleasantly disposes of all things." What is more wonderful than incorporeal might making and ruling the corporeal world? What more beautiful than its ordering and adorning the material world?

lii, 101. All admit that these things are perceived by the body, and that the mind is better than the body. Will not the mind by itself have some object that it can perceive which must be far more excellent and far nobler? We are put in mind by the things of which we are judges to look to that standard by which we judge. We turn from artistic works to the law of the arts, and we shall behold with the mind the form by comparison with which all the things are tarnished which its very goodness has made beautiful. "For the invisible things of God from the creation of the world are clearly seen, being understood by the things that are made, even his eternal power and Godhead" (Rom. 1:20). This is the return from temporal to eternal things, and the transformation of the old man into the new. What can fail to urge man to strive for virtue, when his very vices urge him? Curiosity seeks nothing but knowledge, which cannot be certain knowledge unless it be knowledge of eternal things which remain ever the same. Pride seeks nothing but power, which has reference to facility in acting. But power is attained only by the perfect soul which is submissive to God and which with great love turns towards his kingdom. Bodily pleasure seeks nothing but rest, and there is no rest save where there is no poverty and no corruption. We must beware of the creatures of the lower regions, i.e., of severer penalties after this life, where there can be no reminder of truth because there is no reasoning. And there is no reasoning because there is no shining of "the light that lighteth every man coming into this world" (John 1:9). Wherefore, let us hasten and walk while it is day lest darkness come upon us. Let us hasten to be set free from the second death, where no one is who is mindful of God, and where no one will make confession to God.

liii, 102. But unhappy men make light of what they have come to know, and rejoice in novelties. They take greater pleasure in learning than in knowing, though knowledge is the end of learning. They hold facility in acting to be a poor thing and prefer the battle to the victory, though victory is the end of battle. Those who care little for bodily health prefer to eat too much rather than to eat just enough for satiety. They prefer to enjoy sexual acts rather than to suffer no such agitation. Some even prefer to sleep rather than not to be drowsy. And yet the end of all these desires is *not* to be hungry or thirsty, *not* to seek intercourse with a woman, *not* to be weary.

103. Those who desire these true ends first put off curiosity; for they know that certain knowledge which is within, and they enjoy it as far as they can in this life. Then they put off obstinacy and receive facility in acting, knowing that it is a greater and easier victory not to resist the animosity of any one. And they remain of this opinion so far as they can in this life. Lastly, they seek bodily tranquillity by abstaining from things that are not necessary for living this life. So they taste how sweet is the Lord. They have no doubt as to what will be after this life, and their perfection is nourished by faith, hope and charity. After this life, knowledge will be made perfect. For now we know in part, but when that which is perfect is come, knowledge will not

be in part. There will be perfect peace, for there will be no other law in my members fighting against the law of my mind, but the grace of God through Jesus Christ our Lord will set us free from the body of this death. To a great extent we agree with the adversary while we are with him in the way. The body will be entirely whole without lack or weariness; for this corruptible will put on incorruption in its due time and order, when the resurrection of the flesh comes. There is no marvel if this is given to those who, in knowing, love truth alone, and, in action, love peace alone, and, in the body, love wholeness and nothing besides. What they most love in this life will be made perfect for them after this life.

liv, 104. To those who make a bad use of so good a thing as the mind, desiring visible things outside the mind which ought to remind them to behold and love intelligible things, to them will be given outer darkness. The beginning of this darkness is fleshly knowledge and the weakness of the bodily senses. Those who delight in strife will be aliens from peace and involved in frightful difficulties. The beginning of the greatest difficulty is war and contention. And this I suppose is signified by the fact that their hands and feet are bound, i.e., all facility of working is taken from them. Those who want to hunger and thirst, to burn with lust and be weary, so that they may have pleasure in eating and drinking, in lying with a woman, and in sleeping, love indigence which is the beginning of the greatest woes. What they love will be made perfect for them, for they will be where there is weeping and gnashing of teeth.

105. There are many who love all these vices together. Their whole life is a round of seeing spectacles, striving, eating, drinking, sleeping, having sexual intercourse. They have nothing in their thoughts but to embrace the phantasms which arise out of a life like that, and from their deceptions to set up rules of superstition or impiety to deceive themselves. To these they adhere even when they try to abstain from the enticements of the flesh. They do not make a good use of the talent committed to them, i.e., keenness of mind in which all seem to excel who are called learned, polished or elegant, but keep it bound up in a napkin or buried in the earth, i.e., wrapt up in voluptuous and superfluous things, and crushed beneath earthly cupidities. Therefore their hands and feet will be bound, and they will be sent into outer darkness where there will be weeping and gnashing of teeth. Not because they loved these woes—for who could love them?—but because the things they loved were the beginnings

of these woes, and necessarily bring those who love them to this evil plight. Those, who love the journey rather than the return home or the journey's end, are to be sent into distant parts. They are flesh and spirit continually on the move and never reaching home.

106. But he who makes a good use even of his five bodily senses, to believe and praise the works of God, to cultivate love of God, to seek tranquillity of thought and action, and to know God, *he* enters into the joy of his Lord. The talent is taken from him who made a bad use of it, and is given to him who made a good use of his five talents. Not indeed that keenness of intellect can be transferred from one to another. What is meant is that clever people who neglect their minds and are impious can lose their gift, and that diligent and pious people who are of a slower understanding can nevertheless reach understanding. The talent was not given to him who had received two talents, for he who lives aright both in thought and action already has all he needs. It was given to him who had received five. For he has not yet sufficient mental strength to contemplate eternal things who puts his trust in visible and temporal things. But he can acquire it who praises God, the maker of all sensible things; who trusts God by faith, waits on God in hope, and seeks him in love.

lv, 107. This being so, my dearly beloved friends and brethren, I exhort you as I exhort myself to run with all possible speed after that to which God calls us by his wisdom. Let us not love the world since all that is in the world is lust of the flesh, lust of the eye, and the pride of the world. Do not let us love to corrupt or be corrupted by fleshly pleasure, lest we come to a yet more miserable corruption of grief and torment. Do not let us love strife, lest we be given over to the power of the angels who rejoice in strife, to be humbled, bound and beaten. Let us not love spectacles, lest we wander from the truth and love shadows and are cast into darkness.

108. Let not our religion consist in phantasms of our own imagining. Any kind of truth is better than any fiction we may choose to produce. And yet we must not worship the soul, though the soul remains true even when we entertain false imaginations about it. Stubble, which is nevertheless real, is better than light fabricated at will by the vain thought of him who imagines it; and yet it would be madness to hold stubble, which we can perceive and touch, to be worthy of our worship. Let not our religion be the worship of human works. The workmen are better than their works, yet we must not worship them.

Let not our religion be the worship of beasts. The worst men are better than beasts, but we must not worship them. Let not our religion be the worship of dead men. If they lived pious lives, it must not be supposed that they seek divine honours. They want us to worship him, in whose light they rejoice to have us as sharers in their merit. They are to be honoured by imitation and not adored with religious rites. If they lived evil lives, wherever they now are, they are not to be worshipped. Let not our religion be the worship of demons, for all superstition is the punishment and the deadly disgrace of men, but it is the glory and triumph of demons.

109. Let not our religion be the worship of lands and waters. Air is purer and clearer than these, though it can also be foggy; we must not worship air. Let not our religion be the worship of the purer and more serene upper air, for it is dark when there is no light. Purer than air is the brightness of fire, which, however, we ought not to worship, since we can kindle and extinguish it at will. Let not our religion be the worship of ethereal and celestial bodies, for although they are rightly preferred to all other bodies, still any kind of life is better than they. If they are animated by a soul, any soul in itself is better than any animated body, and yet no one has ever thought that a vicious soul was to be worshipped. Let not our religion be the worship of the life that trees live, for it is not sentient life. It is of the kind that goes on in the rhythm of our bodies, the sort of life that our bones and hair have, and our hair can be cut without our feeling anything. Sentient life is better than this, and yet we must not worship such life as beasts have.

110. Let not our religion be the worship of the perfectly wise rational soul, as it is found in angels who steadfastly carry on their ministry in the universe or in its parts, or in the best of men who await the reformation of their lower selves. All rational life obeys the voice of unchangeable truth speaking silently within the soul. If it does not so obey it is vicious. Rational life therefore does not owe its excellence to itself, but to the truth which it willingly obeys. The lowest man must worship the same God as is worshipped by the highest angel. In fact it is by refusing to worship him that human nature has been brought low. The source of wisdom and of truth is the same for angel and man, namely the one unchangeable Wisdom and Truth. The very Virtue and changeless Wisdom of God, consubstantial and coeternal with the Father, for our salvation deigned, in the temporal dispensation, to take upon himself our nature in order to

teach us that man must worship what every rational intellectual creature must also worship. Let us believe that the highest angels and most excellent ministers of God want us to join them in the worship of the one God, in contemplation of whom they find their happiness. Even we are not made happy by seeing an angel but by seeing the truth, by which we love the angels too and rejoice with them. We do not grudge that they should have readier access to the truth and enjoy it without obstacle. Rather we love them because we are bidden by our common Lord to hope for the same condition hereafter. So we honour them with love, but not with divine worship. We do not build temples for them. They do not wish to be honoured by us in that way, because they know that when we are good men we are ourselves the temples of the most high God. Accordingly it is written, with complete propriety that an angel once forbade a man to worship him, bidding him worship the one God under whom both angel and man were fellow-servants (Rev. 19:10).

111. Those who invite us to serve and worship themselves as gods are like proud men who, if they could, would like to be worshipped in that way. It is less perilous to endure such men than to worship demons. All lordship of men over men is brought to an end by the death of the lord or of the servant. Servitude under the pride of the evil angels is more to be feared on account of the time that is to follow death. Anyone can easily see that under a human lord we are allowed to have our thoughts free. We fear the lordship of demons because it is exercised over the mind in which is found our only means of beholding and grasping the truth. Wherefore, though we be enchained and subjected to all the powers given to men to rule the state, provided we "render unto Caesar the things that are Caesar's and to God the things that are God's" (Matt. 22:21), there is no need to fear lest anyone should exact such service after we are dead. The servitude of the soul is one thing, the servitude of the body quite another. Just men who have all their joy in God alone congratulate those who praise *him* for their good deeds. But when they are praised themselves, where possible they correct the erring. Where that is not possible, they are so far from being grateful for the error that they are eager to have it corrected. The good angels and all the holy ministers of God are like these, only more holy and pure. We need not fear lest we offend any of them if we avoid superstition, and with their help tend towards God alone, and bind [*religare*] our souls

to him alone without superstition. Hence, it is believed, religion derives its name.

112. One God alone I worship, the sole principle of all things, and his Wisdom who makes every wise soul wise, and his Gift [*munus*] whereby all the blessed are blessed. I am certainly sure that every angel that loves this God loves me too. Whoever abides in him and can hear human prayers, hears me in him. Whoever has God as his chief good, helps me in him, and cannot grudge my sharing in him. Let those who adore or flatter the parts of the world tell me this. What good friend will the man lack who worships the one God whom all the good love, in knowing whom they rejoice, and by having recourse to whom as their first principle they derive their goodness? Every angel that loves his own aberrations and will not be subject to the truth, but desires to find joy in his own advantage, has fallen away from the common good of all and from true beatitude. To such all evil men are given to be subdued and oppressed. But no good man is given over into his power except to be tried and proved. None can doubt that such an angel is not to be worshipped, for our misery is his joy, and our return to God is his loss.

113. Let our religion bind us to the one omnipotent God, because no creature comes between our minds and him whom we know to be the Father and the Truth, i.e., the inward light whereby we know him. In him and with him we venerate the Truth, who is in all respects like him, and who is the form of all things that have been made by the One, and that endeavour after unity. To spiritual minds it is clear that all things were made by this form which alone achieves what all things seek after. But all things would not have been made by the Father through the Son, nor would they be preserved within their bounds in safety, unless God were supremely good. He grudges nothing to any, for he has given to all the possibility to be good, and has given to all the power to abide in the good as far as they would or could. Wherefore it befits us to keep and to worship the Gift [*donum*] of God, equally unchangeable with the Father and the Son, in a Trinity of one substance. We worship one God from whom, through whom and in whom we have our being, from whom we fell away, being made unlike him, by whom we have not been allowed to perish, the principle to which we have recourse, the form we imitate, the grace whereby we are reconciled. We worship one God by whom we were made, and his likeness by whom we are formed for unity, and his peace whereby

we cleave to unity; God who spoke and it was done; and the Word by whom all was made that has substance and nature; and the Gift of his benignity by whom nothing that he made through the Word should perish, but should please and be reconciled to its Creator; one God by whose creative work we live, by whom we are remade so that we may live in wisdom, and by loving and enjoying whom we live in blessedness; one God from whom, through whom, and in whom are all things. To him be glory for ever and ever. Amen.

The Usefulness of Belief

St. Augustine's Review of the "De Utilitate Credendi." Retractations, I, xiv

1. After I had become a presbyter at Hippo-regius I wrote a book entitled *On the Utility of Believing*, addressed to a friend of mine who I knew had been deceived by the Manichees, and was still a victim of that error, and mocked the discipline of the Catholic Faith because it bade men believe, and did not teach them the truth by means of indubitable reason. In that book (iii, 9) I said, "In these precepts and commandments of the Law which Christians may not now lawfully obey, such as the Sabbath, circumcision, sacrifice and the like, there are contained such mysteries that every pious man may understand that there is nothing more pernicious than to take them literally, and nothing more wholesome than to let the truth be revealed by the spirit. Hence, the letter killeth but the spirit quickeneth." I have expounded these words of the apostle Paul differently, and, as it seems to me or rather as it is apparent from the facts, much more suitably in my book entitled, *On the Spirit and the Letter*. But the meaning I have given to them here need not be rejected.

2. Again I said (xi, 25), "In religion two kinds of people are praiseworthy—those who have already found the truth, whom we must judge to be entirely blessed; and those who seek it rightly and earnestly. Of these the former are already in possession. The latter are on the way that leads most certainly to possession." These words of mine are not erroneous if it be understood that those who have found the truth and whom I have described as being in possession are not entirely blessed in this life but in the life for which we hope and towards which we tend by the way of faith. Those are to be judged to have attained the final goal who have arrived where we desire to arrive with all our believing and seeking, that is, with our hold-

ing on the way of faith. But I do not think it is true that they are or ever have been entirely blessed in this life, not because in this life no truth at all can be discovered that can be perceived by the mind and not simply believed by faith, but because, however much of truth is discovered, it is not sufficient to make men entirely blessed. I would not say that the apostle's statement, "Now we see through a glass darkly. . . . Now I know in part," is not perceived by the mind. Clearly it is, but it does not make men entirely blessed. Perfect blessedness is described in these words. "But then face to face. . . . Then I shall know even as I am known." Those who have discovered this must be said to have obtained possession of beatitude, to which the way of faith we are following conducts us, and which we desire to reach by believing. But who the blessed are who are in possession of the blessedness to which the way of faith leads, is a great problem. Unquestionably the holy angels have it. But it may rightly be questioned whether holy men who have died may be said to have possession of it. They have indeed put off the corruptible body which burdens the soul, but they too still await the redemption of their bodies, and their flesh rests in hope, but does not yet shine with the incorruption that will one day be theirs. But whether for this reason they have less power to contemplate the truth with the mind's eye, or "face to face," as it is said, this is not the place to inquire or discuss. In regard to what I said a little later in the same chapter—"To know important, honourable and even divine things is most blessed"—this must also be held to refer to future beatitude. For in this life knowledge, however great, does not mean perfect blessedness, for that which is still unknown is incomparably greater.

3. Again, in the same chapter, I said, "There is a difference between true knowledge, i.e., rational knowledge, and belief in what has been usefully handed down to posterity either by report or in writing. . . . Our knowledge we owe to reason, our beliefs to authority." In popular speech that would seem to mean that we shrink from saying that we *know* what we believe on the testimony of suitable witnesses. It should not be taken in this sense. When we speak strictly we mean, by *knowing*, certain, rational comprehension. But when we are using words as they are used in ordinary parlance, as divine Scripture uses them, we do not hesitate to say that we *know* what we perceive with the bodily senses, or believe on the testimony of witnesses worthy of trust; and at the same time we understand the difference between the two uses of the word *knowing*.

4. Again the words in Chapter xii, "No one doubts that men universally are either foolish or wise," may seem to contradict what is written in *De Libero Arbitrio*, Book III, "As if human nature had no condition intermediate between folly and wisdom." I was then inquiring whether the first man was created wise or foolish or neither. We could not say that he was foolish when he was created without a fault, for folly is a great fault; and it was not quite clear how we could call him wise seeing he could be seduced. And so I offered as a brief suggestion a condition intermediate between folly and wisdom. I was also thinking of little children. We may admit that they bring original sin with them, but we cannot properly call them either wise or foolish, seeing they do not as yet use free will either well or ill. Now in this passage I have said that all men are either wise or foolish, meaning all men who have the use of reason, whereby they are distinguished as men from the animals, as in the sentence, All men wish to be happy. We need not fear that little children will be understood as included, for they cannot as yet will to be happy; and yet the sentence is quite true, obviously.

5. In Chapter xvi, after relating what the Lord Jesus did when he was in the flesh, I added, "Why, you ask, do not such things happen now?" and my reply was, "Because they would not affect us unless they were marvellous, and they would not be marvellous if they were familiar." In saying that, I meant that such great miracles do not happen now, not that no miracles happen even today.

6. In Chapter xviii, at the end of the book, I say that I have not begun to refute the Manichees and to attack their absurdities, nor to say anything important about the Catholic Faith. "I wanted simply if possible to rid you of a false opinion about true Christians maliciously or ignorantly distilled into us, and to stimulate you to learn certain great divine truths. Let this book be as it is. If your mind is somewhat placated, perhaps I shall be more ready to deal with other questions." I did not mean that I had hitherto written nothing against the Manichees, and nothing about Catholic teaching, for the books previously mentioned, published by me, testify that I had not kept silent on either subject. But in this book I had not begun to refute the Manichees or to attack their absurdities or to expound anything important about the Catholic Faith. I hoped that with this as a beginning I should later be writing to Honoratus himself what I had not yet written in this book. The book begins: *Si mihi, Honorate, unum atque idem videretur esse*. . . .

The Usefulness of Belief

INTRODUCTION

NOTHING, IT SEEMS, IS KNOWN OF HONORATUS TO whom this tractate is addressed beyond what may be gleaned from the tractate itself. It is true, a certain Honoratus of Carthage sent a number of exegetical queries to St. Augustine who, in 412, replied in a lengthy Epistle (*Epist.* 140), a veritable treatise in itself on the theme of the Grace of the New Testament. There is nothing in the Epistle to suggest that the two men are identical, though they well may be. It would be pleasant to think that St. Augustine won his case.

The Honoratus of *De Util. Cred.* was a student friend of St. Augustine in his Carthaginian days, and shared in his early enthusiasm for philosophy. Unlike his friend he had not come from a Christian home, and he had a strong aversion to the Manichees which was with difficulty overcome. But as the result of St. Augustine's persuasion he consented to become a hearer in that sect. He was acute enough to observe that the Manichees were more clever at refuting and deriding the tenets of others than at giving convincing proof of the truth of their own. He also suspected the weakness of a position which, while professing to accept the New Testament documents, too frequently attempted to get rid of inconvenient passages by alleging that they had been interpolated. Nevertheless, Honoratus had retained his connection with the sect long after St. Augustine had abandoned it, possibly because he had despaired of finding a satisfactory system to take its place. Catholic Christianity in particular offended him because of its demand for belief upon authority.

This treatise, written shortly after St. Augustine had become a presbyter in Hippo in 391, may be said to show him at his best in controversy; unbending no doubt, but also amiable and reasonable. In his eagerness to win Honoratus for the Catholic Faith, he treats him with the utmost courtesy and respect. He reasons with him as an old friend, pointing out the way he had himself travelled through painful doubt to faith, hoping that Honoratus will be induced to follow it. The brief account of his personal history (sect. 20) most interestingly confirms, so far as it goes, the account in the *Confessions*. Here, too, are to be found his most cogent pleas for the authority of the Catholic tradition. Because it is founded on historical events (the life of Christ and the New Testament miracles), and has obtained world-wide acceptance, and inspired the ascetic life in many, it may well be believed and trusted as a starting-point, at least, for those who seek true religion which is the highest wisdom, important therefore if recondite. Even those who think they can achieve knowledge of truth and of God by reason alone cannot neglect this authoritative tradition.

The main subject of the treatise is the relation of faith and reason. It is perhaps surprising that it should be entitled the *Utility* and not the *Reasonableness* of *Believing*, but this corresponds to a central element of St. Augustine's early thought. Knowing, the result of rational demonstration, is the highest achievement of mind. But it is difficult except for the few who are wise. (Later he came to hold that it was impossible so far as religion is concerned for any man in this life.) Belief is a means to an end, which is knowledge, a necessary means for nearly all men, and not to be despised even by the wise, if only that the many who are foolish may not be discouraged. What is true of the intellectual life is even more obvious of the practical life of duty. Even sceptics, who teach that in the practical life probability is the rule, thereby implicitly recognize belief as the bond of human society. Moreover, historical events, e.g., the life and teaching of Christ, cannot strictly speaking be known, but can only be believed on the ground of credible testimony. Here the argument is developed which was to be expressed later in extreme and epigrammatic form, "I should not believe the Gospel unless the authority of the Catholic Church moved me to do so" (*Against the Fundamental Epistle of Manichaeus*. 6).

ANALYSIS

i, 1—ii, 4. Introductory Address to Honoratus.

Recalling early association in pursuit of wisdom, and explaining the subject and purpose of the treatise.

iii, 5–9. Fourfold Sense of Old Testament Scriptures.

(5) Definitions. (6–8) Examples from the New Testament. (9) Allegory.

iv, 10—vi, 13. Difficulty of Interpretation of Literature.

(10–12) Various possible misunderstandings. (13) Old Testament Scripture peculiarly difficult, but also peculiarly important for religion. It should be approached with respect, and with the aid of the best teachers, as we approach the study of Vergil.

vii, 14—viii, 20. Seeking Religion resembles seeking Culture and Wisdom.

(14) True religion and wisdom are identical. (15) Where opinions differ we must go to the most widely renowned teachers, "that we may err with the human race itself." (16) The best teachers of rhetoric, e.g., are usually surrounded by a mass of pupils, few of whom excel; so also with religious teachers. The multitude of their disciples should not repel us. (18) The Catholic Faith by its weight of authority, its world-wide acceptance and general support is at least the obvious starting-point. (20) Augustine's intellectual pilgrimage from doubt to faith since he left Africa.

ix, 21—xiii, 29. Faith and Reason.

(22) Difference between belief and credulity. (23) The religious inquirer demands that his sincerity be believed. (24) Not everyone can use reason in religion. Those fitted to do so should not grudge the easier way of believing to those less able. (25) Knowing, believing and holding an (uninstructed) opinion. Only rational truth can be known. Events in the past cannot strictly be known but can be believed. In practical life probability is the only guide, and this implies some kind of faith. (26) The stability of human society depends on believing. (27) The foolish must believe and obey the wise, especially in religion, but (28) it is impossible for the foolish to decide who is wise. (29) There will be no earnest search for religious truth unless men first believe that God exists and gives aid to seeking minds.

xiv, 30—xvii, 35. Belief in Christ.

(31) All heretics who hold the Christian name demand belief in Christ on the ground of Scripture. Such belief can only be grounded on Catholic tradition. (32) Christ himself demanded belief, and performed miracles in order to win the belief of men who could not be won by reason. (34) The authority of the Catholic tradition is based on the miracles of Christ in the past by which he gathered a multitude of believers, also on the successful expansion of Christianity, and its continuance. (35) The ascetic lives of many simple Christians also supports its authority.

xviii, 36. Final Appeal to Honoratus to abandon Manichaeism.

The Usefulness of Belief

THE TEXT

To Honoratus

i, 1. If I thought, Honoratus, that there was no difference between a heretic and one who follows heretics, I should judge that my tongue and my pen alike should remain quiescent in this matter. But there is a great difference. A heretic, as I suppose, is one who for some temporal advantage, and chiefly for his own glory and pre-eminence, begets or follows new and false opinions. He who trusts such men is deluded by some illusory appearance of truth or piety. That being so, I thought I ought not to keep silent from you what I think about the discovery and the retaining of truth, for which, as you know, I burned with a great flame of love since my early youth. Truth is far removed from the minds of vain men who have gone too far among worldly concerns and, falling, think there is nothing beyond what they perceive by the senses, these five well-known messengers of the body. Even when they endeavour to withdraw from the senses, they carry with them the impressions and images received from the senses, and think that by their death-dealing and fallacious rule the ineffable sanctuary of truth is to be rightly measured. Nothing is easier, my dear friend, than to say or even to think that one has discovered the truth. How difficult it really is you will, I trust, recognize from this letter of mine. That it may be a help or at least not a hindrance to you and to all into whose hands it may chance to fall, I have prayed to God and do pray. And I hope it may be so, if I am right in feeling that I have taken up my pen with a pious and dutiful mind and with no desire for vain reputation or empty ostentation.

2. My purpose, therefore, is to prove to you, if I can, that the

Manichees rashly and sacrilegiously inveigh against those who, accepting the authority of the Catholic Faith, before they can behold the truth which only the pure heart can behold, are forearmed by believing, and are prepared for being enlightened by God. You know, Honoratus, that I fell among these people for no other reason than that they declared that they would put aside all overawing authority, and by pure and simple reason would bring to God those who were willing to listen to them, and so deliver them from all error. What else compelled me for nearly nine years to spurn the religion implanted in me as a boy by my parents, to follow these men and listen diligently to them, than that they said we were overawed by superstition and were bidden to believe rather than to reason, while they pressed no one to believe until the truth had been discussed and elucidated? Who would not be enticed by these promises, especially if he were an adolescent with a mind eager for truth, but made proud and garrulous by the disputes of learned men in school? Such they found me then, scorning what I took to be old wives' tales, and desirous of swallowing and holding the open and sincere truth which they promised. But again, what reason kept me from wholly cleaving to them? For I remained in the grade they call "hearers" so that I might not give up worldly hopes and duties. The reason was that I observed that they were more clever and ready of wit in refuting others than firm and sure in proving their own doctrines. Why do I speak of myself, who was then a Catholic Christian, and who have now, nearly exhausted and parched after my long thirst, sought again with all avidity the breasts which nourished me, and, weeping and deeply groaning, have pressed them, that there might come forth sufficient to refresh me in my present state and bring back hope of life and salvation? Why do I speak of myself? You were not yet a Christian when you were, by my exhortation, with difficulty induced to hear and find out about these men whom you violently detested. What else delighted you, I pray you to recall, save their great presumption and the promise of a reasoned doctrine? Well, they harangued at great length and with great vigour against the errors of simple people, which I have since learned is extremely easy for anyone to do who is moderately educated; and if they taught us any of their own doctrines we thought we must maintain it because nothing else occurred to us to set our minds at rest. They dealt with us as tricky fowlers are wont to do, who fix their limed twigs near water to deceive thirsty birds. Other water they cover and conceal, or set up terrifying devices to scare the birds from them so that they may fall into their trap, not by their own choice but by lack of any other supply.

3. I might, of course, answer myself by saying that these neat and clever similes, and such censures generally, can be most politely and eloquently used by any adversary against all who teach any doctrine whatever. But I thought it right to put that sort of thing into my letter to warn them to cease to use similar modes of controversy. As Cicero says: "Let us give up trifling commonplaces and let us meet fact with fact, case with case, reason with reason." Let them cease to use the expression which trips from their mouths as by some necessity when some one has left them after long attending their discourses, "Light has passed completely through him." I do not bother so much about them; but you, who are my chief concern, will observe how easy and vain is this method of censuring anyone. I leave this point to your prudence. I have no fear that you will think I was the dwelling-place of light when I was involved in the life of this world, nursing shadowy hopes of a beautiful wife, of the pomp of riches, of empty honours and other pernicious and deadly pleasures. All these things, as you know, I did not cease to desire and hope for when I was their zealous hearer. I do not attribute this to their teaching, for I confess that they carefully warned me to beware of these things. Only, to say that I have been abandoned by light when I have turned away from all these shadowy things and have decided to be content with such a livelihood as is necessary for bodily health, but that I was bright and illumined when I loved these things and was held their prisoner, is the mark of a man who, to put it mildly, has no very clear insight into matters about which he loves too much to prate. But let us come to the controversy itself.

ii, 4. You know well that the Manichees by their censures of the Catholic Faith and chiefly by their destructive criticism of the Old Testament affect the unlearned, who do not quite know how these things are to be understood, and how, being usefully taken, they may go down into the veins and the marrow of souls still unweaned, so to speak. Because some of these things offend ignorant and uncareful minds—the great majority—they can be popularly attacked. Not many have the power to defend them in an equally popular way, because of the mysteries they contain. The few who know how to do this do not love public controversy with its consequent publicity. Hence they are unknown except to those who seek them out. Therefore, concerning the rashness of the Manichees in censuring the Old Testament and the Catholic Faith, listen, I pray you, to the considerations which influence me. I hope and pray that you will accept them in the spirit in which they are written. God, to whom the secrets of my conscience are known, knows that in this little book I am doing nothing in malice, but in the hope that my words may be acceptable in proof of the truth. For a long time now, and with incredible solicitude, I have determined to live for the truth alone. I trust that, while it was very easy for me to err in your company, to keep with you the straight path may not be, to avoid a harsher expression, very difficult indeed. In the hope which I cherish that you will find with me the path of wisdom, I am sure he will not leave me to whom I have dedicated myself, whom day and night I seek to behold, and to whom I often pray even weeping, because I know myself incapable of beholding him, since the eye of my soul has been damaged by my sins and by my being habituated to the plagues of lethargic opinions. As eyes which are scarcely opened after a long period of darkness and blindness turn away and refuse the light which, nevertheless, they desire, especially if one try to point them to the sun, so, in my case, I do not deny that there is an ineffable and unique spiritual good visible to the mind, but I confess with weeping and groaning that I am not yet fitted to contemplate it. Nevertheless, he will not leave me if I make no pretence, if I follow the path of duty, if I love truth and friendship, if I am filled with anxiety lest you be deceived.

iii, 5. The whole Old Testament Scripture, to those who diligently desire to know it, is handed down with a four-fold sense—historical, aetiological, analogical, allegorical. Don't think me clumsy in using Greek terms, because in the first place these were the terms I was taught, and I do not venture to pass on to you anything else than what I have received. You will notice also that amongst us Latins, there are no words in common use to express these ideas. If I were to attempt a translation of them I might be even clumsier. If I were to use circumlocutions I should be less speedy in my exposition. This only I ask you to believe that, however I stray, I write nothing merely in the interests of a proudly inflated style. In Scripture, according to the historical sense, we are told what has been written or done. Sometimes the historical fact is simply that such and such a thing was written. According to the aetiological sense we are told for what cause something has been done or said. According to the analogical sense we are shown that the Old and New

Testaments do not conflict. According to the allegorical sense we are taught that everything in Scripture is not to be taken literally but must be understood figuratively.

6. In all these senses our Lord Jesus Christ and his apostles used Scripture. When it was objected that his disciples plucked ears of corn on the Sabbath day, his answer was taken from history—"Have ye not read what David did when he was hungry and those who were with him; how he entered the house of God and ate the shew-bread, which it was not lawful for him to eat or for those who were with him, but only for the priests" (Matt. 12:3–4). To aetiology belongs the answer Christ gave to his questioners who, when he forbade divorce except for fornication, told them that Moses had allowed divorce if a bill of divorcement were given—"Moses did this on account of the hardness of your hearts" (Matt. 19:8). Here a reason was given why Moses properly gave permission owing to the circumstances of the time, while Christ gave his commandment under different circumstances. It would take a long time to explain the changes of the times and the order of change which is fixed and settled by a wondrous disposition of divine providence.

7. Then there is the analogical sense which shows the agreement of the two Testaments. I need not say that this is used by all whose authority is accepted by the Manichees. It is their own affair to resolve the problem created by their wonted suggestion that many things have been interpolated into the divine Scriptures by I know not what corrupters of the truth. That assertion always seemed to me, even when I was their hearer, utterly invalid. And not to me only but to you (for I well remember), and to all of us who tried to exercise a little more care in judging than did the mass of their followers. But now when many of the passages which troubled me most have been explained and straightened out—those ones especially in dealing with which their oratory reached its climax, giving itself a freer rein in the absence of any adversary—none of their teachings seems to be more shameless, or to use a milder expression, weaker or less cautious, than their assertion that the divine Scriptures have been corrupted, for they can produce no exemplars still extant to prove it. If they said that these writings were not to be accepted because written by men who in their judgment did not write the truth, their cavilling would be more upright or their error more worthy of cultivated people. This they have done with the book called the Acts of the Apostles. When I consider their method I can hardly marvel at it enough.

In a matter like this I do not need man's wisdom but simply an ordinary heart. Obviously there is so much in that book which resembles the things they accept that it seems to me the greatest stupidity not to accept it too, and to say that what offends them in it is false and interpolated. Or if that would be impudent, as it is, why do they attribute some value to the Epistles of Paul or to the Four Books of the Gospel, in which, I suppose, there is a far higher proportion than in the Acts, of passages which they make out to have been interpolated by corrupters. Now that is just the point which I ask you to consider with me, judging quietly and calmly. You know that they endeavour to include Manes, their founder, among the apostles, and say that the Holy Spirit whom the Lord promised to send to his disciples, came to us through Manes. Accordingly, if they accepted the Acts of the Apostles, in which the advent of the Holy Spirit is clearly set forth, they would not find any way of explaining how that passage had been interpolated. Their alleged corrupters of the divine Scriptures must have lived before the time of Manes, and must have belonged to those who wished to mix the Jewish Law with the Gospel. But they cannot attribute the passage about the Holy Spirit to such people, unless possibly they allege that they prophesied and put into their book something that might later be urged against Manes, who said that the Holy Spirit was sent through himself. I shall speak more plainly about the Holy Spirit elsewhere. Let me now return to my theme.

8. I think I have shown sufficiently that Old Testament history, aetiology and analogy are found in the New Testament. It remains to show the existence of allegory. Our Saviour himself used an allegory from the Old Testament when he said: "This generation seeketh a sign, but none shall be given to it but the sign of the prophet Jonah; for as Jonah was in the belly of the whale three days and three nights, so shall the Son of Man be three days and three nights in the heart of the earth" (Matt. 12:39–40). What shall I say of the apostle Paul who in the first Epistle to the Corinthians explains that the history of the Exodus was an allegory of the Christian people that was to be: "I would not have you ignorant, brethren, how that all our fathers were under the cloud and all passed through the sea. And all were baptized unto Moses in the cloud and in the sea, and did all eat the same spiritual food, and did all drink the same spiritual drink. For they drank of the spiritual rock that followed them: and that rock was Christ. But with many of

them God was not well pleased: for they were overthrown in the wilderness. Now these things were our examples that we should not lust after evil things, as they lusted. Neither be ye idolaters as some of them were; as it is written, The people sat down to eat and drink and rose up to play. Neither let us commit fornication, as some of them committed and fell in one day three and twenty thousand men. Neither let us tempt Christ, as some of them tempted and were destroyed by serpents. Neither let us murmur as some of them murmured, and were destroyed of the destroyer. Now all these things happened unto them in a figure, but they were written for our admonition, upon whom the ends of the age are come" (I Cor. 10:1–11). There is another allegory also in the apostle's writings which is very pertinent to the present issue, inasmuch as the Manichees themselves are wont to produce it and point to it. To the Galatians Paul says: "For it is written that Abraham had two sons, the one by a bond-maid, the other by a freewoman. But he who was born of the bond-maid was born after the flesh; but he of the freewoman was by promise. Which things are an allegory: for these are the two covenants; the one from Mount Sinai, which gendereth to bondage, which is Hagar. For Sinai is a mountain in Arabia, and answereth to Jerusalem which now is, and is in bondage with her children. But the Jerusalem which is above is free, which is the mother of us all" (Gal. 4:22–26).

9. Here these wicked men, while they try to make the Law of none effect, at the same time compel us to approve of these Scriptures. They pay attention where it is said that those are in servitude who are under the Law, and above other passages brandish this decisive one: "You who are justified by the Law are banished from Christ. You have fallen from grace" (Gal. 5:4). Now we admit that all this is true. We do not say the Law is necessary save for those for whom servitude is profitable. It was profitably laid down because men, who could not be won from their sins by reason, had to be coerced by threats and terrors of penalties which even fools can understand. When the grace of Christ sets men free from such threats and penalties it does not condemn the Law but invites us now to submit to his love and not to be slaves to fear. Grace is a benefaction conferred by God, which those do not understand who desire to continue under the bondage of the Law. Paul rightly calls them unbelievers, reproachfully, who do not believe that they are now set free by our Lord Jesus from a servitude to which they had

been subjected by the just judgment of God. Hence this other saying of the same apostle: "The Law was our pedagogue in Christ" (Gal. 3:24). God, thus, gave men a pedagogue whom they might fear, and later gave them a master whom they might love. But in these precepts and mandates of the Law which Christians may not now lawfully obey, such as the Sabbath, circumcision, sacrifice and the like, there are contained such mysteries that every pious man may understand there is nothing more pernicious than to take whatever is there literally, and nothing more wholesome than to let the truth be revealed by the spirit. For this reason: "The letter killeth but the spirit quickeneth" (II Cor. 3:6). And again: "The same vail remains in the reading of the Old Testament and there is no revelation, for in Christ the vail is done away" (II Cor. 3:14). It is not the Old Testament that is done away in Christ but the concealing vail, so that it may be understood through Christ. That is, as it were, laid bare, which without Christ is obscure and hidden. The same apostle adds immediately: "When thou shalt turn to Christ the vail will be taken away" (II Cor. 3:16). He does not say: "The Law or the Old Testament will be taken away." It is not the case, therefore, that by the grace of the Lord that which was covered has been abolished as useless; rather the covering has been removed which concealed useful truth. This is what happens to those who earnestly and piously, not proudly and wickedly, seek the sense of the Scriptures. To them is carefully demonstrated the order of events, the reasons for deeds and words, and the agreement of the Old Testament with the New, so that not a point remains where there is not complete harmony; and such secret truths are conveyed in figures that when they are brought to light by interpretation they compel those who wished to condemn rather than to learn, to confess their discomfiture.

iv, 10. Meantime, leaving aside all deep science, let me treat you as I think I should treat my familiar friend, that is according to my own ability, and not as learned men whom I have admired might do. There are three kinds of error to which men are liable when they read. First, they may accept as true what is false, and what the writer knew to be false. Secondly—though this is not so obvious but no less deadly—they may accept as true a false opinion actually held by the writer. Thirdly, they may understand some truth from another's writing, which the writer himself did not understand. In this kind of error there is no little advantage. Indeed, if you consider it carefully you will see that herein lies the whole benefit of reading. An example of the first kind of error is this. Suppose someone were to believe that Rhadamanthus in the underworld hears and judges the cases of the dead because he read it in Vergil's *Aeneid*. Here is a double error. He believes an incredible thing, and the author himself is not to be credited with believing it. Here is an example of the second kind of error. Suppose someone were to take it as true that the soul is composed of atoms and after death is dissolved into the same atoms and perishes, because Lucretius wrote it. He is no less unhappy if in so great a matter he is persuaded to accept as certain what is false, though indeed Lucretius, whose book has deceived him, did hold that opinion. What advantage is it to be certain about a writer's opinion when one has chosen a companion in error and not a deliverer from error? The third kind of error is complementary. Suppose someone were to read a passage in a book of Epicurus in which continence was praised, and were to assert that Epicurus taught that virtue was the Supreme Good, and consequently was not to be blamed. The error of Epicurus in believing that bodily pleasure was man's Supreme Good does no harm to such a reader, for he has not accepted so base and deadly an opinion. Indeed, Epicurus pleases him for no other reason than that he supposes that he, Epicurus, did not hold an opinion that ought not to be held. An error of this kind is not only entirely proper but is often very worthy in a good man. Suppose it were reported to me of one whom I loved that, having reached adult life, he declared to many listeners that he liked boyhood and infancy so much that he wanted to continue in that condition of life; suppose the proof that he said so was so strong that I could not decently deny it; would I seem blameworthy if I judged that when he said it he meant that what pleased him was innocence and a mind free from the cupidities in which the human race is involved, and therefore loved him more than I had done before, yes, even if as a boy he had foolishly loved ignoble ease and too great liberty to play and eat? Suppose he died soon after this was reported to me and I had no opportunity to question him and discover what his opinion really was. Would anyone be so unjust as to be angry with me because I praised his intent and purpose on the basis of the words I had heard? Probably no just judge of such matters would hesitate to praise my high opinion of innocence and my good will in thinking well of a man, though there was some doubt, and I might have thought ill of him.

v, 11. Such being the case as regards readers, let me tell you that conversely there are necessarily the same number of difficulties from the point of view of writers. Either one may write usefully and be misunderstood or both the writing and the understanding may be at fault, or the reader derives an advantage while the writer meant something quite different. Of these three possibilities I make no adverse comment on the first, and the third does not concern me. I cannot blame a writer who is misunderstood through no fault of his own. Nor am I troubled when I see that a writer who has not grasped the truth does not harm his readers. But the best and most admirable situation is found only when good things are written and are properly understood by the readers. Even in this case, because we have to do with two minds, the possibility of error is not completely excluded. For it often happens that the writer's views are sound, and the reader's also, but the latter holds them in a different sense, sometimes a better sense, sometimes an inferior sense, but always profitably. But when we share the views of our author and they are suited to promote good conduct, the cause of truth is served in a high degree and no place is left open to falsehood. Now, when we have to do with very obscure matters this kind of relationship between author and reader is extremely rare, and in my opinion it is not a case where clear knowledge is possible but only faith. How can I find out the intention and meaning of an author who is absent or dead, in such a way that I could give evidence as to them on oath. Even if he were present and could be interrogated, even if he were not a bad man, he could still conceal many things from a sense of duty. But I do not think that the character of an author has much to do with the task of sifting truth. It is most honourable to believe that an author was a good man, whose writings were intended to benefit the human race and posterity.

12. Now let the Manichees tell me how they would classify what they are pleased to call the error of the Catholic Church. If in the first class, the charge is grave, but a long defence is not necessary. It is sufficient to say that we do not so understand the Old Testament as they seem to imagine when they attack us. If in the second class, the charge is no less grave, but the same answer refutes it. If in the third class, there is no indictment at all. Just consider the Scriptures themselves. What exactly do they object to in the books of the Old Testament? Are they good books but badly understood by us? But the Manichees refuse to accept them. Are they bad books and badly understood by us? The previous reply is sufficient here too. Will they say that

they are bad books though well understood by us? But that is simply to absolve living adversaries with whom the case is being argued, and to accuse men long since dead with whom there can be no argument. For my part, I believe that the authors of the Old Testament were great and divine men, who to our profit handed down their writings, and that the Law was promulgated and codified at the command and by the will of God. And I can easily prove it (though I know very few books of this kind) if a calm and not too obstinate mind will give me its attention. I shall do so when you give me a kindly hearing. But when shall I have such an opportunity? Is it not enough for me at present that you should not be deceived as to how the matter stands?

vi, 13. I call my conscience to witness, Honoratus, I call God who dwells in pure souls to witness, that I am convinced there is nothing more wise, more chaste, more religious than those Scriptures which the Catholic Church accepts under the name of the Old Testament. You are amazed, I am sure. For I cannot pretend that I was not formerly of a very different opinion. But there is nothing more rash—and of rashness as a boy I had plenty—than to desert the professed expositors of books which they possess and hand on to their disciples, and instead to go asking the opinion of others who, for no reason I can think of, have declared most bitter war against the authors of these books. Who ever thought of having the obscure and recondite works of Aristotle expounded to him by an enemy of Aristotle? I am speaking of studies in which the student may slip without committing sacrilege. Who ever wished to read or learn the geometrical treatises of Archimedes with Epicurus as his master, who, understanding nothing of them so far as I can judge, nevertheless pertinaciously attacked them in his discourses? Are the Scriptures of the Law, which the Manichees attack vainly and foolishly, so very plain and open to vulgar understanding? These men seem to me to resemble the woman whom they are wont to deride. In her religious simplicity, irritated because a Manichaean woman praised the sun and commended it as an object of worship, she leapt up in her excitement and stamped on the place on the floor illumined by the rays that came in through the window, exclaiming: "Lo, I tread under foot the sun, your God." Utterly foolish and so like a woman! No one denies it. But don't you think the Manichees are just like that, who with floods of oratory and malevolent criticism tear to pieces books which they do not understand, of which they do not know the purpose or the nature, books which look quite simple but, to those who understand, are subtle and divine; and, because the ignorant applaud, think they have achieved something wonderful. All that is in these Scriptures, believe me, is profound and divine. All truth is there, and learning suited to refresh and restore souls, but in such a form that there is no one who may not draw thence all he needs, provided he comes to draw in a spirit of piety and devotion such as true religion demands. To prove that to you would require many reasons and a long discourse. I must get you first not to hate these authors and then to love them, and how else can this be done except by expounding their writings and their teachings. If we hated Vergil, indeed if we did not love him, before we knew anything about him, because our seniors praised him, we should never derive any satisfaction from the innumerable Vergilian questions that are wont to excite and agitate teachers of literature. We should not be willing to listen to anyone who discussed these questions and praised the poet. We should be favourably impressed by any one who tried to show that he was wrong or mad. But now, many teachers try to explain these questions variously according to the capacity of each; and those obtain the greatest applause by whose exposition the poet appears in the best light, so that even those who do not understand him at least believe that he was guilty of no error and that his poems are admirable in all respects. So if in any question the teacher fails to give an answer, we are angry with him, and do not attribute his dullness to the fault of Vergil. If he tried to defend himself by blaming so famous an author he would soon be without pupils and fees. Surely we should show a similar respect to those through whom the Holy Spirit spoke, as agelong tradition has affirmed. But we, intelligent youths forsooth, marvellous explorers of reason, without turning over these books, without seeking teachers, without the slightest suspicion of our own slowness of comprehension, without the slightest heed paid to those whose care it has been that these books should be read, guarded and studied throughout the world and for so long a time—*we* had the temerity to suppose that nothing such men said was to be believed, influenced as we were by their bitter enemies, among whom, because of their false promise of reason, we were compelled to believe and cherish an unheard-of number of fables.

vii, 14. Now I shall, if I may, go on with my task, and I shall endeavour, not meantime to explain the Catholic Faith, but to urge those who care for their souls to examine its great mysteries, and I shall show them that there is hope of divine fruit and of finding truth. No one doubts that he who seeks true religion either believes already that the soul, which is to profit by religion, is immortal, or at least hopes to gain that belief from religion itself. All religion is on account of the soul. No man has any care or anxiety about the condition of his natural body, at any rate after death, if his soul possesses that which will make it blessed. On account of the soul alone or chiefly, therefore, true religion, if there is one, is instituted. But the soul —I know not why and I confess the problem is obscure—the soul errs and is foolish, as we see, until it obtains and comprehends wisdom. Wisdom is perchance true religion. Am I sending you to fables? Am I compelling you to believe anything rashly? I say our soul is ensnared and plunged in folly and error, but seeks the path of truth, if there be any. If this is not your experience, pardon me, and share with me, I pray, your wisdom. But if you recognize in your own heart that it is as I say, let us, I beseech you, seek the truth together.

15. Suppose we have never heard any teacher of such a religion. We are undertaking an entirely new enterprise. We must first, I suppose, seek for men who profess to teach it. Suppose we have discovered that some hold one opinion, some another, and in the diversity of opinions all desire to attract inquirers, each to his own opinion. But suppose that among them there are some of notable celebrity, accepted by nearly all nations. Whether in fact they possess the truth remains a big question. But surely we must first find out about them, so that so long as we err, being human, we may seem to err with the human race itself.

16. But, you say, truth is found among the few. If you know where it is to be found, you are assuming that you know what it is, but my hypothesis is that we are starting our search from scratch. Nevertheless, granted that you are compelled by the force of truth to conjecture that only a few can possess it, you do not know who, in fact, these are. Now suppose the few who know the truth are able to hold the multitude by their authority, and can therefore expound and elucidate their secrets widely. What then? We see that very few attain consummate eloquence, though throughout the whole world the schools of rhetoric thunder in the ears of crowds of young men. Surely those who wish to become good orators will not take alarm at the multitude of the unlearned, and imagine that they must pay attention

to the orations of Caecilius and Erucius rather than to those of Cicero. Everyone wants to study Cicero's works because they are established by the authority of our ancestors. The crowds of the unlearned endeavour to learn what is prescribed for their learning by a few learned men. But very few succeed. Still fewer put their learning into practice. And only a fraction attain to fame. Perhaps true religion is something like that. No doubt the churches are frequented by multitudes of unlearned persons, but that does not prove that among them there is none who is perfectly equipped in these mysterious truths. If no more studied eloquence than the few who become eloquent, our parents would never have sent us to the rhetoricians. But if we were drawn to these studies by the very multitude of students, most of them unlearned, and sought to obtain what only a few can obtain, why should we refuse to see something similar in the case of religion, which we despise to the great danger, perhaps, of our souls? Granted that the truest and most sincere worship of God is likely to be found among a few; suppose these few have the assent of a multitude of people involved though they may be in cupidities and far from true understanding—which undoubtedly can happen—what answer, I ask, could we give to any one who censured our temerity and folly in not seeking diligently from its proper teachers that which we were most eager to find? The multitude scared me away? What about the liberal arts which offer hardly any advantage even for the present life? What about the effort to acquire money, or to obtain honour? What about finding and maintaining good health? Finally, what about the desire for happiness? All men are concerned about these matters, while only a few excel. But certainly no one is deterred from seeking these things because of the multitude of seekers.

17. But it appears, you say, that ridiculous things are taught in the Church. Who asserts it? Enemies forsooth. I do not at present inquire why they are enemies, or with what reason, but enemies they are. When I read a book I take in the knowledge all by myself! Do I indeed? Without some training in the poetic art you would not venture to touch Terentianus Maurus without a teacher. You need Asper, Cornutus, Donatus and innumerable others if you are to understand any poet whose poems and plays apparently win applause. Will you boldly venture without a teacher to study books, which, whatever they may be otherwise, are at least holy and full of divine teachings, and are widely famed with the assent of almost the whole human race? Will

you dare to pass sentence on them without a teacher? If anything occurs in them which seems to you absurd, would you not accuse the slowness and worldly corruption of your own mind —which is common to all fools—before you bring an accusation against books which, maybe, cannot be understood by fools. You would seek for someone both pious and learned, or who was widely reputed to be such, by whose precepts you might be made better, and more learned by his teaching. But such a man, you say, is not easy to find. You would make elaborate inquiries. There is none in the land you live in? What better cause could there be to send you on a journey? There is none, or at least no signs of one, on the mainland? You would take ship. If none were found in the nearest country across the sea, you would proceed to the lands where the history recorded in these books is said to have been enacted. We did nothing of the kind, Honoratus. Instead, by our own arbitrary judgment, we unhappy youths condemned a religion which might have proved to be most holy, and at any rate was still an open question, a religion which has taken possession of the whole world. What if those things in the Scriptures which seem to offend some unskilled persons were put there on purpose, so that when we read anything abhorrent to the feelings of ordinary folk, not to mention prudent and saintly folk, we should the more earnestly look for a hidden meaning. Don't you see how men try to put some fine interpretation on the beloved Alexis in Vergil's Bucolics, for whom the harsh shepherd sang his song? (Eclogue 2.) And how they affirm that the boy about whom Plato is said to have written an amatory poem has some deep significance which escapes the understanding of the unskilled? So a richly endowed poet, it appears, may without sacrilege publish lustful songs.

18. Were we, then, prevented from inquiry into the Catholic Faith by some legal penalty, by the power of adversaries, by the worthless character or ill-repute of its sacred officers, by its recent foundation, by the fact that it must be professed in secret? There is nothing of that kind. No law, divine or human, prohibits inquiry as to the Catholic Faith. Certainly human law allows it to be professed and cherished. About divine law we are assuming that we are still uncertain. No enemy terrifies us if we are weak; but of course truth and the soul's salvation ought to be sought at whatever risk, even if they cannot safely be sought and found. Dignities and powers of all ranks serve this divine cult with the greatest devotion. The name of religion is most honourable and in the highest repute. What then hinders thorough

discussion and pious and careful investigation of the question whether the Catholic Faith be not the religion which a few may know intimately and guard, while it rejoices in the goodwill and favour of all nations?

19. Such being the case, suppose, as I said before, we are now for the first time inquiring to what religion we are to entrust our souls for purification and restoration. Without any doubt we must first consider the Catholic Church. Christians are more numerous than Jews and idolaters combined. Among Christians there are several heresies, but all want to be regarded as Catholics and call others beyond their own group heretics. But there is one Church, all will admit, numerically larger taking the whole world into consideration, and sounder in the truth than all others, as those affirm who know it. The question of truth does not, however, concern us just now. It is enough for our inquiry that there is one Catholic Church to which different heresies give different names, while they are called by names proper to each one which they dare not deny. Hence those who judge without fear or favour can discern to whom properly belongs the Catholic name to which all lay claim. But lest any think there is need of lengthy or superfluous discourse on this point I simply assert that there is one Church in which even human laws are in a manner Christian. Not that I wish to create any prejudice in my own favour here. Only I judge that here is a most suitable starting-point for our inquiry. There is no need to fear that the true worship of God, having no strength of its own to rely on, may seem to need the support of those whom it ought itself to support. But surely it is an entirely happy situation if the truth can be found where there is complete security to seek and to possess it. Otherwise it must be approached and searched for elsewhere, whatever be the danger.

viii, 20. Having established these premises which in my opinion are so just that I ought to win my case with you against any adversary, I shall to the best of my ability relate to you the path I followed when I began to look for the true religion in the spirit in which, as I have shown, it ought to be looked for. When I departed from you across the sea I was already in a state of serious doubt; what was I to hold; what was I to give up? Indeed my hesitation grew greater day by day from the time that I heard the famous Faustus. You remember, his coming to explain all our difficulties was held out to us as a gift from heaven. Well, I recognized that he was no better than the others of the sect, except for a certain eloquence he had. When I got settled in Italy I reasoned with myself and deliberated long, not as to whether I should remain in that sect—for I was already sorry that I had fallen into it—but as to how truth was to be found. No one knows better than you do how I sighed for love of truth. Often it seemed to me that truth could not be found, and my thoughts like a great flood tended to carry me over to the opinion of the academics. But often again, as I reflected to the best of my ability how lively was the human mind, how wise, how penetrating, I could not believe that the truth must ever elude its grasp. Possibly the manner of seeking truth might be concealed and would have to be accepted from some divine authority. It remained to inquire what that authority might be, since among so many dissentient voices each one professed to be able to hand it on to me. An inextricable thicket confronted me, most tiresome to be involved in; and here without any rest my mind was agitated by the desire to find the truth. I gave up my customary intercourse with those whom I intended to abandon; and in such perils nothing remained except to pray with tears and lamentations that divine providence might bring me aid. That I did unremittingly. At this point certain disputations of the Bishop of Milan gave me some hope that I might find the answer to many Old Testament difficulties which, because they were badly explained to us, used to offend us. I made up my mind to continue a catechumen in the Church in which I had been brought up by my parents until either I discovered the truth I was seeking, or was persuaded that nothing was to be got by seeking. If there had been anyone who could have been my teacher he would at that time have found me a most ready and docile pupil. If, therefore, your experience has been of this kind, and you have been similarly anxious about your soul, if now at last you see you have been sufficiently tossed about and wish to bring your toils to an end, follow the way of the Catholic discipline which has been derived from Christ himself and has come down to us through the apostles, and by us will be passed on to posterity.

ix, 21. But that is ridiculous, you say, because that is what all the sects profess to hold and to teach. I cannot deny that all the heretics do make this profession. The difference is that they promise to give to those whom they attract a reason even for their most obscure doctrines. This is the chief charge they bring against the Catholic Church, that it bids those who come to it to believe, while they themselves impose no yoke of belief, but glory in opening the fount of knowledge. Well, you say, what could possibly be said in greater praise of them? Ah, but the situation is not quite like that. They say this without having any ability to fulfil their promise but only to win popularity by prating of reason. The human soul naturally is pleased with such promises. It does not consider its own powers and state of health, and asks for the food of sound men which should only be given to the strong. Thus it sucks in the poison of deceivers. True religion cannot by any means be approached without the weighty command of authority. Things must first be believed of which a man may later achieve understanding if he conduct himself well and prove himself worthy.

22. But you will probably ask to be given a plausible reason why, in being taught, you must begin with faith and not rather with reason. That is easy, provided you remain calm. That we may conveniently proceed, please answer my questions. Tell me first why you think belief ought not to be required. Because, you say, credulity, the characteristic of credulous people, seems to me to be a fault; otherwise we should not be accustomed to use the word credulous as a reproach. If the mistrustful man is at fault because he suspects everything he does not know, how much worse is the credulous man? For they differ in this, that the former doubts too much when he hears of things he does not know, while the latter does not doubt at all. I accept provisionally this opinion and distinction. But you know that the epithet, curious, also usually implies a reproach, whereas to call a man studious is to praise him. Now what, pray, is the difference between these two qualities? You will certainly reply that, though both have to do with keen desire to know, the curious man is one who asks about things which do not concern him, and the studious man, on the contrary, about things which do concern him. Now a man is deeply concerned about his wife and children and their well-being, but if anyone who was away from home went on asking all comers how his wife and children were and what they were doing, he is certainly prompted by a great desire to know, and yet we do not call him studious, although he very much wants to know about things which concern him very closely. Clearly our definition of the studious man breaks down, for, while every studious man wants to know about things which concern him, not every man who does so is to be called studious, but only he who has a strong desire to know such things as contribute to the liberal nurture and equipment of his soul. We might of course rightly say that he "studied" this or that, mentioning whatever it was that specially interested him.

We can say that he "studies" his family if he loves them so much, but we should not think him worthy of the name, studious, without qualification. Nor would I call a man who was desirous of hearing how his family was keeping, "studious of hearing," unless, taking special pleasure in a good report, he wanted to hear one repeatedly. But I might say "he studies" to hear if he was satisfied to hear once. Go back now to the curious man, and tell me whether you think any one is to be called curious who gladly hears a fable which will bring him no advantage, inasmuch as it is about things that do not concern him, but is satisfied to hear it occasionally and without undue eagerness, at a banquet for example, or in some circle or meeting. I don't suppose so. And yet he clearly cares for the story he gladly hears. Therefore the definition of the curious man must be amended in the same way as that of the studious man. Now see whether the definitions with which we began this discussion must not also be amended. Why should we consider a man to deserve to be called suspicious who suspects something sometime, or to be called credulous who believes something sometime. Accordingly, just as there is a great difference between one who "studies" something and a genuinely studious man, and again between one who cares for a thing and one who is curious about it, so there is a great difference between a believer and a credulous person.

x, 23. But now, you will say, let us see whether we ought to believe in the matter of religion. For even if we admit that to believe is different from being credulous it does not follow that there is nothing wrong in believing in religious matters. Possibly believing and being credulous are two differing degrees of vice like being drunk on one occasion, and being drunken habitually. I do not see how anyone who accepts that as true can ever have a friend. For if to believe anything is base, either it is base to believe a friend, or without such belief I cannot see how anyone can go on speaking about friendship. Here perhaps you will say: I agree one must believe something sometimes, but explain to me now how in religion it is not base to believe before one knows. I shall do so if I can, and so I ask you this question. Which do you think is more blameworthy, to hand on religion to one who is unworthy, or to believe what is said by those who hand it on? If you do not know whom I mean by one who is unworthy, I mean one who comes with a deceitful heart. I dare say you agree that it is more blameworthy to unfold holy secrets to such a man than to believe what religious men affirm concerning religion. You could not decently make any other reply. Now suppose you are in the presence of a man who is going to hand on religion to you, how are you going to assure him that you come in a true frame of mind, that there is no guile or dissimulation in you so far as concerns the matter in hand? You will say your conscience is clear, that you are void of deceit. You will assert this with all the words you are master of, which are, however, only words. For you cannot lay bare the lurking places of your mind, that you may be intimately known as man to man. But if he said: I indeed believe you, but would it not be equitable that you also believe me, seeing that, if I possess any truth, you are going to receive a benefit and I am going to confer one; what would you reply? Surely: Yes, I ought to believe you.

24. But you say: Would it not have been better to have given me a reason so that I might follow where he led without any rashness? Perhaps it would. But it is a difficult matter for you to know God by reason. Do you think that all men are fitted to grasp the reasons by which the human mind is drawn to the knowledge of God? Or are a good many so fitted, or only a few? I think only a few, you say. Do you believe you are of their number? That is not for me to say, you reply. Do you think, then, that your religious teacher ought to believe this of you. Suppose he does so. Then remember that he has twice believed you when you said things he could not be certain of; but you were unwilling to believe him even once when he was speaking about religion. Granted then that you approach religion with a true mind, and that you belong to the small number of those who are able to grasp the reasons by which divine power leads to certain knowledge, do you think that religion is to be denied to other men who are not endowed with so clear a mind? Are they not to be brought to the inmost sanctuary gradually step by step? You see what is obviously the more religious thing to do; for you cannot think that any man who desires so great a possession ought to be abandoned or rejected. But don't you think that he will not attain real truth otherwise than by first believing that he will reach his goal; then by presenting his mind as a suppliant; finally by purifying his life by action in obedience to certain great and necessary precepts? Of course you do. But what of those who can easily grasp divine secrets with certain reason? I dare say you belong to that class. Is it any disadvantage to them to come by the way by which those come who start with believing? I trow not. And yet you ask:

Why must there be delay? Because, even if they do themselves no harm by by-passing faith, they harm others by their example. Hardly anyone thinks of himself as he ought. He who thinks too little of himself must be stimulated. He who thinks too much, must be repressed, so that the former may not be broken by despair, and the latter fall headlong through over-boldness. The easy way to effect this is to compel those who are able to fly, and who might be a dangerous incitement to others, to walk as is safe for those others. True religion provides for this very thing. This has been divinely commanded and handed down by our blessed predecessors and preserved to our own day. To want to disturb or pervert this practice is nothing but to seek a sacrilegious way to true religion. Those who do so, even if they are allowed to, cannot reach their goal. However they may excel in genius, unless God be with them, they merely crawl along the ground. But God is only with those who, seeking him, have also a care for human society. No surer step towards heaven can be found. How can I say that nothing is to be believed when knowledge is impossible? I cannot resist the argument that there cannot be friendship of any kind unless something is believed which cannot be rationally proved. A master is not blamed for trusting the slaves who serve him. But in religion what can be more unfair than that God's ministers should believe us when we profess to be sincere but that we should be unwilling to believe them when they instruct us. Finally, what way can be more sound than first to become fit to receive the truth by believing the things which God has appointed for the preparation and cultivation of the soul? Or, if you are already fitted, to follow a somewhat round-about but entirely safe path rather than to thrust yourself into danger so as to be an example of rashness to others.

xi, 25. It remains for us to consider why we should not follow men who promise to guide us by reason. We have already explained why it is not blameworthy to follow those who bid us believe. But some think that it is not only not blameworthy but in fact praiseworthy to go to these self-styled sponsors of reason. It is not so. In religion two kinds of people are praiseworthy: those who have already found the truth, whom we must judge to be entirely blessed;[1] and those who seek it rightly and earnestly. Of these the former are already in possession. The latter are on the way that leads most certainly to possession.

[1] Cf. *Retract.* I, xiv, 2. Augustine corrects this, and says that such blessedness of possession is not possible in this life.

There are three other classes of men who are certainly to be disapproved and detested. There is the opinionated kind. They think they know what they do not know. The second class is composed of those who realize that they do not know, but do not seek in such a way that they may find. In the third class are those who do not think they know and are unwilling to seek at all. There are also in men three mental activities, closely related but needing to be distinguished, viz., knowing, believing and holding an opinion. If these are considered in themselves the first is always faultless, the second is sometimes so, the third never. To know important, honourable, even divine things is perfect blessedness. To know superfluous things does no harm, but perhaps in learning them we waste time that should be used for more necessary purposes. There is no harm, even, in knowing harmful things, but doing or suffering them is bad. If a man knows how to kill his enemy without danger to himself, the knowledge does not make him guilty as the desire to act on it would. If that desire is lacking nothing could be more innocent. Believing is blameworthy if one believes anything unworthy of God or if one believes too readily in man. In other matters, if anyone believes anything, knowing that he does not know it, there is no fault committed. I believe that most wicked conspirators were once put to death by the virtuous Cicero. Not only do I not know that, but I am quite certain that I cannot possibly know it. To hold an opinion is disgraceful for two reasons. In the first place, he who is persuaded that he already knows cannot learn, even if the thing in question is something that may be learned. And in the second place temerity in itself is the mark of an ill-disposed mind. Suppose someone thinks he knows the fact I have just mentioned about Cicero. Nothing prevents him from learning it, though it cannot be a matter of knowledge strictly speaking. But if he does not know the difference between true knowledge, i.e., rational knowledge, and belief in what has been profitably handed down to posterity either by report or in writing, he certainly errs, and there is no error without disgrace. Our knowledge, therefore, we owe to reason; our beliefs to authority; and our opinions to error. Knowledge always implies belief, and so does opinion. But belief does not always imply knowledge, and opinion never does. If we, now, apply these three modes of mental activity to the five classes of men just mentioned, the two approved classes which we put first, and the three faulty ones which we put next, we find that the first class, the blessed, believe the very truth, the second, the studious lovers of truth, believe upon authority. The first of the faulty classes, i.e., those who are of opinion that they know what they do not know, exhibit faulty credulity. The other two classes believe nothing—both those who seek truth but despair of finding it, and those who do not seek at all. All this applies to matters pertaining to some branch of learning. For in practical life I just cannot see how anyone can refuse to believe altogether. Those who say that in action they follow probability prefer to say that they can know nothing rather than that they believe nothing. Who can approve what he does not believe? And what is the probable, if it is not approved? Wherefore, there can be two classes of opponents of truth, those who reject knowledge only, not faith, and those who condemn both. But whether this latter class can be found in actual life I do not know. I have said all this that we may know that in believing what we do not yet understand we escape the charge of being rashly opinionated. Let those who say we are to believe nothing but what we know beware of that charge which is a disgraceful and unhappy one. But if one diligently considers the difference between thinking one knows, and believing upon authority what one knows one does not know, one will avoid the charge of error and of boorish pride.

xii, 26. Now I ask, if nothing which is not known is to be believed, how will children serve their parents and love them with mutual dutifulness if they do not believe that they are their parents. That cannot be known by reason. Who the father is is believed on the authority of the mother, and as to the mother, midwives, nurses, slaves have to be believed, for the mother can deceive, being herself deceived by having her son stolen and another put in his place. But we believe, and that without any hesitation, what we confess we do not know. Otherwise who does not see that dutifulness, the most sacred bond of the human race, might be violated by the most overbearing wickedness? Who would be so mad as to think him blameworthy who performed the duties due to those whom he believed to be his parents even if they were not his parents in reality? Who, on the other hand, would not think him worthy of banishment who did not love those who were probably his true parents on the ground that he feared he might love those who were not his parents? I could bring many instances to show that nothing would remain stable in human society if we determined to believe nothing that we could not scientifically establish.

27. Again, let me put this to you which I trust will even more

readily have your assent. In matters of religion, that is in the knowing and worshipping of God, those people are not to be listened to who tell us not to believe, promising to give us from the start a reasoned account. No one doubts that men universally are either foolish or wise. By wise I mean not prudent and clever men but those who have, as far as is possible, clear and strongly established knowledge of God and man, and live and conduct themselves in a way that answers to that knowledge. All others, however skilled or ignorant, however excellent or depraved their manner of life, I put in the number of the foolish. If this is so, who with but moderate intelligence can fail to see that for the foolish it is more useful and helpful to obey the precepts of the wise than to live by their own whims? Every deed wrongly done is sin. Nothing can be rightly done unless it proceeds from right reason, and right reason is precisely virtue. Who then can be virtuous unless he is endowed with the mind of a sage? The sage alone does not sin. The fool sins in all that he does except when he obeys a sage, for then his actions proceed from right reason. But he is not to be considered master of his actions, so to speak, seeing he is the instrument and tool, as it were, of the sage. Therefore, if it is better for all men not to sin than to sin, all foolish people would live better lives if they could be servants of wise men. No one doubts that this would be advantageous in less important matters, like trading, agriculture, marrying, begetting and educating children, in short, managing one's worldly affairs; how much more in religion? For human affairs are more easily grasped than divine affairs; and in holier and more excellent things, where we owe greater reverence and obedience, all the more wicked and perilous is the sin of disobedience. You see, then, that if our heart is set on the good religious life, there is nothing for us so long as we are foolish, but to seek out wise men and to obey them, so that we may not suffer the domination of the folly which is in us, and may in time escape from it altogether.

xiii, 28. Here again arises a most difficult question. How can fools find a wise man? Hardly anyone ventures to claim the title openly, yet many do so indirectly. Yet such is their disagreement concerning the very things knowledge of which constitutes wisdom, that either none of them, or at best only one of them can be truly wise. But which it is, I cannot see at all how the foolish man is to decide with any certainty. Nothing can be recognized by signs unless one knows the thing of which these are the signs; and the fool does not know wisdom. Gold and silver and other such things may be recognized at sight even if one does not possess them. But wisdom cannot be seen by the mental eye of anyone who lacks it. Things with which we make contact by a bodily sense are presented to us from without, and with the eye we can see what belongs to another even if we do not ourselves possess it, or anything like it. Things intellectually perceived are within the mind, and possession and seeing are identical. The fool lacks wisdom; therefore he does not know wisdom. He cannot see it with his eyes. He cannot see it and at the same time lack it; and he cannot possess it and be at the same time a fool. He does not know it, and, so long as that is so, he cannot recognize it anywhere. So long as he remains a fool, no one can with absolute certainty discover a wise man, by obeying whom he may be delivered from the evil of his folly.

29. When religion is the object of our quest God alone can provide a solution for this great difficulty. We ought not to be seeking true religion unless we believe that God is, and that he brings help to human minds. For what are we trying so hard to investigate? What do we hope to obtain? What do we desire to reach? Something that we do not believe exists or can possibly be ours? Nothing could be more perverse. In that spirit you would not dare to ask a favour of me, or at least it would be impertinent to do so, yet you come expecting to find religion when you think that God does not exist or, if he does, cares nothing for us. What if religion be such that it cannot be found unless it be sought with the utmost care and assiduity? What if the extreme difficulty of finding it exercises the mind of the seeker to fit it to grasp what it does find? What is more pleasant and familiar to the eyes than the light? Yet after long habituation to darkness they cannot endure it. What is more suitable for a body, exhausted by disease, than food and drink? Yet we see that convalescents are restrained and prevented from venturing to indulge in a satiety for which only strong men are fit, lest food may itself bring back the disease which caused food to be refused. Convalescents, I say. Don't we urge the sick to take some food? Assuredly they would not try so hard to obey us against their inclination did they not believe that so they would recover from their sickness. When will you give yourself to diligent and laborious search, or dare to impose on yourself such thought and care as the thing is worthy of, unless you believe the thing you seek actually exists? Rightly, therefore, and in full accord with the majesty of the Catholic discipline, it is

insisted that those who come to religion must be asked to have faith before everything else.

xiv, 30. What reason, then, pray, will your heretic give me? For, of course, we are speaking of those who desire to be styled Christians. Why does he ask me to refrain from believing, as if from some rash act? He bids me believe nothing. Very well then. Suppose I do not believe there is such a thing as true religion among men. I do not believe it exists. Therefore I do not seek for it. And yet, I suppose, he wants to demonstrate it to some inquirer. For it is written: He that seeks shall find. Unless I had some belief I should not come to him who forbids me to believe. Can there be any greater absurdity than that he should be displeased by my simple faith supported by no knowledge, when it was my simple faith that brought me to him?

31. But all heretics exhort us to believe in Christ? Could they be more inconsistent? Two points are to be pressed home here. First, I must ask them where is the promised reason, where is the rebuke of rashness, where the assured knowledge. If it is disgraceful to believe without a reason why do you expect me and urge me to believe anything without reason given, so that I may be the more easily led by your reason? Will your reason build some strong edifice on a foundation of temerity? I am speaking like those who take offence at our believing. For my part I judge that believing before reasoning, if you are not able to follow reasoning, and cultivating the mind by faith in order to be ready to receive the seeds of truth, is not only most wholesome, but is indeed the only way by which health can return to sick minds. But these men impudently try to get us to believe in Christ though they think believing is to be derided as utterly rash. Again, in the second place, I confess I have come to believe in Christ, and to hold that what he said is true, though supported by no reason. Are you, my fine heretic, going to lead me on from this starting-point? But let me consider for a moment. I myself did not see Christ as it was his will to be seen by men; for it is declared that he was seen by common eyes like mine. From whom did I derive my faith in him, so that I may come to you duly prepared by faith? I see that I owe my faith to opinion and report widely spread and firmly established among the peoples and nations of the earth, and that these peoples everywhere observe the mysteries of the Catholic Church. Why, then, should I not rather ask most diligently of them what Christ taught, seeing that I was brought by their authority to believe that what he taught was profitable? Will *you* indeed give

me a better exposition of his teaching, though I might not have believed *you* if you had urged me to believe that he once existed or still exists? This I have come to believe on the ground of a report confirmed by its ubiquity, by its antiquity, and by the general consent of mankind. But you are so few in numbers, so confused in thought, so recent in time, that no one could imagine that you could offer anything worthy of being received as authoritative. What utter absurdity! "Believe those," you say, "who have taught you that Christ is to be believed; and then learn from us what he taught!" Why on earth should I? Supposing they failed me and could teach me no more, I could be much more easily persuaded not to believe in Christ, than to learn anything about him from others than those by whom I had been taught to believe in him. What amazing audacity or rather absurdity! "You believe in Christ, and I undertake to teach you what he taught." But if I did not believe, you could teach me nothing about him, could you? "But you ought to believe." On your commendation? "Oh no. We instruct by reasoning those who already believe in him." Why then should I believe in him? "Because of firmly rooted report." Does this report reach us through you or through others? "Through others." So I am to believe them in order that you may teach me? Possibly I might, did not my friends give me special warning to have no dealings with you at all, for they say you have pernicious doctrines. "They lie," you will reply. But how am I to believe them about Christ whom they have not seen, and not believe them about you whom they could see but don't want to? "Believe the Scriptures." But if any new or unheard-of writing is produced or commended by a handful of people without reasonable confirmation, we believe not it but those who produce it. Wherefore if you, being so few and unknown, produce Scriptures, we are unwilling to believe. And at the same time you are acting contrary to your promise in demanding faith rather than giving a reason. You will appeal again to tradition and general consent. At long last restrain your obstinacy and your wild lust to propagate your own sect, and advise me rather to consult the leaders of the great mass of believers. This I shall do most diligently and with the greatest possible efforts, so as to learn something about these Scriptures from men apart from whom I should not know there was anything to learn. But do you go back to your lurking place, and lay no more snares in the name of truth which you are trying to take away from those whose authority you yourself admit.

32. Of course, if such men deny that we are to believe in Christ unless some indubitable reason is given, they are not Christians. That is what some pagans urge against us, foolishly but not inconsistently. Who could allow people to profess to belong to Christ, who maintain that nothing is to be believed unless fools are offered an absolutely clear and rational doctrine of God? We see how Christ himself, according to the story which they also accept, demanded faith above everything else and before everything else, because those with whom he was dealing were not yet able to penetrate to the divine secrets. What was the purpose of so many great miracles? He said himself that they were done for no other purpose than that men should believe in him. He led the foolish by faith; you do it by reason. He cried aloud that men should believe; you declaim against faith. He praised those who believed; you rebuke them. Would he have turned water into wine, to mention only one instance, if men would have followed him if he had merely taught them and done no miracle? Is that word not to be taken into account: "Ye believe in God, believe also in me" (John 14:1)? Is the man to be blamed for rashness who would not have the Lord come to his house, believing that by his bare command his boy's sickness would be cured? Christ, therefore, bringing a medicine to heal corrupt morals, by his miracles gained authority, by his authority deserved faith, by faith drew together a multitude, thereby secured permanence of the tradition, which in time corroborated religion. That religion neither the foolish novelty of heretics working deceitfully, nor the ancient error of the nations in violent opposition, will avail to pluck up and destroy in any part.

xv, 33. Wherefore, though I have no ability to teach, I do not cease to utter this warning. Many want to appear wise, and it is not easy to discern whether they are not in reality fools. Pray to God with all intensity of mind, with all your vows, with groans and, it may be, with tears, that he may deliver you from the evil of error, if your heart is set on the happy life. You will obtain your desire more easily if you willingly obey his precepts which are confirmed by the authority of the Catholic Church. The wise man is so closely united with God in his mind that nothing can come between to separate them. God is truth, and no one is wise if he have not truth in his mind. We cannot deny that man's wisdom is a kind of intermediary placed between the folly of man and the pure truth of God. The wise man, so far as it is given to him, imitates God. The foolish man has nothing nearer to him for wholesome imitation than the wise man. But, as has been said, it is not easy by the use of reason to know who is wise. Miracles must be presented to the eyes, of which fools are much readier to make use than of the mind, so that under the constraint of authority men's lives and morals may first be purified, and they may thus become able to follow reason. Since, then, there had to be a human example to imitate, and yet hope was not to be stayed on man, what could better show the mercy and generosity of God than that the pure, eternal and unchangeable Wisdom of God, to whom we must cleave, saw fit to assume human nature? Not only did he do miracles in order to incite us to follow God, but he also suffered those things which deter us from following God. No man can obtain the supreme and most certain good unless he fully and perfectly loves it; and that he cannot do so long as he fears bodily evils and fortuitous circumstances. By being born miraculously and by doing miracles he procured our love, and by dying and rising again he drove away our fears. In everything else he did, which it would take too long to recall, he showed himself such that we could perceive how far the divine clemency would go, and to what heights human infirmity could be raised.

xvi, 34. Here is, believe me, most wholesome authority. Here is the preliminary raising of our minds above their earthly habitation. Here is conversion from love of this world to the true God. It is authority alone which urges fools to hasten to wisdom. So long as we cannot know pure truth it is misery no doubt to be deceived by authority; but it is certainly greater misery not to be moved by it. If the providence of God does not preside over human affairs, there is no need to worry about religion. But if all the best minds are urged to seek and to serve God, openly, as it were, by the outward appearance of the universe, which assuredly must be believed to emanate from some fountain of truest beauty, and, privately, by some inward consciousness, there is no need to give up the hope that God himself has constituted some authority relying on which as on a sure ladder we may rise to him. Putting aside reason, which, as we have often said, is difficult for fools to follow in its purity, this authority has two ways of appealing to us, partly by miracles and partly by the multitude of those who accept it. Neither of these is necessary for the wise man. No one denies that. But the problem now is how we can become wise, that is, how we can cleave to the truth. That, assuredly, the unclean mind cannot do. Uncleanness of the mind, let me briefly explain, is love of anything besides God and the soul. The more pure a man is from such uncleanness the more easily does he behold the truth. To wish to see the truth in order that you may purge your soul is a perverse and preposterous idea, because it is precisely in order that you may see, that it has to be purged. For the man who is not able to behold the truth, in order that he may become able and allow himself to be purified, authority is available, making its appeal, as I have just said and as no one doubts, partly by miracles, and partly by the multitudes of its adherents. By "miracle" I mean something strange and difficult which exceeds the expectation and capacity of him who marvels at it. Among events of this kind there is nothing more suited to the populace, and to foolish men generally, than what appeals to the senses. But again there are two kinds of miracle. Some there are which merely cause wonder; others produce great gratitude and good will. If one sees a man flying one merely marvels, for such a thing brings no advantage to the spectator beyond the spectacle itself. But if one is affected by some grave and desperate disease and at a word of command immediately gets better, love of one's healer will surpass wonder at one's healing. Such things were done when God appeared to men as true Man, as far as was necessary. The sick were healed. Lepers were cleansed. To the lame the power to walk was restored; to the blind, sight; to the deaf, hearing. The men of that time saw water turned into wine; five thousand satisfied with five loaves of bread, waters walked upon, the dead raised. Of these miracles some looked to the body, conferring on it an obvious benefit, others looked to the mind, conveying to it a hidden signal. But all of them had regard to men, bearing testimony to them of the majesty of Christ. So at that time divine authority drew the erring minds of mortal men towards itself. But why, you say, do such things not happen now? Because they would not affect us unless they were marvellous, and they would not be marvellous if they were familiar. Take the alternation of day and night, the unvarying order of the heavenly bodies, the annual return of the four seasons, the leaves falling and returning to the trees, the endless vitality of seeds, the beauty of light, colour, sounds, odours, the varieties of flavours. If we could speak to someone who saw and sensed these things for the first time, we should find that he was overwhelmed and dizzy at such miracles. But we make light of all these things, not because they are easy to understand—for what is more obscure than their causes?—but because we are continually aware of them.

Christ's miracles, therefore, were done at the most opportune moment so that a multitude of believers might be drawn together, and that authority might be turned to profitable account in the interests of good morals.

xvii, 35. Morals, of course, have a certain value in gaining the minds of men. But we find it easier to disapprove and detest wickedness, usually the result of the prevalence of lusts, than to abandon it or change it for the better. Do you think that too little regard has been paid to the human condition, in that no earthy or fiery object, in short no object accessible to the bodily senses, is to be worshipped as God? Not a few learned men have maintained that God is to be approached through the intellect alone. But unlearned folk too, male and female, in many diverse nations, both believe and declare this. Think of abstinence limiting itself to the slenderest ration of bread and water. Think of fasts continued not for one day only but for several days together. Think of chastity caring not at all for marriage and offspring. Think of endurance that makes light of crosses and flames; of liberality that distributes its patrimony to the poor; of contempt of this world not stopping short of a longing for death. What does all this mean? Few do these things. Still fewer do them rightly and wisely. But the populace hear and approve, favour and in the end love such men. They blame their own weakness in not being able to perform such deeds, wherein they show that they are not without some advancement of mind God-ward, some sparks of virtue. All this has divine providence accomplished through the predictions of the prophets, through the incarnation and teaching of Christ, through the journeys of the apostles, through the reproaches, crosses, blood and deaths of the martyrs, through the laudable lives of the saints, and in every case through miracles worthy of such achievements and virtues, and suitable to the various times. When, therefore, we see such fruit progressively realized by God's aid, shall we hesitate to place ourselves in the bosom of his Church? For it has reached the highest pinnacle of authority, having brought about the conversion of the human race by the instrumentality of the Apostolic See and the successions of bishops. Meantime heretics have barked around it in vain, and have been condemned partly by the judgment of the common people, partly by the weighty judgment of councils, partly also by the majesty of miracles. To be unwilling to give it the first place is assuredly the mark of consummate impiety or of heady arrogance. If there is for souls no certain way to wisdom and salvation unless faith prepares them for the use of reason, how is it possible to be more ungrateful for the help of God than to want to resist an authority so strongly established? Every kind of scholastic discipline, however humble or easy to acquire, demands a teacher or a master if it is to be acquired. What is more rashly proud than to be unwilling to learn to understand the books of the divine oracles from their own interpreters and to be ready to condemn them without understanding them?

xviii, 36. Wherefore, if my reasoning and my pleading affect you, and you have, as I trust, a true care for your own good, I hope you will listen to me and commit yourself in pious faith, keen hope and simple charity to good teachers of Catholic Christianity; that you will not cease to pray to God, by whose goodness alone we were created, by whose justice we pay the penalty for our sins, by whose clemency we are delivered. Thus you will never lack the precepts and discourses of learned men who are truly Christian, nor books, nor quiet thoughts, enabling you easily to find what you are seeking. Abandon utterly those verbose and unhappy Manichees (what gentler adjectives could I use?) who search too much for the source of evil and never find anything but evil. They often stir up their hearers to inquire into that problem, but when they are eager they teach them things they ought not to hear. It would be better to be continually asleep than to be awake in that manner. Into the lethargic they instil frenzy. Both of these diseases are deadly, but they differ in that the lethargic die without troubling others, while a frenzied person is dangerous to many sane people, especially to those who wish to help him. God is not the Author of evil. He never repented of anything he had made. His mind is disturbed by no emotional storms. No particular part of the earth is his Kingdom. He neither approves nor commands any crimes or evil deeds. He never lies. The Manichees used to influence us by aggressively brandishing these truths and insinuating that the contrary was Old Testament doctrine; which is utterly false. I grant they were right in attacking statements which attribute evil to God. But what have I discovered? In attacking such statements they were not attacking Catholic doctrine. So I hold fast the truth I learned from them, and I reject the false opinion they taught me. But many other things the Catholic Church has taught me which these men of bloodless bodies and crass minds cannot aspire to teach: that God is not corporeal; that no part of him can be perceived by the bodily eyes; that none of his substance and nature is in any way violable or mutable, compounded or moulded to a pattern. If you grant me all this—and in no other way may we think of God—all the devices of the Manichees are brought to naught. How it comes to be that God neither begat nor created evil; that there is no nature or substance, or ever has been or will be, which God did not either beget or create; and that he nonetheless delivers us from evil; all this can be proved by reasons so compelling that it is impossible to doubt it, especially for you and people like you, if at any rate piety and peace of mind are added to a good disposition. For without these spiritual qualities nothing at all can be understood of these deep matters. This is no story worthless as smoke, no mere Persian fable to which it is enough to lend an ear and a mind not subtle but quite puerile. Not as the Manichees have it in their folly is the truth. It is far, far different. But since my discourse has gone to much greater length than I expected, let me put an end to this book. You remember my purpose. I have not yet begun to refute the Manichees or to attack their absurdities. Nor have I expounded much of the Catholic Faith. I wanted only, if I could, to rid you of a false opinion about true Christians maliciously and ignorantly distilled into us, and to stimulate you to learn certain great divine truths. Let this book, then, be as it is. If your mind is somewhat placated, perhaps I shall be more ready to deal with the other questions.

The Nature of the Good

St. Augustine's Review of "De Natura Boni."
Retractations, II, ix

The book *Of the Nature of the Good* is against the Manichees. There it is shown that God is unchangeable by nature and is the supreme good, that other natures whether spiritual or corporeal derive their existence from him, and that, so far as they are natures, they are good. Also it is shown what evil is, and whence it springs, what great evils the Manichees attribute to the good nature and what good things they attribute to the evil nature; for their error has conjured up two opposing "natures." The book begins: "The supreme good beyond all others is God."

The Nature of the Good

INTRODUCTION

THE *De Natura Boni*, WRITTEN IN 404, IS THE last of the Anti-Manichaean writings, coming soon after the massive *Contra Faustum.* No special occasion for writing is mentioned, and it seems strange that St. Augustine did not rather continue his refutation of the *Fundamental Epistle* of Manes, for which, he tells us, he had made some preparation. The fragment which survives is in some respects more interesting than this work, but it is already accessible in translation, and the *De Natura Boni* has interesting features of its own.

It falls into three sections.

A. i–xxiii. A summary but reasoned account of the Augustinian metaphysic—God, the Supreme Being and the Supreme Good, from whom all other beings derive existence and value, all being good by nature each in its degree. Evil is nothing but the corruption of natural good. Sin is voluntary and is exactly compensated by its penalty, in a perfect world.

B. xxiv–xxxix. Proof of the doctrine, point by point, is adduced from Scripture "so that the less intelligent may believe on authority."

C. xl–xlviii. An attempt is made to show that (1) the Manichees are inconsistent, attributing many good qualities to their "Evil Nature," and many bad qualities to their "Good Nature." (2) Manichaeism leads to certain abominable practices, at least so it is rumoured. Passages from the *Thesaurus* and the *Fundamental Epistle* of Manes are quoted to show that the suspicion is not without foundation in their authoritative writings.

The Nature of the Good Against the Manichees

THE TEXT

i. The Supreme Good beyond all others is God. It is thereby unchangeable good, truly eternal, truly immortal. All other good things derive their origin from him but are not part of him. That which is part of him is as he is, but the things he has created are not as he is. Hence if he alone is unchangeable, all things that he created are changeable because he made them of nothing. Being omnipotent he is able to make out of nothing, i.e., out of what has no existence at all, good things, both great and small, celestial and terrestrial, spiritual and corporeal. Because he is just, he did not make the things he made out of nothing to be equal to him whom he begat of himself. Therefore, all good things throughout all the ranks of being, whether great or small, can derive their being only from God. Every natural being, so far as it is such, is good. There can be no being which does not derive its existence from the most high and true God. All are not supremely good, but they approximate to the supreme good, and even the very lowest goods, which are far distant from the supreme good, can only derive their existence from the supreme good. Every mutable spirit and every corporeal thing, that is, the whole of created nature, was made by God, for everything that exists is either spirit or body. God is immutable Spirit. Mutable spirit is a created thing, but it is better than corporeal things. Body is not spirit, though in a different sense we speak of the wind as spirit because it is invisible to us, and yet we feel its not inconsiderable force.

ii. There are those who cannot understand that every natural being, that is, every spiritual and corporeal existent, is good by nature. They are impressed by the wickedness of spirits and the mortality of bodies, and so they endeavour to maintain that there is another nature besides that which God has made, viz., that of malignant spirit and mortal body. On their account we think that what we say can be brought to bear on their understanding, in this way. They admit that there can be no good thing save from the most high and true God. Now this is true and is sufficient to correct them if they will but pay attention.

iii. We, Catholic Christians, worship God, from whom are all good things, great or small, all measure great or small, all form great or small, all order great or small. All things are good; better in proportion as they are better measured, formed and ordered, less good where there is less of measure, form and order. These three things, measure, form and order, not to mention innumerable other things which demonstrably belong to them, are as it were generic good things to be found in all that God has created, whether spirit or body. God transcends all measure, form and order in his creatures, not in spatial locality but by his unique and ineffable power from which come all measure, form and order. Where these three things are present in a high degree there are great goods. Where they are present in a low degree there are small goods. And where they are absent there is no goodness. Moreover, where these three things are present in a high degree there are things great by nature. Where they are present in a low degree there are things small by nature. Where they are absent there is no natural thing at all. Therefore, every natural existent is good.

iv. If we ask whence comes evil, we should first ask what evil is. It is nothing but the corruption of natural measure, form or order. What is called an evil nature is a corrupt nature. If it were not corrupt it would be good. But even when it is corrupted, so far as it remains a natural thing, it is good. It is bad only so far as it is corrupted.

v. Of course it is possible that one nature even when corrupted may still be better than another nature which has remained uncorrupted, because the one has a superior, the other an inferior measure, form and order. According to the estimation of men, judging by what they see before them as they look, corrupted gold is better than uncorrupted silver, and corrupted silver is better than uncorrupted lead. Among spiritual natures of greater potency a rational spirit, even when corrupted by an evil will, is better than an irrational spirit that is uncorrupted; and any spirit, even when corrupted, is better than any body even when uncorrupted. For the thing which when present gives life to a body is better than the body to which it gives life. However corrupt the created spirit of life may become, it can still give life to its body. Hence even when corrupted it is better than its body though the latter be uncorrupted.

vi. If corruption take away from corruptible things all measure, form and order, nothing at all will remain in existence. Similarly any nature which cannot be corrupted will be the supreme good, as God is. Any nature which can be corrupted has some good in it, for corruption could not harm it except by taking away or diminishing what is good in it.

vii. To his most excellent creatures, that is to rational spirits, God has given the power not to be corrupted if they do not will to be; but remain obedient under the Lord their God and cleave to his incorruptible beauty. But if they will not remain obedient and are willingly corrupted by sin, they are unwillingly corrupted by penalties. God is the good, so that it can be well with no one who deserts him; and among his creatures the rational nature is so great a good that no other good save God can make it happy. Sinners are ordained to punishment. This order is contrary to their nature, and is therefore penalty. But it suits their fault and is therefore just.

viii. Other things created out of nothing which are inferior to rational spirit can be neither happy nor miserable. Since they are themselves good, because of the degree of measure and form they possess, and since, though the good in them be small or even minimal, they could not have existed save by the act of the good God most high; they are so ordered that the weaker yield to the stronger, and the feebler to those that have greater might, and the less powerful to the more powerful. So terrestrial things have peace with celestial things, being as it were submissive to things which are more excellent than they are. When things pass away and others succeed them there is a specific beauty in the temporal order, so that those things which die or cease to be what they were, do not defile or disturb the measure, form or order of the created universe. A well-prepared speech is beautiful even though all its syllables and sounds pass in succession as if they are born and die.

ix. The nature and quantity of the penalty due to each fault is determined by the judgment of God, not by that of man. When it is remitted to the converted, that is proof of the great goodness of God. When it is paid as due there is no inequity with God. It is a better order that a thing [*natura*] should suffer punishment justly than that it should rejoice in sin with impunity. So long as it retains some measure, form and order there is still some good in it no matter into what extremity it may come. If these were all together taken away and destroyed completely there would be no good because there would be nothing left.

x. Corruptible natures would not be natures at all unless they derived being from God. Nor would they be corruptible if they were part of him. They would then be as he is. The fact that they have some measure, form and order is due to their having been created by God. And they are not immutable because they were made out of nothing. It is sacrilegious audacity to equate nothing and God as we do if we want to make that which he created out of nothing equal to that which is born of God.

xi. No hurt whatever can be done to the divine nature, nor can any other nature which is less than divine be hurt unjustly. No doubt some people by sinning do harm unjustly. Their will to harm unjustly is counted against them, but the power by which they are permitted to do the harm comes only from God, who knows, though they do not, what those ought to suffer whom he permits them to harm.

xii. If those who want to introduce a nature other than that which God has made would only pay attention to these clear and certain facts, they would not be filled with such blasphemies as to impute so much good to the supreme evil, and to impute to God so many evils. As I said above, it is sufficient for their correction if they would only pay attention to what truth compels them to confess even against their will, that all good things come from God alone. Good things whether they are great or small all come from one source, that is from the supreme good, which is God.

xiii. Let us, therefore, recall all the good things we can which are worthy to be attributed to God as their author, and let us see whether when they are removed anything will remain in existence. All life, potency, health, memory, virtue, intelligence, tranquillity, plenty, sense, light, sweetness, measure, beauty, peace—all these things whether great or small, and other similar things which may occur to one, and especially those things which are found universally in spiritual or corporeal existence, measure, form and order, come from the Lord God. Whoever willingly makes a bad use of these good things will, by the divine judgment, pay the penalty. But wherever none of them is present at all, absolutely nothing will remain in existence.

xiv. Of these good things, if any of them is present in a small degree it is given a bad name to distinguish that condition from conditions in which it is present in a higher degree. For example, because there is greater beauty in the form of a man, by comparison with it the beauty of an ape is called deformity. And this misleads the unknowing. They think that the one is good and the other bad. They do not notice that the body of the ape has its own proper measure, correspondence of limbs on both sides, concord of all its parts, readiness in self-defence, and other qualities which it would take a long time to pursue.

xv. That what we are saying may be understood and satisfy those whose intelligence is rather slow, or even compel the pertinacious who resist the most patent truth to confess the truth, let us ask whether corruption can harm the body of an ape. If it can, and the ape can become more hideous, what is diminished if not such beauty as it has, which is a good thing? So long as its body continues to exist some beauty will remain. So if the destruction of good implies the destruction of existence nature is good. We say that the slow is the opposite of the swift, but if anyone does not move at all he cannot be said to be slow. We say that a low voice is the opposite of a shrill one, or a harsh voice of a musical one. But if you take away completely every kind of sound there is silence with no sound at all. We are accustomed to contrast silence with sound as contraries for the very reason that silence means the absence of sound. We speak of clear and obscure as contraries, but obscurity may have some light. If it has none at all, the darkness that results from the complete absence of light is like the silence which is the result of the complete absence of sound.

xvi. Qualitative deprivations are so ordered throughout the universe of nature that, for those who consider them wisely, their vicissitudes are not without propriety. By not causing light to shine on certain places and during certain times God made darkness quite as appropriately as day. If by keeping silent we interpose a suitable pause in our speech, how much more does he, the perfect artificer of all things, suitably and appropriately cause these deprivations? Hence, in the *Hymn of the Three Youths*, Light and Darkness alike praise God, that is, cause his praise to arise from the hearts of those who give full and right consideration to them.

xvii. No nature is evil so far as it is naturally existent. Nothing is evil in anything save a diminishing of good. If the good is so far diminished as to be utterly consumed, just as there is no good left so there is no existence left. Not merely no such existence as the Manichees introduce, in which there is so much good that their blindness is wonderfully great, but no such existence as anyone can imagine.

xviii. Not even matter which the ancients called "Hyle" is to be called evil. I do not mean what Manes in his stupid vanity ignorantly calls "Hyle," that is to say the power that forms bodies. He is rightly said to be introducing a second god. None but God can form and create bodies. Nor are bodies created without measure, form and order being created with them. Now I imagine that even the Manichees admit that these things are good and can only come from God. By "Hyle" I mean matter completely without form and quality, out of which are formed the qualities we perceive, as the ancients said. Hence wood is called "Hyle" in Greek, because it is suitable material for workmen, not that it makes anything but that something may be made out of it. That "Hyle" is not to be called evil. It has no form by which we can perceive it. Indeed, it can hardly be conceived because it is so utterly without form. But it has the capacity to receive form. If it could not receive the form imposed on it by the artificer it could not be called material either. Now if form is a good thing, so that those who have a superior form are called beautiful [*formosi*], doubtless even capacity for form is a good thing. Wisdom is a good thing, and no one doubts that capacity for wisdom is also a good thing. And because every good thing comes from God, no one should doubt that matter, if there is such a thing, derives its existence from God alone.

xix. Gloriously and divinely our God said to his servant: "I am who I am. Say to the children of Israel: He who is hath sent me unto you" (Ex. 3:14). He truly is because he is unchangeable. Every change causes that which was to cease to be. Therefore he truly is who is unchangeable. All other things which he made received existence from him each in its own degree. To him who supremely is there can be no contrary except that which is not. Consequently, just as all that is good comes from him, so from him comes all that has natural existence, since all that has natural existence is good. Every nature is good, and every good thing is from God. Therefore all nature is from God.

xx. Some think that pain whether in mind or body is the chief evil. But there cannot be pain except in things naturally good. For pain means that something that has been is in a sense striving against extinction, because what has been was good. When it is being compelled to become better the pain serves a useful purpose, otherwise it is useless. Mental pain is caused by the will's resisting a greater power. Bodily pain is caused by the senses resisting a more powerful body. But evils that have no accompanying pain are worse. It is worse to rejoice in iniquity than to suffer in corruption. There cannot be no rejoicing except by acquiring inferior good things. Iniquity is the abandonment of the better things. In the body a wound that gives pain is better than a painless festering which is specifically called corruption. The mortal flesh of our Lord did not see, i.e., suffer, corruption, as was foretold in the prophecy: "Thou wilt not give thy Holy One to see corruption" (Ps. 16:10). Who denies that he was wounded by the driving in of the nails and pierced with the spear? Take festering, which men call specifically a corruption of the body. Now if there is still something deep in the wound which it can consume, the corruption grows as good is diminished. But if there is nothing left to consume, there will be no festering since there is no good left. There will be nothing for corruption to corrupt; and there will be no festering, for there will be nothing to fester.

xxi. Tiny little things are in the common usage of speech said to be moderate because some measure remains in them. Without that they would not even be moderate but would not exist at all. Things which have gone too far are called immoderate and are blamed for being over-large. But even these must be kept within bounds under God, who has disposed all things by measure, number and weight.

xxii. We may not say that God has measure, in case that is taken to mean that he has an end. Yet is he not without measure by whom measure is given to all things so that they may in some measure exist. On the other hand we must not say that God has measure, as if it were imposed upon him from elsewhere. If we call him the supreme measure we perhaps say something significant, at any rate if we understand the supreme good by what we call the supreme measure. All measure, so far as it is measure, is good, and we cannot speak of things as moderate, modest or modified without implied praise of them. In another sense we speak of measure as implying end, and we say "measureless" meaning "endless." Sometimes that too implies praise, as in the words: "Of his kingdom there shall be no end" (Luke 1:33). The writer might have said "there shall be no measure [*modus*]" provided *modus* was understood to mean end [*finis*]. For, of course, he who reigns in no measure [*nullo modo* = in no way] simply does not reign at all.

xxiii. Measure, form and order are said to be bad when there is less of them than there ought to be. Or it may be because they are not suited to things as they ought to be. Or they may be called bad because they are alien and incongruous. For example, someone may be said to have acted in a bad manner [*modus*] because he did less than he ought or more than he ought, or because he acted unsuitably or in a wrong way in the particular situation. The action which is blamed as having been done in a bad manner is justly blamed for no other reason than that it did not preserve *modus*. We speak of a form or appearance as being bad because it is inferior not in size but in comeliness when it is compared with more comely and beautiful forms. The reason is that it does not suit the things which wear it, and appears alien and unsuitable; as, for example, if a man were to walk naked in the market-place, an action which would give no offence if it took place in the baths. Likewise order is said to be bad when too little order is observed. It is not order but disorder that is bad, where there is less order than there ought to be, or where such order as there is is not as it ought to be. Nevertheless, wherever there is some measure, form and order there is some good and something naturally existing. Where there is no measure, form or order there is neither good nor existence.

xxiv. These things which we hold according to our faith, and which reason also demonstrates, can be fortified by testimonies from the divine Scriptures, so that the less intelligent who cannot follow the argument may believe on divine authority, and so may deserve to reach understanding. Those who understand, and are less instructed in ecclesiastical sacred books, are not to think that we have produced them out of our heads, and that they are not in the Scriptures. That God is immutable is written thus in the Psalms: "Thou shalt change them and they shall be changed; but thou art the same" (Ps. 102:26–27). And in the Book of Wisdom it is written of Wisdom itself: "Abiding in herself she reneweth all things" (Wisdom 7:27). The apostle Paul says: "To the invisible, incorruptible, only wise God" (I Tim. 1:17). The apostle James writes: "Every good gift and every perfect gift is from above, and cometh down from the Father of lights, with whom is no variableness, neither shadow of turning" (James 1:17). Because the Son was not made, but all things were made through him, it is written: "In the beginning was the Word, and the Word was with God, and the Word was God. He was in the beginning with God. All things were made through him and without him nothing was made" (John 1:1–3).

xxv. We are not to listen to the nonsense of men who think that in this passage "nothing" must mean something. They think that they can force us to this absurd and vain conclusion because the word *nihil* is put at the end of the sentence. You see, say they, "nothing was made," and seeing it was made it is therefore something. They have lost all sense in their eagerness to contradict. They do not understand that there is no difference between saying "without him was made nothing" and saying "without him nothing was made." In either case they could equally well say that nothing is something because it was made. Take something that really exists. What difference is there between saying, "without him there was made a house" and saying, "without him a house was made"? The point is that something was made without him, in this case a house. So when it is said: "without him was made nothing" "nothing" does not mean something, when words are truly and properly used. No matter where "nothing" is placed in the sentence, it makes nothing of a difference. Who would be willing to hold conversation with men who when they hear the expression "nothing of a difference" can say: Therefore there is some difference because nothing is something? Those who have sound brains see quite clearly that my meaning is exactly the same whether I say "nothing of a difference" or "a difference of nothing." And yet these contentious people might say to somebody, What have you done? and if he replied that he had done nothing, they might slander him, saying, You have done something because you have done nothing, for nothing is something. There is the Lord himself putting that word at the end of a sentence where he says: "In secret have I said nothing" (John 18:20). Let them read and hold their peace.

xxvi. All things which God did not beget of himself but made through his Word, he made not out of things which already existed but out of what did not exist at all, i.e., out of nothing. Thus the apostle says: "Who calleth those things which be not as though they were" (Rom. 4:17). But it is written more clearly in the Book of the Maccabees. "I beseech thee, my child, lift thine eyes to the heaven and the earth and all that are therein. See and know that the things were not of which the Lord God made us" (II Maccabees 7:28). There is also what is written in the Psalms. "He spake and they were made" (Ps. 148:5). Clearly he did not beget these things of himself, but made them by his Word and command. What he did not beget he made of nothing; for there was nothing else out of which he might have made them. Of him the apostle says most openly: "Since of him and through him and in him are all things" (Rom. 11:36).

xxvii. "Of him" does not have the same meaning as "out of him" [*de ipso*]. What is *de ipso* may also be said to be *ex ipso*. But not everything that is *ex ipso* can be correctly said to be *de ipso*. Of him are the heaven and the earth for he made them. But they are not "out of him" because they are not parts of his substance. If a man beget a son and make a house both are "of him" but the son is of his substance, the house is of earth and wood. This is because he is a man who cannot make anything of nothing. But God, of whom and through whom and in whom are all things, had no need of any material which he had not made himself, to help his omnipotence.

xxviii. By these words "Of him and through him and in him are all things" we must understand all natures that naturally exist. For sins are not of him. They do not observe nature but vitiate it. In many ways Holy Scripture testifies that sins come from the will of the sinners; especially in that passage where the apostle writes: "And thinkest thou this, O man, that judgest them which do such things, and doest the same, that thou shalt escape the judgment of God? Or despisest thou the riches of his goodness and forbearance and long-suffering, not knowing that the goodness of God leadeth thee to repentance? But after thy hardness and impenitent heart treasurest up unto thyself wrath against the day of wrath and revelation of the righteous judgment of God; who will render to every man according to his deeds" (Rom. 2:3–6).

xxix. Though all things which God has made are in him, those who sin do not defile him. Of his wisdom it is written: "She pervadeth all things by reason of her pureness, and nothing defiled can find entrance into her" (Wisdom 7:24). We must therefore believe God to be incapable of defilement as he is incapable of corruption and change.

xxx. That God made also the lesser good things, that is, earthly and mortal things, may without hesitation be understood from that passage of the apostle where he speaks of our carnal members. "Whether one member suffer, all the members suffer with it; or one member be honoured all the members rejoice with it." Again: "God hath set the members every one of them in the body, as it hath pleased him." And again: "God hath tempered the body together, having given more abundant honour to that part which lacked; that there should be no schism in the body, but that the members should have the same care one for the other" (I Cor. 12:18–26). This measure, form and order which the apostle praises in our carnal members can be found in the flesh of all animals both great and small. For flesh of all kinds is ranked among earthly goods, that is to say among the lowest good things.

xxxi. The kind and magnitude of the penalty due to any particular sin is a matter for the judgment of God, not man. Therefore it is written: "O the depth of the riches both of the wisdom and the knowledge of God! How unsearchable are his judgments, and his ways past finding out!" (Rom. 11:33). That sins are forgiven, to those who are converted, by the goodness of God, is sufficiently proved by the fact that Christ was sent; who died on our behalf not in his divine nature but in our nature which he assumed of a woman. The apostle thus preaches the goodness and love of God towards us: "God commendeth his own love towards us, in that, while we were yet sinners, Christ died for us. Much more then, being now justified by his blood, shall we be saved from wrath through him. For if, while we were enemies, we were reconciled to God through the death of his Son, much more, being reconciled, shall we be saved by his life" (Rom. 5:8–10). Because there is no iniquity with God when sinners pay the due penalty, he writes thus: "What shall we say? Is God unrighteous who visiteth with wrath?" (Rom. 3:5). In one passage he briefly indicates that there are both goodness and severity in God. "Behold, then, the goodness and severity of God: toward them that fell, severity; but toward thee, goodness, if thou continue in his goodness" (Rom. 11:22).

xxxii. That the power of those who do harm comes from God alone is thus stated in Scripture. It is wisdom that speaks: "By me kings reign, and tyrants by me rule the earth" (Prov. 8:15). The apostle says: "There is no power but of God" (Rom. 13:1). That this is rightly so, it is written in the book of Job: "He makes the hypocrite king on account of the perversity of the people" (Job 34:30, LXX). Of the people of Israel God says: "I have given them a king in my wrath" (Hos. 13:11). For it is not unjust that the wicked should receive power to harm so that the patience of the good should be proved and the iniquity of the bad should be punished. By the power given to the devil Job was proved that his justice might be made apparent; Peter was tempted so that he might not think too highly of himself; Paul was buffeted that he might not be puffed up; and Judas was condemned to hang himself. God himself, therefore, did all things justly by the power he gave to the devil. Not for performing these just actions, but for the wicked will to do hurt, which came from the devil himself, will he in the end be awarded punishment, when it will be said to the impious accomplices who have persevered in his iniquity: "Depart into the eternal fire which my Father hath prepared for the devil and his angels" (Matt. 25:41).

xxxiii. Because the bad angels were not made bad by God but became bad by sinning, Peter says this in his Epistle: "God spared not the angels that sinned, but cast them down and committed them to pits of infernal darkness to be reserved for punishment in the judgment" (II Pet. 2:4). Peter thus shows that there is still due to them the penalty of the last judgment, of which the Lord says: "Depart into the eternal fire which is prepared for the devil and his angels." Of course they have even now received as a prison by way of penalty this infernal lower murky air in which we live. It is indeed called heaven but it is not the heaven in which the stars exist, but this lower region whose murk piles up in clouds and where birds fly. It is also called the cloudy heaven, and we speak of the birds of the heaven. For this reason the apostle Paul calls these same wicked angels against whose envy we fight when we live pious lives, "Spiritual powers of wickedness in celestial places" (Eph. 6:12). And that this should not be understood to refer to the superior heavens, he says clearly in another passage: "According to the prince of the power of the air, who now worketh in the sons of disobedience" (Eph. 2:2).

xxxiv. Because sin or iniquity is not a seeking of things evil by nature but an abandonment of the better things, this is found written in Scripture. "Every creature of God is good" (I Tim. 4:4). Every tree that God planted in paradise was good. Man, therefore, did not desire anything evil by nature when he touched the forbidden tree. But by departing from what was better he himself committed an act that was evil. The Creator is better than any of his creatures, and his command should not have been disobeyed by touching what was forbidden, even though it was good. The better was abandoned and a creaturely good sought which it was contrary to the command of the Creator to touch. God had not planted a bad tree in paradise.

But he who had forbidden that tree to be touched was better than the tree.

xxxv. The reason for the prohibition was to show that the rational soul is not in its own power but ought to be subject to God, and must guard the order of its salvation by obedience, or by disobedience be corrupted. Hence God called the tree which he had forbidden to be touched the Tree of the Knowledge of Good and Evil, because anyone who had touched it contrary to the prohibition would discover the penalty of sin, and so would be able to distinguish between the good of obedience and the evil of disobedience.

xxxvi. Who could be so mad as to think that a creature of God, especially one planted in paradise, can be found fault with? Even the thorns and thistles which the earth produced according to the will of God in judgment, in order to afflict the sinner by making him labour, are not rightly to be found fault with. Even such herbs have measure, form and order, and anyone who soberly considers them will find them worthy of praise. But they are evil to the being who had to be disciplined in this way because of the fault of his sin. As I said, therefore, sin is not a seeking of something evil by nature, but an abandonment of what is better. So the deed is the evil thing, not the thing of which the sinner makes an evil use. Evil is making a bad use of a good thing. Hence the apostle reproaches some whom the divine judgment has condemned, who worshipped and served the creature rather than the Creator. He does not find fault with the creature, for, whoever does that, does injustice to the Creator, but he reproaches those who have abandoned the better thing and made a bad use of a good thing.

xxxvii. If all natural things would preserve their proper measure, form and order, there would be no evil. But if anyone willingly makes a bad use of these good things, he cannot overcome the will of God, who knows how to subject even the unjust to a just order. If they by the wickedness of their wills have made a bad use of his good things, he by the justice of his power makes a good use of their evil deeds, rightly ordaining them to punishment who have perversely ordained themselves to sin.

xxxviii. Even the eternal fire which is to torment the impious is not an evil thing. It has its own measure, form and order, debased by no iniquity. But torment is evil to the damned for whose sins it is the due reward. Nor is light an evil thing because it hurts the weak-eyed.

xxxix. The eternal fire is not eternal as God is, for though it is without end it is not without beginning. God has no beginning. Again, though it is applied perpetually to the punishment of sinners, it is nonetheless mutable by nature. God alone has true eternity, true immortality and absolute immutability, for he cannot be changed at all. It is one thing not to be changed when there is a possibility of change; quite another when there is no such possibility. A man is said to be good, but not as God is, of whom it is said: "None is good but God alone" (Mark 10:18). The soul is said to be immortal, but not as God is, of whom it is said: "He alone hath immortality" (I Tim. 6:16). A man is said to be wise, but not as God is, of whom it is said: "To the only wise God" (Rom. 16:27). So the fire is said to be eternal, but not as God is whose immortality alone is true eternity.

xl. Since these things are so according to the Catholic faith and sound doctrine, and also according to truth as it is clear to those who have understanding, none can harm the divine nature; the divine nature can inflict harm on no one unjustly, nor suffer anyone to do harm and to go unpunished. "He who doeth hurt," says the apostle, "shall receive again for the hurt he hath done; and there is no respect of persons with God" (Col. 3:25).

xli. If the Manichees would think of these things in the fear of God and without the pernicious desire to defend their error, they would not blaspheme most wickedly by introducing two natures, one good which they call God, and the other evil which God did not make. So great is their error, silliness, and indeed madness, that they cannot see what they are doing. In effect they attribute to what they call the supreme evil by nature all these great good things: life, potency, safety, memory, intelligence, moderation, virtue, plenty, sensation, light, sweetness, dimension, numbers, peace, measure, form and order. And to the supreme good they attribute these great evils: death, sickness, forgetfulness, madness, perturbation, impotence, neediness, stupidity, blindness, pain, iniquity, dishonour, war, lack of moderation, deformity, perversity. They tell us that the princes of darkness lived in their natural element, and were safe in their kingdom, and had both memory and intelligence. At any rate they tell us that the prince of darkness made a speech such as he could not have made, and such as his hearers could not have listened to, unless they had memory and intelligence. These powers of darkness, we are told, had suitably tempered minds and bodies, and reigned in mighty potency. They were plentifully supplied with all their elements, and could perceive themselves and the light which was their neighbour. They had eyes wherewith to see it afar off. Now eyes without some light in them could not have seen light. That is why eyes are rightly called luminaries. They enjoyed their pleasures sweetly. Their limbs were well-proportioned and their dwellings well-planned. At any rate unless there was some kind of beauty they would not have loved their marriages, nor would their bodies have consisted of parts that harmonized; and without that the events recorded in the silly tale could not have taken place. If they had no peace of any kind they would not have obeyed their prince. If they had no measure, they would do nothing but eat and drink and play the savage and act in other unsocial ways. Even so, they would not have been determined by their particular forms unless they had some kind of measure. As it is, we are told that they performed such actions that there is no denying them fitting measure. If there were no form there would be no natural quality. If there were no order there would not be some ruling and others ruled; they would not live harmoniously with their elements; in short their limbs would not be arranged in their fitting places, as is assumed by the vain Manichee fable. On the other hand, on their vain showing, the divine nature is dead and Christ resuscitates it. It is sick and he heals it. It is forgetful and he brings it to remembrance. It is foolish and he teaches it. It is disturbed and he makes it whole again. It is conquered and captive and he sets it free. It is in poverty and need, and he aids it. It has lost feeling and he quickens it. It is blinded and he illumines it. It is in pain and he restores it. It is iniquitous and by his precepts he corrects it. It is dishonoured and he cleanses it. It is at war and he promises it peace. It is unbridled and he imposes the restraint of law. It is deformed and he reforms it. It is perverse and he puts it right. All these things, they tell us, are done by Christ not for something that was made by God and became distorted by sinning by its own free will, but for the very nature and substance of God, for something that is as God is.

xlii. What can be compared to blasphemies such as these? Nothing at all, if you consider the errors of other perverse sects. Nay, if you compare the error we have been describing with another Manichee error, which we have not yet mentioned, that sect will be proved to allege still worse and more execrable blasphemies against the divine nature. They tell us that certain souls, parts of the substance of God and sharers in the divine nature, as they will have it, went down, not of their own accord but at the command of their Father, to fight against the race of darkness, which the Manichees call the evil nature; that they were defeated and taken captive and were imprisoned for ever in a horrible sphere of darkness. These souls, of course, did not sin voluntarily. In this way, according to their vain profane babbling, God freed part of himself from a great evil, but condemned another part of himself which he could not liberate from the enemy, and yet celebrated a triumph as if the enemy had been defeated. What wicked and incredible audacity to say or believe or proclaim such things about God! When they try to defend this they fall with closed eyes into worse error. For they say that mixing with the evil nature causes the good divine nature to undergo such evils; by itself it cannot and could not have suffered the like. As if an incorruptible nature is to be praised because it does itself no harm, and not because nothing else can harm it. Now, if natural darkness harmed the divine nature, and the divine nature harmed natural darkness, the fact that they did each other harm mutually means that there are two evils. But the race of darkness was of a better mind, for if it did harm it did it unwillingly. It did not wish to harm the divine good but to enjoy it. God wanted to blot out his enemy as Manes vapours most openly in his deadly *Fundamental Epistle*. Forgetting what he had written a little earlier—"His glorious realms are founded upon a bright and blessed earth so that they can never be either moved or shaken by anyone"—he goes on to say, "The Father of most blessed light knew that a great destruction and devastation, arising from the realm of darkness, was threatening his holy realms unless some excellent brilliant and mighty divine power should intervene to overcome and at the same time destroy the stock of darkness. If that were blotted out perpetual rest would be achieved for the inhabitants of the realm of light." You see, he feared destruction and devastation threatening his realms. And yet they were founded upon a bright and blessed earth so that none could ever move or shake them! Because of this fear he determined to harm a neighbouring race and tried to destroy it and blot it out, so that perpetual rest might be achieved for the inhabitants of the realm of light. Why did he not add "and a perpetual prison"? Were not those souls whom he imprisoned for ever in a sphere of darkness also inhabitants of the realm of light? Of them he openly says, "They endured exile from their former bright nature." There he is forced against his will to say that they sinned by their free will, though he will not allow sin to be explained except as due to necessity imposed by the contrary evil nature. He does not know what he is talking about, and is as if he were himself shut up in his imaginary sphere of darkness, seeking for a way out and not finding one. Let him say what he likes to the miserable followers whom he has seduced, by whom he is much more highly honoured than Christ is; so that in return for this honour he sells them his long and profane fables. Let him say what he likes. Let him shut up the race of darkness in a sphere as in a prison, and hem it in with light to which he promised perpetual rest when the enemy was blotted out. The penalty suffered by light is worse than that suffered by darkness. The penalty suffered by the divine nature is worse than that suffered by the hostile race. No doubt the latter is all darkness within, but then it was natural for it to inhabit darkness. But the souls which are of the same nature as God will not be able, he says, to be taken back into the peaceful realms. They will be exiled from the life and liberty of holy light, and will be imprisoned in the aforesaid horrible sphere. And so, he says, "these souls will cleave to the things they have loved, abandoned in the sphere of darkness, procuring for themselves this fate by their deserts." Is not that freedom of the will, with a vengeance? You see how the raving man does not know what he is talking about. By contradicting himself he wages a worse war against himself than against the God of the race of darkness itself. Moreover, if souls that belong to light are condemned because they loved darkness, the race of darkness is unjustly condemned, for it loved the light. The race of darkness loved the light from the beginning. It did not want to blot it out, but to take possession of it, albeit by violence. The race of light determined to blot out the darkness by war, but when defeated came to love darkness. Choose which you will. Either it was compelled by necessity to love darkness or it was voluntarily seduced. If it was by necessity, why is it condemned? If voluntarily, why is the divine nature caught in such iniquity? If the divine nature is compelled by necessity to love darkness, it is vanquished, not victorious. If it loves darkness voluntarily, why do these miserable people hesitate to attribute the will to sin to a being which God made out of nothing rather than to attribute it to the light which he begat?

xliii. If, moreover, we show that even before its fabulous admixture with evil, which they have imagined and foolishly believe, there were great evils in the very nature of light, as they call it, how will it seem possible to add to their blasphemies? Before the battle against darkness took place there was for the light the grim and inevitable necessity of fighting. There is a great evil that existed before evil was mixed with good. Where did that come from, seeing there was as yet no admixture? If there was no necessity to fight but the will was there, whence came that great evil that God was willing to harm his own nature which could not have been harmed by the enemy, by sending it to be cruelly embroiled, shamefully tempted and unjustly condemned? How vast an evil is a will at once pernicious, deadly and cruel, before there was any admixture of evil from the hostile race! Did he perhaps not know that this would happen to his members; that they would come to love darkness and become enemies of the holy light, as Manes says, that is, enemies not only of their God but also of the Father from whom they sprang? Whence came this great evil in God that he should be thus ignorant, before there was any admixture of evil from the hostile race? If he knew it would happen, either there was eternal cruelty in him, if he had no grief for the coming defilement and damnation of his nature, or eternal misery, if he did grieve. Whence came this great evil in your supreme good, before there was any admixture of your supreme evil? If the particle of the divine nature which is held fast in the eternal prison of the afore-mentioned sphere, did not know that this fate was threatening it, even so there was eternal ignorance in the divine nature. If it did know, there was eternal misery. Whence came that great evil before there was any admixture of evil from the hostile race? Perchance it was filled with such charity that it rejoiced because through its punishment perpetual rest was achieved for the other inhabitants of light? Let him anathematize this suggestion who sees how impious it is to make it. If the particle of the divine nature did indeed behave in this way, and did not become hostile to the light, perhaps it could be praised not as divine but as a man might be praised who was willing to suffer some evil for his country. But that evil could only be for a time not for eternity. But they say that the imprisonment in the sphere of darkness was eternal, and that it was the divine nature that was so imprisoned, nothing less. It would surely be a most iniquitous, execrable and unspeakably sacrilegious joy if the divine nature should rejoice in loving darkness and becoming the enemy of the holy light. Whence came this gross and wicked evil before there was any admixture of evil from the hostile race? Who could endure such perverse and impious folly as to attribute so much good to the supreme evil, and so much evil to the supreme good, which is God?

xliv. They say that this part of the divine nature permeates all things in heaven and earth and under the earth; that it is found in all bodies, dry and moist, in all kinds of flesh, and in all seeds of trees, herbs, men and animals. But they do not say of it, as we say of God, that it is present untrammelled, unpolluted, inviolate, incorruptible, administering and governing all things. On the contrary, they say that it is bound, oppressed, polluted but that it can be released and set free and cleansed not only by the courses of the sun and moon and powers of light, but also by their elect. To what sacrilegious and incredible shame this kind of nefarious error urges, if it does not persuade, them, it is horrible to relate. They say that the powers of light are transformed into beautiful males who are set before women of the race of darkness, while others are transformed into beautiful women who are set before males of the race of darkness. By their beauty they inflame the unclean lust of the princes of darkness. Thus the vital substance, i.e., the divine nature, which they say is held bound in their bodies, escapes from their members when they are relaxed in concupiscence, and is thus released, purged and set free. This is what these unhappy folk read and say and hear and believe. This is set down in the seventh book of their Thesaurus, the name they give to a certain writing of Manes where these blasphemies are written. "Then the blessed Father, who has shining ships as dwellings or lodging places, in his clemency brings aid to set his vital substance free from the impious bonds and straits and torments in which it is held. By his invisible nod he transforms his powers which he has in his shining ship, and causes them to show themselves to the adverse powers which are set in the different parts of the heavens. These are of both sexes, male and female. Hence he makes the aforesaid powers appear partly in the shape of beardless boys to women of the adverse race, partly in the shape of fair virgins to males of the opposite race. He knows that all these hostile powers are easily taken in because of the deadly unclean lust that is congenital to them, and will yield to the beautiful forms they see, and will so be dissolved. Know that our blessed Father is identical with these powers of his, which for a necessary purpose he transforms into the undefiled likeness of boys and virgins. He uses these as his proper instruments, and by them accomplishes his will. The shining ships are full of these divine powers which are set over against members of the infernal race as in a kind of marriage. Quickly and easily, in a moment, they achieve their purpose. When reason demands that they should appear to males they show themselves in the form of beautiful virgins. Again, when they have to come to women they put off the appearance of virgins and take on that of beardless boys. At the comely sight ardour and concupiscence grow, and the prison of evil thoughts is broken, and the living soul which was held bound in their members is released and escapes and mingles with the purest air which is its native element. Souls that are completely purified board the shining ships which are prepared to carry them away and to transport them to their fatherland. Anyone who still shows the taint of the adverse race goes down step by step through fiery heat, gets mixed up with trees and plants and the like and is stained with divers colours. Out of that great shining ship the figures of boys and virgins appear to the hostile powers whose home is in the heavens and whose nature is fiery. At the fair sight the part of life which is held bound in their members is released and brought down by heat to earth. In the same way the highest power, that inhabits the ship of vital waters, appears by means of his messengers in the shape of boys and holy virgins to the powers whose nature is cold and moist, which also are set in the heavens. To those which are female it appears in the form of boys, and to males in the form of virgins. By this diversity of divine and beautiful forms the princes of cold and moist stock, whether male or female, are brought to naught and the vital element in them escapes. What remains is brought down to earth by cold and is mingled with all the species of earth." Who could bear stuff of this kind? Who could believe, I do not say, that it is true, but that it could even be spoken? Fancy anyone afraid to anathematize the teaching of Manes and not afraid to believe that God could do or suffer anything like that!

xlv. They tell us that the part of the divine nature that is mixed with evil is purged by their elect, by eating and drinking, forsooth. For they say it is held bound in all foods, and when these are consumed by the holy elect who eat and drink them for the refreshment of their bodies, the divine nature is released, sealed and set free. The miserable people do not notice that it is vain for them to deny what is, not surprisingly, believed about them, if they will not anathematize these books and cease to be Manichees. For if, as they say, there is a part of God bound in all seeds, which is purged by the elect by eating them, who would not in all good faith believe that they do what is done by the celestial powers and the princes of darkness according to their Thesaurus, and especially as they say that their flesh belongs to the race of darkness, and do not hesitate to believe and affirm that the vital substance, a part of God, is held bound there too? If it is to be released and purged by eating, as their deadly error forces them to admit, who does not see and abominate the awful and nefarious baseness that must ensue?

xlvi. They say that Adam, the first man, was created by certain of the princes of darkness so that the light might not escape from them. In the Epistle which they call *Fundamental*, Manes has described how the prince of darkness, whom they introduce as the father of the first man, addressed the other princes of darkness, his associates; and how he acted. "With wicked fabrications he addressed those who were present saying: What do you think about this great light that arises. You see how it moves the heavens and shakes the greatest powers. It is better, therefore, for you to give up to me the portion of light which you have in your power. Thus I shall make an image of the great one who has appeared gloriously, so that we shall be able to reign free at last from our dark way of life. Hearing this they had long deliberation, and thought it right to give what was demanded. They did not think that otherwise they would be able to keep the light under their yoke. So they thought it better to offer it to their prince, in good hope that in this way they would continue to reign. We must consider how they gave up the light they had. The truth is scattered over all the divine scriptures and the celestial secret documents, but it is not difficult to learn how it is given to the wise to know it. It is known openly and face to face by whosoever will behold it truly and faithfully. The multitude of those who had assembled was mixed, including both males and females, so he drove them to have intercourse. . . . Their offspring resembled their parents, obtaining all their great powers. Their prince rejoiced in these as an outstanding gift and consumed them. As we see it happening even now, the evil nature that forms bodies draws its power to make forms from this source; so the aforesaid prince accepted the offspring of his companions with all the sense and prudence they derived from their parents, together with the light that had been transmitted to them at birth, and ate them up. From that food he acquired many powers, among which was not only fortitude but, much more, astuteness and bad feeling derived from the savage race of their parents. Then he called to himself his own wife, who came of the same stock as he did, and, as the others had done, he sowed the multitude of evils which he had devoured, and added something of his own thought and power, so that his sense formed and marked out all that he poured forth. His wife received this as well-tilled earth is wont to receive seed, for in her were constructed and knit together the images of all the celestial and terrestrial powers, that what was formed should have the likeness of the whole world."

xlvii. O monstrous crime! O execrable destruction and rottenness of souls deceived! I will not say how horrible it is to say that the divine nature is thus bound. Let those who are grievously deceived and poisoned with this deadly error notice this. They profess that part of God can be released and purged by eating. But if it is bound by the intercourse of male and female, by necessity this horrible error compels them to release it not only from bread, vegetables and apples, which are the only things they appear in public to accept; but they must also release and purge the part of God by sexual intercourse, if it has been conceived in the womb, and can be bound there. Some are said to have confessed in a public tribunal that they have done this, not only in Paphlagonia but even in Gaul, as I heard from a Catholic Christian at Rome. When they are asked by what written authority they do these things, I hear they produce the passage from the Thesaurus which I quoted a moment ago. When this charge is made against them they are accustomed to reply that one of their number, that is one of the elect, broke away and made a schism and founded this foul heresy. So it is quite clear that though some of them may not behave in that way, those who do, get the idea from their books. Let them then throw away these books if they abhor the crime, which they are urged to commit if they retain the books. If they do not commit it they try to live cleanly, contrary to the teaching of the books. What do they do when we say to them: Either purge out the light from as many seeds as you can, and don't refuse to do what you assert you do not do; or anathematize Manes who says that in all seeds there is a part of God and that it is bound in sexual intercourse, and that the portion of light, i.e., a part of God, which comes as food for the elect, is purged when they eat it? You see what he is persuading you to do, and yet you still hesitate to anathematize him. What do they do, I say, when we say this to them? To what subterfuges they resort! Either they must anathematize such nefarious doctrine, or they must behave in such a wickedly shameful way that by comparison all the evils they attribute to the divine nature, which I have just said were intolerable, must seem tolerable: I mean, that it was compelled to wage war; that it was secure in eternal ignorance, or troubled by eternal grief and fear when the corruption of admixture with evil came upon it and the prison of eternal damnation; that when the war had been waged it was taken captive, oppressed and polluted; and that after a false victory had been gained, it was to live for ever fixed in a horrible sphere separated from its original felicity. By comparison with the moral obliquities taught or practised by the Manichees, these doctrinal errors must seem tolerable, even though, considered in themselves, they are not to be endured.

xlviii. How great is thy patience, O merciful and compassionate Lord, long-suffering, very pitiful and true, who causest thy sun to rise upon the good and the evil, and causest the rain to fall on the just and the unjust; who desirest not the death of the sinner but rather that he be converted and live; who chidest little by little and givest place for penitence, so that men may give up their evil and believe in thee, Lord; who by thy patience dost bring men to penitence, though many according to their hard and impenitent heart heap up for themselves wrath in the day of wrath, and of the revelation of thy just judgment when thou renderest to every man according to his works; who forgettest all the iniquities of man in the day when he is converted from his wickedness to thy mercy and truth. Grant us the gift that by our ministry, whereby thou hast willed that this execrable and utterly horrible error should be refuted, others may be set free as many have already been. May they deserve to receive remission of the sins and blasphemies wherewith in ignorance they have offended thee, whether through the sacrament of thy Baptism, or through the sacrifice of a broken spirit and a contrite humbled heart, in penitential sorrow. Such power has thy almighty mercy, thy authority, the truth of thy Baptism, and the keys of the kingdom of heaven given to thy Holy Church, that there is no need to despair even of such men so long as by thy patience they dwell upon the earth; especially those who know how evil it is to think or speak such things of thee, and yet are kept in that malignant profession because of some temporal and earthly advantage which they are accustomed to enjoy, or hope to obtain; if only they will accept thy correction and fly for refuge to thy ineffable goodness, and to all the enticements of the carnal life will prefer life celestial and eternal.

Faith and the Creed

St. Augustine's Review of "Faith and the Creed." Retractations, I, xvii

About the same time while still a presbyter I discoursed concerning *Faith and the Creed* in the presence and at the bidding of the bishops who were holding a plenary Council of the whole African Church at Hippo-regius. At the earnest request of several of them who were on specially friendly terms with me, I wrote down my discourse in a book. I spoke of the articles of the faith but not in the exact terms in which they are delivered to Competents to be retained in the memory. When I was dealing with the resurrection of the flesh in that book I said, "According to the Christian Faith, which is infallible, the body will rise again. Whoever thinks that incredible is paying attention to the flesh as it now is, and does not consider it as it will be. For in the time of angelic change there will be no more flesh and blood, but body only." That, and all that I said about the transformation of terrestrial into celestial bodies, I based on the apostle's words: "Flesh and blood shall not possess the kingdom of God." But if anyone concludes from that that the earthly body we now have is changed into a celestial body by the resurrection in such a way that it will not have its members as at present, and that there will be no fleshly substance, without doubt he is to be corrected by the example of the Lord's body. For not only was he visible with the same members after the resurrection, but he could be touched; and he verbally confirmed the fact that he had flesh, saying, "Handle me and see; for a spirit hath not flesh and bones as ye behold me having." Clearly, the apostle did not mean to deny that there would be the substance of flesh in the kingdom of God, but meant by the terms "flesh and blood," either men who live after the flesh, or corrupt flesh, of which of course there will be none then. When he said that "flesh and blood shall not possess the kingdom of God" he can perfectly well be understood as explaining what he immediately added: "Neither shall corruption possess incorruption." It is difficult to persuade unbelievers as to this; but whoever will read the last book of the *De Civitate Dei* will find that I have dealt with it as carefully as I could.

Faith and the Creed

INTRODUCTION

THE PLENARY COUNCIL OF THE AFRICAN CHURCH mentioned above was held at Hippo in October 393, doubtless summoned and presided over by Aurelius, who in 390 had become Bishop of Carthage. In 391 the new primate had written to St. Augustine, then recently ordained, and the latter's reply is extant (*Epist.* 22). From this we gather that the two men were already on the most friendly terms, and were of one mind as to reforms necessary in the African Church. Indeed it might appear that it was the presbyter who suggested to the primate the desirability of holding a reforming Council. If he did not specifically offer Hippo as its venue, he at least gave Aurelius to understand that the Bishop of Hippo would willingly support him. This correspondence shows that already St. Augustine's importance was widely recognized, and this would account for the remarkable fact that he, a presbyter and a recent one at that, was invited to address the bishops on so important a theme. Indeed the Christians of Hippo were already in fear lest some vacant church might call him away to be its bishop.

The discourse is a plain, straightforward exposition of the Creed, article by article, with a defence of its doctrine, when called for, against the philosophers, the heretics (Sabellians, Arians, Apollinarians and Manichees) and the schismatics (Novatianists and Donatists). The tenets of these sects are briefly described and repelled, but their names are not mentioned. Some of the articles of the Creed are very briefly handled, but some are dealt with at length and very interestingly. For example: The Omnipotence of God the Father Almighty (2); The Divinity of the Word (3–7); The Temporal

Dispensation for man's salvation; the Incarnation and the Virgin Birth (8–12); The Holy Spirit and the Trinity (16–20); The Resurrection of the Flesh (23–24). The opening chapter briefly explains the use of the Creed, and its relation to theology.

Faith and the Creed

THE TEXT

i, 1. It is written and confirmed by the strong authority of apostolic teaching that the just shall live by faith. And faith imposes on us a duty to be fulfilled both by the heart and by the tongue. "With the heart man believeth unto righteousness; and with the mouth confession is made unto salvation" (Rom. 10:10). We must therefore be mindful both of righteousness and of salvation. Though we are to reign hereafter in eternal righteousness, we cannot be saved from the present evil age unless, earnestly seeking the salvation of our neighbours, we profess with the mouth the faith which we hold in our heart. We must see to it with careful and pious vigilance that that faith shall not be violated in any way for us by the fraudulent craft of the heretics. But the Catholic Faith is made known to the faithful in the Creed, and is committed to memory, in as short a form as so great a matter permits. In this way for beginners and sucklings, who have been reborn in Christ but have not yet been strengthened by diligent and spiritual study and understanding of the divine Scriptures, there has been drawn up in few words a formula they must accept in faith, setting forth what would have to be expounded in many words to those who are making progress and are raising themselves up to attain the divine doctrine in the assured strength of humility and charity. Under colour of the few words drawn up in the Creed many heretics have endeavoured to conceal their poison. But the divine mercy withstands and resists them by the instrumentality of spiritual men, whose merit has permitted them not only to receive and believe the Catholic Faith as expressed in these words, but also to know and understand it by revelation from God. It is written "Except ye believe ye shall not understand" (Isa. 7:9, LXX).

But the exposition of the Faith serves to fortify the Creed, not that it is given to be committed to memory or repeated instead of the Creed by those who obtain the grace of God. But it guards the things contained in the Creed against the wiles of heretics with full Catholic authority and with a stronger defence.

ii, 2. Some have endeavoured to argue that God the Father is not omnipotent. Not indeed that they have ventured to put it in that way, but their teaching proves that this is their opinion and belief. When they say that there is something which God omnipotent did not create, but of which he made the world, beautifully ordered as they admit, they so far deny that God is omnipotent in that they believe he could not have made the world unless, in making it, he had used a material which already existed and which he had not made. They base their argument on the ordinary carnal observation that smiths and builders and other workmen cannot put their art into effect without the aid of material already to hand. So they understand that the maker of the world is not omnipotent, if he could not have made the world without the aid of some kind of material which he had not himself made. If they admit that the world was made by an omnipotent God they must admit that he made what he has made out of nothing. If he were omnipotent there could be nothing of which he was not the Creator. Even if he did make something out of something else, as he made man out of clay, he did not make it out of something which he had not himself made. For he made the earth out of nothing, and clay comes from the earth. If he made the heaven and the earth, i.e., the world and all it contains, out of some matter—as it is written: Thou didst create the world out of invisible, or even, as some copies read, formless matter (Wisdom 11:17)—we must by no means believe that the matter out of which the world was made, however formless or invisible, could have existed as it was by itself, as if it were co-eternal and coeval with God. Only from God omnipotent did it receive whatever mode of being it had, and whatever potentiality it had to receive other different forms. For it is by his gift that any formed thing not only has its being but even is capable of receiving form. There is this difference between what is formed and what is capable of receiving form. That which is formed has already received form. That which is "formable" is capable of receiving form. He who gives form to things also gives capacity for form, for from him and in him is the unchangeable form which is the highest form of all. He is one, who has given to everything not only its beauty but also its power to be beautiful. Most correctly, therefore, do we believe that God has made all things of nothing; for if the world was made out of matter, matter itself was made of nothing, to be, by God's gift and appointment, the primal "formable" substance from which all that has form should be formed. We have said this in order that no one should suppose that Scripture contradicts itself when it says, in one place, that God made all things of nothing, and in another, that the world was made of formless matter.

3. Accordingly, believing *in God the Father Almighty* we ought to believe that there is no creature which has not been created by his omnipotence. Moreover, because he created all things through his Word which is also called the Power and Wisdom of God, and is hinted at by many other titles which commend the Lord Jesus Christ to our faith as the Son of God, our Saviour and ruler; and because none could generate the Word by whom all things are made save he who made all things through him; iii. we also believe *in Jesus Christ our Lord, the Only Son of God, Only-begotten of the Father*. We must not think that the Word is like our words which proceed from our mouths and are passed on by vibrations in the air and abide no longer than the sound of them remains. That Word abides unchangeable. For of him Scripture says, speaking of wisdom: "Remaining in herself she reneweth all things" (Wisdom 7:27). He is called the Word also because through him the Father is made known. For as by our words, when we speak truly, our mind lets him who hears them know something, and by signs of that kind brings to the knowledge of another what we hold secretly in our heart, so wisdom whom God the Father begat is most appropriately called his Word, because through him the Father who dwells in utmost secrecy becomes known to worthy minds.

4. But there is a vast difference between our minds and the words with which we try to show what is in our minds. We do not beget verbal sounds but make them; and in making them we make use of the body as material. Now there is a great difference between mind and body. When God begat the Word, the Begetter was "he who is." He did not make the Word out of nothing nor out of any ready-made material but from his eternal nature. This is what we, too, try to do when we speak the truth, though not when we lie, if we closely consider the purpose we have in mind in speaking. What else are we trying to do but to bring our mind, as far as it can be done, into contact

with the mind of him who listens to us, so that he may know and understand it? We remain in ourselves and take no step outside ourselves, but we produce a token whereby there may be knowledge of us in another; so that, if opportunity is afforded, one mind, as it were, produces another mind to indicate its meaning. We do this with words and sounds and looks and bodily gestures—so many devices that serve our purpose to make known what is within our minds. But we cannot produce anything exactly like our minds, and so the mind of the speaker cannot make itself known with complete inwardness. Hence also there is room for lying. But God the Father had the will and the power to make himself most truly known to those who were destined to know him, and to make himself known he begat one who is like himself, and who is called the Power and Wisdom of God because God operated through him and arranged all things. Wherefore it is written of wisdom that she "reacheth from one end of the world to the other with full strength, and ordereth all things graciously" (Wisdom 8:1).

iv, 5. Wherefore the only-begotten Son of God was not made by the Father, because, as the Evangelist says, "All things were made through him" (John 1:3). Nor was he born of time for the eternally wise God has his Wisdom with him eternally. Nor is he unlike the Father, i.e., less in any way, for the apostle says: "Who being in the form of God thought it not robbery to be equal with God" (Phil. 2:6). Hence the Catholic Faith excludes those who say that the Son is the same as the Father [i.e., Sabellians], because the Word could not be with God unless it were with God the Father, and he who is alone is equal to none. Likewise those are excluded who say that the Son is a creature, though not as the other creatures [i.e. the Arians]. Any creature however great, if it be a creature, is fashioned and made. To fashion is the same as to create, although in the usage of the Latin language "to create" is sometimes used as a synonym for "to beget." The Greeks, however, observe the distinction. What we call a "creature" they call a *κτίσμα* or a *κτίσις*. If we wish to speak without ambiguity we must say not *creare* but *condere*. Therefore if the Son is a creature, however great he may be, he is made. We believe in him by whom all things were made, not in him by whom other things were made; and we cannot accept any other sense of the word "all" except as including whatever has been made.

6. "The Word became flesh and dwelt among us" (John 1:14). The Wisdom who was begotten of God deigned to be

created among men [*creari*]. Here it is pertinent to quote Proverbs 8:22 (after LXX) "The Lord created me in the beginning of his ways." The beginning of his ways is the Head of the Church, which is Christ incarnate, through whom there was to be given us an example of living, i.e., a certain way by which we might reach God. We had fallen through pride; for it was said to the first creature of our race: "Taste and ye shall be as Gods" (Gen. 3:5). We cannot return except through humility. Now our restorer deigned to show in his own person an example of this humility, i.e., of the way by which we must return. "For he thought it not robbery to be equal with God, but emptied himself, taking the form of a servant" (Phil. 2:6). So the Word by which all things were made was created man in the beginning of his ways. According to his nature as the only-begotten, he has no brothers. But according to his nature as first-born, he has deigned to call brethren all who, after him and by means of his headship, are born again into the grace of God by adoption as sons, as the apostolic teaching proclaims. Being Son by nature he was born uniquely of the substance of the Father, being what the Father is, God of God, Light of Light. We are not light by nature, but we are illumined by that light, according as we are able to shine in wisdom. "He was the true light that lighteth every man coming into this world" (John 1:9). To the Faith we profess with regard to eternal things we add the temporal dispensation of our Lord, which he deigned to carry through for us and to overrule for our salvation. According to his nature as only-begotten Son of God, it cannot be said of him that he was, or that he will be, but only that he is. What was is not now, and what will be is not yet. But he is unchangeable without variation or temporal condition. I think there is no other reason for the name by which he proclaimed himself to his servant Moses. For when he asked by whom he should say he had been sent if the people to whom he was sent should scorn him, he received the answer: "I Am who I Am"; and it was added: "Say to the children of Israel, He who is hath sent me unto you" (Ex. 3:14).

7. From this I am sure it is manifest to spiritual minds that there can be no thing which is the opposite of God. For if God is and this Word [*sc.* I AM] can properly be said of God alone, God has nothing opposite to him. What is true abides unchangeably. What changes, once was and is not now, or will be and is not yet. If we were asked what is the opposite of white, we should answer, black. If we were asked what is the opposite of hot, we should reply, cold. If we were asked what is the opposite

of swift, we should reply, slow; and so on. But if the question is asked what is the opposite of that which is, the correct answer is: that which is not.

8. But since, by what I have called a temporal dispensation, our mutable nature was assumed by the unchangeable Wisdom of God, for our salvation and restoration, by the act of God's loving-kindness, we also put faith in temporal things done on our behalf for our salvation. For we believe *in the Son of God who was born by the Holy Spirit of the Virgin Mary*. By the gift of God, that is, by the Holy Spirit, there was shown towards us such humility on the part of God most high that he deigned to take upon him the whole of human nature in the womb of a Virgin, inhabiting the body of his Mother and being born of it, while leaving it pure and entire. The heretics have many insidious ways of attacking this temporal dispensation. But anyone who holds the Catholic Faith and believes that the Word assumed the whole of human nature, body, soul and spirit, is sufficiently armed against them. The incarnation took place for our salvation, so we must take care not to suppose that any part of our nature was unassumed. Otherwise it will have no part in salvation. Apart from the shape of the limbs, which differs in the different classes of living creatures, man is not different from the cattle except in having a rational spirit, which is also called a mind. How could it be sane to believe that the divine Wisdom assumed that part of our nature which we have in common with the cattle, but did not assume the part which is illumined by the light of wisdom, and is man's characteristic part?[1]

9. Those likewise are to be detested who deny that our Lord Jesus Christ had Mary as his mother on earth. That dispensation did honour to both sexes male and female, and showed that both had a part in God's care; not only that which he assumed, but that also through which he assumed it, being a man born of a woman. We are not obliged to deny the Mother of Christ because he said: "Woman, what have I to do with thee? Mine hour is not yet come" (John 2:4). Rather he lets us know that he had no mother so far as his divine nature is concerned, and he was preparing to manifest his majestic character by turning water into wine. When he was crucified, he was crucified in his human character. That was the hour which had not yet come when he spoke as he did, meaning the hour when he would recognize her. For in the hour when he was crucified he recognized his mother's human nature and commended her most

1 This refers to the heresy of Apollinarius.

considerately to his beloved disciple. Nor should we be moved by the other passage where, when it was announced to him that his mother and brethren were present, he replied: "Who is my mother? and who are my brethren?" (Matt. 12:48). Rather he would teach us that if our parents hinder the ministry which is ours to minister the Word of God to the brethren, we ought not to recognize them. Anyone who thinks that he had no mother on earth because he said, "Who is my mother?" must also necessarily think that the apostles had no fathers on earth, because he bade them "call no man your father upon the earth; for one is your Father, which is in heaven" (Matt. 23:9).

10. Nor should our faith be lessened by any reference to "a woman's internal organs," as if it might appear that we must reject any such generation of our Lord, because sordid people think that sordid. "The foolishness of God is wiser than men" (I Cor. 1:25); and "to the pure all things are pure" (Tit. 1:15), as the apostle truly says. Those who think in this way ought to observe that the rays of the sun, which indeed they do not praise as a creature of God but adore as actually God, are poured over evil-smelling drains and other horrible things and do their natural work there without being made foul by any contamination, though visible light is by nature more closely related to visible filth. How much less could the Word of God, who is neither visible nor corporeal, have been polluted by the body of a woman when he assumed human flesh along with a human soul and spirit, within which the majesty of the Word was hidden away from the weakness of the human body? It is manifest that the Word of God could never have been contaminated by the human body, which does not even contaminate the human soul. The soul is not soiled by contact with the body when it rules and animates the body, but only when it lusts after the perishable goods of the body. If these [Manichees] would only avoid stains upon their souls, they would rather fear such lies and sacrilegious doctrines.

v, 11. But our Lord's humility in being born on our behalf was only a small part. In addition, he deigned to die for mortals. "He humbled himself, and became obedient unto death, even the death of the Cross" (Phil. 2:8); lest any of us, even if he could shake off the fear of death, should dread a kind of death which men think most shameful. Accordingly, we believe in him who *was crucified under Pontius Pilate, and buried.* The name of the judge had to be added to mark the date. And when we confess faith in his burial we remember the new tomb which bears testimony to his resurrection to newness of life, as the womb of the Virgin did to his real birth. For just as no other dead body was buried in that tomb before or after, so no other mortal was conceived in that womb before or after.

12. Also we believe that *he rose again from the dead on the third day*, the first-born of his brethren who were to follow him, whom he called into the adoption of the sons of God and deigned to make his co-heirs and co-partners.

vi, 13. We believe that *he ascended into heaven*, the place of beatitude which he promised even to us, saying: "They will be as the angels in heaven" (Matt. 22:30); in that city which is the mother of us all, Jerusalem, eternal in the heavens. It is wont to offend certain impious gentiles or heretics that we believe an earthly body was taken up into heaven. The gentiles mostly ply us eagerly with the arguments of the philosophers who say that an earthly object cannot exist in heaven. They do not know our Scriptures, or how it is written: "It is sown an animal body; it is raised a spiritual body." This does not mean that body is changed into spirit and becomes spirit. The spiritual body is understood as a body so subject to spirit that it may be suited to its celestial habitation, all earthly weakness and corruption being changed and converted into celestial purity and stability. This is the change of which the apostle speaks when he says: "We shall not all sleep, but we shall all be changed" (I Cor. 15:51). That the change is not for the worse but for the better he teaches, saying in the next verse: We shall be changed. It is the merest vain curiosity to ask where and in what manner the Lord's body is in heaven. It does not become our weakness to discuss the secrets of heaven, but it is befitting our faith to think highly and honourably of the dignity of the Lord's body.

vii, 14. We likewise believe that *he sitteth at the right hand of the Father*. Of course we are not to think that God the Father is limited as it were by a human form in such a way that in thinking about him we should imagine a right side and a left side. When it is said that "the Father sits" we are not to think of him as doing so by bending his legs, lest we fall into the sacrilege which the apostle execrates in those who have changed the glory of the incorruptible God into the likeness of corruptible man. It is sinful to set up an image of God in a Christian temple. Much more nefarious is it to do so in the heart which is truly the temple of God if it be cleansed from earthly cupidity and error. We are to understand "At the right hand of God" to mean in supreme blessedness where righteousness is, and peace and joy;

just as the goats are placed on the left hand (Matt. 25:35), i.e., in misery, on account of their iniquities, toils and torments. To say that "God sits" signifies not the position of his members, but his judicial power, which his divine majesty never lacks, but which ever metes out to men their deserts. But at the last judgment the brightness of the only-begotten Son of God, Judge of the living and of the dead, will be much more manifest among men so that none shall doubt it for ever.

viii, 15. We also believe that at the right time, *Thence he will come to judge the quick and the dead.* Possibly these names signify the righteous and the sinners. Or it may be that those are called quick whom he will then find alive upon the earth, while the dead are those who will be raised at his coming. In any case the temporal dispensation is not like his divine generation; for it has both a past and a future. Our Lord was on the earth, is now in heaven and will come in shining raiment to judge the quick and the dead. He will come as he ascended according to the authority of Scripture in the Acts of the Apostles. And of this temporal dispensation it is written in the Apocalypse: "Thus saith he who is and who was and who is to come" (Rev. 1:8).

ix, 16. Having considered and commended to faith the divine generation of our Lord and the dispensation with regard to his manhood, in order to complete what we believe about God, we add: *And in the Holy Spirit.* The Holy Spirit is not by nature less than the Father or the Son, but is, if I may say so, consubstantial and co-eternal with them. That Trinity is one God. Not that Father, Son and Holy Spirit are identically the same. But the Father is Father, the Son is Son and the Holy Spirit is Holy Spirit, and this Trinity is one God, as it is written: "Hear O Israel, the Lord thy God is one God" (Deut. 6:4). And yet if we are asked about the several Persons, e.g., is the Father God, we shall reply, he is God. If the same question is asked about the Son, we shall give the same answer. Nor if the same question were asked about the Holy Spirit ought we to say anything else than that he is God. But we have to be very careful to avoid the sense in which it is said of men: "Ye are gods" (Ps. 82:6). These are not gods by nature who are made and fashioned by the Father through the Son by the gift of the Holy Spirit. The Trinity is signified when the apostle says: "For of him and through him and to him are all things" (Rom. 11:36). Therefore, although when we are asked about the several Persons and answer that each is God, whether it be the Father or the Son or the Holy Spirit, no one is to think that we worship three Gods.

17. It is not surprising that we speak like this about an ineffable nature, for something similar is met with even in things which we see with our bodily eyes and judge with our bodily senses. When we are asked about a fountain we cannot call it a river, and when we are asked about a river we cannot call it a fountain; and if we take a drink from a fountain or a river we cannot call it either a fountain or a river. But we describe all these three things, together or severally, as water. If I ask whether what is in the fountain or in the river or in the tumbler is water, in each case the reply must be that it is; and yet we do not say that there are three waters but only one. Certainly we must take care that no one imagines that the ineffable substance of the Divine Majesty is like a visible corporeal fountain or river or tumbler of water. For the water which is now in the fountain does not remain there but flows out into the river; and when a drink is taken from a fountain or a river it does not remain in the place from which it is taken. Accordingly it can happen that the same water can belong successively to the fountain, the river and the drinking vessel. But in the Divine Trinity the Father cannot be now the Son and again the Holy Spirit. In a tree the root is simply the root, the trunk the trunk and the branches are nothing but branches. We do not use the word "root" of the trunk or the branches. Nor does the wood which belongs to the root pass in any way into the trunk or the branches, but remains only in the root. And yet the rule remains that the root is wood and the trunk and the branches are wood, but we cannot say there are three woods but one only. Possibly because of a difference in strength these portions of a tree may be so unlike that it would not be absurd to speak of three kinds of wood. At least all admit that if three goblets are filled from one fountain, we may speak of three goblets but not of three waters, but of water in the singular only. If you were asked about the goblets severally you would reply that there is water in each of them, although there is no passage from one to the other as we observed there was from the fountain into the river. These corporeal examples have been given not because they bear any real resemblance to the divine nature, but because they show the unity of visible things, and to let you understand that it is possible for three things not only severally but also together to be designated by a singular noun; so that no one may be surprised and think it absurd that we call the Father and the Son and the Holy Spirit God, but hold that in that Trinity there are not three Gods but One only, one substance.

18. Many learned and spiritual men have discoursed in many books about the Father and the Son, trying to explain, as far as men can explain to men, how the Father and the Son are not one Person but one substance, and what the Father is in himself and what the Son is in himself: how the Father begets, and the Son is begotten; how the Father is not of the Son, but the Son is of the Father; how the Father is the principle of the Son, whence he is called the Head of Christ (I Cor. 11:3), though Christ also is principle but not of the Father. He is the image of the Father, though in no way dissimilar but altogether and indistinguishably equal. These things are dealt with at greater length by those whose purpose it is to expound more fully than we are doing the profession of the whole Christian faith. The Son as Son has received existence from the Father, while the Father has not received existence from the Son. So far as, according to the temporal dispensation, the Son in ineffable compassion assumed human nature, a mutable creature, in order to change it for the better, many things are found written in Scripture which mislead the impious minds of heretics who wish to teach rather than to learn, and give them an excuse for thinking that the Son is not equal to the Father, nor of the same substance. Such are: "The Father is greater than I" (John 14:28). "The head of the woman is the man; and the head of the man is Christ, and the head of Christ is God" (I Cor. 11:3). "Then shall the Son also himself be subject unto him that put all things under him." (I Cor. 15:28) "I go to my Father and your Father, to my God and your God" (John 20:17). And some other similar passages. These things are not written to signify any inequality of nature or substance. Otherwise these other passages would be false:—"I and the Father are one" (John 10:30); "He who hath seen me hath seen the Father" (John 14:9); "The Word was God" (John 1:1)—for he was not made, since all things were made through him; "He thought it not robbery to be equal with God" (Phil. 2:6). And there are other such passages. The former passages are written partly on account of the economy of the incarnation, for it is said that he emptied himself—not that Wisdom was changed, for he is completely unchangeable, but that he wished to make himself known to men in this humble manner. Partly, then, on account of this economy these passages were written which the heretics falsely interpret; but partly also for this reason that the Son owes the Father his existence, but owes him also his equality with the Father. The Father on the other hand owes his existence to none.

19. But great and learned commentators of the divine Scriptures have not as yet discussed the doctrine of the Holy Spirit with the same fullness and care, so that we may easily understand his peculiar character as Holy Spirit, by which he is to be distinguished from the Father and the Son. But they declare that he is the gift of God, so that we may believe that God gives no gift inferior to himself. They take care, however, to declare that the Holy Spirit is not begotten of the Father like the Son, for Christ is unique. Nor was he begotten of the Son as if he were the grandson of the Father, most high. Moreover, he owes his existence to the Father from whom are all things. He does not exist in himself; that would be to set up two independent principles instead of one, which is utterly false and absurd, and is the mark not of the Catholic Faith but of the error of some heretics. Some have even dared to believe that the Holy Spirit is the communion or deity, so to speak, of the Father and the Son, their θεότης as the Greeks call it. So, as the Father is God and the Son is God, the very deity which embraces both—the Father who begets the Son and the Son who cleaves to the Father—is equated with God by whom the Son is begotten. This "deity," by which they would have understood the mutual love and charity of both Father and Son, they say is called the Holy Spirit, and they adduce many proofs from Scripture for their opinion. For example: "The love of God is shed abroad in our hearts by the Holy Spirit which is given unto us" (Rom. 5:5). There are many other similar testimonies. And because we are reconciled to God through the Holy Spirit, whence also he is called the gift of God, they would have it clearly indicated that the Holy Spirit is the Love of God. For we are not reconciled to him save through Love, whereby we are also called sons. For we are not under fear as slaves, but perfect love casteth out fear, and we have received the Spirit of liberty "whereby we cry Abba, Father" (Rom. 8:15). Because by love we are reconciled and brought back to friendship, and can know all the secret things of God, it is of the Holy Spirit that it is written: "He will bring you into all truth" (John 16:13). Hence the confidence in preaching the truth which filled the apostles when the Spirit came is rightly attributed to Love. For diffidence comes from fear which is excluded by perfect Love. Likewise he is called the gift of God, because no one enjoys what he knows unless he loves it. To enjoy the Wisdom of God is nothing else but to cleave to him in love; and no one has an abiding grasp of anything unless he loves it. Moreover he is called *Holy*

Spirit, since whatever is made holy is made holy in order to abide for ever. And there is no doubt that the word sanctity is derived from *sancire*, to make holy. Above all the asserters of this opinion make use of this testimony from Scripture: "That which is born of the flesh is flesh and that which is born of the Spirit is Spirit. For God is a Spirit" (John 3:6; John 4:24). Here he speaks of our regeneration which is not after the flesh according to Adam, but after the Holy Spirit according to Christ. If, they say, it is the Holy Spirit that is spoken of in the words, God is a Spirit, it ought to be observed that what is said is that God is a Spirit, not that the Spirit is God. Hence the deity of the Father and the Son is here called God, that is the Holy Spirit. Besides, there is this other testimony where the apostle John says that God is love. He does not say love is God but God is love, so that deity may be understood to be love. There is of course no mention of the Holy Spirit in that passage where many things are linked together: "All things are yours, and ye are Christ's and Christ is God's" (I Cor. 3:21, 23); and in the other passage: "The head of the woman is the man, and the head of the man is Christ and the head of Christ is God" (I Cor. 11:3). But they say that this is due to the fact that where things are linked together the link that holds them together is not usually included among them. Hence those who read with close attention seem to recognize the Trinity in the passage where it is written: "Of him and through him and in him are all things." "Of him" points to him who owes existence to none; "through him" points to the Mediator; and "in him" points to him who contains all things and binds them together.

20. This view is contradicted by those who think that that communion, whether we call it Deity or Love or Charity, is not a substance. They want to have the Holy Spirit explained according to his substance, and do not understand that God could not be said to be love unless love were a substance. They are influenced by ordinary corporeal experience. If two bodies are joined together so as to be set side by side, the junction is not a body. For if the two things which had been joined together are separated, nothing else remains. The "junction" cannot be understood to have moved away, as the bodies parted company. Let such people make for themselves a clean heart so that they may be able to see that there cannot be in the substance of God both substance and accidents. All that can be understood to be there is substance. It is easy to speak about such things and even to believe them, but they cannot be seen as they are save by the

pure heart. Whatever the true view may be in this matter, we must hold with unshaken faith that the Father is God and the Son is God and the Holy Spirit is God; that there are not three Gods, but that the Trinity is One God; that the persons are not diverse in nature but are of the same substance; that the Father is not now the Son and now the Holy Spirit; but that the Father is always the Father and the Son always the Son and the Holy Spirit always the Holy Spirit. We must not rashly affirm anything about invisible things as if we knew, but only as those who believe. These things can only be seen by the pure heart. He who, in this life, sees them in part and in an enigma, as it is written, cannot by speaking about them let another see them, who is hindered by uncleanness of heart. "Blessed are the pure in heart for they shall see God" (Matt. 5:8). This is our faith concerning God our maker and renewer.

x, 21. We are commanded to love not only God but also our neighbour; as it is written: "Thou shalt love the Lord thy God with all thy heart and with all thy soul and with all thy mind and thy neighbour as thyself." Unless the Christian faith gather men together into a society in which brotherly love can operate, it remains less fruitful. Hence we believe [in] *the Holy Church*, that is to say, *the Catholic Church*. Heretics and schismatics also call their congregations churches. But heretics do violence to the faith by holding false opinions about God; and schismatics, although they believe as we believe, have broken away from brotherly love by wicked separations. Wherefore heretics do not belong to the Catholic Church which loves God; nor do schismatics, for the Church loves its neighbour, and easily forgives his sins because it prays to be forgiven by him who has reconciled us to himself, blotting out all past transgressions and calling us to new life. Until we attain perfect life we cannot be without sins, but it makes all the difference what kind of sins we commit.

22. There is no need now to deal with the differences between sins, but we must by all means believe that our sins will not be forgiven if we are inexorable in refusing to forgive. We accordingly believe in *the forgiveness of sins*.

23. Man consists of three parts, spirit, soul and body. Sometimes there are said to be only two, for soul and spirit are spoken of often as one thing, whereof the rational part, which beasts lack, is called spirit. Then the life-force by which we are united to our bodies is called the soul. Finally there is the body which, because it is visible, is called our lowest part. This whole

creature "groaneth and travaileth until now" (Rom. 8:22), but has put forth the first-fruits of the spirit because it has believed God and has already a good will. The spirit is also called mind, of which the apostle says: "I serve the law of God with my mind" (Rom. 7:25). In another place he says: "God is my witness, whom I serve in my spirit" (Rom. 1:9). But the soul is called "flesh" so long as it desires carnal goods. For part of it resists the spirit, not by nature but by sinful custom and habit. Hence it is written: "With my mind I serve the law of God, but with the flesh the law of sin." This custom has been changed into a veritable natural state in his mortal descendants by the sin of the first man. Therefore it is written: "We too were at one time by nature the children of wrath," that is, of the punishment by which we were made to serve the law of sin (Eph. 2:3). The soul is by nature perfect when it is subject to its own spirit, and follows the spirit as the spirit follows God. The natural [*animalis*, soulish] man receiveth not the things of the Spirit of God. The soul is not so speedily subjected to the spirit in order to perform good works, as the spirit is subjected to God to produce true faith and a good will. Sometimes its impulse to seek carnal and temporal things is with difficulty restrained. But sometimes it is cleansed and recovers the stability of its nature under the mastery of the spirit—for the spirit is the head of the soul as Christ is the head of the spirit. Hence there is no need to despair of the body, too, being restored to its proper nature, but not so speedily as the soul, still less speedily than the spirit, but at the opportune time, at the last trump, when the dead shall arise incorruptible and we shall be changed (I Cor. 15:52). Therefore we believe in *the resurrection of the flesh.* That is to say; not merely is the soul restored which is now called "flesh" (in Scripture) on account of its carnal affections, but also this visible flesh, which is naturally flesh and which gives its name to the soul on account of the latter's carnal affections in spite of its higher nature—this visible flesh, properly so-called, we must believe without hesitation, rises again from the dead. The apostle Paul seems to have directly pointed his finger at the flesh when he wrote: "*This* corruptible must put on incorruption." When he says *This* he as good as points with his finger. That which is visible can be pointed at in this way. The soul cannot be pointed at, though it can be called corruptible because it is corrupted by moral vices. [Therefore Paul is here speaking of flesh in its natural acceptation.] When we read: "This mortal must put on immortality," again the visible flesh is signified, for again we have the same demonstrative pronoun. For the soul can be said to be mortal as well as corruptible on account of its moral vices. The death of the soul is to depart from God (cp. Ecclesiasticus 10:12). This first sin committed in paradise is related in the sacred books.

24. The body will rise again according to the Christian faith which is infallible. He who finds this incredible is fixing his attention on what the flesh is like now, and is not considering what it will be like hereafter. When it has been changed into an angelic thing, there will be no longer flesh and blood, but simply body. Speaking of flesh the apostle says: "There is one flesh of beasts, another of birds, another of fishes and serpents. There are also bodies celestial and bodies terrestrial." Notice he does not say celestial flesh, but celestial and terrestrial bodies (I Cor. 15:40). All flesh is corporeal, but every body is not flesh. Among terrestrial things wood is a corporeal thing but is not flesh, while the body of man and beast is also flesh. Among celestial things there is no flesh, but simple and shining bodies, which the apostle calls spiritual; but some call them ethereal. So he does not deny the resurrection of the flesh when he says: "Flesh and blood shall not possess the kingdom of God," but declares what flesh and blood are to become. If any man does not believe that common flesh can be changed into a nature of this sort, he is to be led on to faith by gradual steps. If you ask him whether earth can be changed into water, that will not seem to him incredible because there is no great distance between these two elements. Again if you ask whether water can be changed into air, he will agree that that is not absurd because these two elements are close neighbours. Let him next be asked about air, whether it can be transformed into an ethereal body, and again the close relation of the two elements will make it plausible. Now when he has admitted the possibility that earth can be transmuted by these stages into ethereal body, why should it not be possible directly when God so wills it, who once made it possible for a human body to walk upon the waters? Why should he not believe that it can happen without these intermediate steps, "in the twinkling of an eye," as it is written (I Cor. 15:52); just as smoke is often turned into flame with marvellous speed? Our flesh is no doubt derived from the earth. Philosophical arguments in proof of the assertion that no earthly object can be in heaven are often urged against faith in the resurrection of the flesh; and yet the philosophers admit that any body can be changed and transformed into any other.

When the resurrection of the body has taken place we shall be freed from our temporal condition, and shall enjoy eternal life in ineffable charity and with a constancy that knows no corruption. Then shall it be as it is written: "Death is swallowed up in victory. O Death, where is thy sting? O Death, where is thy contention?" (I Cor. 15:54).

24. This is the faith which is handed over to young Christians, expressed in a few words, which they are to hold faithfully. These few words are made known to believers, that, believing, they may subject themselves to God, being so subject may live righteous lives, living righteously they may cleanse their hearts, and with a pure heart may know what they believe.

To Simplician — on Various Questions. Book I

St. Augustine's Review of "De Quaestionibus Ad Simplicianum." Retractations, II, i

1. Of the books which I wrote after I became a bishop the first two are *Answers to divers Questions addressed to Simplician* who succeeded the Blessed Ambrose as Bishop of Milan. In the first book I have set forth my answer to two questions concerning passages from the Epistle of Paul the Apostle to the Romans. The first concerns Romans 7:7–25. Whereas the apostle says, "The law is spiritual but I am carnal etc.," showing that the flesh wars against the spirit, I have expounded his words as if he were describing the man who is still under the law and not yet under grace. Long afterwards I learned that these words could also describe the spiritual man and indeed in all probability do so. The second question concerns Romans 9:10–29. In answering this question I have tried hard to maintain the free choice of the human will, but the grace of God prevailed. Not otherwise could I reach the understanding that the apostle spoke with absolute truth when he said, "Who made thee to differ? What hast thou that thou didst not receive? But if thou didst receive it, why dost thou glory as if thou didst not receive it?" This truth Cyprian the martyr too wanted to make clear, and he expressed it completely in a phrase "In nothing must we glory since nothing is ours."

2. In the second book other questions are treated and solved according to our poor capacity. They all come from the so-called Books of Kings. The first concerns the words, "The spirit of the Lord came upon Saul" whereas in another place it is written, "An evil spirit from the Lord came upon Saul." In expounding this I said, "Though to will is in the power of any man, ability to perform is not in his power." The reason for saying this is precisely that we do not say a thing is in our power

unless what we will is done. Then willing is the first and chief consideration. The will is there immediately when we will; but we receive from above the power to live aright, when the will is prepared by the Lord. The second question is what is the meaning of the words, "I repent that I have made Saul King"? The third is whether the unclean spirit that was in the priestess of Delphi could have brought it to pass that Samuel appeared to Saul and spoke with him. The fourth explains "King David entered and sat before the Lord." The fifth deals with the words of Elijah: "O Lord, thou hast brought evil upon this widow with whom I sojourn, in slaying her son."

To Simplician — on Various Questions. Book I

INTRODUCTION

In the Eighth Book of the Confessions Augustine tells us how in his growing spiritual distress he went to consult Simplician, an aged presbyter of Milan and a trusted friend and counsellor of Ambrose. To him he unfolded the tale of his wanderings in the maze of error; and from him he received encouragement to persevere in the study of the Platonists because in their works "God and his Word are everywhere implied." Simplician also told him about Victorinus, the translator of Plotinus, in whose conversion he had had a part. Victorinus, an African by birth, had acquired wide-spread fame as an orator in Rome, and had so gained the friendship of many Senators. One day he announced to Simplician that in his reading of the Bible and the Christian writers he had become convinced of the truth of Christianity, but he hesitated long before at last he openly confessed his faith by accepting Baptism publicly in the church in Rome. Subsequently he suffered for his faith under the law of Julian which excluded Christians from the teaching profession. The story naturally set Augustine on fire to imitate him. Simplician's spiritual help at this juncture put Augustine deeply in his debt, and between the two men there was forged a bond of regard and affection.

In 397 Simplician succeeded Ambrose as Bishop of Milan, some eighteen months after Augustine had become coadjutor-Bishop of Hippo. The latter's first literary work as bishop was to reply in two books to certain questions of Biblical interpretation sent to him by Simplician. He says they were written "at the very beginning of my episcopate," and there is nothing to suggest that the elevation of Simplician had already taken place. Of these two books, the first contains the answers to Simplician's first two questions, a detailed exegesis of two difficult passages from the Epistle to the Romans; and it is here translated not only as a good example of Augustine's exegetical work, but also because it is generally held to mark an important stage in his understanding of St. Paul. Augustine himself recognized this, and pointed it out in two of his latest works (*De Praedestinatione Sanctorum*, iv, 8 and *De Dono Perseverantiae*, xx, 52).

Even before his conversion, and doubtless owing to the influence of Ambrose, Augustine had been reading the Epistles of St. Paul, and had found in them something that spoke to his condition, perhaps even more directly than did the Platonist books (*Confessions*, VII, xxi). His copy was lying on his table when Pontician called (*ibid.*, VIII, vi), whose story of St. Antony moved him profoundly and introduced the final scene in the drama of his conversion. When the voice heard in the garden bade him "Take up and read," it was to this book he turned. Opening it at random and chancing to light on Romans 13:13, he saw there a divine call to abandon the world and his conversion was complete. He took the book with him to Cassiciacum and there read it through carefully from beginning to end (*Contra Acad.*, II, ii, 5), clear evidence that his whole activity during that period is not reflected in the Dialogues. Most likely a Pauline influence modifies and colours his Platonism from the beginning, and in time it becomes very marked, notably in *De Vera Religione*. It is not surprising, therefore, that during his presbyterate he should have devoted much of his attention to the Pauline Epistles. He wrote a commentary on Galatians, and planned another on Romans, but on such a gigantic scale that he abandoned it when he had dealt only with the first five verses of the address. Somewhat earlier a group of clergy in Carthage, which included Augustine, were studying the Epistle to the Romans, and he made some comments which at the request of the brethren he committed to writing under the title of "Exposition of certain Propositions from the Epistle to the Romans." Simplician's Questions concerned two of the passages which had there been briefly dealt with.

The First Question concerns the crucial passage which has been and still is much disputed by theologians, Romans 7:7–25. Augustine's new treatment of it is long and more elaborate but the interpretation remains as in the earlier Exposition. His main concern is to defend the Old Testament Law as a good thing against its detractors. It brings sin to consciousness and makes it more sinful through imparting to it the character of deliberate and conscious transgression of the divine commandment. It cannot give the power to perform that which is right. Nevertheless it points out the way of righteousness, and produces anxiety with regard to guilt so that the soul may be prepared to receive grace. To be under the law is a higher state than to have no law. Augustine still accepts the view that in this passage the apostle is speaking in the character of a man set under the law and not yet under grace. Controversy with the Pelagians forced him later to abandon this view (*Contra Duas Epistolas Pelagianorum*, I, viii). He came to see that baptized Christians and even apostles could not in this life attain a state of perfect peace and righteousness. Even under grace the impulses of concupiscence have always to be resisted. Here he discovers the principle, so important to Luther and the Reformers, *Simul Justus et Peccator*.

The Second Question has to do with the interpretation of Romans 9:10–29. Here the much harder problem of the relation of grace and free-will is faced. (2) The clue to its solution is to be sought in the purpose of the Epistle as a whole, which is to show that no man may glory in his own good works. (3) This is strikingly illustrated in the extreme case of Jacob's being chosen and Esau's being rejected before either was born or had done aught of good or evil. There could have been no question of selection, or election, on the strength of good works performed, or even of faith, in either case. (5) The suggestion must be ruled out that the selection was made on the ground of the presence or absence of faith or good works which God foresaw would be forthcoming. (7) Faith is due to the calling of God and must be numbered among the gifts of grace. It is therefore not meritorious. (8) If we say that God graciously calls a man, bestows faith upon him and the power to do good works, no difficulty arises; but (10) why does he not do so in all cases? Is it because some are willing to hear and believe, and others are unwilling? For we cannot believe unwillingly. (12) Formally we have the power to will, but the good will is the gift of God, so that even willing is not wholly ours. (13) What, then, of those who reject God's call? Can they frustrate his gracious purpose? Rather we must say that some are effectually called, others not so. To some the call is made in such a way that they will hear and obey. Others are hardened. (16) Two truths are sure (*a*) There is no unrighteousness with God. (*b*) He treats men differently "as he wills." There is a higher hidden justice which is, however, reflected in human affairs. A creditor may exact or remit a debt, and in neither case is he chargeable with injustice. Certainly the debtors have no cause for complaint. Man may not question the ways of God. (17) Like the potter with the clay, God makes vessels, some to honour, some to dishonour. (19) All men are made of one lump, a *massa peccati*, and some are to be saved, others are to be lost. (21) To those whom he wills to save God provides a motive adequate to win them to faith and obedience. (22) Election, therefore, precedes justification. God elects of his mere good pleasure those who are to be justified so that they may attain eternal life. Without election there can be neither faith nor obedience. But God's judgments are inscrutable and his ways past finding out. For all that he does he is to be praised.

Augustine here has taken a step beyond his earlier Exposition, due, as he tells us repeatedly, to a better understanding of certain Pauline expressions, notably "The election of grace." There he was endeavouring to hold a balance between grace and free-will. "It is ours to believe and to will; it is God's to give to those who believe and are willing the power to do good works, through the Holy Spirit by whom love is spread abroad in our hearts." Now he teaches that God must himself graciously prepare the heart for faith, so that faith too is to be numbered among the gifts of grace, no less than the power to do good; and man's salvation is, therefore, wholly the work of God. The moral difficulty involved in the assertion that God arbitrarily selects some and not others for his gracious aid is met with an appeal to his omnipotence and inscrutable justice. Man may not question his Maker's judgments. "Give what thou commandest, and command what thou wilt." The position is now reached in all its essential features which provoked the protest of Pelagius, and which had to be defended against the Pelagians from 411 onwards to the end of Augustine's life.

To Simplician — on Various Questions. Book I

THE TEXT

Preface

Very pleasing and agreeable is the honour you have done me, Father Simplician, in sending me your questions. If I did not try to answer them I should be not only contumacious but also ungrateful. The problems which you have propounded for me to solve from the apostle Paul I had already discussed in writing. But not content with my former inquiry and exposition, in case I might have overlooked anything through negligence, I have investigated with greater care and attention these same apostolic words and the tenor of his sentences. For you would not have judged that they should be treated again, if the understanding of them were easy and ready to hand.

First Question. Romans 7:7–25

1. Your first question asks me to interpret the passage beginning: "What shall we say then? Is the law sin? God forbid," down to, "I consent unto the law that it is good," and so on down to, "O wretched man that I am! Who shall deliver me from the body of this death? Thanks be unto God through Jesus Christ our Lord" (Rom. 7:7–25). In this passage the apostle seems to me to represent himself as a man set under the law, and to speak in that character. And because just before he had said: "We have been discharged from the law of death wherein we were holden; so that we serve in newness of the spirit and not in the oldness of the letter," and might by these words seem to have found fault with the law he added forthwith: "What shall we say, then? Is the law sin? God forbid. Howbeit I had not known sin but by the law. For I had not known concupiscence except the law had said Thou shalt not covet."

2. But again, if the law is not sin but introduces sin, even so it is found fault with in these words. Therefore we must understand that the law was given not to introduce sin nor to extirpate it, but simply to make it known; by the demonstration of sin to give the human soul a sense of its guilt in place of a secure sense of its innocence. Sin cannot be overcome without the grace of God, so the law was given to convert the soul by anxiety about its guilt, so that it might be ready to receive grace. Accordingly he does not say: "Without the law I had not committed sin," but: "I had not *known* sin except through the law." And again, he does not say: "I had no concupiscence except the law had said Thou shalt not covet," but: "I had not *known* concupiscence except the law had said, Thou shalt not covet." Hence it appears that concupiscence was not implanted in him by the law, but was made known to him.

3. The consequence was that concupiscence was even increased, since it could not be resisted when grace was not yet received. For concupiscence acquires greater strength when in addition there is violation of a law. It is aggravated when it is done against the law, and becomes a worse sin than if there had been no law prohibiting it. Accordingly he adds: "Sin, finding occasion through the commandment wrought in me all manner of concupiscence." Sin, then, existed before the law, but did not reach its full sinfulness because there was so far no violation of a law. So in another passage he says: "Where there is no law there is no breaking of the law."

4. He goes on: "Without the law sin is dead." That is as if he said, "sin is latent," in other words, "is thought to be dead." He is going to say that more clearly a little later. "I lived without the law once," he says, i.e., no fear of death because of sin terrified me, because sin was not made manifest when there was no law. "But when the commandment came, sin revived," i.e., became manifest, "and I died," i.e., I knew that I was dead—because the guilt of breaking the law was threatened by the certain punishment of death. Indeed when he says that sin revived when the commandment came, he makes it perfectly clear that sin had lived before and had been known, I suppose, in the sin of the first man, since he had received and violated a commandment. In another place he says: "The woman being beguiled fell into transgression" (I Tim. 2:14). And again: "After the likeness of Adam's transgression, who is a figure of him who was to come" (Rom. 5:14). In any case, nothing can be said to revive which did not live at some previous time. But sin was dead,

that is, hidden, all the time that men were born mortal and lived without the commandment of the law, following the desires of the flesh in ignorance because there was no prohibition. Therefore he says: "I lived without the law once." Thereby he shows that he is not speaking in his own person but generally in the person of "the old man." But "when the commandment came, sin revived and I died; the commandment which was unto life I found to be unto death." But if the commandment is obeyed it surely gives life. But it was found to be unto death because it was disobeyed. Now, what is done contrary to the commandment is sin, just as it was sinful even before the commandment was given, but now it is more abundantly and perniciously sinful, because it is done knowingly and in transgression of the commandment.

5. "For sin," he says, "finding occasion through the commandment deceived me and thereby slew me." Sin became sweeter, wrongly using the law to increase desire which it was intended to forbid. Thereby it deceived him. Sweetness is deceptive because it is followed by much bitterness in the shape of punishment. Men who have not yet received spiritual grace find greater pleasure in doing what is forbidden, and so sin deceives them with its false sweetness. When there is added the sense of the guilt of transgression, sin slays.

6. Accordingly "the law is holy and the commandment holy, just and good." It commands what ought to be commanded, and prohibits what ought to be prohibited. "Was that which is good, then, made death to me? God forbid." The fault lies in making a bad use of the commandment, which in itself is good. "The law is good if one use it lawfully" (I Tim. 1:8). But he makes a bad use of the law who does not subject himself to God in humble piety, so that, with the aid of grace, he may become able to fulfil the law. He who does not use the law lawfully receives it to no other end than that his sin, which was latent before the prohibition, should be made apparent by his transgression. And this above measure, for it is not only sin but it is also contrary to direct commandment. So he goes on: "Sin, that it might be shown to be sin, worked death in me through that which is good, that through the commandment sin might become exceeding sinful." Here he makes clear in what sense he wrote the words, "Without the law sin was dead," not that it did not exist but that it was not made apparent, and also what he meant by saying that "sin revived"—not simply that that should exist which already existed before the law, but that it

should be made apparent by being committed against the law. That is what he is saying here. "Sin, that it might be shown to be sin, worked death in me through that which is good." He does not say that there should be sin, but that it should be shown to be sin.

7. Then he gives the cause why it should be so. "We know that the law is spiritual but I am carnal." Thus he clearly shows that the law cannot be fulfilled except by spiritual persons, and there cannot be such save by grace. The more one is assimilated to the spiritual law, the more one attains to a spiritual disposition, the more one fulfils the law. The more one delights in it, the less one is afflicted by its burdensomeness, and the more one is quickened by its light. "For the commandment of the Lord is pure, enlightening the eyes; and the law of the Lord is perfect, converting the soul" (Ps. 19:8). When grace forgives sins and infuses a spirit of charity, righteousness ceases to be hard and becomes even pleasant. When he said "I am carnal," he raised the question of what carnal means. People are called carnal in some degree who are already under grace, redeemed by the blood of the Lord and regenerated by faith. To such the apostle writes: "I could not speak to you, brethren, as to spiritual but as carnal. As babes in Christ I have given you milk to drink not meat." In so saying he shows that they had been regenerated by grace, for they were babes in Christ, and had to be given milk to drink, and he still calls them carnal. He who is not yet under grace but is under the law, is carnal in the sense that he is not yet regenerate from sin but is still sold under sin. The price of deadly pleasure includes the sweetness which deceives, and gives delight in doing contrary to the law, which is all the more pleasant the less it is lawful. No one can enjoy that sweetness as the price of his condition without being compelled to serve lust as a chattel-slave. He who knows that an act is prohibited and rightly prohibited, and yet does it, knows that he is the slave of an overmastering desire.

8. "That which I do I know not." This does not mean that he does not know that he is sinning, for that would contradict what he said above. "Sin, that it might be shown to be sin, worked death in me through that which is good." "I had not known sin save by the law." Obviously when he can use expressions like these he cannot mean that he is ignorant of having sinned. He uses the word as the Lord is going to use it when he will say to the impious "I know you not." Nothing escapes the notice of God, "for the face of the Lord is against them that do evil, to

destroy the memory of them from the earth." Sometimes we say we do not know, meaning that we do not approve. So when he says "That which I do I know not" he means "I approve not." And he makes this clear in what follows, "Not what I would, that do I practise, but what I hate that I do." Here he says he *hates* what he had just said he did not know. Now of those to whom the Lord will say "I know you not" it is also said "Thou, O Lord, dost hate all the workers of iniquity" (Ps. 5:5).

9. "If what I would not, that I do, I consent unto the law that it is good." What he would not is what is also forbidden by the law. Therefore, he consents unto the law, not of course in so far as he does what the law prohibits, but in so far as he does not will to do what he in fact does. He is overcome because he is not yet free by grace, but he already knows through the law that he is doing wrong, and he does not really want to do that. And he continues: "So now it is no more I that do it, but sin that dwelleth in me." He does not mean that he did not consent to do the wrong, but that he consented to the law's disapprobation of the wrong. He is still speaking in the person of a man under the law and not yet under grace, who is brought to do wrong by some dominant desire, and by some deceptive sweetness associated with prohibited sin. But he disapproves of this because of his knowledge of the law. "It is no more I that do it," he says, because he is overcome when he does it. It is a desire that does it, when we yield to an overmastering one. Grace brings it about that we do not yield, and that the human mind is strengthened to resist desire. Of grace he will be speaking later.

10. "For I know that in me, that is, in my flesh, dwelleth no good thing." So far as knowledge goes he consents unto the law, but so far as action is concerned he yields to sin. If it is asked how he knows that in his flesh dwelleth no good thing, which means that sin dwells there, how but from his inherited mortality and from his addiction to pleasure? The former is the penalty of original sin, the latter of repeated sinning. We are born into this life with the former, and add to the latter as we live. These two things, nature and custom conjoined, render cupidity strong and unconquerable. This is what he calls sin which, he says, dwells in his flesh, obtaining a certain domination and kingdom, so to speak there. Hence the Psalmist says, "I would rather be a slave in the house of the Lord, than dwell in the tents of sinners" (Ps. 84:10), as if a slave does not dwell in the place where he is a slave. He no doubt means that "to dwell" must

be understood as implying a certain rank. If by grace we achieve the condition described in another passage in these words, "That sin may not reign in our mortal body that we should obey the lusts thereof," then sin cannot be said properly to dwell there.

11. "To will is present with me, but to do that which is good I find not." To those who do not rightly understand these words he seems by them to take away free will. Yet how does he do that when he says "To will is present with me"? If that is so, actual willing is certainly within our power; that it is not in our power to do that which is good is part of the deserts of original sin. This is not the original nature of man, but the penalty of his guilt, whereby mortality was brought in as a second nature, from which the grace of our Creator sets us free, if we submit ourselves to him by faith. These are the words of a man set under the law and not yet under grace. He who is not yet under grace does not do the good he wills but the evil which he does not will, being overcome by concupiscence which derives its strength from the fact, not simply that he is mortal, but also that he is burdened by the weight of custom. But if he does what he wills not, it is no longer he that does it, but the sin that dwells in him, as has been said and explained above.

12. "I find then a law, that, when I would do good, evil is present with me." That is, I find the law is good for me when I wish to do what the law commands, though it is easier to do evil, which is present with me. When he said above "To will is present with me" he was referring to its facility. There is nothing easier for a man under the law than to will to do good and yet to do evil. He has no difficulty in willing, but it is not so easy to do what he wills. It is easy to do what he hates even against his will; just as a man thrown headlong has no difficulty in reaching the bottom, though he does not want to and indeed hates it. So I interpret the word "is present." So the man set under the law and not yet liberated by grace gives testimony to the law that it is good. He does so by the very fact that he blames himself for acting contrary to the law. He finds it a good thing for him, because he wants to do what it commands, but cannot because he is overcome by concupiscence. Thus he sees himself involved in the guilt of transgression, so that he may implore the grace of the Liberator.

13. "I delight in the law of God after the inward man" that is, the law which says, "Thou shalt not covet." "But I see another law in my members warring against the law of my mind,

and bringing me into captivity under the law of sin which is in my members." A "law in his members" is the name he gives to the burden of mortality under which we groan, being heavy-laden. A body which is corrupted burdens the soul. So it often happens that what is not right gives pleasure and cannot be resisted. This sorely pressing burden he calls a law, because it has been imposed as a punishment by the divine judgment, by God who gave man previous warning, saying, "In the day ye eat thereof ye shall surely die" (Gen. 2:17). This law "warreth against the law of the mind" which says, "Thou shalt not covet." In this law man rejoices after the inner man. But before he is under grace the other law so wars against his mind that it brings him into captivity under the law of sin, that is, under itself. In repeating "which is in my members" he shows that this is the same law as that referred to earlier as "another law in my members."

14. All this is said to show that a man who is thus taken captive ought not to presume on his own strength. Paul rebuked the Jews for proudly glorying in the works of the law, though concupiscence attracted them to what was unlawful; since the law in which they gloried said, "Thou shalt not covet." The man who is conquered, damned and taken captive, who is not victorious even though he has received the law but is rather made a transgressor, such a man must humbly cry, "O wretched man that I am, who will deliver me from the body of this death? Thanks be to God through Jesus Christ our Lord." In this mortal life one thing remains for free will, not that a man may fulfil righteousness when he wishes, but that he may turn with suppliant piety to him who can give the power to fulfil it.

15. In this whole closely argued passage of the apostle which we have expounded, possibly some may think that the apostle feels that the law is an evil thing. There are also these other passages: "The law came in that sin might abound" (Rom. 5:20); "The ministration of death engraved in letters of stone" (II Cor. 3:7); "The power of sin is the law" (I Cor. 15:56); "Ye are dead to the law by the body of Christ, that ye may become the property of another, even of him who rose from the dead. ... Sinful passions which were through the law wrought in our members to bring forth fruit unto death. But now we have been discharged from the law of death wherein we were holden so that we may serve in newness of the spirit, and not in oldness of the letter" (Rom. 7:4-6). And we can find other passages in the apostle of similar import. But notice, he does not mean to con-

demn the law. He says these things because the law increases concupiscence by prohibiting it, and makes a man guilty as a transgressor of the law. The law commands what men in their infirmity are not able to fulfil, unless they turn piously to the grace of God. Those are said to be under the law over whom it exercises dominion, that is, those whom it punishes, and it punishes all transgressors. Those who have received the law break it, unless through grace they obtain power to do what it commands. So it is that the law does not exercise dominion over those who are under grace, and fulfil it by love, though they were condemned when they were under the fear of the law.

16. If the apostle's words induce us to think that he is finding fault with the law, what are we to make of these: "I delight in the law of God after the inward man"? He actually praises the law when he says that. But it may be replied that here the apostle is speaking of another law, the law of Christ, and not the law which was given to the Jews. So I ask which law is he speaking of when he says, "The law came that sin might abound." They reply "No doubt, that which the Jews received." Is he then speaking of the same law when he says, "Sin taking occasion by the commandment wrought all manner of concupiscence in me"? What is the difference between "wrought all manner of concupiscence in me," and, "that sin might abound"? Observe also that that other statement is in complete agreement, "that sin by the commandment might become exceeding sinful." That is the same thing as "that sin might abound." If we show that the commandment is a good thing from which sin took occasion to work all manner of concupiscence and to become exceeding sinful, we have shown at the same time that the law is good which came that sin might abound, i.e., might work all manner of concupiscence and become exceeding sinful. Let them hear the apostle's own words. "What shall we say, then? Is the law sin? God forbid." This, they say, is said of the law of Christ, that is, of the law of grace. Then, what do they understand of what follows? "I had not known sin but by the law. I had not known concupiscence did not the law say, Thou shalt not covet. But sin took occasion through the commandment to work all manner of concupiscence in me." The context of the words indicates sufficiently of what law he is speaking when he says, "Is the law sin? God forbid." Obviously, the law by whose commandment occasion was given to sin to work all manner of concupiscence; the law, therefore, which came in afterwards that sin might abound; the law which

they suppose to be evil. What could be more clear than what he says soon after? "The law is holy, and the commandment holy, just and good." Again they say this does not refer to the law given to the Jews, but is spoken of the Gospel. That is the unspeakably blind perversity of the Manichees. They pay no attention to the completely frank and clear sequel; "Was that which is good made death to me? God forbid. But sin, that it might be shown to be sin, by working death to me through that which is good; that through the commandment sin might become exceeding sinful"; that is, by a commandment that was holy, just and good, which nevertheless came that sin might abound, i.e., become exceeding sinful.

17. Why, then, if the law is good, is it called a "ministration of death"? Because "sin, that it might be shown to be sin, worked death for me through that which is good." Do not marvel when it is said of the preaching of the Gospel, "We are a sweet savour of Christ unto God, in them that are being saved and in them who perish, to the one a savour of life to life, to the other a savour of death to death" (II Cor. 2:15–16). Now the law is called a "ministration of death" to the Jews, for whom it was written on stone, to symbolize their hardness of heart. But this does not apply to those who fulfil the law in charity. For charity is the fulfilment of the law (Rom. 13:10). The law which was graven with letters of stone says, "Thou shalt not commit adultery; thou shalt not kill; thou shalt not steal; thou shalt not covet," etc. That law the apostle says is fulfilled by charity. "He that loveth his neighbour hath fulfilled the law. For, Thou shalt not commit adultery; Thou shalt not kill; Thou shalt not steal; Thou shalt not covet; and if there be any other commandment, all are summed up in this word, Thou shalt love thy neighbour as thyself" (Rom. 13:8–9). For of course this, too, is written in the same law. Why, if the law is good, is it "the power of sin" (I Cor. 15:56)? Because sin wrought death by that which is good, that it might become exceeding sinful, i.e., might acquire greater powers by becoming also transgression. Why, if the law is good, are we "dead to the law by the body of Christ"? Because we are dead to the law's condemnation, being set free from the disposition which the law condemns and punishes. The more usual practice is to speak of law as something that threatens, terrifies and punishes. So the same precept, which is law to those who fear it, is grace to those who love it. Hence the saying in the Gospel: "The law was given through Moses; grace and truth came by Jesus Christ" (John 1:17). The same law,

that is, that was given through Moses to be feared, was made grace and truth by Jesus Christ so that it might be fulfilled. So the words, " ye are dead to the law," should be taken to mean, ye are dead to the punishment threatened by the law through the body of Christ, through which are remitted the sins which bound us to the law's punishments. If the law is good, why did "sinful passions, which were through the law, work in our members to bring forth fruit unto death" (Rom. 7:5)? Here he wants us to understood the sinful passions, of which I have already often spoken as an increase of concupiscence due to the prohibition, and as guiltily deserving punishment because of transgression. Death is wrought through that which is good that sin might become exceeding sinful by the commandment. If the law is good, why are we "set free from the law of death wherein we were holden, so that we may serve in newness of spirit and not in oldness of the letter" (Rom. 7:6)? The law is "letter" to those who do not fulfil it in the spirit of charity to which the New Testament belongs. So those who are dead to sin are freed from the letter, which holds guilty those who do not fully obey what is written. The law is nothing else than a "letter" to those who can read it but cannot fulfil it. It is not unknown to those for whom it was written. But because it is known merely in so far as it is written and not as something loved and performed, to such people it is nothing but "letter"; a "letter" which brings no aid to those who read it, but bears witness to their sins. Those who are renewed by the spirit are freed from its condemnation, so that they are no longer bound to the letter for punishment, but are joined to understanding through righteousness. Hence "the letter killeth, but the spirit giveth life" (II Cor. 3:6). The law, when merely read and not understood or fulfilled, killeth. In that case it is called "the letter." But the spirit giveth life, because the fulfilment of the law is charity "shed abroad in our hearts by the Holy Spirit which is given to us" (Rom. 5:5).

The Second Question. Romans 9:10–29

1. Now I think it is time to turn to the second question you have propounded, which concerns the interpretation of Romans 9:10–29, from "Not only so, but Rebecca also conceived" down to "We had been made like unto Gomorrah." You ask that the whole passage be discussed, and indeed it is rather obscure. But, to be sure, I know your regard for me and am certain that you would not bid me expound that passage unless you had prayed

the Lord to give me the ability to do so. With confidence in his help I approach the task.

2. First I shall try to grasp the apostle's purpose which runs through the whole Epistle, and I shall seek guidance from it. It is that no man should glory in meritorious works, in which the Israelites dared to glory, alleging that they had served the law that had been given to them, and that for that reason they had received evangelical grace as due to their merits. So they were unwilling that the same grace should be given to the Gentiles, as if they were unworthy of it unless they undertook to observe the Jewish sacred rites. This problem arose and is settled in the Acts of the Apostles. The Jews did not understand that evangelical grace, just because of its very nature, is not given as a due reward for good works. Otherwise grace is not grace. In many passages the apostle frequently bears witness to this, putting the grace of faith before works; not indeed that he wants to put an end to good works, but to show that works do not precede grace but follow from it. No man is to think that he has received grace because he has done good works. Rather he could not have done good works unless he had received grace through faith. A man begins to receive grace from the moment when he begins to believe in God, being moved to faith by some internal or external admonition. But the fullness and evidentness of the infusion of grace depends on temporal junctures and on sacramental rites. Catechumens are not unbelievers, otherwise Cornelius did not believe in God, although by his prayers and alms he showed himself worthy to have an angel sent to him. But these good deeds would have had no effect had he not already believed; and he would not have believed had he not been called by some secret admonition coming through visions of the mind or spirit, or by more open admonitions reaching him through the bodily senses. In some there is the grace of faith, but not enough to obtain the kingdom of heaven, as in catechumens, or in Cornelius himself before he was incorporated into the Church by participation in the sacraments. In others there is so much grace that they are already reputed to belong to the body of Christ and the holy temple of God. "The temple of God is holy," says the apostle, "which temple ye are" (I Cor. 3:17). And the Lord himself says: "Except a man be born again of water and the Holy Spirit, he shall not enter into the kingdom of heaven" (John 3:5). There are therefore inchoate beginnings of faith, which resemble conception. It is not enough to be conceived. A man must also be born if he is to attain to

eternal life. None of these beginnings is without the grace of God's mercy. And good works, if there are any, follow and do not precede that grace, as has been said.

3. This is the truth the apostle wanted to urge; just as in another passage he says, "By the grace of God we are saved, and that not of ourselves. It is the gift of God. It is not of works, lest any man should boast" (Eph. 2:8, 9). And so he gave a proof from the case of those who had not yet been born. No one could say that Jacob had conciliated God by meritorious works before he was born, so that God should say of him, "The elder shall serve the younger." So "Not only so," he says, was Isaac promised in the words, "At this time I will come, and Sarah shall have a son" (Rom. 9:9). Now Isaac had not conciliated God by any previous meritorious works so that his birth should have been promised, and that in Isaac "Abraham's seed should be called" (Gen. 21:12). That means that those are to belong to the lot of the saints in Christ who know that they are the sons of promise; who do not wax proud of their merits, but account themselves co-heirs with Christ by the grace of their calling. When the promise was made that they should be this they did not as yet exist and so could have merited nothing. "Rebecca also having conceived by one, even by our father Isaac . . ." He is most careful to note that it was by one act of coition that twins were conceived so that nothing could be attributed to the merits of the father, as if someone might say the son was born such as he was because his father had such or such a disposition when he lay with his wife; or that his mother was disposed in such a way when she conceived a son. Both were begotten and conceived at one and the same time. And for another reason he stresses this fact, so as to give no opportunity to astrologers or to those who are called calculators of nativities, who conjecture the characters and destinies of those who are born from their natal hours. They can find absolutely no explantion why there was so great a diversity in these twins when they were conceived at one moment of time, and under the same position of the stars and the heavens, so that it was quite impossible to discover any thing wherein the one differed from the other. They can easily learn if they will that the replies they sell to poor deluded folk have no basis in any kind of scientific knowledge, but only in chance guess-work. But to return to the matter in hand, these things are related to break and cast down the pride of men who are not grateful for the grace of God but dare to glory in their own merits. "For the children being not yet born and having done

nothing either good or evil, not of works but of him that calleth, it was said unto her, the elder shall serve the younger." Grace is therefore of him who calls, and the consequent good works are of him who receives grace. Good works do not produce grace but are produced by grace. Fire is not hot in order that it may burn, but because it burns. A wheel does not run nicely in order that it may be round, but because it is round. So no one does good works in order that he may receive grace, but because he has received grace. How can a man live justly who has not been justified? How can he live holily who has not been sanctified? Or, indeed, how can a man live at all who has not been vivified? Grace justifies so that he who is justified may live justly. Grace, therefore, comes first, then good works. As he says in another place, "To him that worketh, the reward is not reckoned as of grace, but as of debt" (Rom. 4:4). There is, of course, the passage where he speaks of immortality after good works, as if he really demands it as his due, for he says: "I have fought the good fight, I have finished the course, I have kept the faith. Henceforth there is laid up for me the crown of righteousness, which the Lord the righteous judge, shall render to me at that day" (II Tim. 4:7–8). Do you think, perhaps, that because he said "shall render" he meant that it was his due? But when "he ascended on high and took captivity captive, he" did not render but "*gave* gifts to men." How could the apostle speak presumptuously as of a debt being paid back to him, unless he had first received grace which was not due to him, being justified by which, he fought the good fight? For he was a blasphemer, a persecutor and injurious; but he obtained mercy as he testifies himself, believing in him who justifies, not the pious, but the ungodly, in order that by justifying him he may make him godly.

4. "Not of works but of him that calleth it was said unto her, The elder shall serve the younger." The point of this is made clear by the preceding words, "When they were not yet born and had done nothing either good or evil." Clearly it was not of works but of him that calleth. But here we must inquire why he says, "That the purpose of God according to election might stand." How can election be just, indeed how can there be any kind of election, where there is no difference? If Jacob was elected before he was born and before he had done anything at all, for no merit of his own, he could not have been elected at all, there being nothing to distinguish him for election. If Esau was rejected for no fault of his own because he too was not born

and had done nothing when it was said, "The elder shall serve the younger," how can his rejection be said to be just? How are we to understand what follows if we judge according to the standards of equity? "Jacob have I loved, but Esau have I hated." Now that is written in the Prophet Malachi (1:2–3) who prophesied long after they were born and dead. Yet the sentence seems to be referred to which was spoken before they were born or had done anything. "The elder shall serve the younger." But how could there be election, or what kind of election could there be, if there was no distinction of merits because they were not yet born and had done nothing? Possibly there was some distinction in their natures? Who could support such a conclusion, seeing that they sprang from one father, one mother, one act of intercourse, one creator? From the same land the same Creator can produce different kinds of living creatures. Can it be that the Creator produced from one human marriage and embrace twin offspring so diverse that he loved the one and hated the other? There would then be no election before that which was chosen existed. If Jacob was created good so that he might be loved, how could he be loved before he existed, in order that he might become good? Accordingly he was not elected that he might become good, but having been made good, he could be elected.

5. Could it be "according to election" because God has foreknowledge of all things, and foresaw the *faith* that was to be in Jacob even before he was born? No one merits justification by his good works, since unless he is justified he cannot do good works. Nevertheless God justifies the Gentiles by faith, and no one believes except of his own free will. So God, foreseeing that Jacob would believe of his own free will, by his foreknowledge elected to justify one not yet born? If election is by foreknowledge, and God foreknew Jacob's faith, how do you prove that he did not elect him for his works? Neither Jacob nor Esau had yet believed, because they were not yet born and had as yet done neither good nor evil. But God foresaw that Jacob would believe? He could equally well have foreseen that he would do good works. So just as one says he was elected because God foreknew that he was going to believe, another might say that it was rather because of the good works he was to perform, since God foreknew them equally well. How then does the apostle show that it was not of works that it was said, "The elder shall serve the younger"? If the reason for its not being of works was that they were not yet born, that applies also to faith; for before they

were born they had neither faith nor works. The apostle, therefore, did not want us to understand that it was because of God's foreknowledge that the younger was elected to be served by the elder. He wanted to show that it was not of works, and he stressed that by saying, "When they were not yet born and had done neither good nor evil." He could have said, if he wished to, that God already knew what each was going to do. We have still to inquire why that election was made. It was not of works, because being not yet born they had done no works. But neither was it of faith, because they had not faith either. What, then, was the reason for it?

6. Are we to say that there could have been no election unless there had been, even when they were in their mother's womb, some difference of faith or works, or merit of some kind? But the apostle says, "That the purpose of God according to election might stand." That is why we have to ask the question. Possibly we are to make a distinction here. Perhaps we should connect the words, "That the purpose of God according to election might stand," with what precedes rather than with what follows. It may mean not that the elder shall serve the younger *in order that* the purpose of God according to election may stand, but rather that children, who are not yet born and have done nothing, are given as an example that no election is here to be understood. If we read, "When they were not yet born and had done neither good nor evil, that the purpose of God according to election might stand," it would mean that they had done neither good nor evil, so that there could be no election on account of his good deeds of the one who had done good. There could be no election on account of good works, according to which the purpose of God might stand. So, "not of works but of him that calleth," that is, of God who justifies the ungodly by grace calling him to faith, "it was said to her, The elder shall serve the younger." So that the purpose of God does not stand according to election, but election is the result of the purpose of God. That is to say, it is not because God finds good works in men so that he may elect them, that his justifying purpose stands; but because his purpose to justify them that believe stands, he consequently finds good works which he can elect for the kingdom of heaven. If there was no election there could be no elect, and it would have been wrong to say, "Who shall lay any charge against God's elect?" (Rom. 8:33). Election does not precede justification, but follows it. No one is elected unless he is different from him who is rejected. It is written that "God

elected us before the foundation of the world" (Eph. 1:4). I do not see how that could be except by the way of foreknowledge. But here, when he says "Not of works but of him that calleth," he wants us to understand that it is not by election through merits, but by the free gift of God, so that no man may exult in his good works. "By the grace of God are we saved; and that not of ourselves; for it is the gift of God, not of works that no man should glory" (Eph. 2:8).

7. But the question is whether faith merits a man's justification, whether the merits of faith do not precede the mercy of God; or whether, in fact, faith itself is to be numbered among the gifts of grace. Notice that in this passage when he said, "Not of works," he did not say, "but of faith it was said to her, The elder shall serve the younger." No, he said, "but of him that calleth." No one believes who is not called. God calls in his mercy, and not as rewarding the merits of faith. The merits of faith follow his calling rather than precede it. "How shall they believe whom they have not heard? And how shall they hear without a preacher?" (Rom. 10:14). Unless, therefore, the mercy of God in calling precedes, no one can even believe, and so begin to be justified and to receive power to do good works. So grace comes before all merits. Christ died for the ungodly. The younger received the promise that the elder should serve him from him that calleth and not from any meritorious works of his own. So the Scripture "Jacob have I loved" is true, but it was of God who called and not of Jacob's righteous works.

8. What then of Esau, of whom it is written that "he shall serve the younger," and "Esau have I hated"? How could he have merited this by evil deeds of his own doing, since these things were spoken before he was born, and before he had done aught of good or evil? Possibly, just as Jacob received the promise without any meritorious acts of his own, so Esau was hated though he had done no evil to merit hatred. If God predestined Esau to serve his younger brother because he foreknew the evil works that he was to do, he must also have predestined Jacob to be served by his elder brother because he foreknew his future good works. In that case it would be false to say that it was not of works. If it is true that it was not of works—and that is proved by the fact that it was said before they were born and before they had done any works at all—or of faith—for again, similarly, there could be no faith in children not yet born—how did Esau deserve to be hated before he was born? That God made one he was to love is unquestionably true. But it is

absurd to say that he made some one he was going to hate. For another Scripture says, "Thou abhorrest none of the things which thou didst make; for never wouldest thou have formed anything if thou didst hate it" (Wisdom 11:24). By what merit did the sun deserve to be made as it is? How did the moon offend so as to be made so much inferior? How did the moon earn the right to be made so much brighter than the other stars? All these were created good each in its own kind. God would not say "The sun have I loved, but the moon I have hated," or "The moon have I loved, but the stars have I hated," as he said "Jacob have I loved, but Esau have I hated." He loved them all though he ordained them in different degrees of excellence, for God saw that they were good when they were created at his Word. That he hated Esau is unjust unless the hatred was merited by injustice on Esau's part. If we admit this, then Jacob must be loved because he had merited to be loved by his justice. And if that is true, it is false to say that it was not of works. Could it possibly be from the righteousness of faith? But what support for that view can you get from the words, "When they were not yet born"? Not even the righteousness of faith can exist in one who is not yet born.

9. The apostle saw the questions that might arise in the mind of the hearer or reader of these words, and so he immediately added, "What shall we say, then? Is there unrighteousness with God? God forbid." And as if to teach us how there is no unrighteousness, he goes on, "For he saith to Moses, I will have mercy on whom I will have mercy, and I will show compassion to him on whom I will have compassion." Does he solve the question in these words or at least narrow it down? If God will have mercy on whom he will have mercy and show compassion to whom he will show compassion, our chief difficulty remains, which is, why did his mercy fail in Esau's case? Why was not Esau too made good by God's mercy as Jacob was made good? Perhaps the real import of the words is this. If God will have mercy on a man so as to call him, he will also have mercy on him so that he may believe; and on him on whom he in mercy bestows faith he will show compassion, i.e., will make him compassionate, so that he may also perform good works. So we are admonished that no one ought to glory or exult in his works of mercy as if he had propitiated God by meritorious works of his own. God gave him the power to be merciful when he showed compassion on whom he would show compassion. If anyone boasts that he has merited compassion by his faith, let him know

that God gave him faith. God shows compassion by inspiring faith in one on whom he had compassion in giving to one who was still an unbeliever a share in his calling. For already the believer is distinguished from the ungodly. "What hast thou that thou didst not receive? But if thou didst receive it, why dost thou glory, as if thou hadst not received it (I Cor. 4:7)?

10. This is all right, but why was this mercy withheld from Esau, so that he was not called and had not faith inspired in him when called, and was not by faith made compassionate so that he might do good works? Was it because he was unwilling? If Jacob had faith because he willed it, then God did not give him faith as a free gift, but Jacob gave it to himself, and so had something which he did not receive. Or can no one believe unless he wills, or will unless he is called, and can no one be called unless God by calling him also gives him faith? For no one can believe unless he is called, although none can believe against his will. "How shall they believe whom they have not heard? And how shall they hear without a preacher?" No one, therefore, believes who has not been called, but not all believe who have been called. "For many are called but few are chosen" (Matt. 22:14). The chosen are those who have not despised him who calls, but have believed and followed him. There is no doubt that they believed willingly. What then of what follows? "So then it is not of him that willeth, nor of him that runneth, but of God that hath mercy." Does it mean that we cannot even will unless we are called, and that our willing is of no avail unless God give us aid to perform it? We must both will and run. It would not be said in vain, "On earth peace to men of good will" (Luke 2:14). And, "Even so run that ye may attain" (I Cor. 9:24). But it is not of him that willeth, nor of him that runneth, but of God that hath mercy, that we obtain what we wish and reach what we desire. Esau, then, was unwilling and did not run. Had he been willing and had he run, he would have obtained the help of God who by calling him would have given him the power both to will and to run, had he not been reprobate by despising the calling. There are two different things that God gives us, the power to will and the thing that we actually will. The power to will he has willed should be both his and ours, his because he calls us, ours because we follow when called. But what we actually will he alone gives, i.e., the power to do right and to live happily for ever. But Esau was not yet born and consequently could be neither willing nor unwilling in all these matters. Why was he rejected when he was still in the womb?

We come back to that difficulty, troubled not only by the obscurity of the question but also by our own abundant repetition.

11. Why was Esau rejected when he was not yet born and could neither believe him who called, nor despise his calling, nor do aught either good or evil? If it was because God foreknew that his will was to be evil in the future, why was not Jacob approved because God foreknew that his will was to be good? If you admit that anyone could have been approved or rejected for some quality he did not yet possess, but because God foreknew that he would possess it in the future, it follows that he could also have been approved for the works which God foreknew that he would perform some day, though he had as yet performed none of them. You will get no support at all for that view from the fact that they were not born when it was said, "The elder shall serve the younger." You will not be able to show from that that, because neither of them had done any works, it could be said that the call was not "of works."

12. If you pay close attention to these words, "Therefore it is not of him that willeth, nor of him that runneth, but of God that hath mercy," you will see that the apostle said that, not only because we attain what we wish by the help of God, but also with the meaning which he expresses in another passage, "Work out your own salvation with fear and trembling; for it is God which worketh in you both to will and to do of his good pleasure" (Phil. 2:12, 13). There he clearly shows that the good will itself is wrought in us by the working of God. If he said, "It is not of him that willeth, nor of him that runneth, but of God that hath mercy," simply because a man's will is not sufficient for us to live justly and righteously unless we are aided by the mercy of God, he could have put it the other way round and said, "It is not of God that hath mercy, but of the man that willeth," because it is equally true that the mercy of God is not sufficient of itself, unless there be in addition the consent of our will. Clearly it is vain for us to will unless God have mercy. But I do not know how it could be said that it is vain for God to have mercy unless we willingly consent. If God has mercy, we also will, for the power to will is given with the mercy itself. It is God that worketh in us both to will and to do of his good pleasure. If we ask whether a good will is a gift of God, I should be surprised if anyone would venture to deny that. But because the good will does not precede calling, but calling precedes the good will, the fact that we have a good will is rightly attributed to God who calls us, and the fact that we are called cannot be

attributed to ourselves. So the sentence, "It is not of him that willeth, nor of him that runneth, but of God that hath mercy" cannot be taken to mean simply that we cannot attain what we wish without the aid of God, but rather that without his calling we cannot even will.

13. But if that calling is the effectual cause of the good will so that every one who is called follows it, how will it be true that "Many are called but few are chosen"? If this is true, and consequently not everyone who is called obeys the call, but has it in the power of his will not to obey, it could be said correctly that it is not of God who hath mercy, but of the man who willeth and runneth, for the mercy of him that calleth is not sufficient unless the obedience of him who is called follows. Possibly those who are called in this way, and do not consent, might be able to direct their wills towards faith if they were called in another way; so that it would be true that "Many are called but few are chosen." Many, that is to say, are called in one way, but all are not affected in the same way; and those only follow the calling who are found fit to receive it. It would be no less true that "it is not of him that willeth, nor of him that runneth, but of God that hath mercy." For God calls in the way that is suited to those who follow his calling. The call comes also to others; but because it is such that they cannot be moved by it and are not fitted to receive it, they can be said to be called but not chosen. And again it would not be true that it is not of God who hath mercy but of man who willeth and runneth. For the effectiveness of God's mercy cannot be in the power of man to frustrate, if he will have none of it. If God wills to have mercy on men, he can call them in a way that is suited to them, so that they will be moved to understand and to follow. It is true, therefore, that many are called but few chosen. Those are chosen who are effectually [*congruenter*] called. Those who are not effectually called and do not obey their calling are not chosen, for although they were called they did not follow. Again it is true that "it is not of him that willeth, nor of him that runneth, but of God that hath mercy." For, although he calls many, he has mercy on those whom he calls in a way suited to them so that they may follow. But it is false to say that "it is not of God who hath mercy but of man who willeth and runneth," because God has mercy on no man in vain. He calls the man on whom he has mercy in the way he knows will suit him, so that he will not refuse the call.

14. Here someone will say, why was not Esau called in such

a way that he would be willing to obey? We see that people are variously moved to believe when the same facts are shown or explained to them. For example, Simeon believed in our Lord Jesus Christ when he was still a little child, for the Spirit revealed the truth to him. Nathanael heard but one sentence from him, "Before Philip called thee, when thou wast under the fig tree I saw thee" (John 1:48); and he replied, "Rabbi, thou art the Son of God; thou art the King of Israel." Long after, Peter made the same confession, and for that merit heard himself pronounced blessed, and that the keys of the Kingdom of Heaven were to be given to him. His disciples believed on him when by a miracle in Cana of Galilee water was turned into wine, which the evangelist John records as the beginning of the signs of Jesus. He stirred many to believe by his words, but many did not believe though the dead were raised. Even his disciples were terrified and shattered by his cross and death, but the thief believed at the very moment when he saw him not highly exalted but his own equal in sharing in crucifixion. One of his disciples after his resurrection believed, not so much because his body was alive again, as because of his recent wounds. Many of those who crucified him, who had despised him while he was working his miracles, believed when his disciples preached him and did similar miracles in his name. Since, then, people are brought to faith in such different ways, and the same thing spoken in one way has power to move and has no such power when spoken in another way, or may move one man and not another, who would dare to affirm that God has no method of calling whereby even Esau might have applied his mind and yoked his will to the faith in which Jacob was justified? But if the obstinacy of the will can be such that the mind's aversion from all modes of calling becomes hardened, the question is whether that very hardening does not come from some divine penalty, as if God abandons a man by not calling him in the way in which he might be moved to faith. Who would dare to affirm that the Omnipotent lacked a method of persuading even Esau to believe?

15. But why do we ask such a question? The apostle himself goes on. "The Scripture saith unto Pharaoh, For this very purpose did I raise thee up, that I might show in thee my power, and that my name might be published abroad in all the earth." The apostle adds this as an example to prove what he had said above, that "it is not of him that willeth, nor of him that runneth, but of God that hath mercy." As if some one had said to

him, What is the source of this doctrine of yours? His reply is "The Scripture saith unto Pharaoh" etc. Thus he shows that it is not of him that willeth but of God that hath mercy. And he concludes with these words: "So then he hath mercy on whom he will, and whom he will he hardeneth." Earlier he had not stated both of these truths. He said: "It is not of him that willeth, nor of him that runneth, but of God that hath mercy"; but he did not say "It is not of him that is unwilling, nor of him that contemneth, but of God who causeth the hardening of the heart." So by putting both sides—he hath mercy on whom he will have mercy, and whom he will he hardeneth—we are given to understand that the new statement agrees with the former one, viz., the hardening which God causes is an unwillingness to be merciful. We must not think that anything is imposed by God whereby a man is made worse, but only that he provides nothing whereby a man is made better. But if there be no distinction of merits who would not break out into the objection which the apostle brings against himself? "Thou wilt say then unto me, Why doth he still find fault? For who withstandeth his will?" God often finds fault with men because they will not believe and live righteously, as is apparent from many passages of Scripture. Hence faithful people who do the will of God are said to walk blamelessly, because Scripture finds no fault with them. But he says, "Why does he find fault? Who withstandeth his will" though "he hath mercy on whom he will and whom he will he hardeneth." Let us look at what was said above and let it direct our interpretation as the Lord himself gives us aid.

16. The apostle said a little before, "What shall we say, then? Is there unrighteousness with God? God forbid." Let this truth, then, be fixed and unmovable in a mind soberly pious and stable in faith, that there is no unrighteousness with God. Let us also believe most firmly and tenaciously that God has mercy on whom he will and that whom he will he hardeneth, that is, he has or has not mercy on whom he will. Let us believe that this belongs to a certain hidden equity that cannot be searched out by any human standard of measurement, though its effects are to be observed in human affairs and earthly arrangements. Unless we had stamped upon these human affairs certain traces of supernal justice our weak minds would never look up to or long for the holy and pure ground and source of spiritual precepts. "Blessed are they who hunger and thirst after righteousness, for they shall be filled." In the drought of our mortal condition in this life it would be a case of being burnt up rather than of

merely thirsting, did not some gentle breath of justice from on high scatter showers upon us. Human society is knit together by transactions of giving and receiving, and things are given and received sometimes as debts, sometimes not. No one can be charged with unrighteousness who exacts what is owing to him. Nor certainly can he be charged with unrighteousness who is prepared to give up what is owing to him. This decision does not lie with those who are debtors but with the creditor. This image or, as I said, trace of equity is stamped on the business transactions of men by the Supreme Equity. Now all men are a mass of sin, since, as the apostle says, "In Adam all die" (I Cor. 15:22), and to Adam the entire human race traces the origin of its sin against God. Sinful humanity must pay a debt of punishment to the supreme divine justice. Whether that debt is exacted or remitted there is no unrighteousness. It would be a mark of pride if the debtors claimed to decide to whom the debt should be remitted and from whom it should be exacted; just as those who were hired to work in the vineyard were unjustly indignant when as much was given to the others as was duly paid to themselves (Matt. 20:11 ff.). So the apostle represses the impudent questioner. "O man, who art thou that repliest against God?" A man so speaks back to God when he is displeased that God finds fault with sinners, as if God compelled any man to sin when he simply does not bestow his justifying mercy on some sinners, and for that reason is said to harden some sinners; not because he drives them to sin but because he does not have mercy upon them. He decides who are not to be offered mercy by a standard of equity which is most secret and far removed from human powers of understanding. "Inscrutable are his judgments, and his ways past finding out" (Rom. 11:33). He justly finds fault with sinners because he does not compel them to sin. Justly also he has mercy on some that they may have this calling, to be heartily penitent when God finds fault with sinners, and to turn to his grace. He finds fault, therefore, both justly and mercifully.

17. To be sure, no one resists his will. He aids whom he will and he leaves whom he will. Both he who is aided and he who is left belong to the same mass of sin. Both deserve the punishment which is exacted from the one and remitted to the other. If you are troubled by this, "O man, who art thou that repliest against God?" I think "man" has the same meaning here as in that other passage: "Are ye not men and walk according to man?" There the word denotes carnal and animal people to whom it is said, "I could not speak unto you as unto spiritual but as unto

carnal . . . for ye were not yet able to bear it, nay not even now are ye able, for ye are yet carnal" (I Cor. 3:1–3). And again, "The animal (natural) man receiveth not the things of the Spirit of God" (I Cor. 2:14). So the apostle continues in our present passage. "O man who art thou that repliest against God? Does the thing formed say to him that formed it, Why didst thou make me thus? Hath not the potter power over the clay, from the same lump to make one vessel unto honour and another unto dishonour?" Possibly he shows clearly enough that he is speaking to the carnal man because he refers to the clay from which the first man was formed; and because, as I have recalled, according to the same apostle all die in Adam, he speaks as if all formed one mass. Though one vessel is made unto honour and another unto dishonour, nevertheless that which is made unto honour must begin as carnal and rise to the spiritual state. Though they were made unto honour and were already born in Christ, yet because he was addressing them still as children he even calls them carnal, saying, "I could not speak unto you as unto spiritual, but as unto carnal. As babes in Christ I gave you milk to drink, not meat, for ye were not able to bear it, nay not even now are ye able, for ye are yet carnal." He says they are carnal though they have been born in Christ and are babes in Christ and must be fed with milk. In adding "Nor are ye yet able" he shows that those who make progress will one day be able, because, seeing that they have already been spiritually re-born, grace has begun its work in them. These people were, therefore, already "vessels made unto honour," to whom it could nevertheless be rightly said, "O man, who art thou that repliest against God?" If that can be rightly said to such people, much more can it be said to those who either are not yet so regenerated, or even have been made unto dishonour. Only let us hold fast with unshakable faith the fact that there is no unrighteousness with God; so that, whether he remits or exacts the debt, he cannot rightly be charged with unrighteousness by him from whom he exacts it; and he who receives remission ought not to glory in his own merits. The former pays back nothing but what he owes, and the latter has nothing that he has not received.

18. At this point we must try, if the Lord will help us, to see how both of these Scripture passages can be true: "Thou hatest nothing that thou hast made" and "Jacob I have loved, but Esau have I hated." The potter, remember, made one vessel unto honour and another unto dishonour. Now, if he hated

Esau because he was a vessel made unto dishonour, how could it be true that "Thou hatest nothing which thou hast made." For in that case God hated Esau though he had himself made him a vessel unto dishonour. This knotty problem is solved if we understand God to be the artificer of all creatures. Every creature of God is good. Every man is a creature as man but not as sinner. God is the creator both of the body and of the soul of man. Neither of these is evil, and God hates neither. He hates nothing which he has made. But the soul is more excellent than the body, and God is more excellent than both soul and body, being the maker and fashioner of both. In man he hates nothing but sin. Sin in man is perversity and lack of order, that is, a turning away from the Creator who is more excellent, and a turning to the creatures which are inferior to him. God does not hate Esau the man, but hates Esau the sinner. As it is said of the Lord, "He came unto his own, and his own received him not" (John 1:11). To them also he said himself, "For this cause ye hear not, because ye are not of God" (John 8:47). How can they be "his own" and yet be "not of God"? The first statement must be taken as regarding them as men whom the Lord himself had made, the second as regarding them as sinners whom the Lord rebuked. They are both men and sinners, men as fashioned by God, sinners by their own wills. Was not Jacob a sinner, then, seeing that God loved him? But God loved in him, not the sin which he had blotted out, but the grace which he had freely given him. Christ died for the ungodly not that they should remain ungodly, but that they should be justified and converted from their impiety, believing in him who justifies the ungodly. For God hates impiety. In some he punishes it with damnation, in others he removes it by justification, doing what he judges right in his inscrutable judgments. Those of the number of the godless whom he does not justify he makes "vessels unto dishonour"; but he does not hate that in them which he has made, though of course they are hateful in so far as they are godless. In so far as he has made them vessels, he made them for some use, that "vessels made unto honour" may learn from the penalties duly ordained for the evil. Accordingly, God does not hate them as men or as vessels, that is, not in so far as he created them and ordained their punishment. He hates nothing which he has made. In making them vessels of perdition he makes them for the correction of others. He hates their impiety which he did not make. A judge hates theft, but he does not hate sending the thief to the mines. The thief is responsible for the crime, the judge for the sentence. So God, in making vessels of perdition from the lump of the impious, does not hate what he does, i.e., his work of ordaining due penalty for those who perish; for thereby those on whom he has mercy may find an opportunity of salvation. So it was said to Pharaoh, "For this very purpose did I raise thee up, that I might show in thee my power and that my name might be published abroad in all the earth." This demonstration of the power of God and proclamation of his name in all the earth is of advantage to those to whom it is a calling perfectly suited to their condition, so that they may learn from it to fear and to correct their ways. So the apostle goes on: "What if God, willing to show his wrath, and to make his power known, endured with much long-suffering vessels of wrath fitted unto destruction. . . ?" Through all this you can hear as an undertone, "Who art thou that repliest against God?" That must be understood as a recurring refrain—if God, willing to show his wrath, endured vessels of wrath, who art thou that repliest against God? But not only is it to be understood with the words just quoted, but also with the words that follow, "That he might make known the riches of his glory upon vessels of mercy." There is no advantage for vessels fitted unto destruction that God patiently endures them, to destroy them in due order and to use them as a means of salvation for those on whom he has mercy. But there is advantage for those for whose salvation God uses this means. As it is written, "The just shall wash his hands in the blood of the wicked" (Ps. 58:10), i.e., he shall be cleansed from evil works by the fear of God when he sees the punishment of sinners. That God shows his wrath in bearing with vessels of wrath avails to set a useful example to others, but also to "make known the riches of his glory upon vessels of mercy which he prepared unto glory." The hardening of the ungodly demonstrates two things—that a man should fear and turn to God in piety, and that thanks should be given for his mercy to God who shows by the penalty inflicted on some the greatness of his gift to others. If the penalty he exacts from the former is not just, he makes no gift to those from whom he does not exact it. But because it is just, and there is no unrighteousness with God who punishes, who is sufficient to give thanks to him? For he remits a debt which, if God wanted to exact it, no man could deny was justly due.

19. "Us he also called, not from the Jews only, but also from the Gentiles." That is to say, we also are vessels of mercy which he has prepared unto glory. He did not call all the Jews, but

some of them. Nor did he call all the Gentiles but some of them. From Adam has sprung one mass of sinners and godless men, in which both Jews and Gentiles belong to one lump, apart from the grace of God. If the potter out of one lump of clay makes one vessel unto honour and another unto dishonour, it is manifest that God has made of the Jews some vessels unto honour and others unto dishonour, and similarly of the Gentiles. It follows that all must be understood to belong to one lump. Then the apostle begins to bring forward prophetic attestation to both of these classes, but he reverses the order. For he had spoken first of the Jews and then of the Gentiles, but he first brings forward testimony concerning the Gentiles and then concerning the Jews. "As Hosea says, I will call that my people which was not my people, and her beloved, which was not beloved. And it shall be, that in the place where it was said, Ye are not my people, there they shall be called sons of the living God." This must be understood as spoken of the Gentiles because they had no one fixed place of sacrifices as the Jews had at Jerusalem. The apostles were sent to the Gentiles that all who believed, wherever they believed, might in that place offer a sacrifice of praise, because God had given them the power to become sons of God. "And Isaiah crieth concerning Israel." Lest it should be believed that all Israelites had gone to perdition, he teaches that from among them, too, some were made vessels unto honour, others unto dishonour. "If," he says, "the number of the children of Israel be as the sand of the sea, a remnant shall be saved." The multitude of the others are vessels fitted for destruction. "The Lord will consummate his Word upon earth and cut it short" that is, he will save by grace those who believe, using the short way of faith and not the innumerable observances which like a servile yoke pressed hard upon the Jewish multitude. By grace he consummated his Word to us and cut it short upon earth, saying "My yoke is easy and my burden is light" (Matt. 11:30). A little later the apostle writes, "The word is nigh thee, in thy mouth and in thy heart; that is the word of faith which we preach, because if thou shalt confess with thy mouth that Jesus is Lord, and shalt believe in thy heart that God raised him from the dead, thou shalt be saved. For with the heart man believeth unto righteousness; and with the mouth confession is made unto salvation" (Rom. 10:8 ff.). This is the finished and short Word that God has done upon earth. By its perfection and brevity the thief was justified who, when all his limbs were nailed to the cross, had these two free; with the heart he believed unto righteousness, and with the mouth he made confession unto salvation. For this merit he was told immediately: "To-day thou shalt be with me in paradise." Good works would have followed if after receiving grace he had continued to live for a time among men. They certainly did not precede so that he might have merited that grace, for he had been crucified as a robber, and from the cross was translated to paradise. "And as Isaiah had prophesied, Except the Lord of Sabaoth had left us a seed, we had become as Sodom, and had been made like unto Gomorrah." "Had left us a seed" in this passage is equivalent to "a remnant shall be saved" in the other. For the rest perished as a due punishment, being vessels of perdition. That all did not perish as in Sodom and Gomorrah is due not to any merit of their own but to the grace of God that left a seed from which should spring another harvest throughout the whole earth. So he writes a little later. "Even so then at this present time a remnant is saved by the election of grace. But if it is by grace, it is no more of works: otherwise grace is no more grace. What then? That which Israel sought he did not obtain; but the election obtained it, and the rest were blinded" (Rom. 11:5 ff.). The vessels of mercy obtained it and the vessels of wrath were blinded. Yet all were of the same lump as in the fulness of the Gentiles.

20. There is a certain passage of Scripture which is highly relevant to the matter we are dealing with, and which wonderfully confirms what I have been urging. It is in the book which some call Jesus Sirach and others Ecclesiasticus. There it is written: "All men are from the ground, and Adam was created of earth. In the abundance of his discipline the Lord separated them and changed their ways. Some of them he blessed and exalted. Some he sanctified and brought nigh to himself. Some of them he cursed and brought low, and turned them to their dissensions. As the clay is in the potter's hand to form and fashion it, and all his ways are according to his good pleasure, so is man in the hand of him that made him, and he will render to him according to his judgment. Good is set over against evil, and life over against death. So is the sinner over against the godly. Thus look upon all the works of the most High, two and two, one against another" (Ecclesiasticus 33:10 ff.). First God's discipline is commended. "In the abundance of his discipline God separated them"—from what if not from the blessedness of paradise. "And he changed their ways"—that they might now live as mortals. Then, of all was formed one mass coming from

inherited sin and the penalty of mortality, though God formed and created what was good. In all there is form and the fitting together of the body in such concord of the members that the apostle can use it as an illustration of how charity is obtained. In all the spirit of life vivifies the earthly members, and man's whole nature is wonderfully attuned as the soul rules and the body obeys. But carnal concupiscence now reigns as a result of the penalty of sin, and has thrown the whole human race into confusion, making of it one lump in which the original guilt remains throughout. And yet he goes on: "Some of them he blessed and exalted. Some he sanctified and brought nigh to himself. Some he cursed and brought low, and turned them to their dissensions." He continues in words like those of the apostle: "Has not the potter power over the clay, of the same lump to make one vessel unto honour and another unto dishonour?" He has the same similitude: "As the clay is in the potter's hand to form and to fashion it, and all his ways are according to his good pleasure, so is man in the hand of him that made him." The apostle says: "Surely there is no unrighteousness with God?" Sirach adds: "He will render unto him according to his judgment." Just punishments are allotted to the damned. But even this is put to a good use, for those learn from it who have obtained mercy, as he says: "Good is set over against evil, and life over against death, so is the sinner over against the godly. So look upon all the works of the most High; two and two, one against the other." The better stand out and learn from comparison with the worse. Now these better are made better by grace. He hardly says that a remnant shall be saved, but he goes on to speak as one of the remnant. "I awaked up last, as one that gleaneth after the grape-gatherers." How does he prove that it was not for his own merits but by the mercy of God? "By the blessing of God I hoped, and filled my winepress as one that gathereth grapes." Though it awaked last, because, as it is said, the last shall be first, a people hoping in the blessing of God gleaned from the remnant of Israel and filled its winepress from the riches of the harvest which the whole earth produces.

21. The apostle, therefore, and all those who have been justified and have demonstrated for us the understanding of grace, have no other intention than to show that he that glories should glory in the Lord. Who will call in question the works of the Lord who out of one lump damns one and justifies another? Free will is most important. It exists, indeed, but of what

value is it in those who are sold under sin? "The flesh," says he, "lusteth against the spirit and the spirit against the flesh so that ye may not do the things that ye would" (Gal. 5:17). We are commanded to live righteously, and the reward is set before us that we shall merit to live happily for ever. But who can live righteously and do good works unless he has been justified by faith? We are commanded to believe that we may receive the gift of the Holy Spirit and become able to do good works by love. But who can believe unless he is reached by some calling, by some testimony borne to the truth? Who has it in his power to have such a motive present to his mind that his will shall be influenced to believe? Who can welcome in his mind something which does not give him delight? But who has it in his power to ensure that something that will delight him will turn up, or that he will take delight in what turns up? If those things delight us which serve our advancement towards God, that is due not to our own whim or industry or meritorious works, but to the inspiration of God and to the grace which he bestows. He freely bestows upon us voluntary assent, earnest effort, and the power to perform works of fervent charity. We are bidden to ask that we may receive, to seek that we may find, and to knock that it may be opened unto us. Is not our prayer sometimes tepid or rather cold? Does it not sometimes cease altogether, so that we are not even grieved to notice this condition in us. For if we are grieved that it should be so, that is already a prayer. What does this prove except that he who commands us to ask, seek and knock, himself gives us the will to obey? "It is not of him that willeth, nor of him that runneth, but of God that hath mercy." We could neither will nor run unless he stirred us and put the motive-power in us.

22. If by the words "a remnant according to the election of grace" we are to understand not election of the justified to eternal life, but election of those who are to be justified, that kind of election is verily hidden, and cannot be known by us who must regard all men as parts of one lump. If, however, some are able to know it, I confess my own weakness in this matter. If I am allowed speculatively to examine such election of men to saving grace, I have nothing to go by but the greater abilities of some, or their relative freedom from sin, or, may I add if you please, their honourable and profitable doctrines. In that case the man would seem to be fit to be elected to grace who was snared and stained by the most trifling sins (for who indeed has no sins?), or who had a keen mind, or was cultivated

in the liberal arts. But if I set up this standard of judgment, he will deride me who has chosen the weak things of the world to confound the strong, and the foolish things of the world to confound the wise. Looking to him I should be ashamed; and being corrected I in turn would mock at many who are pure by comparison with some sinners, and many who are cultivated orators by comparison with certain fishermen. Don't we see that many of our faithful people walking in the way of God cannot be compared for ability, I will not say with certain heretics, but even with comic actors? Don't we see some, men and women, living blamelessly in pure marriage, who are either heretics or pagans or are so luke-warm in the true faith and the true Church that we marvel to see them surpassed not only in patience and temperance but also in faith, hope and charity by harlots and actors who have been suddenly converted? The only possible conclusion is that it is wills that are elected. But the will itself can have no motive unless something presents itself to delight and stir the mind. That this should happen is not in any man's power. What did Saul will but to attack, seize, bind and slay Christians? What a fierce, savage, blind will was that! Yet he was thrown prostrate by one word from on high, and a vision came to him whereby his mind and will were turned from their fierceness and set on the right way towards faith, so that suddenly out of a marvellous persecutor of the Gospel he was made a still more marvellous preacher of the Gospel. And yet what shall we say? "Surely there is no unrighteousness with God" who exacts punishment from whom he will and remits punishment to whom he will; who never exacts what is not due, and never remits what he might not exact? "Is there unrighteousness with God? God forbid." Why then does he deal thus with this man and thus with that man? "O man, who art thou?" If you do not have to pay what you owe, you have something to be grateful for. If you have to pay it you have no reason to complain. Only let us believe if we cannot grasp it, that he who made and fashioned the whole creation, spiritual and corporeal, disposes of all things by number, weight and measure. But his judgments are inscrutable and his ways past finding out. Let us say Halleluia and praise him together in song; and let us not say, What is this? or, Why is that? All things have been created each in its own time.

SELECT BIBLIOGRAPHY

The Translation has been made from the Benedictine Edition of the Complete Works of St. Augustine (first printed at Paris 1679, reprinted at Venice 1729; final edition in Migne, *Patrologia Latina*, 1841), except *De Utilitate Credendi* where the Vienna edition in *Corpus Scriptorum Ecclesiasticorum Latinorum* was available.

Prosper Alfaric: *L'Évolution Intellectuelle de S. Augustin*, I. Nouroy, Paris 1918.

Bloch (editor): *A Monument to Saint Augustine*. Sheed and Ward, London 1945.

Vernon J. Bourke: *Augustine's Quest of Wisdom*. Milwaukee, Wis., 1944.

John Burnaby: *Amor Dei: A Study of the Religion of St. Augustine*. Hodder and Stoughton, London 1938.

J. Gibb and W. Montgomery: *The Confessions of St. Augustine: Introduction, Text and Notes*. Cambridge Patristic Texts, 1908.

Étienne Gilson: *Introduction à l'Étude de Saint Augustin*. Librairie Philosophique Vrin, Paris 1929.

Adolph Harnack: *History of Dogma* (English translation from third German edition by James Millar), V. Williams and Norgate, London 1898.

Karl Holl: *Augustin's Innere Entwickelung: Gesammelte Aufsätze zur Kirchengeschichte*, III. 1928.

Henri-Irénée, Marrou: *Saint Augustin et la Fin de la Culture antique*. Boccard, Paris 1938.

W. Montgomery: *St. Augustine: Aspects of his Life and Thought*. Hodder and Stoughton, London 1914.

W. J. Sparrow-Simpson: *St. Augustine's Conversion*. S.P.C.K., 1930.

INDEXES

General Index

Biblical References